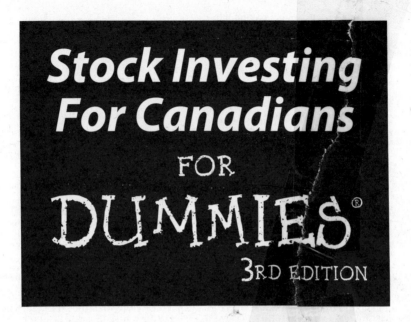

# Stock Investing For Canadians FOR DUMMIES®

## 3RD EDITION

### by Andrew Dagys and Paul Mladjenovic

John Wiley & Sons Canada, Ltd

**Stock Investing For Canadians For Dummies,® 3rd Edition**

Published by
**John Wiley & Sons Canada, Ltd**
6045 Freemont Boulevard
Mississauga, Ontario, L5R 4J3

www.wiley.com

For general information on John Wiley & Sons Canada, Ltd., including all books published by Wiley Publishing, Inc., please call our distribution centre at 1-800-567-4797. For reseller information, including discounts and premium sales, please call our sales department at 416-646-7992. For press review copies, author interviews, or other publicity information, please contact our publicity department, Tel. 416-646-4582, Fax 416-236-4448.

For technical support, please visit www.wiley.com/techsupport.

Wiley also publishes its books in a variety of electronic formats. Some content that appears in print may not be available in electronic books.

Library and Archives Canada Cataloguing in Publication Data

Dagys, Andrew

     Stock investing for Canadians for dummies / by Andrew Dagys and Paul Mladjenovic. — 3rd ed.

Includes index.

ISBN 978-0-470-73684-5

1. Stocks.  2. Investments.  3. Investments—Handbooks, manuals, etc.
4. Investments—Canada—Handbooks, manuals, etc. I. Mladjenovic, Paul J
II. Title.

HG5152.D23 2009         332.63'22         C2009-905899-5

Printed in the United States

3 4 5 BRR 14

WILEY

# About the Authors

**Andrew Dagys, CMA,** is a best-selling author who has written and co-authored several books, including *Investing Online For Canadians For Dummies* (CDG Books Canada, 2000; Wiley, 2001) and *The Financial Planner For 50+* (Prentice Hall, 2000). Andrew has contributed columns to *Canadian Living, Forever Young,* and other publications. He has appeared on *Canada AM* and several popular CBC broadcasts to offer his insights on the Canadian and world investment landscapes.

An avid investor, Andrew uses online resources to advantage to identify compelling investment opportunities. For years, his business, The Treetop Group, has helped match some of those opportunities with the financial needs of his Canadian clients. Andrew also enjoys speaking to business and general audiences about the latest investment trends, always in the context of current world realities, and about new developments in high technology that can empower Canadians to enhance their lifestyles. He lives in Toronto with his wife, Dawn-Ava, and their three children — Brendan, Megan, and Jordan.

Andrew looks forward to your comments and can be reached at aj-dagys@rogers.com.

**Paul Mladjenovic** is a certified financial planner practitioner, writer, and public speaker. His business, PM Financial Services, has helped people with financial and business concerns since 1981. In 1985 he achieved his CFP designation. Since 1983, Paul has taught thousands of budding investors through popular national seminars such as "The $50 Wealthbuilder" and "Stock Investing Like a Pro." Paul has been quoted or referenced by many media outlets, including Bloomberg, MarketWatch, Comcast, CNBC, and a variety of financial and business publications and Web sites. As an author, he has written the books *The Unofficial Guide to Picking Stocks* (Wiley, 2000) and *Zero-Cost Marketing* (Todd Publications, 1995). In recent years, Paul accurately forecast many economic events, such as the rise of gold, the decline of the U.S. dollar, and the housing crisis. He edits the financial newsletter Prosperity Alert, available at no charge at www.supermoneylinks.com. Paul's personal Web site can be found at www.mladjenovic.com.

# Dedication

Andrew dedicates this book to his supportive wife, Dawn-Ava, and their wonderful children — Brendan, Megan, and Jordan. He thanks God for them all. He commends those Canadians who have the courage to invest wisely in the face of a challenging and rapidly changing world.

Paul dedicates this book to his beloved Fran, Adam, and Joshua and his loving, supportive family — he thanks God for you. He also dedicates this book to the millions of investors who deserve more knowledge and information to achieve lasting prosperity.

# Authors' Acknowledgements

Once again, Andrew thanks his editor, Robert Hickey, who gave him the opportunity to write this book. More important, Robert was instrumental through his dedication to excellence in making this book even stronger than the previous edition. Andrew also thanks his copy editor, Kelli Howey, for her fantastic editorial work. She navigated through a significant amount of new material and provided thoughtful insights and creative recommendations. Alanna McCracken provided a thorough technical review, ensuring that all information in the book was accurate and current.

Andrew appreciates the efforts and contributions of Lindsay Humphreys, Project Editor. She kept the project moving along. Additional thanks go to all of the dedicated people at Wiley Canada who work hard behind the scenes.

Finally, Andrew thanks Robert Harris, with whom he has had a long-standing and highly enjoyable business relationship. He especially thanks Robert for allowing him the privilege of entering the world of writing in Canada.

Paul thanks Georgette Beatty, his project editor, who has guided him from day one. Her patience, professionalism, and guidance have kept him sane and productive. Todd Lothery, Paul's copy editor, is a pro who took Paul's bundle of words and turned them into worthy messages.

Paul's technical editor, Juli Erhart-Graves, is a great financial pro whom he appreciates. She made sure his logic is sound and his facts are straight.

Paul's gratitude again goes out to his fantastic acquisitions editor, Stacy Kennedy, for making this thir3rd edition happen. *For Dummies* books don't magically appear at the bookstore; they happen because of the foresight and efforts of people like Stacy. Wiley is fortunate to have her (and the others also mentioned)!

Fran, Lipa Zyenska, Paul appreciates your great support during the writing and updating of this book. It's not always easy dealing with the world, but with you by his side, he knows that God has indeed blessed him. Te amo!

Lastly, Andrew and Paul want to acknowledge you, the reader. Over the years, you've made the *For Dummies* books what they are today. Your devotion to these wonderful books helped build a foundation that played a big part in the creation of this book and many more yet to come. Thank you!

## Publisher's Acknowledgements

We're proud of this book; please send us your comments at http://dummies.custhelp.com. For other comments, please contact our Customer Care Department within the U.S. at 877-762-2974, outside the U.S. at 317-572-3993, or fax 317-572-4002.

Some of the people who helped bring this book to market include the following:

### *Acquisitions and Editorial*

**U.S. Project Editor:** Georgette Beatty

**Editor:** Robert Hickey

**Copy Editor:** Kelli Howey

**Project Editor:** Lindsay Humphreys

**Technical Editor:** Alanna McCracken

**Cartoons:** Rich Tennant
(www.the5thwave.com)

### *Composition*

**Vice-President, Publishing Services:**
Karen Bryan

**Project Coordinator:** Lynsey Stanford

**Layout and Graphics:**
Wiley Indianapolis Composition Services

**Proofreader:** Lisa Young Stiers

**Indexer:** Slivoskey Indexing Services

---

**John Wiley & Sons Canada, Ltd**

**Bill Zerter,** Chief Operating Officer

**Jennifer Smith,** Publisher, Professional & Trade Division

**Publishing and Editorial for Consumer Dummies**

**Diane Graves Steele,** Vice President and Publisher, Consumer Dummies

**Kristin Ferguson-Wagstaffe,** Product Development Director, Consumer Dummies

**Ensley Eikenburg,** Associate Publisher, Travel

**Kelly Regan,** Editorial Director, Travel

**Composition Services**

**Debbie Stailey,** Director of Composition Services

# Contents at a Glance

Introduction .................................................. 1

## Part I: The Essentials of Stock Investing ..................... 9
Chapter 1: Welcome to the World of Stock Investing ................................. 11
Chapter 2: Taking Stock of Your Current Financial Situation and Goals ................. 19
Chapter 3: Defining Common Approaches to Stock Investing ....................... 35
Chapter 4: Recognizing the Risks ......................................................... 45
Chapter 5: Say Cheese: Getting a Snapshot of the Market with Indexes ................. 61

## Part II: Before You Invest ..................................... 73
Chapter 6: Gathering Information ........................................................ 75
Chapter 7: Going for Brokers ............................................................. 97
Chapter 8: Investing for Growth ........................................................ 117
Chapter 9: Investing for Income ........................................................ 131
Chapter 10: Getting a Grip on Economics ............................................ 143
Chapter 11: Money, Mayhem, and Votes ............................................. 153

## Part III: Picking the Winners ................................. 163
Chapter 12: Financial-Statement Boot Camp ...................................... 165
Chapter 13: Silly Income-Statement Tricks ....................................... 185
Chapter 14: Silly Balance-Sheet Tricks ............................................ 195
Chapter 15: Looking at What the Insiders Do: Corporate Hijinks .............. 207
Chapter 16: Five Minutes for Misconduct ......................................... 219
Chapter 17: Analyzing Industries .................................................... 227
Chapter 18: Emerging-Sector Opportunities ...................................... 237

## Part IV: Investment Strategies ............................... 253
Chapter 19: Choosing between Investing and Trading ........................... 255
Chapter 20: Selecting a Strategy That's Just Right for You ..................... 265
Chapter 21: Understanding Brokerage Orders and Trading Techniques .............. 273
Chapter 22: Keeping More of Your Money from the Taxman ..................... 289

## Part V: The Part of Tens .............................. 305

Chapter 23: Ten Ways to Profit Before the Crowd Does.............................307
Chapter 24: Ten Ways to Protect Your Stock Market Profits.................................313
Chapter 25: Ten Red Flags for Stock Investors ...................................319
Chapter 26: Ten Challenges and Opportunities for Stock Investors.....................325

## Part VI: Appendixes .............................. 331

Appendix A: Financial Ratios....................................................333
Appendix B: Resources for Stock Investors ..............................343

## Index .............................. 357

# Table of Contents

*Introduction* .................................................................... *1*

About This Book ...............................................................2
Conventions Used in This Book .......................................3
What You Don't Have to Read...........................................3
Foolish Assumptions.........................................................3
How This Book Is Organized ............................................4
    Part I: The Essentials of Stock Investing ....................4
    Part II: Before You Invest ...........................................5
    Part III: Picking the Winners .......................................5
    Part IV: Investment Strategies ...................................6
    Part V: The Part of Tens .............................................6
    Part VI: Appendixes ....................................................7
Icons Used in This Book ...................................................7
Where to Go from Here......................................................7

*Part 1: The Essentials of Stock Investing* ...................... *9*

**Chapter 1: Welcome to the World of Stock Investing** ..............**11**

Understanding the Basics.................................................12
Preparing to Buy Stocks ..................................................12
Knowing How to Pick Winners .........................................13
    Recognizing stock value...........................................13
    Understanding how market capitalization affects stock value ......14
    Sharpening your investment skills ............................15
Boning Up on Strategies and Tactics ..............................16

**Chapter 2: Taking Stock of Your Current Financial Situation and Goals** ............................................................**19**

Establishing a Starting Point ...........................................20
    Step 1: Making sure you have an emergency fund ..........21
    Step 2: Listing your assets in decreasing order of liquidity ..........21
    Step 3: Listing your liabilities ...................................24
    Step 4: Calculating your net worth ...........................26
    Step 5: Analyzing your balance sheet........................27
Funding Your Stock Program ...........................................28
    Step 1: Tallying up your income ................................29
    Step 2: Adding up your outflow.................................30
    Step 3: Creating a cash-flow statement ...................31
    Step 4: Analyzing your cash flow ..............................32
    Another option: Finding investment money in tax savings..........32
Setting Your Sights on Your Financial Goals.....................33

**Chapter 3: Defining Common Approaches to Stock Investing . . . . . . .35**

Matching Stocks and Strategies with Your Goals......................................36
Investing by Time Frame .............................................................................37
    Focusing on the short term .................................................................37
    Considering intermediate-term goals................................................38
    Preparing for the long term ................................................................39
Investing for a Purpose................................................................................40
    Making loads of money quickly: Growth investing..........................40
    Making money steadily: Income investing.........................................41
Investing for Your Personal Style ...............................................................43
    Conservative investing........................................................................43
    Aggressive investing............................................................................44

**Chapter 4: Recognizing the Risks . . . . . . . . . . . . . . . . . . . . . . . . . . . . .45**

Exploring Different Kinds of Risk................................................................46
    Financial risk ........................................................................................46
    Interest-rate risk...................................................................................48
    Market risk.............................................................................................51
    Inflation risk..........................................................................................52
    Tax risk...................................................................................................53
    Political and governmental risks ........................................................53
    Personal risks .......................................................................................54
    Emotional risk .......................................................................................55
Minimizing Your Risk ...................................................................................56
    Gaining knowledge...............................................................................56
    Staying out until you get a little practice..........................................56
    Putting your financial house in order ...............................................57
    Diversifying your investments ...........................................................58
Weighing Risk against Return .....................................................................59

**Chapter 5: Say Cheese: Getting a Snapshot of the Market
with Indexes . . . . . . . . . . . . . . . . . . . . . . . . . . . . . . . . . . . . . . . . . . . . . . .61**

Knowing How Indexes Are Measured .........................................................61
Checking Out the Indexes............................................................................63
    The Dow Jones Industrial Average ....................................................63
    The Toronto Stock Exchange/TMX.....................................................65
    Standard & Poor's 500..........................................................................67
    Wilshire Total Market Index ...............................................................68
    Nasdaq indexes ....................................................................................69
    Russell 3000 Index................................................................................69
    International indexes.............................................................................70
Using the Indexes Effectively .....................................................................71
    Tracking the indexes ...........................................................................71
    Investing in indexes.............................................................................71

## *Part II: Before You Invest* ............................................... **73**

### **Chapter 6: Gathering Information** .................................**75**

Looking to Stock Exchanges for Answers.....................................76
Understanding Stocks and the Companies They Represent...................77
    Accounting for taste and a whole lot more ..........................77
    Understanding how economics affects stocks......................78
Staying on Top of Financial News................................................82
    Figuring out what a company's up to.................................83
    Discovering what's new with an industry............................83
    Knowing what's happening with the economy ....................83
    Seeing what politicians and government bureaucrats are doing ....84
    Checking for trends in society, culture, and entertainment .........84
Reading (and Understanding) Stock Tables....................................85
    52-week high......................................................86
    52-week low........................................................86
    Name and symbol ...............................................87
    Dividend ..........................................................87
    Volume ............................................................88
    Yield................................................................89
    P/E..................................................................89
    Day last............................................................90
    Net change ........................................................90
Using News about Dividends ...................................................90
    Looking at important dates .......................................91
    Understanding why these dates matter............................92
Evaluating (Avoiding?) Investment Tips........................................93
    Consider the source ..............................................93
    Get multiple views ................................................93
Gathering Data from SEDAR and EDGAROnline.............................94

### **Chapter 7: Going for Brokers** ...................................**97**

Defining the Broker's Role.......................................................97
Distinguishing between Investment Advisers and Discount Brokers.....98
    Investment advisers ..............................................99
    Discount brokers ................................................100
Choosing a Broker ..............................................................102
    Revisiting your personal investing style..........................102
    Making the decision.............................................103
Online Investing Services ......................................................104
    Getting online trading services for less ..........................105
    Trading online at a discount .....................................105
    Checking out special features ....................................106
    Opening your online brokerage account ........................108

Types of Brokerage Accounts ....................................................... 109
  Cash accounts ........................................................................ 109
  Margin accounts ..................................................................... 110
  Option accounts ..................................................................... 110
Evaluating Brokers' Recommendations ....................................... 111
  Understanding basic recommendations ................................. 111
  Asking a few important questions ......................................... 112
Brokerage Reports: The Good, the Bad, and the Ugly ................ 113
  The good ................................................................................. 114
  The bad ................................................................................... 114
  The ugly ................................................................................... 115

**Chapter 8: Investing for Growth . . . . . . . . . . . . . . . . . . . . . . . . . . . . . .117**

Understanding Growth Stocks ..................................................... 118
Analyzing Growth Stocks for the Very First Time ...................... 119
  Making the right comparison ................................................. 119
  Checking out a company's fundamentals .............................. 120
  Looking for leaders and megatrends ..................................... 120
  Considering a company with a strong niche ........................ 121
  Noticing who's buying and/or recommending the stock ...... 122
  Learning investing lessons from history .............................. 123
  Evaluating the management of a company ........................... 123
  Making sure a company continues to do well ....................... 126
Exploring Small-Caps and Speculative Stocks ........................... 126
  Avoid IPOs, unless . . . ........................................................... 127
  If it's a small-cap stock, make sure it's making money ........ 128
  Investing in small-cap stocks requires analysis .................. 129

**Chapter 9: Investing for Income . . . . . . . . . . . . . . . . . . . . . . . . . . . . . . .131**

Understanding the Basics of Income Stocks .............................. 131
  Getting a grip on dividends and dividend rates ................... 132
  Recognizing who's well-suited for income stocks ............... 132
  Checking out the advantages of income stocks ................... 133
  Watching out for the disadvantages of income stocks ........ 133
Analyzing Income Stocks ............................................................. 135
  Understanding your needs first ............................................. 135
  Checking out yield ................................................................. 137
  Checking the stock's payout ratio ........................................ 139
  Diversifying your stocks ........................................................ 140
  Examining the company's bond rating .................................. 140
Exploring Some Typical Income Stocks ...................................... 141
  Utilities ................................................................................... 141
  Real estate stocks and investment trusts ............................ 142
  Royalty (energy) trusts .......................................................... 142

### Chapter 10: Getting a Grip on Economics ......................143

Breaking Down Microeconomics versus Macroeconomics ..................144
  Microeconomics..................................................................144
  Macroeconomics..................................................................145
Understanding Important Concepts in Economic Logic ......................145
  Supply and demand ...........................................................146
  Wants and needs................................................................146
  Dynamic analysis versus static analysis.................................147
  Cause and effect................................................................148
Surveying a Few Schools of Economic Thought...............................148
  The Marx school ...............................................................148
  The Keynes school.............................................................149
  The Austrian school ..........................................................150
Understanding Some Current Economic Issues Facing
  Stock Investors................................................................151
  Inflation .........................................................................151
  Government intervention ...................................................152

### Chapter 11: Money, Mayhem, and Votes ......................153

Tying Together Politics and Stocks...........................................154
  Seeing the general effects of politics on stock investing..............154
  Ascertaining the political climate.........................................156
  Distinguishing between nonsystemic and systemic effects.........158
  Understanding price controls ..............................................159
Poking into Political Resources ..............................................160
  Government reports to watch for..........................................160
  Web sites to surf ..............................................................162

## Part III: Picking the Winners ...................... 163

### Chapter 12: Financial-Statement Boot Camp ...................165

Reading the Income Statement ..............................................165
  Revenues........................................................................166
  Cost of sales....................................................................166
  Gross margin ...................................................................167
  Selling, general, and administrative (SG&A) ...........................167
  Research and development (R&D).........................................168
  Depreciation and amortization .............................................168
  Reserves.........................................................................168
  Interest and taxes .............................................................169
  Income from continuing operations.......................................169
  Extraordinary items...........................................................170

Impairments, investments, and other write-downs......................171
Net income.................................................................................172
The Balance Sheet.................................................................................172
Cash and cash equivalents........................................................173
Inventory.....................................................................................175
Fixed assets................................................................................176
Investments................................................................................177
Intangible assets........................................................................178
Payables......................................................................................179
Long-term liabilities..................................................................179
Owner's equity...........................................................................180
The Statement of Cash Flows...............................................................181
Cash flow from operations........................................................182
Cash flow from investing activities..........................................182
"Free" cash flow.........................................................................183
Cash flow from financing activities..........................................183
Introducing Ratio Analysis..................................................................183

**Chapter 13: Silly Income-Statement Tricks................185**
How Did All This Start?.........................................................................186
Revealing Revenue Manipulation........................................................188
Accelerating sales......................................................................188
Paying with cash, credit card, or stock?..................................188
Creating revenue out of thin air..............................................188
Moving revenue in mysterious ways........................................189
Hiding Expenses: Capitalizing Costs..................................................189
Small fry......................................................................................190
Big fry..........................................................................................190
Related-party transactions.......................................................190
Sussing Out Stock Options...................................................................191
How options work......................................................................191
What to watch for.......................................................................191
Reviewing Reserves...............................................................................192
Taking On Tax Losses............................................................................193
Pro Forma Performance.........................................................................193
Picky, picky.................................................................................193
The good news is . . ..................................................................194

**Chapter 14: Silly Balance-Sheet Tricks.................195**
Accounts Receivable: Allowing for Returned Stuff............................196
Message to auditor: It's the economy, stupid!........................196
Red flags and other signs..........................................................196
Increasing Profits through Inventories...............................................197
Making Acquisitions Look So Good......................................................198

Special Charges and More Big Baths ........................................198
Hiding Liabilities: Off-Balance-Sheet Obligations ....................199
    Leasing transactions...............................................200
    Securitization transactions.....................................200
    Commitments and contingencies ............................201
    Creation of unconsolidated or special-purpose entities (SPEs) ....201
Pension Plans...........................................................202
    Accounting impact, too..........................................202
    Oh, and one more thing . . . ....................................203
Tricks of the Trade: Other Things to Watch Out For...................203
    Smoke and mirrors ...............................................203
    And materiality rabbits, too ....................................203
    Buzzwords and other warning signs .........................204

**Chapter 15: Looking at What the Insiders Do: Corporate Hijinks . . .207**
Tracking Insider Trading ...............................................208
    U.S. insider trading information................................208
    Canadian insider trading information .........................209
Looking at Insider Transactions ......................................210
    Learning from insider buying...................................210
    Picking up tips from insider selling ...........................212
Considering Corporate Stock Buybacks ..............................213
    Boosting earnings per share....................................214
    Beating back a takeover bid ....................................214
    Exploring the downside of buybacks .........................215
    Ordinary stock splits.............................................216
    Reverse stock splits..............................................216

**Chapter 16: Five Minutes for Misconduct . . . . . . . . . . . . . . . . . . . . . .219**
Ruin at the Top: Corporate Governance Risk.........................220
    The role of the board of directors.............................220
    How the BOD manages risks ...................................220
    Senior management's role in good governance:
      Rolling up the sleeves...................................221
    Management's role in controlling risk ........................222
    Back to the BOD...................................................223
Misbehavin': Ethical Risk...............................................223
    Fraud.................................................................223
    Conflict of interest ...............................................224
A Bad Rep: Reputational Risk...........................................224
Information and Technology Risks .....................................225
    Piracy................................................................225
    Privacy...............................................................226

**Chapter 17: Analyzing Industries** . . . . . . . . . . . . . . . . . . . . . . . . . . .**227**

Interrogating the Industries . . . . . . . . . . . . . . . . . . . . . . . . . . . . . . 228
Which category does the industry fall into? . . . . . . . . . . . . . . . 228
Is the industry growing? . . . . . . . . . . . . . . . . . . . . . . . . . . . . . . . . 229
Are the industry's products or services in demand? . . . . . . . . . 231
What does the industry's growth rely on? . . . . . . . . . . . . . . . . . 231
Is the industry dependent on another industry? . . . . . . . . . . . . 232
What are the leading companies in the industry? . . . . . . . . . . . 232
Is the industry a target of government action? . . . . . . . . . . . . . 233
Outlining Key Industries . . . . . . . . . . . . . . . . . . . . . . . . . . . . . . . . . . 233
Moving in: Real estate . . . . . . . . . . . . . . . . . . . . . . . . . . . . . . . . . 234
Driving it home: Automotive . . . . . . . . . . . . . . . . . . . . . . . . . . . . 235
Talking tech: Computers and related electronics . . . . . . . . . . . 235
Banking on it: Financials . . . . . . . . . . . . . . . . . . . . . . . . . . . . . . . 236

**Chapter 18: Emerging-Sector Opportunities** . . . . . . . . . . . . . . . . . . . .**237**

Bullish Opportunities . . . . . . . . . . . . . . . . . . . . . . . . . . . . . . . . . . . . 239
Commodities . . . . . . . . . . . . . . . . . . . . . . . . . . . . . . . . . . . . . . . . . 239
Oil and gas . . . . . . . . . . . . . . . . . . . . . . . . . . . . . . . . . . . . . . . . . . . 240
Alternative energy . . . . . . . . . . . . . . . . . . . . . . . . . . . . . . . . . . . . 241
Gold and other precious metals . . . . . . . . . . . . . . . . . . . . . . . . . 241
Healthcare . . . . . . . . . . . . . . . . . . . . . . . . . . . . . . . . . . . . . . . . . . . 242
Defending the nation . . . . . . . . . . . . . . . . . . . . . . . . . . . . . . . . . . 243
A Bearish Outlook . . . . . . . . . . . . . . . . . . . . . . . . . . . . . . . . . . . . . . . 244
Avoiding consumer discretionary sectors . . . . . . . . . . . . . . . . . 244
A warning on real estate . . . . . . . . . . . . . . . . . . . . . . . . . . . . . . . 245
The great credit monster . . . . . . . . . . . . . . . . . . . . . . . . . . . . . . . 246
Cyclical stocks . . . . . . . . . . . . . . . . . . . . . . . . . . . . . . . . . . . . . . . . 247
Geographic regions: Stalled economic engines . . . . . . . . . . . . 248
Important Considerations for Bulls and Bears . . . . . . . . . . . . . . . . 250
Conservative and bullish . . . . . . . . . . . . . . . . . . . . . . . . . . . . . . . 250
Aggressive and bullish . . . . . . . . . . . . . . . . . . . . . . . . . . . . . . . . . 251
Conservative and bearish . . . . . . . . . . . . . . . . . . . . . . . . . . . . . . 251
Aggressive and bearish . . . . . . . . . . . . . . . . . . . . . . . . . . . . . . . . 251

*Part IV: Investment Strategies* . . . . . . . . . . . . . . . . . . . . . . . **253**

**Chapter 19: Choosing between Investing and Trading** . . . . . . . . . . .**255**

The Differences between Investing and Trading . . . . . . . . . . . . . . . 255
The time factor . . . . . . . . . . . . . . . . . . . . . . . . . . . . . . . . . . . . . . . 256
The psychology factor . . . . . . . . . . . . . . . . . . . . . . . . . . . . . . . . . 257
Checking out an example . . . . . . . . . . . . . . . . . . . . . . . . . . . . . . . 257

Tools of the Canadian Trader ................................................................. 260
  Technical analysis .......................................................................... 260
  Brokerage orders .......................................................................... 261
  Advisory services .......................................................................... 261
The Basic Rules of Trading...................................................................... 262

**Chapter 20: Selecting a Strategy That's Just Right for You . . . . . . . .265**

Laying Out Your Plans ............................................................................. 265
  Living the bachelor life: Young single with no dependants ......... 266
  Going together like a horse and carriage: Married
    with children.............................................................................. 266
  Getting ready for retirement: Over 40 and either single
    or married .................................................................................. 267
  Kicking back in the hammock: Already retired............................. 267
Allocating Your Assets.............................................................................. 268
  Investors with less than $10,000 .................................................. 268
  Investors with $10,000 to $50,000 ................................................ 269
  Investors with $50,000 or more..................................................... 269
Knowing When to Sell ............................................................................. 270

**Chapter 21: Understanding Brokerage Orders and
Trading Techniques . . . . . . . . . . . . . . . . . . . . . . . . . . . . . . . . . . . . . .273**

Checking Out Brokerage Orders.............................................................. 274
  On the clock: Time-related orders................................................ 274
  At your command: Condition-related orders ............................... 276
  The joys of technology: Advanced orders.................................... 281
Pass the Margin, Please ........................................................................... 282
  Examining marginal outcomes ...................................................... 282
  Maintaining your balance .............................................................. 284
Going Short and Coming Out Ahead ...................................................... 285
  Setting up a short sale.................................................................... 286
  Oops! Going short when prices grow taller.................................. 286
  Feeling the squeeze ....................................................................... 287

**Chapter 22: Keeping More of Your Money from the Taxman . . . . . . .289**

Interest Income......................................................................................... 290
Dividend Income....................................................................................... 291
Stock Dividends and Splits ..................................................................... 292
Capital Gains and Losses......................................................................... 292
  Capital-gains deduction ................................................................. 293
  Superficial losses ........................................................................... 293
  Reserves........................................................................................... 293
Oil, Gas, and Mineral Stock Investments .............................................. 294
Mutual Funds............................................................................................. 294

The Tax-Wise REIT .................................................................. 295
Deferred-Income Tax Shelters and Plans.................................. 296
    Registered Retirement Savings Plans (RRSPs)................... 296
    Registered Retirement Income Funds (RRIFs) ................... 300
    Registered Education Savings Plans (RESPs)...................... 300
    There's a catch................................................................... 302
Tax-Free Savings Accounts..................................................... 302
    Investigating the TFSA rules .............................................. 303
    Comparing TFSAs to RRSPs ............................................... 303

## Part V: The Part of Tens .................................... 305

### Chapter 23: Ten Ways to Profit Before the Crowd Does .......... 307

Use Your Instincts .................................................................. 307
Take Notice of Praise from Consumer Groups .......................... 308
Check Out Powerful Demographics .......................................... 308
Look for a Rise in Earnings...................................................... 308
Analyze Industries .................................................................. 309
Stay Aware of Positive Publicity for Industries ......................... 310
Watch Megatrends .................................................................. 310
Keep Track of Politics ............................................................. 310
Recognize Heavy Insider or Corporate Buying.......................... 311
Follow Institutional Investors .................................................. 311

### Chapter 24: Ten Ways to Protect Your Stock Market Profits ....... 313

Accrue Cash ........................................................................... 313
Spread Your Money across Several Stocks................................ 313
Buy More of a Down (Yet Solid) Stock...................................... 314
Apply Long-Term Logic............................................................ 314
Use the Almighty Stop-Loss Order ........................................... 314
Use the Almighty Trailing-Stop Order....................................... 315
Set Up Broker Triggers............................................................ 315
Consider the Put Option .......................................................... 316
Check Out the Covered Call Option .......................................... 316
When All Else Fails, Sell .......................................................... 317

### Chapter 25: Ten Red Flags for Stock Investors .................. 319

Earnings Slow Down or Head South .......................................... 319
Sales Slow Down .................................................................... 320
Debt Is Too High or Unsustainable ........................................... 321
Analysts Are Exuberant Despite Logic....................................... 321
Insider Selling........................................................................ 322
A Bond Rating Cut .................................................................. 322
Increased Negative Coverage................................................... 322

Industry Problems ...........................................................................323
Political Problems ...........................................................................323
Funny Accounting: No Laughing Here!.............................................323

**Chapter 26: Ten Challenges and Opportunities for Stock Investors . . . . . . . . . . . . . . . . . . . . . . . . . . . . . . . . . .325**

Debt, Debt, and More Debt..............................................................325
Derivatives......................................................................................326
Real Estate ......................................................................................326
Inflation ..........................................................................................327
Pensions and Unfunded Liabilities .................................................327
The Growth of Government .............................................................328
Recession/Depression.....................................................................328
Commodities ...................................................................................329
Energy .............................................................................................329
Dangers from Left Field...................................................................329

**Part VI: Appendixes . . . . . . . . . . . . . . . . . . . . . . . . . . . . . . . 331**

**Appendix A: Financial Ratios. . . . . . . . . . . . . . . . . . . . . . . . . . .333**

Liquidity Ratios...............................................................................334
Current ratio...............................................................................334
Quick ratio .................................................................................335
Operating Ratios.............................................................................335
Return on equity (ROE)..............................................................335
Return on assets (ROA) .............................................................336
Sales to receivables ratio (SR) ..................................................336
Solvency Ratios...............................................................................337
Debt to net equity ratio..............................................................337
Working capital ..........................................................................338
Common Size Ratios.......................................................................338
Valuation Ratios..............................................................................339
Price-to-earnings ratio (P/E)......................................................339
Price to sales ratio (PSR) ...........................................................340
Price to book ratio (PBR)............................................................341

**Appendix B: Resources for Stock Investors . . . . . . . . . . . . . . . . . . .343**

Basics of Investing...........................................................................343
Financial Planning Sources.............................................................344
General Investing Supersites...........................................................344
Investor Research and Analysis Resources .....................................345
Books and pamphlets..................................................................346
Special books of interest to stock investors ...............................347

        Periodicals and magazines ................................................348
        Company research and analyst evaluations ..................348
        Industry analysis ............................................................349
        External factors that affect market value ....................349
        Investment news sources ..............................................350
        Press releases ................................................................350
    Tax Resources ......................................................................350
    Stock Investing Web Sites ..................................................351
        Stock exchanges ............................................................351
        Investors' associations and organizations ..................352
        Stock screens ................................................................352
        Quotes ............................................................................352
        Charts ............................................................................353
        Earnings and earnings estimates ................................353
        Technical analysis ........................................................353
        Insider trading ..............................................................354
        Fraud ..............................................................................354
        Public filings ................................................................354
        IPOs ................................................................................355

*Index* ................................................................ *357*

# Introduction

*S*tock Investing For Canadians For Dummies, 3rd Edition, has been an honour for us to write. We are grateful we can share our thoughts, information, and experience with such a large and devoted group of Canadian readers.

This edition is our most important one so far because so much change, volatility, and uncertainty have become part of today's stock market. It's not your grandparents' stock market anymore! Recently, all too many well-known stocks have ceased to exist — including the "safe" stocks your grandma and grandpa used to buy — because the companies behind those stocks went bankrupt. You know many of the names because they featured prominently in 2009's headlines.

In today's world landscape, the opportunities for great gains (and even greater losses) have reached an extreme. In some ways, our current market reminds us of Dickens' famous novel opener: "It was the best of times, it was the worst of times . . ." In terms of what faces us now — economic uncertainty, terrorism, war, political instability, rising inflation, persistent unemployment, and so on — these seem like the worst of times. Yet when we think of the tools, strategies, and investing vehicles available for you to build (and protect) wealth, it's clear these can be the best of times.

At the time of this writing, we still do not know in which direction the stock market will likely go. We never really do. As you see in this book, stock markets march to the beat of many drums, including economic ones. No one knows when we will truly emerge from the Great Recession that sank the stock market to a painful low in March 2009. If we have already emerged, then any Canadian who invested near those 2009 lows has likely done very well since then, and everyone can still benefit from a rising stock market. However, if the rebound in the Canadian and world economy was just a head fake — or if terrorism, political strife, or other nerve-fraying world events arise to undermine economic recovery — then expect the stock markets to dip again, perhaps even re-testing the low levels we've already experienced.

What can or should Canadian stock investors do? Like with so many of life's lessons, being successful at stock investing takes diligent effort, experience, and knowledge. Even if you suffer an unfortunate loss in the stock market, that in itself affords a valuable learning experience — but only if you understand why the loss occurred in the first place. We can definitely help you understand stock investing fundamentals, and help you avoid some of the big mistakes others have already made. We can also help you better understand and hopefully not repeat any past stock investing mistakes you yourself may have made. It is our pleasure and purpose to help you succeed!

In the face of all of this uncertainty, today's most effective stock investors will be those who are nimble, prepared to make quick decisions, and perceptive to changes that are relevant to stock investing. This book helps you get to that state, and shows you how to make important connections to the events and drivers that move stocks in one direction or another. In all the years that we've counselled and educated investors, the single difference between success and failure, between gain and loss, boils down to one word: _knowledge_. Welcome to this book — and welcome to the intriguing and exciting world of stock investing!

# About This Book

The stock market has been a cornerstone of the Canadian investor's passive wealth-building program for more than a century and continues in this role. This decade has been one wild roller-coaster ride for stock investors. Fortunes have been made and lost. Even with all the media attention, all the talking heads on radio and television, and the reams of books promising great profits, the investing public still didn't avoid losing trillions in a historic stock market debacle. Sadly, even the so-called experts who understand stocks didn't see the economic and geopolitical forces that acted like a tsunami on the market. With just a little more knowledge and a few wealth-preserving techniques, more investors could have held onto their hard-earned stock market fortunes. Cheer up, though: This book gives you an early warning on those megatrends and events that will affect your stock portfolio. Other books may tell you about stocks, but this book tells you about stocks, what affects them, and other stock investing fundamentals.

This book is designed to give you a realistic approach to making money in stocks. It provides the essence of sound, practical stock investing strategies and insights that have been market-tested and proven from nearly 100 years of stock market history. We don't expect you to read it cover to cover, although we'd be delighted if you read every word! Instead, this book is primarily designed as a reference tool. Feel free to read the chapters in whatever order you choose. You can flip to the sections and chapters that interest you or those that include topics you need to know more about.

_Stock Investing For Canadians For Dummies,_ 3rd Edition, is different from the "get rich with stocks" titles that have crammed the bookshelves in recent years. It doesn't take a standard approach to the topic; it doesn't assume that stocks are a sure thing and the be-all, end-all of wealth building. In fact, at times in this book, we tell you when _not_ to invest in stocks.

This book can help you succeed not only in up markets but also in down markets. Bull markets and bear markets come and go, but the informed Canadian investor can keep making money no matter what. To give you an extra edge, we've included information about the investing environment for stocks. Whether it's politics or hurricanes (or both), you need to know how the big picture affects your stock investment decisions.

# Conventions Used in This Book

To make navigating through this book easier, we've established the following conventions:

- **Boldface** text points out keywords or the main parts of bulleted items.
- *Italics* highlight new terms that are defined.
- Monofont is used for Web addresses.

When this book was printed, some of the Web addresses needed to run across two lines of text. Note that we did not add hyphens to indicate the breaks; when using these Web addresses you can just type in exactly what you see, pretending the line break doesn't exist.

# What You Don't Have to Read

Sidebars (grey boxes of text) in this book give you a more in-depth look at certain topics — they further illuminate a particular point, but aren't crucial to your understanding of the rest of the book. Feel free to read the sidebars or skip them.

You can also pass over the text that accompanies the Technical Stuff icon (see the section "Icons Used in This Book"). Text associated with this icon gives some technical details about stock investing that are certainly interesting and informative, but even if you don't read it you will still come away with the information you need.

# Foolish Assumptions

We figure you've picked up this book for one or more of the following reasons:

- You're a beginner and want a crash course on stock investing that's an easy read.

✔ You're already a stock investor, and you need a book that allows you to read only those chapters that cover specific stock investing topics of interest to you.

✔ You need to review your own situation with the information in the book to see whether you missed anything when you invested in that hot stock your brother-in-law recommended.

✔ You need a great gift! When Uncle Gus is upset over his poor stock picks, give him this book so he can get back on his financial feet. Be sure to get a copy for his broker, too. (Odds are the broker was the one who made those picks to begin with.)

# How This Book Is Organized

We've taken care to lay out information in a straightforward format. The parts progress in a logical approach that any Canadian interested in stock investing can follow very easily.

## Part 1: The Essentials of Stock Investing

This part is for everyone. Understanding the essentials of stock investing and investing in general will only help you, especially in these uncertain economic times. Stocks may even touch your finances in ways not readily apparent. For example, stocks aren't only in individual accounts; they're also in mutual funds and Canadian pension plans.

An important point is that stocks are really financial tools that are a means to an end. Investors should be able to answer the question, "Why am I considering stocks at all?" Stocks are a great vehicle for wealth building, but only if investors realize what they can accomplish and how to use them. Chapter 2 explains how to assess your current financial situation and personal goals, and Chapter 3 defines common approaches to stock investing.

One essential of stock investing is recognizing and understanding risk. All too many Canadians ignore risk, and they do so at their peril. Chapter 4, on risk, is one of the most important chapters serious stock investors should read. You can't avoid every type of risk out there (life itself embodies risk). However, this chapter can help you recognize it and find ways to minimize it in your stock investing program. Chapter 5 rounds out the essentials by showing you how stock market performance is measured.

# *Part II: Before You Invest*

When you're ready to embark on your second career as a stock investor, you need to use some critical resources to gather information about the stocks you're interested in. Fortunately, you live in the information age. We pity the investors from the 1920s who didn't have access to so many resources, but today's investors are in an enviable and very empowered position. This part tells you where to find valuable and timely information and how to use it to be a more knowledgeable investor. Chapter 6 is a great starting place for your information gathering; we show you how to stay on top of financial news and read stock tables, among other topics.

When you're ready to invest, you'll invariably have to turn to a Canadian broker. Several types of brokers are out there, so know which is which. The wrong broker can make you . . . uh . . . broker. Chapter 7 helps you choose. We also explain how stocks can be used for both growth and income purposes, and discuss the characteristics of each; see Chapters 8 and 9 for more information.

New to this edition is Chapter 10, which gives you the lowdown on how a grasp of basic economics can make you more successful with your stock investing strategy. What with the economy being front row centre in the media these days, we thought we'd show you how the economy ties in to stock investing. In Chapter 11, we also show you how politics affects the stock market as well as individual stocks.

# *Part III: Picking the Winners*

Where do you turn to find specific information about a company's financial health? We tell you about the financial documents to review to make a more informed decision. We also show you how to make sense of the data.

Looking through company financial information is critical to stock investing, and we clarify what financial statements really mean. One of the things some investors all too often fail to do is to extract the story told by these financial statements. Instead, they rely on others to do this homework for them — financial analysts with different agendas or levels of knowledge. Many analysts still fail to see instances of questionable accounting tricks that so many companies continue to espouse. The bottom line is that if you want it done right, learn to do it yourself. Read a company's valuable financial information — it's the key to picking winners! Chapters 12 to 14 take you on that journey.

Chapter 15 urges you to keep an eye on what company insiders are doing, and we explain what it may mean if a company's management is buying or selling the same stock you're considering. In Chapter 16, we revisit risk and introduce even more risks you should know about. Together, these chapters will help you avoid making stock investing mistakes.

We also show you in Chapter 17 how important it is to analyze industries before investing in individual stocks. We close out this part with Chapter 18, which presents for your consideration some relevant and timely emerging-sector opportunities.

We compare buying stock to choosing goldfish — if you're looking at a bunch, you want to make sure you pick the healthiest ones to buy. With stocks, you also need to pick companies that are healthy. Part III helps you do that.

# Part IV: Investment Strategies

Even the stocks of great companies can fall in a bad investing environment. This is where it pays to be aware of the "macro" picture. If stocks were goldfish, the macro would be the pond or the goldfish bowl — and even healthy goldfish can die if the water is toxic. Therefore, monitor the investing environment for stocks. Part IV reveals tips, strategies, and resources that you shouldn't ignore.

Investing is a long-term activity but stocks can also be short-term opportunities; therefore, we discuss stock trading in Chapter 19. In Chapter 20 we provide guidance on selecting an investing strategy that's right for your personal and financial situations.

You may be an investor, but that doesn't mean you have deep pockets. Chapter 21 tells you how to buy stocks with low (or no) transaction costs. If you're going to buy the stock anyway, why not save on commissions and other costs?

After you spend your time, money, and effort to grow your money in the world of stocks, you have yet another concern: holding on to your hard-earned gains. This challenge is summarized in one word: taxes. Sound tax planning is crucial for everyone who works hard. After all, taxes are the biggest expense in your lifetime (right after children!). See Chapter 22 for more information on how the Canada Revenue Agency treats stock investing.

# Part V: The Part of Tens

We wrap up the book with a hallmark of *For Dummies* books — the Part of Tens. These chapters give you a mini crash course in stock investing, including tips on how to profit with stocks before the crowd does (Chapter 23) and how to protect those profits (Chapter 24). We also provide a list of ten red flags for stock investors (Chapter 25), along with ten challenges and opportunities that face stock investors (Chapter 26).

## Part VI: Appendixes

Don't overlook the appendixes. We pride ourselves on these resources we provide to our students and readers so they can make informed investment decisions. Whether the topic is stock investing terminology, economics, or avoiding capital gains taxes, we include a treasure trove of resources to help you.

In Appendix A, we explain key financial ratios. These important numbers help you better and more quickly determine whether to invest in a particular company's stock. And whether you prefer a bookstore, the library, or the Internet, Appendix B gives you some great places to turn to for help.

## Icons Used in This Book

When you see this icon, we're reminding you about some information to always keep stashed in your memory, whether you're new to investing or an old pro.

The text attached to this icon may not be crucial to your success as an investor, but it may enable you to talk shop with investing gurus and better understand the financial pages of your favourite business publication or Web site.

This icon flags a particular bit of advice that just may give you an edge over other investors.

Pay special attention to this icon, because the advice can prevent headaches, heartaches, and financial aches.

## Where to Go from Here

You may not need to read every chapter to make you more confident as a stock investor, so feel free to jump around to suit your personal needs. Because every chapter is designed to be as self-contained as possible, it won't do you any harm to cherry-pick what you really want to read. But if you're like us, you may still want to check out every chapter because you never know when you may come across a new tip or resource that will make a profitable difference in your stock portfolio. We want you to be successful so we can brag about you in the next edition!

# Part I

# The Essentials of Stock Investing

The 5th Wave                    By Rich Tennant

EARLY INVESTORS TRACKING A STOCK

# In this part . . .

The latest market turmoil and uncertainty tell investors to get back to square one. Your success is dependent on doing your homework before you invest your first dollar in stocks. Most investors don't realize that they should be scrutinizing their own situations and financial goals at least as much as they scrutinize stocks. How else can you know which stocks are right for you? Too many people risk too much simply because they don't take stock of their current needs, goals, and risk tolerance before they invest. The chapters in this part tell you what you need to know to choose the stocks that best suit you.

# Chapter 1

# Welcome to the World of Stock Investing

*In This Chapter*

▶ Knowing the essentials

▶ Doing your own research

▶ Recognizing winners

▶ Exploring investment strategies

$S$tock investing was the hot thing during the late 1990s — a trend just like hula hoops and pet rocks. With the new millennium, however, a reversal of fortunes occurred as the bear market of 2000–02 rocked our world (a *bear market* is a prolonged period of falling prices — in this case, stock prices). This decade has been a wild roller-coaster ride that saw the market hit new highs in 2008, although it was down in ugly fashion in 2009. During this time, the public figured out that stock investing isn't for wild-eyed amateurs or dart-throwers (or the worst . . . wild-eyed amateur dart-throwers!).

We wrote much of this Canadian 3rd edition with current events and market conditions on our radar screen. The year 2009 witnessed some ominous events that will make stock investing very interesting (to say the least) for the foreseeable future. Don't let that scare you, though; informed investors have made money in all sorts of markets — good, bad, and even ugly.

As we write this the jury is still out whether North America will remain in a low interest rate environment; or whether we'll step into a new inflationary spiral like we did in the 70s when governments printed and pumped too much money into the North American economy. It seems for now that today's rise in money supply is being offset by deflation, thanks in part to persistent unemployment, offshore competition, and weak domestic economic output. As Canadians navigate through these new economic realities, it will become very important to select good stocks that can actually benefit from any given economic state. Recognizing the overall environment you're investing in is something we'll help you with, and it will help you preserve your nest egg and even make you wealthier.

The purpose of this book is not only to tell you about the basics of stock investing, but also to let you in on some solid strategies that can help you profit from the stock market. But before you invest your first dollar you need to understand the basics of stock investing, which we introduce in this chapter.

# Understanding the Basics

The basics are so basic that few people are paying much attention to them. Perhaps the most basic — and therefore most important — thing to grasp is the risk you face whenever you do anything (like putting your hard-earned money in an investment like a stock). When you lose track of the basics, you lose track of why you invested to begin with. Find out more about risk (and the different kinds of risk) in Chapters 4 and 16. (Yes, two chapters — understanding risk is *that* important!)

When the late comedian Henny Youngman was asked, "How is your wife?" he responded, "Compared to what?" This also applies to stocks. When you're asked, "How is your stock?" you can very well respond that it's doing well, especially when compared to an acceptable yardstick such as a stock index (like the TSX, or the S&P 500). Find out more about indexes in Chapter 5.

The bottom line in stock investing is that you shouldn't immediately send your money to a brokerage account or go to a Web site and click "buy stock." The first thing you should do is find out as much as you can about what stocks are, and how and when to use them to achieve your wealth-building goals. Chapters 2 and 3 help you assess your current financial situation and help you understand common approaches to stock investing.

Now is the time to get straight exactly what a stock is. A *stock* is a type of security that indicates ownership in a corporation and represents a claim on part of that corporation's assets and earnings. The two primary types of stocks are common and preferred. *Common stock* (what we cover throughout this book) entitles the owner to vote at shareholders' meetings and receive any dividends the company issues. *Preferred stock* doesn't usually confer voting rights, but it does include some rights that exceed those of common stock. Preferred stockholders, for example, have priority in certain conditions, such as receiving dividends before common stockholders in the event the corporation goes bankrupt or becomes insolvent.

# Preparing to Buy Stocks

Gathering information is critical in your stock-investing pursuits, and is best done two times: before you invest, and after. Obviously, you should become more informed before you invest your first dollar, but you also need to stay informed about what's happening to the company whose stock you buy, and also about the industry and the general economy. To find the best information sources, check out Chapter 6.

When you're ready to invest, you need a brokerage account. How do you know which broker to use? Chapter 7 provides some answers and resources to help you choose a broker.

# Knowing How to Pick Winners

When you get past the basics, you can get to the meat of stock picking. Successful stock picking isn't mysterious, but it does take some time, effort, and analysis. And the effort is worthwhile, because stocks are a convenient and important part of most investors' portfolios. Read the following sections and be sure to leapfrog to the relevant chapters to get the inside scoop on hot stocks.

## Recognizing stock value

Imagine that you like eggs and you're buying them at the grocery store. In this example, the eggs are like companies, and the prices represent the prices you would pay for the companies' stock. The grocery store is the stock market. What if two brands of eggs are similar, but one costs 50 cents a carton and the other costs 75 cents? Which would you choose? Odds are you'd look at both brands, judge their quality, and — if they're indeed similar — take the cheaper eggs. The eggs at 75 cents are overpriced. The same is true of stocks. What if you compare two companies that are similar in every respect but have different share prices? All things being equal, the cheaper price has greater value for the investor.

But the egg example has another side. What if the quality of the two brands of eggs is significantly different, but their prices are the same? If one brand of eggs is stale, of poor quality, and priced at 50 cents and the other brand is fresh, of superior quality, and also priced at 50 cents, which would you get? We'd take the good brand because they're better eggs. Perhaps the lesser eggs are an acceptable purchase at 10 cents, but they're definitely overpriced at 50 cents. The same example works with stocks. A poorly run company isn't a good choice if you can buy a better company in the marketplace at the same — or a better — price.

Comparing the value of eggs may seem overly simplistic, yet it provides an egg-cellent depiction of the heart of stock investing. (Sorry, we couldn't resist.) Eggs and egg prices can be as varied as companies and stock prices. As an investor, you must make it your job to find the best value for your investment dollars. Otherwise, you end up with egg on your face. (You saw that one coming too, right?)

## Understanding how market capitalization affects stock value

You can determine a company's value (and thus the value of its stock) in many ways. The most basic way is to look at the company's market value, also known as *market capitalization* (or market cap). Market capitalization is simply the value you get when you multiply all the outstanding shares of a stock by the current price of a single share.

Calculating the market cap is easy. If a company has 1 million shares outstanding and its share price is $10, the market cap is $10 million.

Small cap, mid cap, and large cap aren't references to headgear; they're references to how large a company is as measured by its market value. The five basic stock categories of market capitalization are:

- ✔ **Micro cap (under $250 million):** These stocks are the smallest and hence the riskiest available.

- ✔ **Small cap ($250 million to $1 billion):** These stocks fare better than the micro caps and still have plenty of growth potential. The key word here is "potential."

- ✔ **Mid cap ($1 billion to $10 billion):** For many investors, this category offers a good compromise between small caps and large caps. These stocks have some of the safety of large caps while retaining some of the growth potential of small caps.

- ✔ **Large cap ($10 billion to $50 billion):** This category is usually best reserved for conservative stock investors who want steady appreciation with greater safety. Stocks in this category are frequently referred to as *blue chips.*

- ✔ **Ultra cap (over $50 billion):** These stocks are also called *mega caps* and obviously refer to companies that are the biggest of the big. U.S. stocks such as General Electric and Exxon Mobil are examples. (No ultra caps exist in Canada — not even Research In Motion qualifies.)

From a safety point of view, a company's size and market value do matter. All things being equal, large-cap stocks are considered safer than small-cap stocks. That's because larger companies generally have better operational controls than smaller ones, so their risks are more mitigated. However, small-cap stocks have greater potential for growth. These tend to be leaner, meaner, and more responsive to market and customer needs. They often exploit opportunities more quickly.

Compare these stocks to trees: Which tree is sturdier, a giant B.C. redwood or a small oak tree that's just a year old? In a great storm, the redwood holds up well, while the smaller tree has a rough time. But you also have to ask yourself which tree has more opportunity for growth. The redwood may not have much growth left, but the small oak tree has plenty of growth to look forward to.

For beginning investors, comparing market cap to trees isn't so far-fetched. You want your money to branch out without becoming a sap.

Although market capitalization is important to consider, don't invest (or not invest) based solely on it. It's just one measure of value. As a serious investor, you need to look at numerous factors that can help you determine whether any given stock is a good investment. Keep reading — this book is full of information to help you decide.

## Sharpening your investment skills

Canadian investors who analyze a company can better judge the value of its stock and profit from buying and selling it. Your greatest asset in stock investing is knowledge (and a little common sense). To succeed in the world of stock investing, keep in mind these key success factors:

- **Understand why you want to invest in stocks.** Are you seeking appreciation (capital gains) or income (dividends)? Look at Chapters 8 and 9 for information on these topics.

- **Get a good grounding in economics.** It could save your financial life! In Chapter 10, we include some basic (but very interesting) points on economics. We suspect that as a group stock investors are woefully underinformed in economics now more than ever, and are therefore at greater risk (translation: they're prone to bad stock decisions!). Check it out — you'll be glad you did.

- **Stay on top of political trends.** Stocks succeed or fail in large part because of the political environment in which they operate. Politics (see Chapter 11) is definitely something you should know about in the context of stock investing.

- **Do some research on the numbers behind a company.** Look at the company whose stock you're considering to see whether it's a profitable and financially stable business worthy of your investment dollars. Chapters 12, 13, and 14 help you scrutinize the all-important financial reports of companies.

✔ **Investigate the people running the companies you're considering investing in.** Sometimes, what people tell you to do with stocks is not as revealing as what people are actually doing. This is why we like to look at company insiders before we buy or sell a particular stock. To find out more about insider buying and selling, read Chapter 15.

✔ **Choose a winning industry to choose a winning stock.** You'll frequently see stock prices of mediocre companies in hot industries rise higher and faster than solid companies in floundering industries. Therefore, choosing the industry is very important. Find out more about analyzing industries in Chapter 17.

✔ **Understand and identify megatrends.** Doing so makes it easier for you to make money. This edition spends more time on — and provides more resources for — helping you see the opportunities in emerging sectors and avoid the problem areas (see Chapter 18 for details).

# Boning Up on Strategies and Tactics

Successful investing isn't just what you invest in; it's also the way you invest. We're very big on strategies that take into account your risk tolerance, stage of life, preferred type of brokerage account, and tax situation.

✔ **Recognize that the turbulent markets you've witnessed recently are likely to continue for some time.** Choosing between investing over the long term (buy and hold) and trading stocks over a shorter time frame (buy and sell quickly) may be necessary. Even though we are not huge proponents of stock trading, we agree that during these volatile times it may be appropriate to a limited extent. Delve into basic stock trading concepts in Chapter 19.

✔ **Use investing strategies like the pros do.** In other words, how you go about investing can be just as important as what you invest in. Chapter 20 highlights techniques for investing to help you make more money from your stocks.

✔ **Understand how to strategically place orders to buy and sell stocks with the broker you select.** Chapter 21 shows you how to be effective in executing orders.

✔ **Keep more of the money you earn.** After all your great work in getting the right stocks and making the big bucks, you should know about keeping more of the fruits of your investing. We cover taxes in stock investing in Chapter 22.

Actually, every chapter in this book offers you valuable guidance on some essential aspect of the fantastic world of stocks. The knowledge you pick up and apply from these pages has been tested over nearly a century of stock picking. The investment experience of the past — the good, the bad, and some of the ugly — is here for your benefit. Use this information to make a lot of money (and make us proud!). And don't forget to check out the appendixes, where we provide a wide variety of investing resources and financial ratios.

## Stock market insanity

Have you ever noticed a stock going up even though the company is reporting terrible results? How about seeing a stock nosedive despite the fact that the company is doing well? What gives? Well, judging the direction of a stock in a short-term period — over the next few days or weeks — is almost impossible.

Yes, in the short term, stock investing is irrational. The price of a stock and the value of its company seem disconnected and crazy. The key phrase to remember is "short term." A stock's price and the company's value become more logical over an extended period of time. The longer a stock is in the public's view, the more rational the performance of the stock's price. In other words, a good company continues to draw attention to itself; hence, more people want its stock, and the share price rises to better match the company's value. Conversely, a bad company doesn't hold up to continued scrutiny over time. As more and more people see that the company isn't doing well, the share price declines. Over the long run, a stock's share price and the company's value eventually become equal for the most part.

# Chapter 2

# Taking Stock of Your Current Financial Situation and Goals

. . . . . . . . . . . . . . . . . . . . . . . . . . . . . . . . . . . . . . . . . . . . . . . . . . .

*In This Chapter*

▶ Preparing your personal balance sheet

▶ Looking at your cash-flow statement

▶ Determining your financial goals

. . . . . . . . . . . . . . . . . . . . . . . . . . . . . . . . . . . . . . . . . . . . . . . . . . .

**Y**es, you want to make the big bucks. Or maybe you just want to get back the big bucks you lost in stocks during the bear market (a long period of falling prices) of 2000–02, or perhaps in the tumultuous volatility of 2008–09. (Investors who followed the guidelines from the 1st and 2nd editions of this book did much better than the crowd!) Either way, you want your money to grow so that you can have a better life. But before you make reservations for that Caribbean cruise you're dreaming about, you have to map out your action plan for getting there. Stocks can be a great component of most wealth-building programs, but you must first do some homework on a topic you should be very familiar with — yourself. That's right. Understanding your current financial situation and clearly defining your financial goals are the first steps in successful investing.

Let us give you an example. Paul met an investor at one of his seminars who had a million dollars worth of Procter & Gamble (PG) stock, and he was nearing retirement. He asked Paul if he should sell his stock and be more growth-oriented, investing in a batch of *small-cap* stocks (that is, stocks of a company worth $250 million to $1 billion; see Chapter 1). Because he already had enough assets to retire on at that time, Paul told him he didn't need to get more aggressive. In fact, Paul said that he had too much tied to a single stock, even though it was a solid, large company. What would happen to his assets if problems arose at PG? It seemed obvious to tell him to shrink his stock portfolio and put that money elsewhere, such as paying off debt or adding investment-grade bonds for diversification.

This chapter is undoubtedly one of the most important chapters in this book. At first, you may think it's more suitable for some general book on personal finance. Wrong! Unsuccessful investors' greatest weakness is not understanding their financial situation and how stocks fit in. Often, we counsel people to stay out of the stock market if they aren't prepared for the responsibilities of stock investing — they haven't been regularly reviewing the company's financial statements or tracking the company's progress.

Investing in stocks requires balance. Investors sometimes tie up too much money in stocks, putting themselves at risk of losing a significant portion of their wealth if the market plunges. Then again, other investors place little or no money in stocks and therefore miss out on excellent opportunities to grow their wealth. Investors should make stocks a part of their portfolios, but the operative word is *part*. Let stocks take up only a *portion* of your money. A disciplined investor also has money in bank accounts, investment-grade bonds, precious metals, and other assets that offer growth or income opportunities. Diversification is the key to minimizing risk. (For more on risk, see Chapters 4 and 16.)

# Establishing a Starting Point

Whether you're already in stocks or you're looking to get into stocks, you need to decide how much money you can afford to invest. No matter what you hope to accomplish with your stock investing plan, the first step to take as a budding investor is figuring out how much you own and how much you owe. To do this, prepare and review your personal balance sheet. A *balance sheet* is simply a list of your assets and your liabilities, and what each item is currently worth, so you can arrive at your *net worth*: total assets minus total liabilities. We know that these terms sound like accounting mumbo jumbo, but knowing your net worth is important to your future financial success, so we urge you to just do it!

Composing your balance sheet is simple. Pull out a pencil and a piece of paper. For the computer savvy, a spreadsheet software program accomplishes the same task. Gather all your financial documents, such as bank and brokerage statements and other such paperwork — you need figures from these documents. Then follow the steps that we outline in the following sections. Update your balance sheet at least once each year to monitor your financial progress. (Is your net worth going up or not?)

Your personal balance sheet is really no different from balance sheets that huge companies like CN (Canadian National Railway Company) prepare. (The main difference is a few zeros, but you can use our advice in this book to work on changing that.) In fact, the more you find out about your own balance sheet, the easier it is to understand the balance sheets of companies in which you're seeking to invest.

# Step 1: Making sure you have an emergency fund

First, list cash on your balance sheet (see the next step for more on listing your assets). Your goal is to have, in reserve, at least three to six months' worth of your gross living expenses in cash. The cash is important because it gives you a cushion. Three to six months is usually long enough to get you through the most common forms of financial disruption, such as losing your job and needing time to find a new one.

If your monthly expenses (or *outflow*) are $2,000, you should have at least $6,000 — and probably closer to $12,000 — in a secure, Canada Deposit Insurance Corporation (CDIC)–insured, interest-bearing bank account or other relatively safe interest-bearing vehicle, such as a money market fund. Consider this account an emergency fund and not an investment. Don't use this money to buy stocks.

Too many Canadians don't have an emergency fund, meaning that they put themselves at risk. Walking across a busy street while wearing a blindfold is a great example of putting yourself at risk, and in recent years investors have done the financial equivalent. Investors piled on tremendous debt, put too much money into investments (such as stocks) that they didn't understand, and had little or no cash savings to fall back on. One of the biggest problems of this decade was that savings were sinking to record lows while debt levels were reaching new heights. People then sold many of their stocks because they needed funds for — you guessed it — paying bills and debt.

Resist the urge to start thinking of your investment in stocks as a savings account generating over 20 percent per year. This is dangerous thinking! If your investments tank, or if you lose your job, you will have financial difficulty. This cash-flow trouble, in turn, will affect your stock portfolio (you might have to sell some stocks in your account just to get money to pay the bills). An emergency fund exists to help you through a temporary cash crunch.

# Step 2: Listing your assets in decreasing order of liquidity

Liquid assets aren't references to beer or cola (unless you're Molson, Labatt, Sleeman, or Cott). Instead, *liquidity* refers to how quickly you can convert a particular *asset* (something you own that has value) into cash. If you know the liquidity of your assets, including investments, you have some options when you need cash to buy some stock (or pay some bills). All too often, people are short on cash and have too much wealth tied up in *illiquid investments* such as real estate, leading to what the Governor of the Bank of Canada would call a "liquidity crisis." *Illiquid* is just a fancy way of saying that you don't have the immediate cash to meet a pressing need. (Hey, we've all had those moments!) Review your assets and take measures to ensure you have enough liquid assets (along with your illiquid assets).

Listing your assets in order of liquidity on your balance sheet gives you an immediate picture of which assets you can quickly convert to cash and which assets you can't. If you need money *now,* you can see that cash in hand, your chequing account, and your savings account are at the top of the list. The items last in order of liquidity become obvious; they're things like real estate and other assets that can take a long time to convert to cash.

Selling real estate can take many months, especially in a buyer's market like the one most Canadian provinces are currently experiencing. Investors who don't have adequate liquid assets run the danger of selling assets too quickly — possibly at a loss — because they scramble to accumulate the cash for their short-term financial obligations. For stock investors, this scramble may include prematurely selling stocks that they originally intended to use as long-term investments.

Table 2-1 shows a typical list of assets in order of liquidity. Use it as a guide for making your own asset list.

**Table 2-1   John Q. Investor: Personal Assets as of December 31, 2000**

| Asset Item | Market Value | Annual Growth Rate % |
|---|---|---|
| **Current Assets** | | |
| Cash on hand and in chequing | $150 | 0 |
| Bank savings accounts and GICs | $500 | 2% |
| Stocks | $2,000 | 11% |
| Mutual funds | $2,400 | 9% |
| Other assets (such as collectibles) | $240 | |
| **Total Current Assets** | **$5,290** | |
| **Long-Term Assets** | | |
| Auto | $1,800 | –10% |
| Residence | $150,000 | 5% |
| Real estate investments | $125,000 | 6% |
| Personal stuff (such as jewellery) | $4,000 | |
| **Total Long-Term Assets** | **$280,800** | |
| **Total Assets** | **$286,090** | |

The first column of Table 2-1 describes the asset. You can quickly convert *current assets* to cash — they're more liquid; *long-term assets* have value, but you can't necessarily convert them to cash quickly — they aren't very liquid.

Please take note. Stocks are listed as short-term in the table above. The reason for this is that this balance sheet is meant to list items in order of liquidity. Liquidity is best exemplified in the question, "How quickly can I turn this asset into cash?" Because a stock can be sold and converted to cash very quickly, it is a good example of a liquid asset. (However, that is not the main purpose for buying stocks.)

The second column gives the current market value for that item. Keep in mind that this value is not the purchase price or original value; it's the amount you would realistically get if you sold the asset in the current market at a given moment.

The third column tells you how well that investment is doing compared to one year ago. If the percentage rate is 5 percent, that item increased in value by 5 percent from a year ago. You need to know how well all your assets are doing. Why? To adjust your assets for maximum growth or to get rid of assets that are losing money. Assets that are doing well are kept (in fact, you may want to increase your holdings), and assets that are down in value are candidates for removal. Perhaps you can sell these losers and reinvest the money elsewhere. In addition, the realized loss has tax implications (see Chapter 22).

Figuring the annual growth rate (in the third column) as a percentage isn't difficult. Say that you buy 100 shares of the stock Gro-A-Lot Corp. (GAL), and its market value on December 31, 2008 is $50 per share, for a total market value of $5,000 (100 shares × $50 per share). When you check its value on December 31, 2009, you find out the stock is at $60 per share, meaning your shares now have a total market value of $6,000 (100 shares × $60 per share). The annual growth rate is 20 percent. You calculate this by taking the amount of the gain ($60 per share – $50 per share = $10 gain per share), which is $1,000 (100 shares × the $10 gain), and dividing it by the value at the beginning of the time period ($5,000). In this case, you get 20 percent ($1,000 ÷ $5,000). What if GAL also generates a dividend of $2 per share during that period; now what? In that case, GAL generates a total return of 24 percent. To calculate the total return, add the appreciation ($10 per share × 100 shares = $1,000) and the dividend income ($2 per share × 100 shares = $200), and then divide that sum ($1,000 + $200, or $1,200) by the value at the beginning of the year ($50 per share × 100 shares, or $5,000). The total is $1,200 ($1,000 of appreciation + $200 total dividends), or 24 percent ($1,200 ÷ $5,000).

The last line of Table 2-1 lists the total current market value of current and long-term assets. The third column answers the question, "How well did this particular asset grow from a year ago?"

## Step 3: Listing your liabilities

*Liabilities* are simply the bills that you're obligated to pay. Whether it's a credit card bill or a mortgage payment, a liability is an amount of money you have to pay back eventually (with interest). If you don't keep track of your liabilities, you may end up thinking that you have more money than you really do.

Table 2-2 lists some common liabilities. Use it as a model when you list your own. List the liabilities according to how soon you need to pay them; for example, credit card balances tend to be short-term obligations, and mortgages are long-term debts.

| Table 2-2 | Listing Personal Liabilities | |
|---|---|---|
| *Liabilities* | *Amount* | *Paying Rate %* |
| Credit cards | $4,000 | 20% |
| Personal loans | $13,000 | 10% |
| Mortgage | $100,000 | 5% |
| Total Liabilities | $117,000 | |

The first column in Table 2-2 names the type of debt. Don't forget to include student loans and auto loans if you have any of these. Never avoid listing a liability because you're embarrassed to see how much you really owe. Be honest with yourself — doing so helps you improve your financial health.

The second column shows the current value (or current balance) of your liabilities. List the most current balances to see where you stand with your creditors.

The third column reflects how much interest you're paying for carrying that debt. This information is an important reminder of how debt can be a wealth zapper. Credit card debt can have an interest rate of 19 percent or more, and to add insult to injury, the Canada Revenue Agency (CRA) doesn't even allow these interest fees to be tax deductible. Using a credit card to make even a small purchase costs you if you maintain a balance. Within a year, a $50 sweater at 19 percent ends up costing $59.50 when you add in the potential interest you pay.

When you compare your liabilities in Table 2-2 and your personal assets in Table 2-1, you may find opportunities to reduce the amount you pay for interest. Say, for example, that you pay 15 percent on a credit card balance of $4,000 but also have a personal asset of $5,000 in a bank savings account that's earning 2 percent in interest. In this case, you may want to consider taking $4,000 out of the savings account to pay off the credit card balance. Doing so saves you $520: The $4,000 you have in the bank is earning only $80 (2 percent of $4,000), while you are paying $600 on the credit card balance (15 percent of $4,000).

If you can't pay off high-interest debt, at least look for ways to minimize the cost of carrying the debt. The most obvious ways include the following:

✔ **Replacing high-interest cards with low-interest cards:** Many companies offer incentives to consumers, including signing up for credit cards with favourable rates that can be used to pay off high-interest cards.

✔ **Replacing unsecured debt with secured debt:** Credit cards and personal loans are *unsecured* (you haven't put up any collateral or other asset to secure the debt); therefore, they have higher interest rates because the creditor considers this type of debt to be riskier. Sources of secured debt (such as home equity line accounts and brokerage accounts) provide you with a means to replace your high-interest debt with lower-interest debt. You get lower interest rates with *secured debt* because it's less risky for the creditor — the debt is backed up by collateral (your home or your stocks).

The Office of the Superintendent of Bankruptcy Canada reported that 103,621 people declared bankruptcies in Canada for the 12-month period ending March 31, 2009. In 2005, that figure was about 85,000. (In the U.S., the personal bankruptcy figure hit 1.6 million people in the 12-month period ended March 31, 2009. It has hovered around the one-million mark during the past decade.) Clearly, many Canadians continue to get tripped up in debt traps and need to make a serious 180-degree turn with respect to their saving habits. Every Canadian should make a diligent effort to control and reduce any personal debt, or risk his or her personal wealth being wiped out during periods of economic decline. Those who do not keep their debts to a minimum will probably have to sell off their stocks just to stay solvent. Remember, Murphy's Law states that you *will* sell your stock at the worst possible moment. Don't go there!

## I owe, I owe, so off to work I go

Debt is one of the biggest financial problems in North America today. Companies and individuals holding excessive debt (to buy assets or finance growth) contributed to the stock market's massive decline in March 2009 and the current overall economic weakness. If individuals managed their personal liabilities more responsibly, the general economy would be much better off. Even when the Canadian or American economy looks unstoppable, sooner or later you have to pay the piper. This may mean working longer and harder than you had hoped. Remember: Stock prices may go up and down, but debt stays up until it is either paid down or the debtor files for bankruptcy. As of 2009, American and Canadian debt combined has surpassed a mind-boggling $51 trillion — which means that consumers, businesses, and governments will continue to be financially challenged during this decade and into the next. Yes, the stock market will be affected!

## Step 4: Calculating your net worth

Your *net worth* is an indication of your total wealth. You can calculate your net worth with this basic equation: Total assets (Table 2-1) less total liabilities (Table 2-2) equals net worth (net assets or net equity).

Table 2-3 shows this equation in action with a net worth of $169,090 — a very respectable number. For many investors, just being in a position where assets exceed liabilities (a positive net worth) is great news. Use Table 2-3 as a model to analyze your own financial situation. Your mission (if you choose to accept it — and you should) is to ensure that your net worth increases from year to year as you progress toward your financial goal.

| Table 2-3 | Figuring Your Personal Net Worth | |
|---|---|---|
| *Totals* | *Amounts ($)* | *Increase from Year Before* |
| Total assets (from Table 2-1) | $286,090 | +5% |
| Total liabilities (from Table 2-2) | ($117,000) | –2% |
| Net worth (total assets less total liabilities) | $169,090 | +3% |

# Step 5: Analyzing your balance sheet

Create a balance sheet based on the prior steps in this chapter to illustrate your current finances. Take a close look at it and try to identify any changes you can make to increase your wealth. Sometimes reaching your financial goals can be as simple as refocusing the items on your balance sheet (use the above table as a general guideline). Here are some brief points to consider:

✔ **Is the money in your emergency (or rainy-day) fund sitting in an ultra-safe account and earning the highest interest available?** Bank money market accounts or money market funds are recommended. The safest type of account is a Canadian or U.S. Treasury money market fund. The Canada Deposit Insurance Corporation (CDIC) backs Canadian banks, and the Federal Deposit Insurance Corporation (FDIC) backs American banks. Canadian and U.S. Treasury securities (which usually comprise money market funds) are backed by the "full faith and credit" of their respective federal government.

✔ **Can you replace depreciating assets with appreciating assets?** Say you have two stereo systems. Why not sell one and invest the proceeds? You may say, "But I bought that unit two years ago for $500, and if I sell it now, I'll only get $300." And that's your choice. You need to decide what helps your financial situation more — a $500 item that keeps shrinking in value (a *depreciating asset*) or $300 that can grow in value when invested (an *appreciating asset*).

✔ **Can you replace low-yield investments with high-yield investments?** Maybe you have $5,000 in a bank GIC earning 3 percent. You can certainly shop around for a better rate at another bank, but you can also seek alternatives that offer a higher yield, such as Canada Savings Bonds or short-term bond funds.

✔ **Can you pay off any high-interest debt with funds from low-interest assets?** For example, if you have $5,000 earning 2 percent in a taxable bank account and a $2,500 debt on a credit card charging 18 percent (nondeductible), you may as well pay off the credit card balance and save on the interest.

✔ **If you're carrying debt, are you using that money to gain an investment return that is greater than the interest you're paying?** Carrying a loan with an interest rate of 8 percent is acceptable if that borrowed money is yielding more than 8 percent elsewhere. Suppose that you have $6,000 in cash in a brokerage account. If you qualify, you can actually make a stock purchase greater than $6,000 by using *margin* (essentially a loan from the broker). You can buy $12,000 of stock using your $6,000 in cash, with the remainder financed by the broker. Of course, you pay interest on that margin loan. But what if the interest rate is 6 percent and the stock you're about to invest in has a dividend that yields 9 percent? In that case, the dividend can help you pay off the margin loan and you keep the additional income.

✔ **Can you sell any personal stuff for cash?** You can replace unproductive assets with cash from garage sales and auction Web sites.

✔ **Can you use your home equity to pay off consumer debt?** Borrowing against your home has more favourable interest rates, and this interest is still tax deductible. (Be careful about your debt level. See Chapter 20 for warnings about debt and other concerns.)

Paying off consumer debt by using funds borrowed against your home is a great way to wipe the slate clean. What a relief it is to get rid of your credit card balances! Just don't turn around and run up the consumer debt again. You can get overburdened and experience financial ruin (not to mention homelessness). Not a pretty picture.

The important point to remember is that you can take control of your finances with discipline (and with the advice we offer in this book).

# Funding Your Stock Program

If you're going to invest money in stocks, the first thing you need is . . . money! Where can you get that money? If you're waiting for an inheritance to come through, you may have to wait a long time, considering all the advances being made in healthcare lately. (What's that? You were going to invest in healthcare stocks? How ironic.) Yet, the challenge still comes down to how to fund your stock program.

Many investors can reallocate their investments and assets to do the trick. *Reallocating* simply means selling some investments or other assets and reinvesting that money into stocks. It boils down to deciding which investments or assets you can sell or liquidate. Generally, consider those investments and assets that give you a low return on your money (or no return at all). If you have a complicated mix of investments and assets, you may want to review your options with a financial planner. Reallocation is just one part of the answer; your cash flow is the other part.

Ever wonder why there's so much month left at the end of the money? Consider your cash flow. Your *cash flow* refers to what money is coming in (income) and what money is being spent (outflow). The net result is either a positive cash flow or a negative cash flow, depending on your cash management skills. Maintaining a positive cash flow (more money coming in than going out) helps you increase your net worth tremendously (mo' money, mo' money, mo' money!). A negative cash flow ultimately depletes your wealth and wipes out your net worth if you don't turn it around immediately. The following sections show you how to analyze your cash flow. The first step is to do a cash-flow statement.

Don't confuse a cash-flow statement with an income statement (also called a "profit and loss statement" or an "income and expense statement"). A cash-flow statement is simple to calculate because you can easily track what goes in and what goes out.

With a cash-flow statement (see Table 2-6), you ask yourself three questions:

- ✓ **What money is coming in?** In your cash-flow statement, jot down all sources of income. Calculate your income for the month and then for the year. Include everything — salary or wages, interest, dividends, and so on. Add them all up to get your grand total for income.

- ✓ **What is your outflow?** Write down all the things that you spend money on. List all your expenses. If possible, categorize them into essential and nonessential expenses — this lets you get an idea of all the expenses that you can reduce without affecting your lifestyle. But before you do that, make as complete a list as possible of what you spend your money on.

- ✓ **What's left?** If your income is greater than your outflow, then you have money ready and available for stock investing. No matter how small the amount seems, it definitely helps. We've seen fortunes built when people started to diligently invest as little as $25 to $50 per week or per month. If your outflow is greater than your income, then you better sharpen your pencil. Cut down on nonessential spending and/or increase your income. If your budget is a little tight, hold off on your stock investing until your cash flow improves.

## Step 1: Tallying up your income

Using Table 2-4 as a worksheet, list and calculate the money you have coming in. The first column describes the source of the money; the second indicates the monthly amount from each respective source; and the third indicates the amount projected for a full year. Include all income, such as wages, business income, dividends, interest income, and so on. Then project these amounts for a year (multiply by 12) and enter those amounts in the third column.

| **Table 2-4** | **Listing Your Income** | |
|---|---|---|
| *Item* | *Monthly $ Amount* | *Yearly $ Amount* |
| Salary and wages | | |
| Interest income and dividends | | |
| Business net (after taxes) income | | |
| Other income | | |
| Total Income | | |

This is the amount of money you have to work with. To ensure your good financial health, don't spend more than this amount. Always be aware of and carefully manage your income.

## Step 2: Adding up your outflow

Using Table 2-5 as a worksheet, list and calculate the money that's going out. What amount of money are you spending, and on what? The first column describes the source of the expense; the second indicates the monthly amount; and the third shows the amount projected for a full year. Include all the money you spend on essential expenses, including credit card and other debt payments; household expenses, such as food, utility bills, and medical expenses; and miscellaneous expenses, such as shinny hockey arena fees. Also include money spent for nonessential expenses such as video games and porcelain busts of John Diefenbaker. (All right, perhaps hockey fees aren't all that essential!)

| Table 2-5 | Listing Your Expenses (Outflow) | |
|---|---|---|
| *Item* | *Monthly $ Amount* | *Yearly $ Amount* |
| Payroll taxes | | |
| Rent or mortgage | | |
| Utilities | | |
| Food | | |
| Clothing | | |
| Insurance (drug plan, auto, homeowners, and so on) | | |
| Telephone | | |
| Real estate taxes | | |
| Auto expenses | | |
| Charity donations | | |
| Recreation | | |
| Credit card payments | | |
| Loan payments | | |
| Other | | |
| Total | | |

*Payroll taxes* is just a category in which to lump all the various taxes that the government takes out of your paycheque. Feel free to include each individual tax on its own line, if you prefer. The important thing is to create a comprehensive list that is meaningful to you. You may notice that the outflow doesn't include items such as payments to a Registered Retirement Savings Plan (RRSP), Tax Free Savings Account (TFSA), or other savings vehicles. Yes, these items do impact your cash flow, but they're not expenses. The amounts that you invest (or that your employer invests on your behalf) are essentially assets that benefit your long-term financial situation, as opposed to an expense that doesn't help you build wealth.

## Step 3: Creating a cash-flow statement

Okay, you're almost finished. The last step is creating a cash-flow statement so that you can see (all in one place) how your money moves — how much comes in and how much goes out, and where it goes.

Plug the amount of your total income (from Table 2-4) and the amount of your total expenses (from Table 2-5) into the Table 2-6 worksheet to see your *cash flow*. Do you have a positive cash flow — more cash coming in than going out — so that you can start investing in stocks (or other investments), or are expenses overwhelming your income? Doing a cash-flow statement isn't just about finding money to fund your stock program. First and foremost, it's about your financial well-being. Are you managing your finances well, or not?

| Table 2-6 | Looking at Your Cash Flow | |
|---|---|---|
| *Item* | *Monthly $ Amount* | *Yearly $ Amount* |
| Total income (from Table 2-4) | | |
| Total outflow (from Table 2-5) | | |
| Net Inflow/Outflow | | |

Recall our earlier warning that Canada's personal bankruptcy levels recently reached a record high, and the U.S. also has sustained record numbers of personal bankruptcies — in these cases, personal debt and expenses far exceeded whatever income was generated. This should serve as yet another reminder to all Canadians to watch their cash flow. Keep your income growing and your expenses and debt as low as possible.

# Step 4: Analyzing your cash flow

Use your cash-flow statement to identify sources of funds for your investment program. The more you can increase your income and the more you can decrease your outflow, the better. Scrutinize your data. Where can you improve the results? Here are some questions to ask yourself:

- How can you increase your income? Do you have hobbies, interests, or skills that can generate extra cash for you?

- Can you get more paid overtime at work? How about a promotion or a job change?

- Where can you cut expenses?

- Have you categorized your expenses as either essential or nonessential?

- Can you lower your debt payments by refinancing or consolidating loans and credit card balances?

- Have you shopped around for lower insurance or telephone rates?

- Have you analyzed the tax withholdings in your paycheque to make sure you aren't overpaying your taxes (just to get your overpayment back from the Canada Revenue Agency next year as a refund)?

# Another option: Finding investment money in tax savings

It's always a good idea to sit down with your tax adviser and try to find ways to reduce your taxes. A home-based business, for example, is a great way to gain new income and increase your tax deductions, resulting in a lower tax burden. Your tax adviser or professional accountant (someone with a CA, CMA, or CGA designation) can make recommendations that will work for you.

One tax strategy to consider is doing your stock investing in a tax-sheltered account, such as an open or locked-in self-directed RRSP. Another option is a Tax Free Savings Account (TFSA). Again, check with your qualified tax adviser for deductions and strategies available to you. For more on the tax implications of stock investing, including TFSA rules, see Chapter 22.

# *Setting Your Sights on Your Financial Goals*

Consider stocks to be tools for living, just like any other investment — no more, no less. Stocks are the tools you use (one among many) to accomplish something — to achieve a goal. Yes, successfully investing in stocks is the goal you're probably shooting for if you're reading this book. Take a moment to complete the following sentence: "I want to be successful in my stock investing program to accomplish _____." You must consider stock investing as a means to an end. When people buy a computer, they don't (or shouldn't) think of buying a computer just to have a computer. People buy a computer because doing so helps them achieve a particular result, such as being more efficient in business, playing fun games, or having a nifty paperweight (tsk, tsk).

Know the difference between long-term, intermediate-term, and short-term goals and then set some of each. *Long-term* refers to projects or financial goals that need funding five or more years from now; *intermediate-term* goals need funding two to five years from now; and *short-term* goals need funding less than two years from now.

Stocks, in general, are best suited for long-term goals such as these:

✔ Achieving financial independence (think retirement funding)

✔ Paying for future postsecondary education costs

✔ Paying for any long-term expenditure or project

Some categories of stock (such as conservative or blue-chip) may be suitable for intermediate-term financial goals. If, for example, you will retire four years from now, conservative stocks are appropriate. If you're optimistic about the stock market and confident that stock prices will rise, then go ahead and invest. However, if you're negative about the market (you're *bearish,* or you believe that stock prices will decline), you may want to wait until the economy starts to forge a clear path.

Stocks generally aren't suitable for short-term investing goals because stock prices can behave irrationally within a short period of time. Stocks fluctuate from day to day, so you don't know what the stock will be worth in the near future. You may end up with less money than you expected. For investors seeking to reliably accrue money for short-term needs, short-term bank GICs or money market funds are more appropriate.

In recent years, investors have sought quick, short-term profits by trading and speculating in stocks. Lured by the fantastic returns generated by the stock market in the late 1990s, investors saw stocks as a get-rich-quick scheme. It is very important for you to understand the differences between *investing, saving,* and *speculating.* Which one do you want to do? Knowing the answer to this question is crucial to your goals and aspirations. Investors who don't know the differences tend to get burned. Here's some information to help you distinguish among these three actions:

✔ *Investing* **is the act of putting your current funds into securities or tangible assets for the purpose of gaining future appreciation, income, or both.** You need time, knowledge, and discipline to invest. The investment can fluctuate in price but has been chosen for long-term potential.

✔ *Saving* **is the safe accumulation of funds for a future use.** Savings don't fluctuate and are generally free of financial risk. The emphasis is on safety and liquidity.

✔ *Speculating* **is the financial world's equivalent to gambling.** An investor who speculates is seeking quick profits gained from short-term price movements in that particular asset or investment.

These distinctly different concepts are often confused, even among so-called financial experts. For your purposes, though, please make sure you know the differences among investing, saving, and speculating before you invest in stocks. In fact, avoid speculating altogether when you are starting out in the world of stock investing.

# Chapter 3

# Defining Common Approaches to Stock Investing

*In This Chapter*

▶ Figuring out what strategy matches your goals

▶ Deciding what time frame fits your investment strategy

▶ Looking at your purpose for investing: growth versus income

▶ Determining your investing style: conservative versus aggressive

"*I*nvesting for the long term" isn't just some perfunctory investment slogan. It's a culmination of proven stock market experience that goes back many decades. Unfortunately, investor buying and selling habits have deteriorated in recent years due to impatience. Today's investors think that short term is measured in days, intermediate term is measured in weeks, and long term is measured in months. Yeesh! It's no wonder that so many folks are complaining about lousy investment returns. Investors have lost the profitable art of patience!

What should you do? Become an investor with a time horizon greater than one year. Give your investments time to grow. Everybody dreams about emulating the success of someone like Warren Buffett, but few emulate his patience (a huge part of his investment success).

Stocks are tools you can use to build your wealth. When used wisely, for the right purpose, and in the right environment, they do a great job. But when improperly applied, they can lead to disaster. In this chapter, we show you how to choose the right types of investments based on your short- and long-term financial goals. We also show you how to decide on your purpose for investing (growth or income investing) and your style of investing (conservative or aggressive).

# Matching Stocks and Strategies with Your Goals

Various stocks are out there, and so are various investment approaches. The key to success in the stock market is matching the right kind of stock with the right kind of investment situation. You have to choose both the stock and the approach that match your goals. (Refer to Chapter 2 for more on defining your financial goals.)

Before investing in a stock, ask yourself, "When do I want to reach my financial goal?" Stocks are a means to an end. Your job is to figure out what that end is — or, more important, *when* it is. Do you want to retire in ten years or next year? Must you pay for your kid's university education next year or 18 years from now? The length of time you have before you need the money you hope to earn from stock investing determines what stocks you buy. Table 3-1 gives some guidelines for choosing the kind of stock that's best suited to the type of investor you are and the goals you have.

| Table 3-1 | Stock Types, Financial Goals, and Investor Types | |
|---|---|---|
| *Type of Investor* | *Time Frame for Financial Goals* | *Type of Stock Most Suitable* |
| Conservative (worries about risk) | Long-term (over 5 years) | Large-cap stocks and mid-cap stocks |
| Aggressive (high tolerance to risk) | Long-term (over 5 years) | Small-cap stocks and mid-cap stocks |
| Conservative (worries about risk) | Intermediate-term (2 to 5 years) | Large-cap stocks, preferably with dividends |
| Aggressive (high tolerance to risk) | Intermediate-term (2 to 5 years) | Small-cap stocks and mid-cap stocks |
| Occasional | Short-term (2 years or less) | Stocks are typically not suitable for fulfilling short-term goals. Instead, look at vehicles such as savings accounts and money market funds. |

*Dividends* are payments made to an owner (unlike *interest,* which is payments to a creditor). Dividends are a great source of income, and companies that issue dividends tend to have more stable stock prices as well. For more information on dividend-paying stocks, see the section "Investing for a Purpose" in this chapter, and Chapter 9.

Table 3-1 gives you general guidelines, but keep in mind that not everyone can fit into a particular profile. Every investor has a unique situation, set of goals, and level of risk tolerance. Remember that the terms *large cap, mid cap,* and *small cap* refer to the size (or *market capitalization,* also known as *market cap*) of the company. All factors being equal, large companies are safer (less risky) than small companies. For more on market caps, see the section "Investing for Your Personal Style" later in this chapter.

# Investing by Time Frame

Are your goals long-term or short-term? Answering this question is important because individual stocks can be either great or horrible choices, depending on the time period you want to focus on. Generally, the length of time you plan to invest in stocks can be short term, intermediate term, or long term. The following sections outline what kinds of stocks are most appropriate for each term length.

With stock performance history as an indicator, investing in stocks becomes less risky as the time frame lengthens. Stock prices tend to fluctuate on a daily basis, but they have a tendency to trend up or down over an extended period of time. Even if you invest in a stock that goes down in the short term, you're likely to see it rise — and possibly go above your initial investment — if you have the patience to wait it out and let the stock price appreciate.

## Focusing on the short term

*Short term* generally means one year or less, although some people extend the period to two years or less. You get the point.

Everyone has short-term goals. Some are modest, such as setting aside money for an exciting vacation in Barbados this year or paying for unwelcome car repair bills. Other short-term goals are more ambitious, such as accruing funds for a down payment to purchase a new home within six months. Whatever the expense or purchase, you need a predictable accumulation of cash soon. If this sounds like your situation, stay away from the stock market!

Because stocks can be so unpredictable in the short term, they're a bad choice for short-term considerations. We continue to marvel in disbelief whenever we hear slick market analysts saying things like, "At $25 a share, XYZ is a solid investment, and we feel that its stock should hit our target price of $40 within six to nine months." You just know that someone will hear that and say, "Gee, why bother with 3 percent at the bank when this stock will rise by more than 50 percent? I better call my broker." The stock may indeed hit that target amount (or even surpass it), or it may not. Most of the time, the stock doesn't reach the target price, and then the investor is disappointed. The stock could even go down! The reason why target prices are frequently (usually) missed is that the analyst is only one person and it's difficult to figure out what millions of investors will do in the short term. The short term can be irrational because so many investors have so many reasons for buying and selling that it's difficult to analyze. If you want to use the money you invest for an important short-term need, you could lose very important cash quicker than you think.

Short-term stock investing is very unpredictable. You can better serve your short-term goals with stable, interest-bearing investments such as guaranteed investment certificates (GICs) and certificates of deposit (CDs), available at chartered banks.

During the raging bull market of the late 1990s, investors watched as some high-profile stocks went up 20 to 50 percent in a matter of months. Hey, who needs a savings account earning a measly interest rate when stocks grow like that! Of course, when the bear market hit from 2000 to 2002 and those same stocks fell 50 to 85 percent, a savings account earning a measly interest rate suddenly didn't seem so bad.

Stocks — even the best ones — fluctuate in the short term. In a negative environment, they can be very volatile. No one can accurately predict the price movement (unless you have some inside information), so stocks are definitely inappropriate for any financial goal that you need to reach within one year. Revisit Table 3-1 for suggestions about your short-term strategies.

## Considering intermediate-term goals

*Intermediate term* refers to financial goals that you plan to reach within five years. If, for example, you want to accumulate funds to put money down for investing in real estate four years from now, some growth-oriented investments may be suitable.

Although some stocks *may* be appropriate for a two- or three-year time period, not all stocks are good intermediate-term investments. Different types and categories of stocks exist. Some stocks are fairly stable and hold their value well, such as the stock of very large or established dividend-paying companies. Other stocks have prices that jump all over the place, such as the stocks of untested companies that haven't been in existence long enough to develop a consistent track record.

## Short-term investing = Speculating

Our case files are littered with examples of long-term stock investors who morphed into short-term speculators. We know of one fellow who had $80,000 and was set to get married within 12 months and then put a down payment on a new home for him and his bride. He wanted to surprise her by growing his nest egg quickly so they could have a glitzier wedding and a larger down payment. What happened? The money instead shrunk to $11,000 as his stock choices pulled back sharply. Ouch! How does

that go again? For better or for worse . . . uh . . . for richer or for poorer? We're sure they had to adjust their plans accordingly. We recall some of the stocks he chose, and now, years later, those stocks have recovered and gone on to new highs.

The bottom line is that investing in stocks for the short term is nothing more than speculating. Your only possible strategy is luck.

If you plan to invest in the stock market to meet intermediate-term goals, consider large, established companies or dividend-paying companies in industries that provide the necessities of life (like the food and beverage industry, or electric utilities). In today's economic environment, we very strongly believe that stocks attached to companies that serve basic human needs should have a major presence in most stock portfolios. They're especially well-suited for intermediate investment goals.

Just because a particular stock is labelled as being appropriate for the intermediate term doesn't mean you should get rid of it by the stroke of midnight on this date five years from now. After all, if the company is doing well and going strong, you can continue holding the stock indefinitely. The more time you give a well-positioned, profitable company's stock to grow, the better you'll do.

## Preparing for the long term

Stock investing is best suited for making money over a long period of time. When you measure stocks against other investments in terms of five to (preferably) ten or more years, they excel. Even investors who bought stocks during the depths of the Great Depression saw profitable growth in their stock portfolios over a ten-year period.

In fact, if you examine any ten-year period over the past 70 years, you see that stocks almost always beat out other financial investments — such as bonds or bank investments — when measured by total return (taking reinvesting and the compounding of capital gains and dividends into account)!

See Chapters 8 and 9 for more about growth and income. As you can see, long-term planning allows stocks to shine. Of course, your work doesn't stop at deciding on a long-term investment. You still have to do your homework and choose stocks wisely because, even in good times, you can lose money if you invest in companies that go out of business. Part III shows you how to evaluate specific companies and industries and alerts you to factors in the general economy that can affect stock behaviour. Appendix B provides plenty of resources you can turn to.

Because you can choose between many different types and categories of stocks, virtually any investor with a long-term perspective should add stocks to his or her investment portfolio. Whether you want to save for your child's university fund or for future retirement goals, carefully selected stocks have proven to be a superior long-term investment for multitudes of Canadians.

# Investing for a Purpose

When the lady was asked why she bungee jumped off the bridge that spanned a massive ravine, she answered, "Because it's fun!" When someone asked the fellow why he dove into a pool that was chock-full of alligators and snakes, he responded, "Because someone pushed me." Your investment in stocks shouldn't happen unless you have a purpose that you understand, like investing for growth or investing for income. Even if an adviser pushes you to invest, be sure she gives you an explanation of how that stock choice fits your purpose before you dive in.

We know of a very nice, elderly lady who had a portfolio brimming with aggressive-growth stocks because she had an overbearing broker. Her purpose should've been conservative, and she should've chosen investments that would preserve her wealth rather than grow it. Obviously, the broker's agenda got in the way. Stocks are just a means to an end. Figure out your desired end and then match the means. To find out more about dealing with brokers, see Chapter 7.

## Making loads of money quickly: Growth investing

When investors want their money to grow, they look for investments that appreciate in value. *Appreciate* is just another way of saying "grow." If you have a stock that you bought for $8 per share and now its value is $30 per share, your investment has grown by $22 per share — that's appreciation. We know we would appreciate it!

Appreciation (also known as *capital gain*) is probably the number-one reason why people invest in stocks. Few investments have the potential to grow your wealth as conveniently as stocks. If you want the stock market to make you loads of money relatively quickly (and if you can assume some risk), head to Chapter 8, which takes an in-depth look at investing for growth.

Stocks are a great way to grow your wealth, but they're not the only way. Many investors seek alternative ways to make money, but many of these alternative ways are more aggressive and carry significantly more risk. You may have heard about people who made quick fortunes in areas such as commodities (like wheat, pork bellies, or precious metals), options, and other more sophisticated investment vehicles. Keep in mind that you should limit risky investments to only a small portion of your portfolio, such as 10 percent of your investable funds. Experienced investors, however, can go as high as 20 percent. As we mention earlier in this section, Chapter 8 goes into greater detail about growth investing.

## Making money steadily: Income investing

Not all investors want to take on the risk that comes with making a killing. (Hey . . . no guts, no glory!) Some people just want to invest in the stock market as a means of providing a steady income. They don't need stock values to go through the ceiling. Instead, they need stocks that perform well consistently.

If your purpose for investing in stocks is to create income, you need to choose stocks that pay dividends. Dividends are typically paid quarterly to shareholders on record.

### Distinguishing between dividends and interest

Don't confuse dividends with interest. Most people are familiar with interest, because that's how you grow your money over the years in the bank. The important difference is that *interest* is paid to creditors, and *dividends* are paid to owners (meaning *shareholders* — and if you own stock, you're a shareholder, because stocks represent shares in a publicly traded company).

When you buy stock, you buy a piece of that company. When you put money in a bank (or when you buy bonds), you basically loan your money. You become a creditor, and the bank or bond issuer is the debtor and, as such, must eventually pay your money back to you with interest.

### Recognizing the importance of an income stock's yield

When you invest for income, you have to consider your investment's yield and compare it with the alternatives. The *yield* is an investment's payout expressed as a percentage of the investment amount. Looking at the yield is a way to compare the income you expect to receive from one investment with the expected income from others. Table 3-2 shows some comparative yields.

| Table 3-2 | | Comparing the Yields of Various Investments | | | |
|---|---|---|---|---|---|
| *Investment* | *Type* | *Amount* | *Pay Type* | *Payout* | *Yield* |
| Smith Co. | Stock | $50/share | Dividend | $2.50 | 5.00% |
| Jones Co. | Stock | $100/ share | Dividend | $4.00 | 4.00% |
| Acme Bank | Bank CD | $500 | Interest | $25.00 | 5.00% |
| Acme Bank | Bank CD | $2,500 | Interest | $131.25 | 5.25% |
| Acme Bank | Bank CD | $5,000 | Interest | $287.50 | 5.75% |
| Brown Co. | Bond | $5,000 | Interest | $300.00 | 6.00% |

To understand how to calculate yield, you need the following formula:

Yield = payout ÷ investment amount

Yield enables you to compare how much income you would get for a prospective investment with the income you would get from other investments. For the sake of simplicity, this exercise is based on an annual percentage yield basis (compounding would increase the yield).

Jones Co. and Smith Co. are both typical dividend-paying stocks; presume in the example presented by Table 3-2 that both companies are similar in most respects except for their differing dividends. How can you tell whether a $50 stock with a $2.50 annual dividend is better (or worse) than a $100 stock with a $4.00 dividend? The yield tells you.

Even though Jones Co. pays a higher dividend ($4.00), Smith Co. has a higher yield (5 percent). Therefore, if you had to choose between those two stocks as an income investor, you would choose Smith Co. Of course, if you truly want to maximize your income and don't really need your investment to appreciate a lot, you should probably choose Brown Co.'s bond because it offers a yield of 6 percent.

Dividend-paying stocks do have the ability to increase in value. They may not have the same growth potential as growth stocks, but at the very least they have a greater potential for capital gain than bank CDs or bonds. Dividend-paying stocks (income investing) are covered in Chapter 9.

# Investing for Your Personal Style

Your investing style isn't a blue-jeans-versus-three-piece-suit debate. It refers to your approach to stock investing. Do you want to be conservative or aggressive? Would you rather be the tortoise or the hare? Your investment personality greatly depends on the term over which you're planning to invest and on your purpose (refer to the previous two sections in this chapter). The following sections outline the two most general investment styles.

## Conservative investing

Conservative investing means that you put your money in something proven, tried, and true. You invest your money in safe and secure places, such as chartered banks and government-backed securities. But how does that apply to stocks? (Table 3-1 gives you suggestions.)

Conservative stock investors want to place their money in companies that exhibit some of the following qualities:

- **Proven performance:** You want companies that show increasing sales and earnings year after year. You don't demand anything spectacular, just a strong and steady performance.

- **Market size:** Companies should be *large cap* (short for large capitalization). In other words, they should have a market value exceeding $10 billion in size. Conservative investors surmise that bigger is safer.

- **Market leadership:** Companies should be leaders in their industries.

- **Perceived staying power:** You want companies with the financial clout and market position to weather uncertain market and economic conditions. It shouldn't matter what happens in the economy or who gets elected as prime minister.

As a conservative investor, you don't mind if the companies' share prices jump (who would?), but you're more concerned with steady growth over the long term.

## *Aggressive investing*

Aggressive investors can plan over the long term or look only to the intermediate term, but in any case they want stocks that resemble Aesop's fabled hare — they show the potential to break out of the pack.

Aggressive stock investors want to invest their money in companies that exhibit some of the following qualities:

- ✔ **Great potential:** The company must have superior goods, services, ideas, or ways of doing business compared to its competition.

- ✔ **Capital gains possibility:** You don't even consider dividends. If anything, you dislike dividends. You feel that the money that would've been dispensed in dividend form is better reinvested in the company. This, in turn, can spur greater growth.

- ✔ **Innovation:** Companies should have technologies, ideas, or innovative methods that make them stand apart from other companies.

Aggressive investors usually seek out small-capitalization stocks, known as *small caps,* because they have plenty of potential for growth. Take the tree example, for instance: A giant redwood may be strong but may not grow much more, whereas a brand-new sapling has plenty of growth to look forward to. Why invest in stodgy, big companies when you can invest in smaller enterprises that may become the leaders of tomorrow? Aggressive investors have no problem investing in obscure companies because they hope that such companies will become another IBM, CN, or Research In Motion. Find out more about growth investing in Chapter 8.

# Chapter 4

# Recognizing the Risks

*In This Chapter*

▶ Considering different types of risk

▶ Taking steps to reduce your risk

▶ Balancing risk against return

*I*nvestors face many risks, most of which we cover in this chapter. The simplest definition of risk for investors is "the possibility that your investment will lose some (or all) of its value." Yet you don't have to fear risk if you understand it and plan for it. You must understand the oldest equation in the world of investing — risk versus return. This equation states the following:

> If you want a greater return on your money, you need to tolerate more risk. If you don't want to tolerate more risk, you must tolerate a lower rate of return.

This point about risk is best illustrated from a moment in one of Paul's investment seminars. One of the attendees told Paul that he had his money in the bank but was dissatisfied with the rate of return. He lamented, "The yield on my money is pitiful! I want to put my money somewhere where it can grow." Paul asked him, "How about investing in common stocks? Or what about growth mutual funds? They have a solid, long-term growth track record." He responded, "Stocks? I don't want to put my money there. It's too risky!" Okay, then. If you don't want to tolerate more risk, then don't complain about earning less on your money. Risk (in all its forms) has a bearing on all your money concerns and goals. That's why it's so important that you understand risk before you invest.

This man — as well as the rest of us — needs to remember that risk is not a four-letter word. (Well, it is a four-letter word, but you know what we mean.) Risk is present no matter what you do with your money. Even if you simply stick your money in your mattress, risk is involved — several kinds of risk, in fact. You have the risk of fire. What if your house burns down? You have the risk of theft. What if burglars find your stash of cash? You also have relative risk. (In other words, what if your relatives find your money?)

Be aware of the different kinds of risk we describe in this chapter, and you can easily plan around them to keep your money growing.

# Exploring Different Kinds of Risk

Think about all the ways that an investment can lose money. You can list all sorts of possibilities. So many that you may think, "Holy cow! Why invest at all?"

Don't let risk frighten you. After all, life itself is risky. Just make sure that you understand the different kinds of risk that we discuss in the following sections before you start navigating the investment world. Be mindful of risk and find out about the effects of risk on your investments and personal financial goals.

## Financial risk

The financial risk of stock investing is that you can lose your money if the company whose stock you purchase loses money or goes belly up. This type of risk is the most obvious, because companies do go bankrupt.

You can greatly enhance the chances of your financial risk paying off by doing an adequate amount of research and choosing your stocks carefully (which this book helps you do — see Part III for details). Financial risk is a real concern even when the economy is doing well. Some diligent research, a little planning, and a dose of common sense help you reduce your financial risk.

In the stock investing mania of the late 1990s, millions of investors (along with many well-known investment gurus) ignored some obvious financial risks of many then-popular stocks. Investors blindly plunked their money into stocks that were bad choices. Consider investors who put their money into 360 Networks, a Canadian company involved in the build-out of fiber optic networks. This company had no profit, was poorly-run, and was way over-indebted. The financial condition of 360 Networks soon went into a full spin and it collapsed in late 2001. Anyone holding shares soon found that they were worthless as the company was delisted from the Toronto Stock Exchange. Canadian investors had lost millions.

Internet and tech stocks littered the graveyard of stock market catastrophes during 2000–01 because investors didn't see (or perhaps didn't want to see) the risks involved with companies that didn't offer a solid record of results (profits, sales, and so on). When you invest in companies that don't have a proven track record, you're not investing, you're speculating.

Fast forward to 2007–08. New risks abound as the headlines rail on about the credit crisis on Wall Street and the subprime fiasco in the wake of the U.S. housing bubble popping. Think about how this crisis impacted investors worldwide as the market went through its stomach-churning roller-coaster ride. A good example of a casualty you didn't want to be part of was the U.S. investment bank Bear Stearns (BSC), which was caught in the subprime buzz saw. Bear Stearns was sky-high at $170 a share in early 2007, yet it crashed to $2 a share by March 2008. Yikes! Its problems arose from massive overexposure to bad debt, and investors could have done some research — the public data were revealing! — and avoided the stock entirely. Fast forward even further to 2009. As you have undoubtedly heard, Bear Stearns was ultimately joined by scores of similar and well-known companies in severe distress. Almost all were jockeying for government bailouts.

Investors who did their homework regarding the financial conditions of companies such as the Internet startups (and later Bear Stearns, among others) would have discovered that these companies had the hallmarks of financial risk — high debt, low (or no) earnings, and plenty of competition. They steered clear, avoiding tremendous financial loss. Investors who didn't do their homework were lured by the status of these companies and lost their shirts.

Of course, the individual investors who lost money by investing in these trendy, high-profile companies don't deserve all the responsibility for their tremendous financial losses; many high-profile analysts and media sources also should have known better. This decade may someday be a case study of how euphoria and the herd mentality (rather than good, old-fashioned research and common sense) ruled the day (temporarily). The excitement of making potential fortunes gets the best of people sometimes, and they throw caution to the wind. Historians may look back at those days and say, "What *were* they thinking?" Achieving true wealth takes diligent work and careful analysis.

In terms of financial risk, the bottom line is . . . well . . . the bottom line! A healthy bottom line means that a company is making money. And if a company is making money, then you can make money by investing in its stock. However, if a company isn't making money, you won't make money if you invest in it. Profit is the lifeblood of any company. See Chapter 12 for the scoop on determining whether a company's bottom line is healthy.

## Interest-rate risk

You can lose money in an apparently sound investment because of something that sounds as harmless as "interest rates have changed." Interest-rate risk may sound like an odd type of risk, but in fact it's a common consideration for investors. Be aware that interest rates change on a regular basis, causing some challenging moments. Banks set interest rates, and the primary institutions to watch closely are the Bank of Canada and the Federal Reserve (the Fed) in the U.S., which are, in effect, national central banks. Both institutions raise or lower their interest rates, actions that in turn cause banks to raise or lower interest rates accordingly. Interest-rate changes affect consumers, businesses, and, of course, investors.

Here's a generic introduction to the way fluctuating interest-rate risk can affect investors in general: Suppose you buy a long-term, high-quality corporate bond and get a yield of 6 percent. Your money is safe, and your return is locked in at 6 percent. Whew! That's 6 percent. Not bad, huh? But what happens if, after you commit your money, interest rates increase to 8 percent? You lose the opportunity to get that extra 2 percent interest. The only way to get out of your 6 percent bond is to sell it at current market values and use the money to reinvest at the higher rate.

The only problem with this scenario is that the 6 percent bond is likely to drop in value because interest rates rose. Why? Say that the investor is Bob and the bond yielding 6 percent is a corporate bond issued by Lucin-Muny (LM). According to the bond agreement, LM must pay 6 percent (called the *face rate* or *nominal rate*) during the life of the bond and then, upon maturity, pay the principal. If Bob buys $10,000 of LM bonds on the day they're issued, he gets $600 (of interest) every year for as long as he holds the bonds. If he holds on until maturity, he gets back his $10,000 (the principal). So far so good, right? The plot thickens, however.

Say that he decides to sell the bond long before maturity and that, at the time of the sale, interest rates in the market have risen to 8 percent. Now what? The reality is that no one is going to want his 6 percent bond if the market is offering bonds at 8 percent. What's Bob to do? He can't change the face rate of 6 percent, and he can't change the fact that only $600 is paid each year for the life of the bond. What has to change so that current investors get the *equivalent* yield of 8 percent? If you said, "The bond's value has to go down" . . . bingo! In this example, the bond's market value needs to drop to $7,500 so that investors buying the bond get an equivalent yield of 8 percent. (For simplicity's sake, I left out the time it takes for the bond to mature.) Here's how that figures:

New investors still get $600 annually. However, $600 is equal to 8 percent of $7,500. Therefore, even though investors get the face rate of 6 percent, they get a yield of 8 percent because the actual investment amount is $7,500. In this example, little, if any, financial risk is present, but you see how interest rate risk presents itself. Bob finds out that you can have a good company with a good bond, yet you still lose $2,500 because of the change in the interest rate. Of course, if Bob doesn't sell, he doesn't realize that loss. (For more on the how and why of selling your stock, review Chapter 20.)

Historically, rising interest rates have had an adverse effect on stock prices. We outline several reasons why in the following sections. Because Canada and especially the U.S. are top-heavy in debt, rising interest rates are an obvious risk that threatens both stocks and fixed-income securities (such as bonds).

### Hurting a company's financial condition

Rising interest rates have a negative impact on companies that carry a large current debt load or that need to take on more debt, because when interest rates rise, the cost of borrowing money rises, too. Ultimately, the company's profitability and ability to grow are reduced. When a company's profits (or earnings) drop, its stock becomes less desirable, and its stock price falls.

### Affecting a company's customers

A company's success comes when it sells its products or services. But what happens if increased interest rates negatively impact its customers (specifically, other companies that buy from it)? The financial health of its customers directly affects the company's ability to grow sales and earnings.

For a good example, consider Magna International (MGA) during 2007–09. The company had soaring sales and earnings during several years leading up to 2007 as the North American automotive industry continued brisk sales of cars and needed automotive parts from Magna. After 2007, the worldwide automotive industry entered a steep slowdown in sales (due to the global credit crisis, tighter auto loan credit requirements, rising interest rates, and so on). Investors took special notice of the fact that almost all automotive sector companies had loads of debt on their balance sheets. This debt, including interest, had to be paid off. The entire auto sector went into an agonizing decline, and the fortunes of Magna followed suit because its success is directly tied to auto sales. By late 2008, Magna's sales were slipping and earnings were dropping as the automotive industry sank deeper into its depression. This was bad news for stock investors. Magna's stock went from more than $96 in 2007 to $20 by March 2009. Ouch! The brakes didn't quite work that time.

### Affecting investors' decision-making considerations

When interest rates rise, investors start to rethink their investment strategies, resulting in one of two outcomes:

- Investors may sell any shares in interest-sensitive stocks that they hold. Interest-sensitive industries include real estate, the debt-saddled automotive sector, and the very sickly U.S. financial sector. Although increased interest rates can hurt these sectors, the reverse is also generally true: Falling interest rates boost the same industries. Keep in mind that interest rate changes affect some industries more than others.

- Investors who favour increased current income (versus waiting for the investment to grow in value to sell for a gain later on) are definitely attracted to investment vehicles that offer a higher yield. Higher interest rates can cause investors to switch from stocks to bonds or GICs.

### Hurting stock prices indirectly

High or rising interest rates can have a negative impact on any investor's total financial picture. What happens when an investor struggles with burdensome debt, such as a second mortgage, credit card debt, or *margin debt* (debt from borrowing against stock in a brokerage account)? He may sell some stock to pay off some of his high-interest debt. Selling stock to service debt is a common practice that, when taken collectively, can hurt stock prices.

As this book goes to press, the stock market and the U.S. economy face perhaps the greatest challenge since the Great Depression — debt. Because Canada's fortunes are tied to the U.S., the same is somewhat true for us. In terms of gross domestic product (GDP), the size of the U.S. economy is about $15 trillion (give or take $100 billion), but the debt level is about $57 trillion (this includes personal, corporate, mortgage, and government debt). (In Canada, the amounts are about one-tenth as much.) This already enormous amount doesn't include $55 trillion of government employment insurance, welfare, and health care liabilities. Additionally (yikes! there's more?), some U.S. financial institutions hold more than $100 trillion worth of derivatives — very complicated and sophisticated investment vehicles that can backfire. Derivatives have, in fact, sunk some large organizations (such as Enron and Bear Stearns), and investors should beware of them. Just check out the company's financial reports. (Find out more in Chapter 13.)

Because of the effects of interest rates on stock portfolios, both direct and indirect, successful investors regularly monitor interest rates in both the general economy and in their personal situations. Although stocks have proven to be a superior long-term investment (the longer the term, the better), every investor should maintain a balanced portfolio that includes other investment vehicles. A diversified investor has some money in vehicles that do well when interest rates rise. These vehicles include money market funds, variable-rate GICs, and other variable-rate investments whose interest rates rise when market rates rise. These types of investments add a measure of safety from interest rate risk to your stock portfolio. (We discuss diversification in more detail later in this chapter.)

## Market risk

People talk about "the market" and how it goes up or down, making it sound like a monolithic entity instead of what it really is — a group of millions of individuals making daily decisions to buy or sell stock. No matter how modern our society and economic system, you can't escape the laws of supply and demand. When masses of people want to buy a particular stock, it becomes in demand, and its price rises. That price rises higher if the supply is limited. Conversely, if no one's interested in buying a stock, its price falls. Supply and demand is the nature of market risk. The price of the stock you purchase can rise and fall on the fickle whim of market demand.

Millions of investors buying and selling each minute of every trading day affect the share price of your stock. This fact makes it impossible to judge which way your stock will move tomorrow, or next week. This unpredictability and seeming irrationality is why stocks aren't appropriate for short-term financial growth.

A good example of market risk with a stock is Apple (AAPL). Had you bought AAPL in January 2007, you could have gotten it for about $75 a share and watched it rise joyfully upward to hit $205 a share by December. At that point some giddy investor may be thinking, "It's time to pop the champagne!" Hold on a second! Within three months of that top, AAPL had a dizzying plunge to under $120 by March 2008. It's typical for stocks to take a relatively long time to climb, but they can fall in a relatively short time. In that example, a long-term, patient investor would still be up, but some short-term folks who jump in and jump out would have been burned.

Markets are volatile by nature; they go up and down, and investments need time to grow. Market volatility is an increasingly common condition that we have to live with. Investors should be aware of the fact that stocks in general (especially in today's marketplace) aren't suitable for short-term goals (one year or less; see Chapters 2 and 3 for more on short-term goals). Despite the fact that companies you're invested in may be fundamentally sound, all stock prices are subject to the gyrations of the marketplace and need time to trend upward.

Investing requires diligent work and research before putting your money in quality investments with a long-term perspective. Speculating is attempting to make a relatively quick profit by monitoring the short-term price movements of a particular investment. Investors seek to minimize risk, whereas speculators don't mind risk because it can also magnify profits. Speculating and investing have clear differences, but investors frequently become speculators and ultimately put themselves and their wealth at risk. Don't go there!

Consider the married couple nearing retirement who decided to play with their money to see about making their pending retirement more comfortable. They borrowed a sizable sum by tapping into their home equity to invest in the stock market. (Their home, which they had paid off, had enough equity to qualify for this loan.) What did they do with these funds? You guessed it: they invested in the high-flying stocks of the day, which were high-tech and Internet stocks. Within eight months, they lost almost all their money.

Understanding market risk is especially important for people who are tempted to put their nest eggs or emergency funds into volatile investments such as growth stocks (or mutual funds that invest in growth stocks, or similar aggressive investment vehicles). Remember, you can lose everything.

## Inflation risk

*Inflation* is the artificial expansion of the quantity of money so that too much money is used in exchange for goods and services. To consumers, inflation shows up in the form of higher prices for goods and services. Inflation risk is also referred to as *purchasing power risk*. This term just means that your money doesn't buy as much as it used to. For example, a dollar that bought you a sandwich in 1980 barely bought you a candy bar a few years later. For you, the investor, this risk means that the value of your investment (a stock that doesn't appreciate much, for example) may not keep up with inflation.

Say you have money in a bank savings account currently earning 4 percent. This account has flexibility — if the market interest rate goes up, the rate you earn in your account goes up. Your account is safe from both financial risk and interest-rate risk. But what if inflation is running at 5 percent? At that point you're losing money.

At the time of this writing, inflation is a very real and a very serious concern and it should not be ignored. We deal more with inflation in Chapter 10.

## Tax risk

Taxes (such as income tax or capital gains tax) don't affect your stock investment directly. Taxes can obviously affect how much of your money you get to keep. Because the entire point of stock investing is to build wealth, you need to understand that taxes take away a portion of the wealth that you're trying to build. Taxes can be risky because if you make the wrong move with your stocks (selling them at the wrong time, for example) you can end up paying higher taxes than you need to. Because Canadian tax laws change so frequently, tax risk is part of the risk-versus-return equation, as well.

It pays to gain knowledge about how the Canada Revenue Agency (CRA) rules can affect your wealth-building program before you make your investment decisions. Chapter 22 covers the impact of taxes in greater detail.

## Political and governmental risks

If companies were fish, politics and government policies (such as taxes, laws, and regulations) would be the pond. In the same way that fish die in a toxic or polluted pond, politics and government policies can kill companies. Of course, if you own stock in a company exposed to political and governmental risks, you need to be aware of these risks. For some companies, a single new regulation or law is enough to send them into bankruptcy. For other companies, a new law could help them increase sales and profits.

What if you invest in companies or industries that become political targets? You may want to consider selling them (you can always buy them back later) or consider putting in stop-loss orders on the stock (see Chapter 21). For example, tobacco companies were the targets of political firestorms that battered their stock prices. Whether you agree or disagree with the political machinations of today is not the issue. As an investor, you have to ask yourself, "How does politics affect the market value and the current and future prospects of my chosen investment?" (See Chapter 11 for more on how politics can affect the stock market.)

Taking the preceding point a step further, we'd like to remind you that politics and government have a direct and often negative impact on the economic environment. And one major pitfall for investors is that many misunderstand even basic economics. Considering all the examples we could find in recent years, we could write a book! Or . . . uh . . . simply add it to this book. Chapter 10 goes into greater detail to help you make (and keep) stock market profits just by understanding rudimentary (and quite interesting) economics. (Don't worry; we keep the dry stuff to a minimum!)

## Personal risks

Frequently, the risk involved with investing in the stock market may not be directly involved with the investment or factors related to the investment; sometimes the risk is with the investor's circumstances.

Suppose that investor Ralph puts $15,000 into a portfolio of common stocks. Imagine that the market experiences a drop in prices that week and Ralph's stocks drop to a market value of $14,000. Because stocks are good for the long term, this type of decrease is usually not an alarming incident. Odds are that this dip is temporary, especially if Ralph carefully chose high-quality companies. Incidentally, if a portfolio of high-quality stocks *does* experience a temporary drop in price, it can be a great opportunity to get more shares at a good price. (Chapter 21 covers orders you can place with your broker to help you do that.)

Over the long term, Ralph would probably see the value of his investment grow substantially. But what if, during a period when his stocks are declining, Ralph experiences financial difficulty and needs quick cash? He may have to sell his stock to get some money.

This problem occurs frequently for investors who don't have an emergency fund or a rainy-day fund to handle large, sudden expenses. You never know when your company may lay you off or when your basement may flood, leaving you with a huge repair bill. Car accidents, emergency repairs, and other unforeseen events are part of life's bag of surprises — for anyone.

You probably won't get much comfort from knowing that stock losses are tax deductible — a loss is a loss (see Chapter 22 for more on taxes). However, you can avoid the kind of loss that results from prematurely having to sell your stocks if you maintain an emergency cash fund. A good place for your emergency cash fund is in either a bank savings account or a money market fund. Then you aren't forced to prematurely liquidate your stock investments to pay emergency bills. (Chapter 2 provides more guidance on having liquid assets for emergencies.)

# *Emotional risk*

What does emotional risk have to do with stocks? Emotions are important risk considerations because the main decision makers are human beings. Logic and discipline are critical factors in investment success, but even the best investor can let emotions take over the reins of money management and cause loss. For stock investing, you're likely to be sidetracked by three main emotions: greed, fear, and love. You need to understand your emotions and what kinds of risk they can expose you to. If you get too attached to a sinking stock, then you don't need a stock investing book — you need Dr. Phil!

## *Paying the price for greed*

In 1998–2000, millions of investors threw caution to the wind and chased highly dubious, risky dot-com stocks. The dollar signs popped up in their eyes (just like slot machines) when they saw that easy street was lined with dot-com stocks that were doubling and tripling in a very short time. Who cares about price/earnings (P/E) ratios and earnings when you can just buy stock, make a fortune, and get out with millions? (Of course, *you* care about making money with stocks, so you can refer to Appendix A to find out more about P/E ratios.)

Unfortunately, the lure of the easy buck can easily turn healthy attitudes about growing wealth into unhealthy greed that blinds investors and discards common sense (such as investing for quick short-term gains in dubious hot stocks rather than doing your homework and buying stocks of solid companies with strong fundamentals and a long-term focus, as we explain in Part III).

## *Recognizing the role of fear*

Greed can be a problem, but fear is the other extreme. People who are fearful of loss frequently avoid suitable investments and end up settling for a low rate of return. If you have to succumb to one of these emotions, at least fear exposes you to less loss.

Also, keep in mind that fear is frequently a symptom of lack of knowledge about what's going on. If you see your stocks falling and don't understand why, fear will take over and you may act irrationally. When stock investors are affected by fear, the tendency is to sell their stocks and head for the exits and/or the life boats. When an investor sees his stock go down 20 percent, what goes through his head? Experienced, knowledgeable investors see that no bull market goes straight up. Even the strongest bull goes up in a zigzag fashion. Conversely, even bear markets don't go straight down, they zigzag down. Out of fear, inexperienced investors will sell good stocks if they see them go down temporarily (the "correction"), while experienced investors see that temporary down move as a good buying opportunity to add to their positions.

### Looking for love in all the wrong places

Stocks are dispassionate, inanimate vehicles, but people can look for love in the strangest places. Emotional risk occurs when investors fall in love with a stock and refuse to sell it, even when the stock is plummeting and shows all the symptoms of getting worse. Emotional risk also occurs when investors are drawn to bad investment choices just because they sound good, are popular, or are pushed by family or friends. Love and attachment are great in relationships with people but can be horrible with investments. To deal with this emotion, investors have to deploy techniques that take the emotion out. For example, you can use brokerage orders (such as trailing stops and limit orders), which can automatically trigger buy and sell transactions and leave some of the agonizing out. Hey, disciplined investing may just become your new passion!

# Minimizing Your Risk

Now, before you go crazy thinking that stock investing carries so much risk you may as well not get out of bed, take a breath. Minimizing your risk in stock investing is easier than you think. Although wealth building through the stock market doesn't take place without some amount of risk, you can practise the following tips to maximize your profits and still keep your money secure.

## Gaining knowledge

Some people spend more time analyzing a restaurant menu to choose a $10 entrée than analyzing where to put their next $5,000. Lack of knowledge constitutes the greatest risk for new investors, but diminishing that risk starts with gaining knowledge. The more familiar you are with the stock market — how it works, factors that affect stock value, and so on — the better you can navigate around its pitfalls and maximize your profits. The same knowledge that enables you to grow your wealth also enables you to minimize your risk. Before you put your money anywhere, you want to know as much as you can. This book is a great place to start — check out Chapter 6 for a rundown of the kinds of information you want to know before you buy stocks, as well as the resources that can give you the information you need to invest successfully.

## Staying out until you get a little practice

If you don't understand stocks, don't invest! Yeah, we know this book is about stock investing, and we think that some measure of stock investing is a good idea for most people. But that doesn't mean you should be 100 percent invested 100 percent of the time. If you don't understand a particular stock (or don't understand stocks, period), stay away until you do understand. Instead, give yourself an imaginary sum of money, such as $100,000, give yourself reasons to invest, and just make believe (an exercise called "simulated stock investing or trading"). Pick a few stocks that you think will increase in value, track them for a while, and see how they perform. Begin to understand how the price of a stock goes up and down, and watch what happens to the stocks you choose when various events take place. As you find out more and more about stock investing, you get better and better at picking individual stocks, and you haven't risked — or lost — any money during your learning period.

A good place to do your imaginary investing is at Web sites such as Marketocracy (`www.marketocracy.com`) and Investopedia's simulator (`http://simulator.investopedia.com`). You can design a stock portfolio and track its performance with thousands of other investors to see how well you do.

## Putting your financial house in order

Advice on what to do before you invest could fill a whole book all by itself. The bottom line is that you want to make sure you are, first and foremost, financially secure before you take the plunge into the stock market. If you're not sure about your financial security, look over your situation with a financial planner. (You can find more on financial planners in Appendix B.)

Before you buy your first stock, here are a few things you can do to get your finances in order:

- ✔ **Have a cushion of money.** Set aside three to six months' worth of your gross living expenses somewhere safe, such as in a bank account or money market fund, in case you suddenly need cash for an emergency (see Chapter 2 for details).

- ✔ **Reduce your debt.** Overindulging in debt was the worst personal economic problem for many Canadians in the late 1990s, and this has continued in recent years. When the U.S. housing bubble popped, millions of foreclosures were the result as homeowners piled on too much debt. In Canada, foreclosures and powers of sale have also increased, but not as dramatically as in the U.S.

- ✔ **Make sure your job is as secure as you can make it.** Are you keeping your skills up to date? Is the company you work for strong and growing? Is the industry you work in strong and growing?

- ✔ **Make sure you have adequate insurance.** You need enough supplemental insurance to cover you and your family's needs in case of illness, death, disability, and so on. Although Canada's provincial health care plans cover many medical expenses, they may not be enough for certain types of illnesses.

# Diversifying your investments

*Diversification* is a strategy for reducing risk by spreading your money across different investments. It's a fancy way of saying, "Don't put all your eggs in one basket." But how do you go about divvying up your money and distributing it among different investments? The easiest way to understand proper diversification may be to look at what you *shouldn't* do:

- ✔ **Don't put all your money in one stock.** Sure, if you choose wisely and select a hot stock you may make a bundle, but the odds are tremendously against you. Unless you're a real expert on a particular company, it's a good idea to have small portions of your money in several different stocks. As a general rule, the money you tie up in a single stock should be money you can do without.

- ✔ **Don't put all your money in one industry.** We know people who own several stocks, but the stocks are all in the same industry. Again, if you're an expert in that particular industry, it could work out. But just understand that you're not properly diversified. If a problem hits an entire industry, you may get hurt.

- ✔ **Don't put all your money in one type of investment.** Stocks may be a great investment, but you need to have money elsewhere too. Bonds, bank accounts, Treasury securities, real estate, and precious metals are perennial alternatives to complement your stock portfolio. Some of these alternatives can be found in mutual funds or exchange-traded funds (ETFs). An *exchange-traded fund* is a fund with a fixed portfolio of stocks or other securities that tracks a particular index but is traded like a stock. Check out Globe Investor (`www.globeinvestor.com/partners/free/etf/`) for more information about Canadian ETFs.

Okay, now that you know what you *shouldn't* do, what *should* you do? Until you become more knowledgeable, follow this advice:

- ✔ **Keep only 10 percent (or less) of your investment money in a single stock.**

- ✔ **Invest in four or five (and no more than ten) different stocks that are in different industries.** Which industries? Choose industries that offer products and services that have shown strong, growing demand. To make this decision, use your common sense (which isn't as common as it used to be). Think about the industries that people need no matter what happens in the general economy, such as food, energy, and other consumer necessities. See Chapter 17 for more information about analyzing industries.

---

## Better luck next time!

A little knowledge can be very risky. Consider the true story of one "lucky" fellow who played the lottery in 1987. He discovered that he had a winning ticket, with the first prize of $412,000. He immediately ordered a Porsche, booked a lavish trip to Hawaii for his family, and treated his wife and friends to a champagne dinner at a posh Hollywood restaurant. When he finally went to collect his prize, he found out that he had to share first prize with over 9,000 other lottery players who also had the same winning numbers. His share of the prize was actually only $45! Hopefully, he invested that tidy sum based on his increased knowledge about risk.

---

# *Weighing Risk against Return*

How much risk is appropriate for you, and how do you handle it? Before you try to figure out what risks accompany your investment choices, analyze yourself. Here are some points to keep in mind when weighing risk versus return in your situation:

- ✔ **Your financial goal:** In five minutes with a financial calculator, you can easily see how much money you're going to need to become financially independent (presuming financial independence is your goal). Say that you need $500,000 in ten years for a worry-free retirement and that your financial assets (such as stocks, bonds, and so on) are currently worth $400,000. In this scenario, your assets need to grow by only 2.25 percent to hit your target. Getting investments that grow by 2.25 percent safely is easy to do because that's a relatively low rate of return.

  The important point is that you don't have to knock yourself out trying to double your money with risky, high-flying investments; some run-of-the-mill bank investments will do just fine. All too often, investors take on more risk than is necessary. Figure out what your financial goal is so that you know what kind of return you realistically need. Flip to Chapters 2 and 3 for details on determining your financial goals.

- ✔ **Your investor profile:** Are you nearing retirement, or are you fresh out of college? Your life situation matters when it comes to looking at risk versus return.

  - If you're just beginning your working years, you can certainly tolerate greater risk than someone facing retirement. Even if you lose big time, you still have a long time to recoup your money and get back on track.

- However, if you're within five years of retirement, risky or aggressive investments can do much more harm than good. If you lose money, you don't have as much time to recoup your investment, and the odds are that you'll need the investment money (and its income-generating capacity) to cover your living expenses after you're no longer employed.

✔ **Asset allocation:** We never tell retirees to put a large portion of their retirement money into a high-tech stock or other volatile investment. But if they still want to speculate, we don't see a problem as long as they limit such investments to 5 percent of their total assets. As long as the bulk of their money is safe and sound in secure investments (such as Canada Savings Bonds), we can sleep well (knowing that *they* can sleep well!).

Asset allocation harkens back to diversification, which we discuss earlier in this chapter. For people in their 20s and 30s, having 75 percent of their money in a diversified portfolio of growth stocks (such as mid-cap and small-cap stocks; see Chapter 1) is acceptable. For people in their 60s and 70s, it's not acceptable. They may, instead, consider investing no more than 20 percent of their money in stocks (mid caps and large caps are preferable). Check with your financial adviser to find the right mix for your particular situation.

# Chapter 5

# Say Cheese: Getting a Snapshot of the Market with Indexes

*In This Chapter*

▶ Defining index basics

▶ Looking at the Dow and other indexes

▶ Exploring indexes for practical use

"**H**ow's the market doing today?" is the most common question that interested parties ask about the stock market. "What did the Dow do?" "How about Nasdaq?" "The TSX?" Invariably, people asking those questions expect an answer regarding how well the market performed that day. "Well, the Dow fell 157 points to 12,500, while the TSX was unchanged at 8,749." The Dow, Nasdaq, and TSX are *indexes,* statistical measures that represent the value of a batch of stocks. You can use indexes as general gauges of stock market activity. From them, you get a basic idea of how well (or how poorly) the overall market (or a portion of it) is doing. In this chapter, we focus our attention on the major North American stock market indexes and how to use them.

## Knowing How Indexes Are Measured

The oldest stock market index is the Dow Jones Industrial Average (DJIA, or simply "the Dow"), which was created by Charles Dow (of Dow Jones fame) in 1896. The Dow covered only 12 stocks then, but the number increased to 30 stocks in 1928, and it remains the same to this day. Because Dow worked long before the age of computers, he kept the calculations of his stock market index simple and did them arithmetically by hand. Dow added up the stock prices of the 12 companies and then divided the sum by 12. Technically, this number is an *average* and not an index (hence the word "average" in the name). For simplicity's sake, we refer to it as an index. Besides, the number gets tweaked nowadays to account for things such as stock splits. (For more on stock splits, see Chapter 15.)

However, indexes and averages get calculated differently. The primary difference is the concept of weighting. *Weighting* refers to the relative importance of the items when they're computed within the index. Several kinds of indexes exist, including:

- **Price-weighted index:** This index tracks changes based on the change in the individual stock's price per share. For example, suppose you own two stocks: Stock A, worth $20 per share, and Stock B, worth $40 per share. A price-weighted index allocates a greater proportion of the index to the stock at $40 than to the one at $20. If the index contained only these two stocks, the index number would reflect the $40 stock as being 67 percent (two-thirds of the total), while the $20 stock would be 33 percent (one-third of the total). The Dow is a good example of a price-weighted index.

- **Market-value-weighted index:** This index, also known as a *capitalization-weighted index,* tracks the proportion of a stock based on its market capitalization (or market value, also called market cap).

  Say that in your portfolio, you have 10 million shares of a $20 stock (Stock A) and 1 million shares of a $40 stock (Stock B). Stock A's market cap is $200 million, while Stock B's market cap is $40 million. Therefore, in a market-value-weighted index, Stock A represents 83 percent of the index's value because of its much larger market cap. Examples of market-value-weighted indexes are the Nasdaq Composite Index and the S&P/TSX Composite Index. (We discuss the Nasdaq and the S&P/TSX indexes later in this chapter.)

- **Broad-based index:** The sample portfolios in the preceding bullets show only two stocks — obviously not a good representative index. Most investing professionals (especially money managers and mutual fund firms) use a broad-based index as a benchmark to compare their progress. A broad-based index provides a snapshot of the entire market. The S&P 500 and the Wilshire 5000 are good examples of broad-based indexes (they also happen to be market-value-weighted indexes; see descriptions of both indexes later in this chapter).

- **Composite index:** This index is a combination of several averages or indexes. An example is the New York Stock Exchange (NYSE) Composite, which tracks all the stocks on the NYSE. Another example is the Nasdaq Composite Index, which is a market-capitalization composite index of 3,000 companies on Nasdaq.

- **Performance-based index:** This index includes not only the appreciation of the stocks represented in the index but also the dividends (and other cash payouts) issued to shareholders. The DAX (the most widely followed German index, composed of 30 major German companies) is a performance-based index.

# Checking Out the Indexes

Although most people consider the Dow, Nasdaq, and Standard & Poor's 500 to be the stars of the financial press, you may find other indexes equally important to follow because they cover other significant facets of the market, such as small-cap and mid-cap stocks, or specific sectors and industries.

For example, if you invest in an Internet stock, check the Internet Stock Index to compare how your stock is doing when measured against the index. You can find indexes that cover industries such as transportation, brokerage firms, retailers, computer companies, and real estate firms. For a comprehensive list of indexes, go to www.djindexes.com (a Dow Jones & Co. Web site). The most reliable and most widely respected indexes are produced not only by Dow Jones but also Standard & Poor's and the major exchanges/markets themselves, such as the TSX, New York Stock Exchange (NYSE), the American Stock Exchange (AMEX), and Nasdaq. Smaller exchanges also issue or provide indexes (such as the Philadelphia Exchange). You can find Web sites for different exchanges in Appendix B.

## The Dow Jones Industrial Average

The most famous stock market barometer is my first example in the previous section — the Dow Jones Industrial Average (DJIA). When someone asks how the market is doing, most investors quote "the Dow." This index is price-weighted and tracks a basket of 30 of the largest and most influential public companies in the stock market. We list the stocks tracked on the Dow and discuss the Dow's drawbacks in the following sections.

### The companies of the Dow

The following list shows the current roster of 30 stocks tracked on the DJIA (in alphabetical order by company, with their stock symbols in parentheses).

Alcoa (AA)

American Express Co. (AXP)

AT&T (T)

Bank of America (BAC)

Boeing (BA)

Caterpillar (CAT)

Chevron (CVX)

Cisco (CSCO)

Coca-Cola Co. (KO)

Disney & Co (DIS)

DuPont (DD)

Exxon Mobil (XOM)

General Electric (GE)

Hewlett-Packard (HPQ)

Home Depot (HD)

Intel (INTC)

International Business Machines (IBM)

Johnson & Johnson (JNJ)

J.P. Morgan Chase (JPM)

Kraft Food Inc. (KFT)

McDonald's (MCD)

Merck (MRK)

Microsoft (MSFT)

Minnesota Mining and Manufacturing (also known as 3M) (MMM)

Pfizer (PFE)

Procter & Gamble (PG)

Travelers Companies (TRV)

United Technologies (UTX)

Verizon (VZ)

Wal-Mart Stores (WMT)

### The drawbacks of the Dow

The Dow has survived as a popular gauge of stock market activity for over a century because it was the first such statistical snapshot of the stock market, which helped it become quickly entrenched as a widely followed and quoted barometer. Although it's an important indicator of the market's progress, the Dow does have one major drawback: it tracks only 30 companies. Regardless of their status in the market, the companies in the Dow represent a limited sampling, so they don't communicate the true pulse of the market. For example, when the Dow surpassed the record 10,000 and 11,000 milestones during 1999 and 2000, the majority of (non-index) companies showed lacklustre or declining stock price movement. (See the "Dow Jones milestones" sidebar in this chapter for more information.)

The roster of the Dow has changed many times during the 100-plus years of its existence. The only original company from 1896 is General Electric. Dow Jones made most of the changes because of company mergers and bankruptcies. However, Dow Jones also made some changes simply to reflect the changing times. In September 2008, as AIG Corp.'s stock was plummeting because of the credit crisis on Wall Street, it was quickly removed from the Dow and replaced with Kraft Foods. At that time, AIG fell from $25 per share to $3 per share within days. Had AIG stayed in the Dow, the Dow would have shown a larger drop, but it maintained a higher level because of the quick replacement. Investors unaware of such moves can be fooled regarding the market's health — another drawback of the Dow.

The Dow isn't a pure gauge of industrial activity, because it also includes a hodgepodge of nonindustrial companies such as J.P. Morgan Chase and AMEX (banks), Home Depot (retailing), and Microsoft (software). During this decade, true industrial sectors like manufacturing had difficult times, yet the Dow rose to record levels.

Given the Dow's shortcomings, serious investors also look at the following indexes:

- ✔ **Broad-based indexes:** The S&P 500 and the Wilshire 5000 are more realistic gauges of the stock market's performance than the Dow. (We discuss these indexes later in this chapter.)

- ✔ **Industry or sector indexes:** These indexes are better gauges of the growth (or lack of growth) of specific industries and sectors. If you buy a gold stock, for example, you should track the index for the precious metals industry.

Dow Jones has several averages, including the Dow Jones Transportation Average (DJTA) and the Dow Jones Utilities Average (DJUA). Dow Jones manages both of these indexes more strictly than the Dow, so they tend to be a more accurate barometer of the market they represent. Find out more about the Dow Jones indexes at www.djindexes.com.

## The Toronto Stock Exchange/TMX

In 2000, the Toronto Stock Exchange became a for-profit company. Soon after, the Toronto Stock Exchange bought out the Canadian Venture Exchange, and the new group of exchanges was renamed the TSX. This transformation ended almost 125 years of using the term "TSE." In mid-2008 the shareholders of TSX Group changed its name to the TMX Group. As of March 2009, the combined resources and entities of the predecessor exchange now sometimes use the name TMX.

The TMX Group's business lines — in various Canadian cities — operate in the currency and derivatives markets as well as in equities, fixed income instruments, and energy:

- ✔ The Toronto Stock Exchange group offers stock issuers access to a public equity market that is world-class.

- ✔ The TSX Venture Exchange group serves the public-venture capital market, which provides access to growth capital for new companies.

- ✔ The Montreal Exchange component provides interest rate, index, and equity derivatives trading and owns a majority interest in the influential Boston Options Exchange (BOX).

- ✔ The Natural Gas Exchange (NGX) is a leading exchange for the trading of natural gas and electricity contracts.

✔ Shorcan, the final piece of the puzzle, is an institutional fixed income trading system that also provides fixed income indexes in Canada.

In Canada, the S&P/TSX 60 Index includes 60 large-capitalization stocks (from the Toronto Stock Exchange) for Canadian equity markets. The index is market-capitalization-weighted, weight-adjusted for things like *share float* (shares readily available to the public), and balanced across ten industry sectors. S&P/TSX 60 constituents are selected for inclusion using Standard & Poor's guidelines concerning company capitalization, liquidity, and fundamentals.

The S&P/TSX 60 serves as the benchmark for related products such as exchange-traded funds and index options. Approximately $9 billion in index products are indexed to the S&P/TSX 60 index. The S&P/TSX 60 is part of the S&P Global 1200, a world equity index that covers more than 30 countries.

The following list shows the current lineup of 60 stocks tracked on the S&P/TSX 60.

Agnico-Eagle Mines (AEM)

Agrium Inc. (AGU)

ARC Energy Trust (AET.UN)

Bank of Montreal (BMO)

Bank of Nova Scotia (Scotiabank) (BNS)

Barrick Gold (ABX)

Bell Canada Enterprises (BCE)

Biovail Corporation (BVF)

Bombardier (BBD.B)

Brookfield Asset Management (BAM.A)

Cameco Corporation (CCO)

Canadian Imperial Bank of Commerce (CIBC) (CM)

Canadian National Railway Company (CN) (CNR)

Canadian Natural Resources Limited (CNQ)

Canadian Oil Sands Trust (COS.UN)

Canadian Pacific Railway Limited (CPR) (CP)

Canadian Tire Corporation Ltd. (CTC.A)

Enbridge Inc. (ENB)

EnCana Corporation (ECA)

Enerplus Resources Fund (ERF.UN)

First Quantum Minerals (FM)

Fortis (FTS)

George Weston Limited (WN)

Gildan Activewear (GIL)

Goldcorp Inc. (G)

Groupe Aeroplan (AER)

Husky Energy Inc. (HSE)

Imperial Oil Limited (IMO)

Inmet Mining (IMN)

Kinross Gold Corporation (K)

Loblaw Companies Limited (L)

Magna International Inc. (MG.A)

Manulife Financial (MFC)

MDS Inc. (MDS)

Metro (MRU.A)

National Bank of Canada (NA)

Nexen Inc. (NXY)

Penn West Energy Trust (PWT.UN)

Petro-Canada (PCA)

Potash Corporation of Saskatchewan (PotashCorp) (POT)

Power Corporation of Canada (POW)

Research In Motion Limited (RIM)

Rogers Communications Inc. (RCI.B)

Royal Bank of Canada (RY)

Saputo (SAP)

Shaw Communications (SJR.B)

Shoppers Drug Mart Inc. (SC)

SNC Lavalin Group (SNC)

Sun Life Financial (SLF)

Suncor Energy Inc. (SU)

Talisman Energy Inc. (TLM)

Teck Cominco Limited (TCK.B)

TELUS (T)

Thomson Reuters Corporation, The (TRI)

Tim Hortons (THI)

Toronto-Dominion Bank (TD)

TransAlta Corporation (TA)

TransCanada (TRP)

Yamana Gold (YRI)

Yellow Pages Income Fund (YLO.UN)

## *Standard & Poor's 500*

The Standard & Poor's 500 (S&P 500) tracks 500 leading publicly traded companies considered to be widely held. The publishing firm Standard & Poor's created this index (we bet you could've guessed that). Because it contains 500 companies, the S&P 500 more accurately represents overall market performance than the DJIA, with its 30 companies. Money managers and financial advisers actually watch the S&P 500 stock index more closely than the Dow. Most mutual funds especially like to measure their performance against the S&P 500 rather than any other index, although mutual funds that concentrate on small-cap stocks usually prefer an index that has more small-cap stocks in it, such as the Russell 2000 (which we discuss later in this chapter).

The S&P 500 doesn't attempt to cover the 500 biggest companies. Instead, it includes companies that are widely held and widely followed. The companies are also industry leaders in a variety of industries, including energy, technology, healthcare, and finance.

Although it's a reliable indicator of the market's overall status, the S&P 500 also has some limitations. Despite the fact that it tracks 500 companies, the top 50 companies make up 50 percent of the index's market value. This situation can be a drawback, because those 50 companies have a greater influence on the index's price movement than any other segment of companies. In other words, 10 percent of the companies have an equal impact to 90 percent of the companies on the same index. Therefore, although the index better represents the market than the DJIA, it doesn't give a perfectly accurate representation of the general market.

Standard & Poor's doesn't set in stone the 500 companies it tracks — S&P can add or remove companies when market conditions change, removing a company if it isn't doing well or goes bankrupt, for instance, and replacing it with a company that's doing better. You can find out more at www.standardandpoors.com.

## Dow Jones milestones

This table shows when the Dow Jones Industrial Average reached each of fourteen 1,000-point milestones and how long it took to reach that point:

| Milestone | Date | How long it took |
| --- | --- | --- |
| 1,000 | Nov. 14, 1972 | 76 years |
| 2,000 | Jan. 8, 1987 | 14 years |
| 3,000 | April 17, 1991 | 4 years |
| 4,000 | Feb. 23, 1995 | 4 years |
| 5,000 | Nov. 21, 1995 | 9 months |
| 6,000 | Oct. 14, 1996 | 11 months |
| 7,000 | Feb. 13, 1997 | 4 months |
| 8,000 | July 16, 1997 | 5 months |
| 9,000 | April 6, 1998 | 9 months |
| 10,000 | March 29, 1999 | 1 year |
| 11,000 | May 3, 1999 | 1 month |
| 12,000 | Oct. 19, 2006 | 7 years and 5 months |
| 13,000 | April 25, 2007 | 6 months |
| 14,000 | July 19, 2007 | 3 months |

As you can see, the Dow took 76 years to hit its first milestone. But it took less and less time to hit each succeeding milestone because the higher the Dow is in a relative sense, the easier it is to jump 1,000 points. For example, it went from 6,000 to 7,000 in only four months.

As the table indicates, most of the milestones happened during the 1982–99 bull market. But the Dow didn't reach a new milestone from 2000–05. After the Dow hit a peak of 11,722 in January 2000, it entered a bear market that lasted three years. A new bull market started in 2003, and the Dow regained its traction and started an ascent to new highs. It finally hit the 12,000 mark in late 2006 (nearly 7½ years after hitting the 11,000 level). Despite hitting the 14,000 plateau in July 2007, it spent the subsequent 12-month period trading sideways in the 11,000–13,000 range. The Dow hit an all-time closing high of 14,164.53 on October 9, 2007, although it is considerably lower today. Oh well . . .

# Wilshire Total Market Index

The Wilshire 5000 Equity Index, often referred to as the Wilshire Total Market Index, is probably the largest stock index in the world. Wilshire Associates started out in 1980 tracking 5,000 stocks. Since then, the Wilshire 5000 has ballooned to cover more than 7,500 stocks. The advantage of the Wilshire 5000 is that it's very comprehensive, covering nearly the entire market (at the very least, the Wilshire 5000 tracks the largest publicly traded stocks). It includes all the stocks on the major stock exchanges (NYSE, AMEX, and the largest issues on Nasdaq), which by default also includes all the stocks covered by the S&P 500. Investors and analysts who seek the greatest representation/performance of the general market look to the Wilshire 5000.

The Wilshire 5000 is a market-value-weighted index that also performs as a broad-based index. The Wilshire indexes are maintained by Wilshire Associates Incorporated, and you can find out more at www.wilshire.com.

## Nasdaq indexes

Nasdaq became a formalized market in 1971. The name used to stand for "National Association of Securities Dealers Automated Quote" system, but now it's simply "Nasdaq" (as if it's a name, like Ralph or Eddie). Nasdaq indexes are similar to other indexes in style and structure. The only difference is that, well, they cover companies traded on the Nasdaq (www.nasdaq.com). The Nasdaq has two indexes, both of which are reported in the financial pages:

- ✔ **Nasdaq Composite Index:** Most frequently quoted on the news, the Nasdaq Composite Index covers about 3,000 companies that trade on Nasdaq. The companies encompass a variety of industries, but the index's concentrationis primarily technology, biotech, alternative energy, and related sectors. The Nasdaq Composite Index hit an all-time high of 5,048 in March 2000 before the worst bear market in its history occurred. The index dropped a whopping 77 percent by 2002 to bottom out at 1,114 in October 2002. As of late 2009, the Nasdaq was at approximately 2,000 (still way below its all-time high, but higher than its bottom six years earlier).

- ✔ **Nasdaq 100 Index:** The Nasdaq 100 tracks the 100 largest companies in Nasdaq based on size in terms of market capitalization. This index is for investors who want to concentrate on the largest companies, which tend to be especially weighted in technology. It provides extra representation of technology-related companies such as Microsoft, Adobe, and Symantec.

Although these indexes track growth-oriented companies, the stocks of these companies are also very volatile and carry commensurate risk. The indexes themselves bear out this risk; in the bear market of 2000 and 2001 (and even extending into 2002), they fell more than 60 percent. In March 2009, the index dropped below 1,300. You can find out more about Nasdaq's indexes at www.nasdaq.com.

## Russell 3000 Index

The Russell 3000 Index is a great example of an index that seeks more comprehensive inclusion of U.S. companies. It's a performance-based index that includes the 3,000 largest publicly traded companies (nearly 98 percent of publicly traded stocks). The Russell 3000 is important because it includes many mid-cap and small-cap stocks. Most companies covered in the Russell 3000 have an average market value of a billion dollars or less.

Russell Investments Group created and maintains the Russell 3000 Index, as well as the Russell 1000 and the Russell 2000. The Russell 2000 contains the smallest 2,000 companies from the Russell 3000, while the Russell 1000 contains the largest 1,000 companies. The Russell indexes don't cover *micro-cap stocks* (companies with a market capitalization under $250 million). You can find out more at www.russell.com.

## International indexes

Investors need to remember that the whole world is a vast marketplace that interacts with and exerts tremendous influence on individual national economies and markets. Whether you have one stock or one mutual fund, keep tabs on how world markets affect your portfolio. The best way to get a snapshot of international markets is, of course, with indexes. Here are some of the more widely followed international indexes:

- **BSE SENSEX (India):** The most widely followed index of Indian stocks is also referred to as the "BSE 30 Index" and is a value-weighted index maintained by the Bombay Stock Exchange (www.bseindia.com).

- **CAC-40 (France):** This market-capitalization-weighted index tracks 40 of the largest public stocks that trade on Paris's stock exchange, the Euronext Paris.

- **DAX (Germany):** This index is similar to our DJIA in that it tracks 30 blue-chip stocks (the largest and most active that trade on the Frankfurt Exchange).

- **FTSE-100 (Great Britain):** Usually referred to as the "footsie," this market-value-weighted index includes the top 100 public companies in the United Kingdom.

- **Halter USX China Index (China):** This index tracks a basket of 50 market-value-weighted U.S. public companies that derive most of their revenues from China.

- **Hang Seng Index (Hong Kong):** This market-value-weighted index tracks the top 45 companies on the Hong Kong Stock Exchange.

- **Nikkei (Japan):** This index is considered Japan's version of the Dow. If you're invested in Japanese stocks or in stocks that do business with Japan, you want to know what's up with the Nikkei.

- **SSE Composite Index (Shanghai):** This is an index of all the stocks that trade on the Shanghai Stock Exchange.

 You can track these international indexes (among others) at major financial Web sites such as www.bloomberg.com and www.marketwatch.com. You may find international indexes useful in your analysis as you watch your stocks' progress. What if you have stock in a company that has most of its customers in Japan? Then the Nikkei can help you get a general snapshot of how well the major companies are doing in Japan, which in turn can be a general barometer of Japan's economic health. If your company's business partners or customers are in the Nikkei and it's plunging, you know it's probably "sayonara" for the company's stock price.

As for us, we're still waiting for the "Galaxy 1 Million Index" — no point in being overweight with Earth stocks, you know.

# Using the Indexes Effectively

You may be wondering which indexes you should be checking out and exactly what you should do with them. The sections that follow give you some idea of how to put all the pieces together.

## Tracking the indexes

The bottom line is that indexes give investors an instant snapshot of how well the market is doing. Indexes offer a quick way to compare the performance of one investor's portfolio with the rest of the market. If the Dow goes up 10 percent in a year and your portfolio shows a cumulative gain of 12 percent, then you know you're doing well. Appendix B lists resources to help you keep up with various indexes.

The problem with indexes is that they can be misleading if you take them too literally as an accurate barometer of stock success. For example, the Dow has changed its roster of companies many times since 1896. Had it not, the Dow's general upward trajectory in the past few decades would have been much different. Laggard stocks have been dropped and replaced with stocks that have shown more promise. Many of the original companies that were in the DJIA in 1896 went out of business or were bought by other companies that aren't reflected in the index.

## Investing in indexes

If the market is doing well but your specific stock isn't, can you find a way to invest in the index itself? Yes, and with investments based on indexes, you can invest in the general market or a particular industry.

Say you want to invest in the DJIA. After all, why try to beat the market if just matching it is sufficient to grow your wealth? Why not have a portfolio that directly mirrors the DJIA? Well, it's too impractical and expensive to invest in all 30 stocks in the DJIA. Fortunately, alternatives can accomplish the act of investing in indexes. Here are the best ways:

✔ **Index mutual funds:** An index mutual fund is much like a regular mutual fund except that it invests only in securities (in this case, stocks) that match as closely as possible the basket of stocks in that particular index. For example, you can find index mutual funds that track the DJIA and the S&P 500. Find out more about index mutual funds at places such as Morningstar (www.morningstar.com) and Globe Investor (www.globeinvestor.com).

✔ **Exchange-traded funds (ETFs):** This is a particular favourite of ours. ETFs have similar characteristics to mutual funds except for a few key differences. An ETF can reflect a basket of stocks that mirror a particular index, but you can trade the ETF like a stock itself. You can transact ETFs like stocks in that you can buy, sell, or go short. You can put stop losses on them, and you can even purchase them on margin (see Chapter 21 for more on stop losses and buying on margin). ETFs can give you the diversification of mutual funds coupled with the versatility of stocks. Examples of ETFs that track indexes are the DJIA ETF (symbol DIA) and the ETF for Nasdaq (QQQ). You can find out more about ETFs at the American Stock Exchange (www.amex.com) and at Globe Investor (www.globeinvestor.com).

# Part II
# Before You Invest

The 5th Wave                                        By Rich Tennant

Defining your investment risk with the:
TOAST RETRIEVING RISK TOLERANCE TEST

LOW RISK | Waits for toast to pop up even though it's burning.

MODERATE RISK | Goes after toast with wooden toast prongs.

HIGH RISK | Goes after toast with all metal butter knife.

ULTRA HIGH RISK | Goes after toast with metal butter knife wearing a wet swim suit and a stainless steel colander on head.

# In this part . . .

When you're about to begin investing in stocks, you should know that different types of stocks exist for different objectives. If you can at least get a stock that fits your situation, you're that much ahead in the game. In this part, you can find out where to start gathering information and discover what stockbrokers can do for you. In addition, you'll find fun chapters on the basics of economics (really!) and the influence of politics that will keep you ahead of the curve — because stock choices are made more intelligently when you know the economic and political environment.

# Chapter 6

# Gathering Information

## In This Chapter

▶ Using stock exchanges to get investment information

▶ Applying know-how from accounting and economics to your investing

▶ Exploring financial issues

▶ Deciphering stock tables

▶ Interpreting dividend news

▶ Recognizing good (and bad) investing advice

▶ Gathering information online

K nowledge and information are two critical success factors in stock investing. (Isn't that true about most things in life?) People who plunge headlong into stocks without sufficient knowledge of the stock market in general, and current information in particular, quickly learn the lesson of the eager diver who didn't find out ahead of time that the pool was only an inch deep (ouch!). In their haste to avoid missing so-called golden investment opportunities, investors too often end up losing money.

Opportunities to *make* money in the stock market will always be there, no matter how well or how poorly the economy and the market are performing in general. There's no such thing as a single (and fleeting) magical moment, so don't feel that if you let an opportunity pass you by, you'll always regret that you missed your one big chance.

For the best approach to stock investing, you want to build your knowledge and find quality information first. Then buy stocks and make your fortunes more assuredly. Basically, before you buy stock, you need to know that the company you're investing in is

✔ Financially sound and growing

✔ Offering products and services that are in demand by consumers

✔ In a strong and growing industry (and general economy)

Where do you start and what kind of information do you want to acquire? Keep reading.

# Looking to Stock Exchanges for Answers

Before you invest in stocks, you need to be completely familiar with the basics of stock investing. At its most fundamental, stock investing is about using your money to buy a piece of a company that will give you value in the form of appreciation or income. Fortunately, many resources are available to help you find out about stock investing. Some of our favourite places are the stock exchanges themselves.

Stock exchanges are organized marketplaces for the buying and selling of stocks (and other securities). The Toronto Stock Exchange (TSX) and the New York Stock Exchange (NYSE) are the premier North American stock exchanges (refer to Chapter 5). They provide a framework for stock buyers and sellers to make their transactions. The TSX and NYSE make money not only from a piece of every transaction but also from fees (such as listing fees) charged to companies and brokers that are members of its exchanges.

The main exchanges for most North American stock investors are the NYSE, TSX, Nasdaq, and the American Stock Exchange (AMEX). Nasdaq technically is not an exchange, but it is a formal market that effectively acts as an exchange. These four exchanges/markets encourage and inform people about stock investing. Because they benefit from increased popularity of stock investing and continued demand for stocks, they offer a wealth of free (or low-cost) resources and information for stock investors. Go to their Web sites to find useful resources such as:

- Tutorials on how to invest in stocks, common investment strategies, and so on

- Glossaries and free information to help you understand the language, practice, and purpose of stock investing

- A wealth of news, press releases, financial data, and other information about companies listed on the exchange or market, usually accessed through an on-site search engine

- Industry analysis and news

- Stock quotes and other market information related to the daily market movements of stocks, including data such as volume, new highs, new lows, and so on

- Free tracking of your stock selections (you can input a sample portfolio, or the stocks you're following, to see how well you're doing)

What each exchange/market offers keeps changing and is often updated, so go exploring at their Web sites:

- ✔ New York Stock Exchange: www.nyse.com
- ✔ TSX: www.tsx.com (also www.tmx.com)
- ✔ Nasdaq: www.nasdaq.com
- ✔ American Stock Exchange: www.amex.com

# Understanding Stocks and the Companies They Represent

Stocks represent ownership in companies. Before you buy individual stocks, you want to understand the companies whose stock you're considering and find out about their operations. It may sound like a daunting task, but you'll digest the point more easily when you realize that companies work very similarly to how you work. They make decisions on a day-to-day basis just as you do.

Think about how you grow and prosper as an individual or as a family, and you see the same issues with businesses and how they grow and prosper. Low earnings and high debt are examples of financial difficulties that can affect both Canadians and companies. You'll understand companies' finances when you take the time to pick up some information in two basic disciplines: accounting and economics. These two disciplines play a significant role in understanding the performance of a firm's stock.

## Accounting for taste and a whole lot more

Accounting. Ugh! But face it: Accounting is the language of business, and believe it or not, you're already familiar with the most important accounting concepts. Just look at the following three essential principles:

- ✔ **Assets minus liabilities equals net worth.** In other words, take what you own (your assets), subtract what you owe (your liabilities), and the rest is yours (net worth)! Your own personal finances work the same way as Microsoft's (except yours have fewer zeros at the end). See Chapter 2 to figure out how to calculate your own net worth.

A company's balance sheet shows you its net worth at a specific point in time (such as December 31). The net worth of a company is the bottom line of its asset and liability picture, and it tells you whether the company is *solvent* (has the ability to pay its debts without going out of business). The net worth of a successful company is regularly growing. To see whether your company is successful, compare its net worth with the net worth from the same point a year earlier. A firm that has a $4 million net worth on December 31, 2008, and a $5 million net worth on December 31, 2009, is doing well; its net worth has gone up 25 percent ($1 million) in one year.

✔ **Income less expenses equals net income.** In other words, take what you make (your income), subtract what you spend (your expenses), and the remainder is your *net income* (or net profit or net earnings — your gain).

A company's profitability is the whole point of investing in its stock. As it profits, the business becomes more valuable, and in turn its stock price becomes more valuable. To discover a firm's net income, look at its income statement. Try to determine whether the company uses its gains wisely, either reinvesting them for continued growth or paying down debt.

✔ **Do a comparative financial analysis.** That's a mouthful, but it's just a fancy way of saying how a company is doing now compared with something else (like a prior period or a similar company).

If you know that the company you're looking at had a net income of $50,000 for the year, you may ask, "Is that good or bad?" Obviously, making a net profit is good, but you also need to know whether it's good compared to something else. If the company had a net profit of $40,000 the year before, you know that the company's profitability is improving. But if a similar company had a net profit of $100,000 the year before and in the current year is making $50,000, then you may want to either avoid that company or see what (if anything) went wrong with it.

Accounting can be this simple. If you understand these three basic points, you're ahead of the curve (in stock investing as well as in your personal finances). For more information on how to use a company's financial statements to pick good stocks, see Chapters 12, 13, and 14.

## Understanding how economics affects stocks

Economics. Double ugh! No, you aren't required to understand "the inelasticity of demand aggregates" (thank heavens!) or "marginal utility" (say what?). But a working knowledge of basic economics is crucial (and we mean crucial) to your success and proficiency as a stock investor. The stock market and the economy are joined at the hip. The good (or bad) things that happen to one have a direct effect on the other.

### Getting the hang of the basic concepts

Alas, many investors get lost on basic economic concepts (as do some so-called experts that you see on TV). We owe our personal investing success to our status as students of economics. Understanding basic economics helps us (and will help you) filter the financial news to separate relevant information from the irrelevant in order to make better investment decisions. Be aware of these important economic concepts:

- **Supply and demand:** How can anyone possibly think about economics without thinking of the ageless concept of supply and demand? *Supply and demand* can be simply stated as the relationship between what's available (the supply) and what people want and are willing to pay for (the demand). This equation is the main engine of economic activity and is extremely important for your stock investing analysis and decision-making process. We mean, do you really want to buy stock in a company that makes porcelain busts of John Diefenbaker if you find out that the company has an oversupply and nobody wants to buy them anyway? (We discuss supply and demand in more detail in Chapter 10.)

- **Cause and effect:** If you pick up a prominent news report and read, "Companies in the table industry are expecting plummeting sales," do you rush out and invest in companies that sell chairs or manufacture tablecloths? Considering cause and effect is an exercise in logical thinking, and believe us, logic is a major component of sound economic thought.

  When you read business news, play it out in your mind. What good (or bad) can logically be expected given a certain event or situation? If you're looking for an effect ("I want a stock price that keeps increasing"), you also want to understand the cause. Here are some typical events that can cause a stock's price to rise (see Chapter 10 for additional info on cause and effect):

  - **Positive news reports about a company:** The news may report that the company is enjoying success with increased sales or a new product.

  - **Positive news reports about a company's industry:** The media may be highlighting that the industry is poised to do well.

  - **Positive news reports about a company's customers:** Maybe your company is in industry A, but its customers are in industry B. If you see good news about industry B, that may be good news for your stock.

  - **Negative news reports about a company's competitors:** If the competitors are in trouble, their customers may seek alternatives to buy from, including your company.

✔ **Economic effects from government actions:** Political and governmental actions have economic consequences. As a matter of fact, nothing (and we mean nothing!) has a greater effect on investing and economics than government. Government actions usually manifest themselves as taxes, laws, or regulations. They also can take on a more ominous appearance, such as war or the threat of war. Government can willfully (or even accidentally) cause a company to go bankrupt, disrupt an entire industry, or even cause a depression. It controls the money supply, credit, and all public securities markets. For more information on political effects, see Chapter 11.

### Gaining insight from past mistakes

Because most investors ignored some basic observations about economics in the late 1990s, they subsequently lost trillions in their stock portfolios. During 2000–09, the U.S. experienced the greatest expansion of total debt in history, coupled with a record expansion of the money supply. The Federal Reserve (or "the Fed"), the U.S. government's central bank, controls both. In Canada, government debt also increased in recent years, albeit less significantly. (In mid-2009 the Bank of Canada increased the money supply as well.) This growth of North American debt and U.S. money supply resulted in more consumer (and corporate) borrowing, spending, and investing. This activity hyperstimulated the stock market for over a decade, and caused stocks to rise until the stock market bubble popped during 2000–02. It was soon replaced with the housing bubble, which popped during 2005–06 and is still hurting the economy in 2010.

Of course, you should always be happy to earn double-digit annual returns with your investments, but such a return can't be sustained and encourages speculation. This artificial stimulation by the Fed and the Bank of Canada resulted in the following:

✔ More and more people depleted their savings. After all, why settle for 3 percent in the Royal Bank when you can get 25 percent in the stock market?

✔ More and more people bought on credit. If the economy is booming, why not buy now and pay later? Consumer credit hit record highs in both Canada and the U.S.

✔ More and more people borrowed against their homes. Why not borrow and get rich now? I can pay off my debt later.

✔ More and more companies sold more goods as consumers took more vacations and bought SUVs, electronics, and so on. Companies then borrowed to finance expansion, open new stores, and so on.

✔ More and more North American companies went public and offered stock to take advantage of more money that was flowing to the markets from banks and other financial institutions.

Beginning in late 2007, spending started to slow down in Canada and the U.S. because consumers and businesses became too indebted. This slowdown in turn caused the sales of goods and services to taper off. However, companies had too much overhead, capacity, and debt because they expanded too eagerly. At this point, businesses were caught in a financial bind. Too much debt and too many expenses in a slowing economy mean one thing: profits shrink or disappear. To stay in business, companies had to do the logical thing — cut expenses. What's usually the biggest expense for companies? People! To stay in business, many companies in Canada and the U.S. started laying off employees. As a result, consumer spending dropped further because more people were either laid off or had second thoughts about their own job security.

As people had little in the way of savings and too much in the way of debt, they had to sell their stock to pay their bills. This trend was one major reason why stocks started to fall in recent years. Earnings started to drop because of shrinking sales from a sputtering economy. As earnings fell, stock prices also fell.

The lessons from the 1990s and from the housing bubble years are important ones for investors today:

✔ Stocks are not a replacement for savings accounts. Always have some money in the bank.

✔ Stocks should never occupy 100 percent of your investment funds.

✔ When anyone (including an expert) tells you that the economy will keep growing indefinitely, be skeptical and read diverse sources of information.

✔ If stocks do well in your portfolio, consider protecting your stocks (both your original investment and any gains) with stop-loss orders. (See Chapter 21 for more on these strategies.)

✔ Keep debt and expenses to a minimum.

✔ If the Canadian economy is booming, a decline is sure to follow as the ebb and flow of the economy's business cycle continues.

## Know thyself before you invest in stocks

If you're reading this book, you're probably doing so because you want to become a successful investor. Granted, to be a successful investor you have to select great stocks, but having a realistic understanding of your own financial situation and goals is equally important. We recall one investor who lost $10,000 in a speculative stock. The loss wasn't that bad because he had most of his money safely tucked away elsewhere. He also understood that his overall financial situation was secure and that the money he lost was "play" money — the loss wouldn't have a drastic effect on his life. But many investors often lose even more money, and the loss does have a major, negative effect on their lives. You may not be like the investor who can afford to lose $10,000. Take time to understand yourself, your own financial picture, and your personal investment goals before you decide to buy stocks.

# *Staying on Top of Financial News*

Reading the financial news can help you decide where or where not to invest. Many newspapers, magazines, and Web sites offer great coverage of the financial world. Obviously, the more informed you are, the better, but you don't have to read everything that's written. The information explosion in recent years has gone beyond overload, and you can easily spend so much time reading that you have little time left for investing. In the following sections, we describe the types of information you need to get from the financial news.

Appendix B of this book provides more information on the following resources, along with a treasure trove of some of the best publications, resources, and Web sites to assist you:

- ✔ The most obvious publications of interest to stock investors are the two Canadian national dailies — the *National Post* (www.nationalpost.com) and *The Globe and Mail* (www.theglobeandmail.com). Other useful publications include *The Wall Street Journal* and *Investor's Business Daily*, U.S. newspapers that also cover world financial news. These leading publications report the news and stock data as of the day before.

- ✔ Some other leading Web sites are CBS's MarketWatch (www.marketwatch.com) and Bloomberg (www.bloomberg.com), which include Canadian company news and information. These Web sites can also give you news and stock data within minutes of a transaction.

## Figuring out what a company's up to

Before you invest, you need to know what's going on with the company. When you read about the company, either from the firm's literature (its annual report, for example) or from media sources, be sure to get answers to some pertinent questions:

- ✔ **Is the company making more net income than it did last year?** You want to invest in a company that's growing.

- ✔ **Are the company's sales greater than they were the year before?** Remember, you won't make money if the company isn't making money.

- ✔ **Is the company issuing press releases on new products, services, inventions, or business deals?** All these achievements indicate a strong, vital company.

Knowing how the company is doing, no matter what's happening with the general economy, is obviously important. To better understand how companies tick, see Chapter 12.

## Discovering what's new with an industry

As you consider investing in a stock, make it a point to know what's going on in that company's industry. If the industry is doing well, your stock is likely to do well, too. But then again, the reverse is also true.

Yes, we've seen investors pick successful stocks in a failing industry, but those cases are exceptional. By and large, it's easier to succeed with a stock when the entire industry is doing well. As you're watching the news, reading the financial pages, or viewing financial Web sites, check out the industry to see that it's strong and dynamic. See Chapter 17 for information on analyzing industries.

## Knowing what's happening with the economy

No matter how well or how poorly the overall economy is performing, you want to stay informed about its general progress. It's easier for the value of stock to keep going up when the economy is stable or growing. The reverse is also true; if the economy is contracting or declining, the stock has a tougher time keeping its value. Some basic items to keep tabs on include the following:

✔ **Gross domestic product (GDP):** This is roughly the total value of output for a particular nation, measured in the dollar amount of goods and services. The GDP is reported quarterly, and a rising GDP bodes well for your stock. When the GDP is rising 3 percent or more on an annual basis, that's solid growth. If it rises at more than zero but less than 3 percent, that's generally considered less than stellar (or mediocre). A GDP under zero (or negative) means that the economy is shrinking (heading into recession).

✔ **The index of leading economic indicators (LEI):** The LEI is a snapshot of a set of economic statistics covering activity that precedes what's happening in the economy. Each statistic helps you understand the economy in much the same way that barometers (and windows!) help you understand what's happening with the weather. Economists don't just look at an individual statistic; they look at a set of statistics to get a more complete picture of what's happening with the economy.

Chapter 10 goes into greater detail on economics and its effect on stock prices.

## Seeing what politicians and government bureaucrats are doing

Being informed about what public officials are doing is vital to your success as a stock investor. Because federal, provincial, and local governments pass literally thousands of laws every year, monitoring the political landscape is critical to your success. The Canadian news media report what the government is doing, so always ask yourself, "How does a new law, tax, or regulation affect my stock investment?"

Because government actions have a significant effect on your investments, it's a good idea to see what's going on. The Canadian Taxpayers Federation (www. taxpayer.com) informs the Canadian public about tax laws and their impact. Chapter 11 gives you more insights into politics and its effect on the stock market. Laws being proposed or enacted by the U.S. government can be found through the Thomas legislative search engine, which is run by the Library of Congress (www.loc.gov).

## Checking for trends in society, culture, and entertainment

As odd as it sounds, trends in society, popular culture, and entertainment affect your investments, directly or indirectly. For example, a headline such as, "The greying of Canada: More people than ever before will be senior citizens" gives you some important information that can make or break your stock portfolio. With that particular headline, you know that as more and more people age, companies that are well positioned to cater to that growing market's wants and needs will do well — meaning a successful stock for you.

Keep your eyes open to emerging trends in society at large. What trends are evident now? Can you anticipate the wants and needs of tomorrow's society? Being alert, staying a step ahead of the public, and choosing stocks appropriately gives you a profitable edge over other investors. If you own stock in a solid company with growing sales and earnings, other investors eventually notice. As more investors buy up your company's stocks, you're rewarded as the stock price increases.

# Reading (and Understanding) Stock Tables

The stock tables in major business publications such as *The Wall Street Journal* and *Investor's Business Daily* are loaded with information that can help you become a savvy investor — *if* you know how to interpret them. You need the information in the stock tables for more than selecting promising investment opportunities. You also need to consult the tables after you invest to monitor how your stocks are doing. The *National Post* (www.nationalpost.com) and *The Globe and Mail* (www.theglobeandmail.com) also produce stock tables for a selection of mostly Canadian equities in their print editions. As well, they let you check just about any stock (U.S. or Canadian) in their online editions.

Looking at the stock tables without knowing what you're looking for or why you're looking is the equivalent of reading *War and Peace* backwards through a kaleidoscope — nothing makes sense. But we can help you make sense of it all (well, at least the stock tables!). Table 6-1 shows a sample stock table to refer to as you read the sections that follow.

Every newspaper's financial tables are a little different, but they give you basically the same information. This section, updated daily, is not the place to start your search for a good stock; it's usually where your search ends. The stock tables are the place to look when you own a stock or know what you want to buy and you're just checking to see the most recent price.

Each item gives you some clues about the current state of affairs for that particular company. The sections that follow describe each column to help you understand what you're looking at.

| Table 6-1 | | A Sample Stock Table | | | | | | |
|---|---|---|---|---|---|---|---|---|
| 52-Wk High | 52-Wk Low | Name (Symbol) | Div | Vol | Yld | P/E | Day Last | Net Chg |
| 21.50 | 8.00 | SkyHighCorp (SHC) | | 3,143 | | 76 | 21.25 | +.25 |
| 47.00 | 31.75 | LowDownInc (LDI) | 2.35 | 2,735 | 5.9 | 18 | 41.00 | −.50 |
| 25.00 | 21.00 | ValueNowInc (VNI) | 1.00 | 1,894 | 4.5 | 12 | 22.00 | +.10 |
| 83.00 | 33.00 | DoinBadlyCorp (DBC) | | 7,601 | | | 33.50 | −.75 |

# 52-week high

The column in Table 6-1 labelled "52-Wk High" gives you the highest price that particular stock has reached in the most recent 52-week period. Knowing this price lets you gauge where the stock is now versus where it has been recently. SkyHighCorp's (SHC) stock has been as high as $21.50, while its last (most recent) price is $21.25, the number listed in the "Day Last" column. (Flip to the "Day last" section for more on understanding this information.) SkyHighCorp's stock is trading very high right now because it's hovering right near its overall 52-week-high figure.

Now, take a look at DoinBadlyCorp's (DBC) stock price. It seems to have tumbled big time. Its stock price has had a high in the past 52 weeks of $83, but it's currently trading at $33.50. Something just doesn't seem right here. During the past 52 weeks, DBC's stock price fell dramatically. If you're thinking about investing in DBC, find out why the stock price fell. If the company is strong, it may be a good opportunity to buy stock at a lower price. If the company is having tough times, avoid it. In any case, research the firm and find out why its stock has declined.

# 52-week low

The column labelled "52-Wk Low" gives you the lowest price that particular stock reached in the most recent 52-week period. Again, this information is crucial to your ability to analyze stock over a period of time. Look at DBC in Table 6-1, and you can see that its current trading price of $33.50 is close to its 52-week low of $33.

Keep in mind that the high and low prices just give you a range of how far that particular stock's price has moved within the past 52 weeks. They could alert you that a stock has problems, or they could tell you that a stock's price has fallen enough to make it a bargain. Simply reading the 52-Wk High and 52-Wk Low columns isn't enough to determine which of those two scenarios is happening. They basically tell you to get more information before you commit your money.

## Name and symbol

The "Name (Symbol)" column is the simplest in Table 6-1. It tells you the company name (usually abbreviated) and the stock symbol assigned to the company.

When you have your eye on a stock for potential purchase, get familiar with its symbol. Knowing the symbol makes it easier for you to find your stock in the financial tables, which list stocks in alphabetical order by the company's name. Stock symbols are the language of stock investing, and you need to use them in all stock communications, from getting a stock quote at your broker's office to buying stock over the Internet.

## Dividend

Dividends (shown under the "Div" column in Table 6-1) are basically payments to owners (shareholders). If a company pays a dividend, it's shown in the dividend column. The amount you see is the annual dividend quoted for one share of that stock. If you look at LowDownInc (LDI) in Table 6-1, you can see that you get $2.35 as an annual dividend for each share of stock that you own. Companies usually pay the dividend in quarterly amounts. If I own 100 shares of LDI, the company pays me a quarterly dividend of $58.75 ($235 total per year). A healthy company strives to maintain or upgrade the dividend for shareholders from year to year. (We discuss additional dividend details later in this chapter.)

The dividend is very important to investors seeking income from their stock investment. For more about investing for income, see Chapter 9. Investors buy stock in companies that don't pay dividends primarily for growth. For more information on growth stocks, see Chapter 8.

## *Volume*

Normally, when you hear the word "volume" on the news, it refers to how much stock is bought and sold for the entire market: "Well, stocks were very active today. Trading volume at the Toronto Stock Exchange hit 350 million shares." Volume is certainly important to watch because the stocks that you're investing in are somewhere in that activity. For the "Vol" column in Table 6-1, though, the volume refers to the individual stock.

*Volume* tells you how many shares of that particular stock were traded that day. If only 100 shares are traded in a day, then the trading volume is 100. SHC had 3,143 shares change hands on the trading day represented in Table 6-1. Is that good or bad? Neither, really. The business news media generally mention volume for a particular stock only when it's unusually large. If a stock normally has a trading volume in the 5,000 to 10,000 range and all of a sudden it's at 87,000, then it's time to sit up and take notice.

Keep in mind that a low trading volume for one stock may be a high trading volume for another stock. You can't necessarily compare one stock's volume against that of any other company. The large-cap stocks like IBM or Microsoft typically have trading volumes in the millions of shares almost every day, while less active, smaller stocks may have average trading volumes in far, far smaller numbers.

The main point to remember is that trading volume far in excess of that stock's normal range is a sign that something is going on with the stock. It may be negative or positive, but something newsworthy is happening with that company. If the news is positive, the increased volume is a result of more people buying the stock. If the news is negative, the increased volume is probably a result of more people selling the stock. What are typical events that cause increased trading volume? Some positive reasons include the following:

- ✔ **Good earnings reports:** The company announces good (or better-than-expected) earnings.

- ✔ **A new business deal:** The firm announces a favourable business deal, such as a joint venture, or lands a big client.

- ✔ **A new product or service:** The company's research and development department creates a potentially profitable new product.

- ✔ **Indirect benefits:** The business may benefit from a new development in the economy or from a new law passed by Parliament.

Some negative reasons for an unusually large fluctuation in trading volume for a particular stock include the following:

- ✔ **Bad earnings reports:** Profit is the lifeblood of a company. When its profits fall or disappear, you see more volume.

- **Governmental problems:** The stock is being targeted by federal or provincial government action, such as a lawsuit or a securities commission (Ontario Securities Commission, for example) probe.

- **Liability issues:** The media report that the company has a defective product or similar problem.

- **Financial problems:** Independent analysts report that the company's financial health is deteriorating.

Check out what's happening when you hear about heavier than usual volume (especially if you already own the stock).

## Yield

In general, yield is a return on the money you invest. However, in the stock tables, *yield* ("Yld" in Table 6-1) is a reference to what percentage that particular dividend is to the stock price. Yield is most important to income investors. It's calculated by dividing the annual dividend by the current stock price. In Table 6-1, you can see that the yield *du jour* of ValueNowInc (VNI) is 4.5 percent (a dividend of $1 divided by the company's stock price of $22). Notice that many companies report no yield; because they have no dividends, their yield is zero.

Keep in mind that the yield reported in the financial pages changes daily as the stock price changes. Yield is always reported as if you're buying the stock that day. If you buy VNI on the day represented in Table 6-1, your yield is 4.5 percent. But what if VNI's stock price rises to $30 the following day? Investors who buy stock at $30 per share obtain a yield of just 3.3 percent (the dividend of $1 divided by the new stock price, $30). Of course, because you bought the stock at $22, you essentially locked in the prior yield of 4.5 percent. Lucky you. Pat yourself on the back.

## P/E

The P/E ratio is the ratio between the price of the stock and the company's earnings. P/E ratios are widely followed and are important barometers of value in the world of stock investing. The P/E ratio (also called the "earnings multiple" or just "multiple") is frequently used to determine whether a stock is expensive. Value investors (such as your authors) find P/E ratios to be essential to analyzing a stock as a potential investment. As a general rule, the P/E should be 10 to 20 for large-cap or income stocks. For growth stocks, a P/E no greater than 30 to 40 is preferable. (See Chapter 12 for details on P/E ratios.)

In the P/E ratios reported in stock tables, *price* refers to the cost of a single share of stock. *Earnings* refers to the company's reported earnings per share as of the most recent four quarters. The P/E ratio is the price divided by the earnings. In Table 6-1, VNI has a reported P/E of 12, which is considered a low P/E. Notice how SHC has a relatively high P/E (76). This stock is considered too pricey because you're paying a price equivalent to 76 times earnings. Also notice that DBC has no available P/E ratio. Usually this lack of a P/E ratio indicates that the company reported a loss in the most recent four quarters.

## Day last

The "Day Last" column tells you how trading ended for a particular stock on the day represented by the table. In Table 6-1, LDI ended the most recent day of trading at $41. Some newspapers report the high and low for that day in addition to the stock's ending price for the day.

## Net change

The information in the "Net Chg" column answers the question, "How did the stock price end today compared with its price at the end of the prior trading day?" Table 6-1 shows that SHC stock ended the trading day up 25 cents (at $21.25). This column tells you that SHC ended the prior day at $21. VNI ended the day at $22 (up 10 cents), so you can tell that the prior trading day it ended at $21.90.

# Using News about Dividends

Reading and understanding the news about dividends is essential if you're an *income investor* (someone who invests in stocks as a means of generating regular income; see Chapter 9 for details). The following sections explain some basics about dividends you should know.

You can find news and information on dividends in newspapers such as *The Globe and Mail*, *National Post*, *The Wall Street Journal*, *Investor's Business Daily*, and *Barron's* (you can find their Web sites online using your favourite search engine, or just check out Appendix B).

## Looking at important dates

To understand how buying stocks that pay dividends can benefit you as an investor, you need to know how companies report and pay dividends. Some important dates in the life of a dividend are as follows:

- **Date of declaration:** This is the date when a company reports a quarterly dividend and the subsequent payment dates. On January 15, for example, a company may report that it is "pleased to announce a quarterly dividend of 50 cents per share to shareholders of record as of February 10." That was easy. The date of declaration is really just the announcement date. If you buy the stock before, on, or after the date of declaration, it won't matter in regard to receiving the stock's quarterly dividend. The date that matters is the date of record (see that bullet later in this list).

- **Date of execution:** This is the day you actually initiate the stock transaction (buying or selling). If you call up a broker (or contact her online) today to buy a particular stock, then today is the date of execution, or the date on which you execute the trade. You don't own the stock on the date of execution; it's just the day you put in the order. For an example, skip to the following section.

- **Closing date (settlement date):** This is the date on which the trade is finalized, which usually happens three business days after the date of execution. The closing date for stock is similar in concept to a real estate closing. On the closing date, you're officially the proud new owner (or happy seller) of the stock.

- **Date of record:** This is used to identify which shareholders qualify to receive the declared dividend. Because stock is bought and sold every day, how does the company know which investors to pay? The company establishes a cut-off date by declaring a date of record. All investors who are official shareholders as of the declared date of record receive the dividend on the payment date, even if they plan to sell the stock any time between the date of declaration and the date of record.

- **Ex-dividend date:** *Ex-dividend* means *without dividend.* Because it takes three days to process a stock purchase before you become an official owner of the stock, you have to qualify (that is, you have to own or buy the stock) *before* the three-day period. That three-day period is referred to as the "ex-dividend period." When you buy stock during this short time frame you aren't on the books of record, because the closing (or settlement) date falls after the date of record. Read the next section to see the effect that the ex-dividend date can have on an investor.

- **Payment date:** The date on which a company issues and mails its dividend cheques to shareholders. (Finally!)

For typical dividends, the events in Table 6-2 happen four times per year.

| Table 6-2 | The Life of the Quarterly Dividend | |
|---|---|---|
| *Event* | *Sample Date* | *Comments* |
| Date of declaration | January 15 | The date the company declares the quarterly dividend |
| Ex-dividend date | February 7 | Starts the three-day period during which, if you buy the stock, you don't qualify for the dividend |
| Record date | February 10 | The date by which you must be on the books of record to qualify for the dividend |
| Payment date | February 27 | The date that payment is made (a dividend cheque is issued and mailed to shareholders who were on the books of record as of February 10) |

## Understanding why these dates matter

Three business days pass between the date of execution and the closing date. Three business days also pass between the ex-dividend date and the date of record. This information is important to know if you want to qualify to receive an upcoming dividend. Timing is important, and if you understand these dates, you know when to purchase stock and whether you qualify for a dividend.

As an example, say that you want to buy ValueNowInc (VNI) in time to qualify for the quarterly dividend of 25 cents per share. Assume that the date of record (the date by which you have to be an official owner of the stock) is February 10. You have to execute the trade (buy the stock) no later than February 7 to be assured of the dividend. If you execute the trade right on February 7, the closing date occurs three days later, on February 10 — just in time for the date of record.

But what if you execute the trade on February 8, a day later? Well, the trade's closing date is February 11, which occurs *after* the date of record. Because you aren't on the books as an official shareholder on the date of record, you aren't getting that quarterly dividend. In this example, the February 7–9 period is called the *ex-dividend period*.

Fortunately, for those people who buy the stock during this brief ex-dividend period, the stock actually trades at a slightly lower price to reflect the amount of the dividend. If you can't get the dividend, you may as well save on the stock purchase. How's that for a silver lining?

# Evaluating (Avoiding?) Investment Tips

Psst. Have I got a stock tip for you! Come closer. You know what it is? *Research!* What we're trying to tell you is that you should never automatically invest just because you get a hot tip from someone. Good investment selection means looking at several sources before you decide on a stock. There's no shortcut. That said, getting opinions from others never hurts — just be sure to carefully analyze the information you get. The following sections present some important points to bear in mind as you evaluate tips and advice from others.

## Consider the source

Frequently, people buy stock based on the views of some market strategist or market analyst. People may see an analyst being interviewed on a television financial show and take that person's opinions and advice as valid and good. The danger here is that the analyst could easily be biased because of some relationship that isn't disclosed on the show.

 It happens on TV all too often. The show's host interviews analyst U.R. Kiddingme from the investment firm Foolum & Sellum. The analyst says, "Implosion Corp. is a good buy with solid, long-term, upside potential." You later find out that Implosion Corp. is paying investment banking fees to the analyst's employer. Do you really think that analyst would ever issue a negative report on a company that's helping to pay the bills? It's not likely. Being suspicious can keep you from being a sucker.

## Get multiple views

One source isn't enough to base your investment decisions on. Well, not unless you have the best reasons in the world for thinking that one particular single source is outstanding and extremely accurate and prescient. A better approach is to scour current issues of independent financial publications, such as *Barron's, Canadian Business, SmartMoney,* and other publications listed in Appendix B. Search the Internet for information, too. Appendix B lists lots of informative Web sites for you to check out.

# Gathering Data from SEDAR and EDGAROnline

In Canada, publicly traded companies are required to file business and financial information with provincial securities regulators. These reports are entered into a government-sponsored database called SEDAR — the System for Electronic Document Analysis and Retrieval (www.sedar.com).

Electronic filing with SEDAR is now a mandatory requirement for most public companies. The rules of who files what were established at the federal level by the Canadian Securities Administrators (CSA) regulatory body and are overseen by each provincial securities regulatory body. SEDAR is a link that enables enterprises to file securities documents and remit filing fees electronically. It saves them time and gives you, the Canadian investor, fast, easy, and free access to important information about companies (and mutual funds, as well).

In the U.S., the peer site is called EDGAROnline (www.freeedgar.com). The EDGAROnline service is even more advanced than SEDAR. In addition to letting you access statutory filings, it also provides registered users with an e-mail alert every time a certain reporting firm files a document and links you to that document.

Individual investors can access downloadable data from both Web sites (EDGAROnline charges a fee but SEDAR is free). This means that you can download SEDAR and EDGAROnline reports to read later. The content available at these Web sites is critical to investors because it contains all significant financial, legal, and other types of statutory (mandatory) declarations that are important in the investment decision-making process. For example, financial statements tell you whether or not a company is fiscally fit. Legal matters (like big lawsuits) that are material (important enough to influence an investor's decision to buy or sell a stock) in nature can also be found at these sites. Any material changes, like a new senior executive appointment or a major shift in operations to China, would also be described in a filing in SEDAR or EDGAROnline.

Be aware of the fact that annual reports may include more than 50 pages, and they often exceed 100 pages. For example, Canadian and U.S. annual reports include financial statements with notes; supplementary data; wordy management discussions of financial conditions and operations results; business descriptions; legal proceedings; shareholder voting matters; insider transactions; executive compensation; and leasing agreements. Fun stuff! So be selective about how much information you want — and need — to download.

When you search the EDGAR databases, you're asked (via a drop-down screen or report number) which type of document you want. The reports are organized in this manner:

- **Annual reports and filings (*10-K Reports* in EDGAR):** Annual reports that include shareholder information covering the firm's fiscal year

- **Quarterly financial statements (*10-Q Reports* in EDGAR):** Quarterly reports that include shareholder information for the company's last quarter

- **Notices of material changes (*8-K Reports* in EDGAR):** Special reports that are the result of a significant contract, lawsuit, or other material event

- **EDGAR S-1 registrations:** Forms required for businesses that want to offer stock to the public, often used for initial public offerings (IPOs); an S-3 registration is used to offer stock to the public in a secondary offering after an IPO

- **Notices of annual or special meetings (*14-A Forms* in EDGAR):** Information about annual general meetings (AGMs) and voting matters such as candidates seeking election to the board of directors, approval of the increase in authorized capital stock, and/or approval of a merger or acquisition

When you want to get big-picture information about a company, take a look at the reports that companies must file with SEDAR or EDGAROnline. By searching these repositories, you can find companies' balance sheets, income statements, and other related information. You can verify what others say and get a fuller picture of a company's activities and financial condition. All this information will help you make better investment decisions.

# Chapter 7

# Going for Brokers

## In This Chapter

▶ Finding out what brokers do

▶ Understanding the difference between investment advisers and discount brokers

▶ Selecting a broker

▶ Considering online brokers

▶ Exploring the types of brokerage accounts

▶ Figuring out what brokers' recommendations mean

▶ Examining brokerage reports

*W*hen you're ready to dive in and start investing in stocks, you first have to choose a broker. It's kind of like buying a car: You can do all the research in the world and know exactly what kind of car you want to buy; still, you need a venue to do the actual transaction. Similarly, when you want to buy stock, your task is to do all the research you can to select the company you want to invest in. Still, you need a broker to actually buy the stock, whether you buy over the phone or online. In this chapter, we introduce you to the intricacies of the investor/broker relationship.

For information on various types of orders you can place with a broker, such as market orders, stop-loss orders, and so on, flip to Chapter 21.

## Defining the Broker's Role

The broker's primary role is to serve as the vehicle through which you either buy or sell stock. When we talk about brokers, we're referring to organizations such as TD Waterhouse, BMO InvestorLine, HSBC InvestDirect, and many others that can buy stock on your behalf. Brokers can also be individuals who work for such firms. Although you can buy some stocks directly from the company that issues them, to purchase most stocks, you still need a broker.

Brokers primarily buy and sell securities, such as stocks (keep in mind that the word *securities* refers to the world of financial or paper investments and that stocks are only a small part of that world). But they can also perform other tasks for you, including the following:

- **Providing advisory services:** Investors pay brokers a fee for investment advice. Customers also get access to the firm's research.
- **Offering limited banking services:** Brokers can offer banking features like interest-bearing accounts, cheque writing, and direct deposit.
- **Brokering other securities:** Brokers can also buy bonds, mutual funds, options, exchange-traded funds, and other investments on your behalf.

Personal stockbrokers make their money from individual investors — like you, and us too — through various fees, including these:

- **Brokerage commissions:** These fees are for buying and/or selling stocks and other securities.
- **Margin interest charges:** Interest is charged to investors for borrowing against their brokerage account for investment purposes.
- **Service charges:** These charges are for performing administrative tasks and other functions. Brokers charge fees to investors for administering Registered Retirement Savings Plans (RRSPs), Registered Education Saving Plans (RESPs), for mailing stocks in certificate form, and for other special services.

The distinction between personal stockbrokers and institutional stockbrokers is important. Institutional brokers make money from institutions and companies through investment banking and securities placement fees (such as initial public offerings and secondary offerings), advisory services, and other broker services. Personal stockbrokers generally offer the same services to individuals and small businesses.

# Distinguishing between Investment Advisers and Discount Brokers

Stockbrokers fall into two basic categories: investment advisers (sometimes known as full-service brokers) and discount brokers. The type you choose really depends on what type of investor you are. In a nutshell, investment advisers are suitable for investors who need some guidance. Discount brokers are better for those investors who are sufficiently confident and knowledgeable about stock investing to manage with minimal help.

# *Investment advisers*

Investment advisers are just what the name indicates. They try to provide as many services as possible for investors who open accounts with them. When you open an account at a brokerage firm, a representative is assigned to your account. This representative may be called an *account executive,* a *registered rep,* or a *financial consultant* by the brokerage firm. This person usually has a securities licence and is knowledgeable about stocks in particular and investing in general.

HSBC InvestDirect, RBC Dominion Securities, and TD Waterhouse Private Investment Advice have many investment advisers. Of course, all brokerage houses now have full-feature Web sites to give you information about their services. Get as informed as possible before you open your full-service account. An investment adviser should be there to help make your fortune, not to help make you . . . uh . . . broker.

## *What they can do for you*

Your investment adviser is responsible for assisting you, answering questions about your account and the securities in your portfolio, and transacting your buy and sell orders. Here are some things that investment advisers can do for you:

✔ **Offer guidance and advice:** The greatest distinction between investment advisers and discount brokers is the personal attention you receive from your account rep. You get to be on a first-name basis with an investment adviser, and you disclose much information about your finances and financial goals. The rep is there to make recommendations about stocks and funds that are likely to be suitable for you.

✔ **Provide access to research:** Investment advisers can give you access to their investment research department, which can give you in-depth information and analysis on a particular company. This information can be very valuable, but be aware of the pitfalls. (See the section "Evaluating Brokers' Recommendations" in this chapter.)

✔ **Help you achieve your investment objectives:** Beyond advice on specific investments, a good rep gets to know you and your investment goals and *then* offers advice and answers your questions about how specific investments and strategies can help you accomplish your wealth-building goals.

✔ **Make investment decisions on your behalf:** Many investors don't want to be bothered when it comes to investment decisions. Investment advisers can actually make decisions for your account with your authorization. This service is fine, but insist they give you a reasonable explanation of their choices.

### What to watch out for

Although investment advisers — with their seemingly limitless assistance — can make life easy for an investor, you need to remember some important points to avoid problems:

- **Advisers and account reps are still salespeople.** Most are honest; some are complete shills. No matter how well they treat you, they're still compensated based on their ability to produce revenue for the brokerage firm. They generate commissions and fees from you on behalf of the company. (In other words, they're paid to sell you things.)

- **Some advisers don't give clear reasons for their decisions.** Once again, whenever your rep makes a suggestion or recommendation be sure to ask why — and request a complete answer that includes the reasoning behind the recommendation. A good adviser is able to clearly explain the reasoning behind every suggestion. If you don't fully understand and agree with the advice, don't take it.

- **Investment advisers can be costly.** Working with an investment adviser costs more than working with a discount broker. Discount brokers are paid simply for performing the act of buying or selling stocks for you. Investment advisers do that and more. Additionally, they provide advice and guidance. Because of that, investment advisers are more expensive (higher brokerage commissions and advisory fees). Also, most investment advisers expect you to invest at least $5,000 to $10,000 just to open an account. Grr . . .

- **Some brokers make bad decisions for you.** Handing over decision-making authority to your rep can be a possible negative because letting others make financial decisions for you is always dicey — especially when they're using *your* money. If they make poor investment choices that lose you money, you may not have any recourse because you authorized them to act on your behalf.

- **Many investment advisers engage in an activity called churning.** *Churning* is basically buying and selling stocks for the sole purpose of generating commissions. Churning is great for investment advisers but really hurts customers. If your account shows a lot of activity, definitely ask for justification. Commissions, especially those charged by investment advisers, can take a big bite out of your wealth. Don't tolerate churning or any other suspicious activity.

## Discount brokers

Perhaps you don't need any hand holding from a broker. You know what you want, and you can make your own investment decisions. All you need is someone to transact your buy/sell orders. In that case, go with a discount broker. They don't offer advice or premium services — just the basics required to perform your stock transactions. Discount brokers let you buy and sell through the Internet or by phone (touch tone or via a live representative who executes orders without providing advice).

Discount brokers, as the name implies, are cheaper to engage than investment advisers. Because you're advising yourself (or getting advice from third parties such as newsletters or independent advisers), you can save on the costs you incur when you pay for an investment adviser.

If you choose to work with a discount broker, you must know as much as possible about your personal goals and needs. You have a greater responsibility for conducting adequate research to make good stock selections. You must be prepared to accept the outcome, whatever that outcome may be.

### What they can do for you

Discount brokers offer some significant advantages over investment advisers, such as

- **Lower cost:** This lower cost is usually the result of lower commissions, and it's the primary benefit of using discount brokers.

- **Unbiased service:** Discount brokers offer you the ability to just transact your stock buy/sell orders only. Because they don't offer advice, they have no vested interest in trying to sell you any particular stock.

- **Access to information:** Established discount brokers offer extensive educational and research materials at their offices or on their Web sites.

### What to watch out for

Of course, doing business with discount brokers also has its downside, including the following:

- **No guidance:** Because you've chosen a discount broker, you *know* not to expect guidance, but the broker should make this fact clear to you anyway. If you're a knowledgeable investor, the lack of advice is considered a positive thing — no interference.

- **Hidden fees:** Discount brokers may shout about their lower commissions, but commissions aren't their only way of making money. Many discount brokers charge extra for services that you may think are included, such as issuing a stock certificate, letting you access certain types of research, or mailing a statement. Ask whether they assess fees for maintaining RRSPs or fees for transferring stocks and other securities (such as bonds) in or out of your account. Find out what interest rates they charge for borrowing through brokerage accounts.

- **Minimal customer service:** If you deal with a discount brokerage firm, find out about its customer-service capability. If you can't transact business on its Web site, find out where you can call for assistance with your order.

# *Choosing a Broker*

Before you choose a broker, you must resolve a few issues. The first issue is the broker's hair colour. Okay, okay, we'll stop the cheap jokes. Really, after you've decided whether to go the investment adviser or discount broker route, make sure you select a reputable brokerage firm.

Look for a firm that's a member in good standing of IIROC — the Investment Industry Regulatory Organization of Canada (`www.iiroc.ca`). IIROC is Canada's self-regulatory organization, which oversees all member investment dealers. It also watches out for trading activity on debt and equity markets in Canada. IIROC was established in 2008 through the merger of the Investment Dealers Association and other regulatory bodies. It sets regulatory and investment industry standards, tries to protect investor interests, and attempts to strengthen market integrity while maintaining smoothly operating capital markets.

In addition to performing the above "reference check," be sure to check out the provincial securities commissions. They have a national group that works toward making securities regulations consistent and standardized across Canada. This group is called the Canadian Securities Administrators (CSA; `www.securities-administrators.ca`). Through the CSA, securities regulators from each of the ten provinces and three territories have teamed up to protect Canadian investors from "unfair, improper, or fraudulent practices" and to foster "fair and efficient capital markets."

However organized they are, provincial securities commissions possess nowhere near the power that's wielded by the more independent regulators of U.S. stock markets. As a result, options and remedies to the Canadian individual stock investor are very limited.

## *Revisiting your personal investing style*

Before you choose a broker, you need to analyze and reassess your personal investing style. When you know yourself and the way you invest, you can proceed to finding the kind of broker that fits your needs. It's almost like choosing shoes: if you don't know your size, you can't get a proper fit. (And if you get it wrong, you can be in for a really uncomfortable future.)

Consider Bob and Ed. Both men are knowledgeable, confident, and competent investors, so they each choose a discount broker — makes sense. Bob likes to trade stocks very frequently. Ed is a buy-and-hold type, but he likes to use margin. *Trading on margin* means using the stocks and other securities in your brokerage account as collateral to purchase more shares. (See Chapter 21 for more on margin.) Which discount broker is suitable for which investor?

Imagine two discount brokers, JumpCo and StayCo. JumpCo charges $9 per trade, and StayCo charges $25. However, when it comes to margin trading, JumpCo charges 10 percent, but StayCo usually charges a full percentage point lower.

In this example, JumpCo is better suited to Bob's style of investing, but StayCo is better for Ed. Because Bob likes to trade frequently, the commission charge makes it more economical. Ed will pay a higher commission, but he'll eventually make his money back through lower margin interest costs.

This example clearly illustrates how different investors can benefit by analyzing themselves and then choosing an appropriate broker.

## *Making the decision*

When the time comes to choose a broker, keep the following points in mind:

- Match your investment style with an IIROC-member brokerage firm that charges the least amount of money for the services you're likely to use most frequently.

- Compare all the costs of buying, selling, and holding stocks and other securities through a broker. Don't look only at commissions; compare other costs, too, such as margin interest and other service charges.

- Contact a few firms before making your selection. Ask them if they are currently seeking accounts like yours. Ask for and call a few references to find out about the broker's strengths and weaknesses.

- If you select the investment adviser route, ask for a recommendation of one or more brokers at the brokerage who would be appropriate to handle your account and then interview them.

- Read articles that compare brokers in publications and newspapers such as *Canadian Business, The Globe and Mail,* and the *National Post.*

Your broker will influence your finances in a big way, so take the time to get to know your new financial friend to decide whether this is the right person for you.

## Interviewing individual brokers

Ask about the individual broker's education and experience. If he or she has successfully completed an appropriate course of study, that points to a certain degree of skill and knowledge required for the job. (The Canadian Securities Institute [www.csi.ca] offers a wide variety of courses and certifications that are required or recommended for individuals beginning or enhancing careers throughout the financial services industry.)

Enquire about the broker's typical client profile. Are clients growth or income investors? Are they young professionals, or persons entering retirement? Brokers with profiles consistent with your own needs will be better tuned to your investment objectives. Knowing that your broker has other clients who are much like you can be reassuring.

Also discuss expected outcomes. Outcomes include the type of services you're seeking, types of research and recommendations to expect, and desired returns.

The Canadian Investor Protection Fund (CIPF) is overseen by the Canadian investment industry and provides coverage for Canadians making investments through its members. It insures brokerage accounts similar to the way the Canada Deposit Insurance Corporation (CDIC) insures bank accounts. CIPF covers a customer's general accounts — up to $1,000,000 — for losses related to securities, commodity and futures contracts, segregated insurance funds, and cash balances. However, the amount of cash losses that you can claim as part of this limit is restricted, and other important coverage restrictions exist. Check out the CIPF Web site (www.cipf.ca) for full and detailed information. By the way — you aren't covered if the market corrects! When a market goes way higher or lower than it should, a natural tendency exists for stock indexes to respond by falling or rising rapidly and settle into a more "normal" state.

Investing is no more than the allocation of capital for use by an enterprise with the idea of achieving a suitable return. He or she who allocates capital best wins!

# Online Investing Services

Investing online has flourished for several reasons. Online investing, via a discount brokerage service (conventional or Internet-centric), lets you buy and sell stocks and other financial instruments using your personal computer and an Internet connection. As we mention earlier, discount brokers provide most online broker services, but many investment advisers work for firms that support online services, as well. Several factors contribute to the popularity of online investing:

✔ **Information aplenty:** The Internet provides quick and easy access to raw investment information (such as a stock quote) as well as refined information (such as a broker's analysis of a company, or other information services previously available only to investment professionals).

✔ **Lower commission rates:** By eliminating the need for actual brokers or advisers, online brokers can offer commission rates that are lower than offline brokers charge. For example, buying 500 shares of Potash Corporation through a traditional investment adviser could cost you about $100 in commissions. Online, the cost is only about $35. Easy account access is another reason for the popularity of online investing. Online brokers conveniently provide you with access to your account and the ability to place orders anytime and anywhere in Canada (or abroad) as long as you have an Internet connection.

✔ **You're in charge:** Control of the investment process appeals to many investors. You can research a company, buy shares in it, monitor its progress, and chat with other shareholders in that company to hear their opinions.

## Getting online trading services for less

As you may have guessed, no two online brokerage services are alike. Furthermore, individual brokerages may change their services and fees to keep pace with their competitors. To find the online broker that best meets your needs, you must investigate the prices, services, and features that various brokers offer.

Make certain that your brokerage doesn't charge you for services that are free elsewhere, or are hidden. Some hidden fees may include:

✔ Fees to close your account.

✔ Fees to withdraw funds from your trading account.

✔ Higher fees for accepting *odd-lot orders* (for example, orders that include increments of fewer than 100 shares).

## Trading online at a discount

You can't measure broker service with a formula. You have to look at both financial and non-financial criteria.

Cost is one factor, as we just found out. Definitely look at how much each broker charges in commission at different volumes of trades. Also assess the quality of online trade execution by talking to others who use a service that you are considering. Are real-time quotes available? Is research material available? What is the overall ease of use of the service? Does the broker provide online screening tools?

Product selection is another important factor. You want to be able to trade things like guaranteed investment certificates (GICs), gold and silver certificates, municipal bonds, futures, Canadian and foreign equities, and so on. A list of investment products to consider is provided later in this chapter.

Response time should be quick. Some online brokers boast trade execution times of less than nine seconds! Phone each firm to see how long it takes for the broker to respond. E-mail each broker under consideration with a few questions; ask for an application to be sent by mail. Again, evaluate the response time.

Table 7-1 lists several discount brokerage services in Canada.

## Checking out special features

Commission structures range widely from firm to firm because some Internet brokers include special or added features. When deciding which broker is best for you, factor in some or all of the features that we list in this section. First, consider whether each broker offers these features in your cash account:

- Confirmation of trades (via e-mail, phone, or Canada Post)
- Consolidation of your money market, investment, and chequing and savings accounts
- Historical review of your trading activities
- Low minimum amount required to open an account
- Low or no fees with minimum equity balance
- Summary of your portfolio's value

| Table 7-1 | You Can Trade at a Discount | | |
|---|---|---|---|
| | *Minimum Online Trade Fee* | *Minimum Automated Telephone Trade Fee* | *Minimum Broker-Assisted Trade Fee* |
| **BMO InvestorLine** 1-800-387-7800 www.bmo investorline.com | $25 for up to 1,000 shares | $25 for up to 1,000 shares | $39 minimum price per trade |
| **CIBC Investor's Edge** 1-800-567-3343 www.investorsedge. cibc.com | $28.95 for up to 1,000 shares | $28.95 for up to 1,000 shares | $35 minimum price per trade |
| **Disnat** 1-800-268-8471 https://www. disnat.com | $29 for up to 1,000 shares | Not available | $35 on orders of up to $2,000 |
| **HSBC InvestDirect** 1-866-865-4722 www. investdirect. hsbc.ca/ | $29 for up to 1,000 shares | Not available | $35 minimum per trade |
| **National Bank Discount Brokerage** 1-800-363-3511 www.nbc.ca | $28.95 for up to 1,000 shares | Not available | $44.95 minimum per trade |
| **Qtrade Canada** 1-877-787-2330 www.qtrade.ca | $19 for up to 1,000 shares | Not available | $40 minimum per trade |
| **RBC Action Direct** 1-800-769-2560 www. rbcdirect investing.com | $28.95 for up to 1,000 shares | $35 for up to 1,000 shares | $35 minimum per trade |
| **Scotia iTRADE (formerly E*TRADE Canada)** 1-888-872-3388 https://www. scotiaitrade.com | $19.99 for up to 1,000 shares | Not available | $35 minimum per trade |
| **ScotiaMcLeod Direct** **1-800-872-3388** www.scotiamcleod direct.com | $28.95 for up to 1,000 shares | 28.95 for up to 1,000 shares | $39.95 minimum per trade |
| **TD Waterhouse** 1-800-465-5463 www.tdwaterhouse. ca | $29 for up to 1,000 shares | $29.95 (TalkBroker) or $35 (TeleMax) | $43 minimum per trade |

Also, find out which of the following types of investments the broker enables you to trade:

✔ Bonds (corporate, agency, or municipal)

✔ Canada and provincial savings bonds

✔ Commercial paper

✔ Government of Canada and U.S. Treasury bills

✔ Guaranteed investment certificates (GICs)

✔ Investment trusts

✔ Mutual funds

✔ Options

✔ Precious metals

✔ Stocks (foreign or domestic)

✔ Treasury notes

Finally, determine whether the brokerage offers the following analytical and research features:

✔ Company profiles and breaking news

✔ Economic forecasts

✔ End-of-day prices automatically sent to you

✔ Real-time online quotes

✔ Reports on insider trading

## Opening your online brokerage account

Internet brokerage firms are basically cash-and-carry enterprises. They all require investors to open an account before trading — a process that takes from one to two weeks to complete. Because most Canadian brokerages don't require minimum account balances, you can open an account with a nominal deposit. However, you can buy only so many shares of EnCana with $300 in your account!

When you place an order, your Internet broker withdraws money from your cash account to cover your trade. If you sell stock or receive a dividend, the Internet broker adds money to your cash account. All Internet brokers require that you complete an application form (which you can download online by following the instructions given at the Web site). The form will ask for your name, address, and social insurance number; your work history; and a personal cheque, certified cheque, or money order for the minimum amount (if any) needed to open an account. Canadian law requires all broker-ages to have your signature on file. The Internet broker then verifies all the information on the form and opens your account. Investors are sent a per-sonal identification number (PIN) by mail. After you receive your PIN, you're ready to begin trading.

# Types of Brokerage Accounts

After you start investing in the stock market, you have to somehow *pay* for the stocks you buy. Most brokerage firms offer investors several different types of accounts, each serving a different purpose. We present three of the most common types in the following sections. The basic difference boils down to how particular brokers view your *creditworthiness* when it comes to buying and selling securities. If your credit isn't great, your only choice is a cash account. If your credit is good, you can open either a cash account or a margin account. After you qualify for a margin account, you can (with addi-tional approval) upgrade it to do options trades.

To open an account, you have to fill out an application and submit a cheque or money order for at least the minimum amount required to establish an account.

## Cash accounts

A *cash account* means just what you think it means. You must deposit a sum of money along with the new account application to begin trading. The amount of your initial deposit varies from broker to broker. Although some brokers have a minimum of $10,000, others let you open an account for as little as $75. Once in a while you may see a broker offering cash accounts with no minimum deposit, usually as part of a promotion. Use the resources in Appendix B to help you shop around. Qualifying for a cash account is usu-ally easy as long as you have cash and a pulse.

With a cash account, your money has to be deposited in the account before the closing (or settlement) date for any trade you make. The closing occurs three business days after the date you make the trade (the date of execution).

In other words, if you call your broker on Monday, October 10, and order 50 shares of CashLess Corp. at $20 per share, then on Thursday, October 13, you better have $1,000 in cash sitting in your account (plus commission). Otherwise, the purchase doesn't go through.

If you have cash in a brokerage account, see whether the broker will pay you interest on the uninvested cash in it, and how much. Some offer a service in which uninvested money earns money market rates.

## Margin accounts

A *margin account* gives you the ability to borrow money against the securities in the account to buy more stock. Because you have the ability to borrow in a margin account, you have to be qualified and approved by the broker. After you're approved, this newfound credit gives you more leverage so that you can buy more stock or do short-selling. (You can read more about buying on margin and short-selling in Chapter 21.)

Why use margin? "Margin" is to stocks what "mortgage" is to real estate. You can buy real estate with 100 percent cash, but many times using borrowed funds makes sense because you may not have enough money or you prefer not to pay all cash. With margin, you could, for example, be able to buy $10,000 worth of stock with as little as $5,000 in cash (or securities owned) sitting in your account. This example assumes a 50-percent margin limit. The balance of the stock purchase is acquired using a loan (margin) from the brokerage firm.

For stock trading, the margin limit is usually 50 percent. (For very conservative stocks, the margin limit can be as high as 70 percent; ask your broker to inform you about margin limits on a stock-by-stock basis.) The interest rate that you pay varies depending on the broker, but most brokers generally charge a rate that's several points higher than their own borrowing rate.

## Option accounts

An *option account* gives you all the capabilities of a margin account (which in turn also gives you the capabilities of a cash account) plus the ability to trade options on stocks and stock indexes. To upgrade your margin account to an options account, your Canadian broker must by law ask you to sign a statement that you're knowledgeable about options and familiar with the risks associated with them.

Options can be a very effective addition to a stock investor's array of wealth-building investment tools. A more comprehensive review of options is available in the book *Stock Options For Dummies* by Alan R. Simon (Wiley).

# Evaluating Brokers' Recommendations

Canadians have become enamoured of a new spectator sport: watching brokers rate stocks on the television financial shows. Frequently these shows feature a dapper market strategist talking up a particular stock. Some stocks have been known to jump significantly right after an influential analyst issues a buy recommendation. Analysts' speculation and opinions make for great fun, and many people take their views very seriously. However, most investors should be very wary when analysts, especially the glib ones on TV, make a recommendation.

## Understanding basic recommendations

Brokers, and their analytical staff, issue their recommendations as a general idea of how much regard they have for a particular stock. The following list presents the basic recommendations (or ratings) and what they mean to you:

- ✔ **Strong buy** and **buy:** Hot diggity dog! These ratings are the ones to get. The analyst loves this pick, and you would be very wise to get a bunch of shares. The thing to keep in mind, however, is that *buy* recommendations are about as common as snow in Alberta. Let's face it, brokers exist to sell stocks!

- ✔ **Accumulate** and **market perform:** An analyst who issues these types of recommendations is positive, yet unexcited, about the pick. This rating is akin to asking a friend whether he likes your new suit and getting the response "it's nice" in a monotone voice. It's a polite reply, but you wish his opinion had been more enthusiastic.

- ✔ **Hold** or **neutral:** Analysts use this language when their backs are to the wall, but they still don't want to yell, "Sell that loser!" This recommendation reminds us of mothers telling kids to be nice — to either say something positive or keep quiet. In this case, this rating is the analyst's way of keeping quiet.

- ✔ **Sell:** Many analysts should have issued this recommendation during 2000 and 2001, but few actually uttered it. They, and some of the brokerage houses they worked for, sold their souls for the almighty dollar! What a shame.

- ✔ **Avoid like the plague:** We're just kidding about this one, but we wish that this recommendation was available. We've seen plenty of stocks that we thought were dreadful investments — stocks of companies that made no money and were in such terrible financial condition that they should never have been considered at all. Yet investors gobble up billions of dollars' worth of stocks that eventually become worthless.

## Asking a few important questions

Don't get us wrong. An analyst's recommendation is certainly a better tip than what you'd get from your barber or your sister-in-law's neighbour, but you want to view recommendations from analysts with a healthy dose of reality. Analysts have biases because their employment depends on the very companies that are being presented. What investors need to listen to when a broker talks up a stock is the reasoning behind the recommendation. In other words, why is the broker making this recommendation?

Keep in mind that analysts' recommendations can play a useful role in your personal stock investing research. If you find a great stock and *then* you hear analysts give glowing reports on the same stock, you're on the right track! Here are some questions and points to keep in mind:

- ✔ **How does the analyst arrive at a rating?** The analyst's approach to evaluating a stock can help you round out your research as you consult other sources such as newsletters and independent advisory services.

- ✔ **What analytical approach is the analyst using?** Some analysts use *fundamental analysis* (looking at the company's financial condition and factors related to its success, such as its standing within the industry and the overall market). Other analysts use *technical analysis* (looking at the company's stock price history and judging past stock price movements to derive some insight regarding the stock's future price movement). Many analysts use a combination of the two. Is this analyst's approach similar to your approach or to those of sources that you respect or admire?

- ✔ **What is the analyst's track record?** Has the analyst had a consistently good record through both bull and bear markets? Major financial publications, such as *Barron's* and *Investor's Digest of Canada* (www.investors digestofcanada.com), and Web sites, such as MarketWatch (market watch.com) and Canoe Money (money.canoe.ca), regularly track recommendations from well-known analysts and stock pickers.

- ✔ **How does the analyst treat important aspects of the company's performance, such as sales and earnings?** How about the company's balance sheet? The essence of a healthy company is growing sales and earnings coupled with strong assets and low debt.

- ✔ **Is the industry that the company is in doing well?** Does the analyst give you insight on this important information? A strong company in a weak industry can't stay strong for long.

- ✔ **What research sources does the analyst cite?** Does the analyst quote the Canadian government or industry trade groups to support his or her thesis? These sources are important because they help give a more complete picture regarding the company's prospects for success. Imagine that you decide on the stock of a strong company. But what if the federal government (through agencies such as the Ontario Securities Commission) is penalizing the company for fraudulent activity? Or what if the company's industry is shrinking or has ceased to grow (making it tougher for the company to continue growing)? The astute investor looks at a variety of sources before buying stock.

✔ **Is the analyst rational when citing a target price for a stock?** When Anna the analyst says, "We think the stock will hit $100 per share within 12 months," is she presenting a rational model, such as basing the share price on a projected price/earnings ratio? The analyst must be able to provide a logical scenario about why the stock has a good chance of achieving the cited target price within the time frame mentioned. You may not necessarily agree with the analyst's conclusion, but the explanation can help you decide whether the stock choice was well thought out.

✔ **Does the company that is being recommended have any ties to the analyst or the analyst's firm?** During 2000–02, the financial industry got bad publicity because many analysts gave positive recommendations on stocks of companies that were doing business with the very firms that employed those analysts. This conflict of interest is probably the biggest reason why analysts were so wrong in their recommendations during that period. Ask your broker to disclose any conflict of interest.

The bottom line with brokerage recommendations is that you shouldn't use them to buy or sell a stock. Instead, use them to confirm your own research. We know that if we buy a stock based on our own research and later discover the same stock being talked up on the financial shows, that's just the icing on the cake. The experts may be great to listen to, and their recommendations can augment your own opinions; however, they're no substitute for your own careful research.

# Brokerage Reports: The Good, the Bad, and the Ugly

Clint Eastwood, where are you? Traditionally, brokerage (analyst) reports — research-based documents with a buy, sell, or hold recommendation that include a stock's target price and the underlying quantitative and qualitative rationale behind that price — have been a good source of information for investors seeking informed opinions about stocks. And they still are, but some brokerage reports have gotten bad press in recent years — and deservedly so.

## The good

Research departments at brokerage firms provide stock reports and make them available for their clients and investment publications. The firms' analysts and market strategists generally prepare these reports. Good research is critical, and brokerage reports can be very valuable. What better source of guidance than full-time experts backed up by million-dollar research departments? Brokerage reports have some strong points:

- ✔ The analysts are certified professionals who should understand the value of a company and its stock. They analyze and compare company data every day.
- ✔ They have at their disposal tremendous information and historical data that they can sift through to make informed decisions.
- ✔ If you have an account with the firm, you can usually access some of the information for free.

During the late 1990s, some of these analysts gained celebrity status as the public fervour over stock investing turned it into a national pastime. Analysts said, "X is a great stock. Buy it." Millions bought. Stocks soared. Brokerage firms made tonnes of money. Analysts got million-dollar bonuses. Common investors became wealthier. And they lived happily ever after! (Ahem, don't stop here. Keep reading . . .)

## The bad

Well, brokerage reports may not be bad in every case, but at their worst they're quite bad. Brokers make their money from commissions and investment banking fees (nothing bad here). However, they can find themselves in the awkward position of issuing brokerage reports on companies that are (or could be) customers for the brokerage firm that employs them (hmm — could be bad). Frequently, this relationship can result in a brokerage report that paints an overly positive picture of a company that's a poor investment (yup, that's bad).

Sometimes, good research can be compromised by conflicts of interest, even when that conflict of interest is disclosed to the public.

As recently as 2008, a very large number of brokerage reports issued glowing praise for companies that were either mediocre or dubious. Investors bought up stocks in the retail, bank, and automotive sectors big time. The sheer demand pushed up stock prices, which gave the appearance of genius to analysts' forecasts, yet they rose essentially as a self-fulfilling prophecy. The stocks were very overvalued and were flying on a wing and a prayer. By March 2009, Canadians saw exactly *how* overvalued they were!

## *The ugly*

Investors lost a tonne of money (yuck, ugly) in 2009. Money that was pains-takingly accumulated over many years of work vanished in a matter of months (even uglier). Retirees who had trusted some smooth-talking but slip-pery analysts saw nest eggs lose 30 to 60 percent in value (yikes, very ugly). In total, Canadian investors lost billions during 2008 and 2009, much of it needlessly. Both Bay Street and Main Street learned some tough lessons.

Regarding research reports from brokerage firms, the following points can help you avoid getting a bad case of the uglies:

- ✔ Always ask yourself, "Is the provider of the report a biased source?" In other words, is the broker getting business in any way from the com-pany that is being recommended?

- ✔ Never, never, *never* rely on just one source of information, especially if it is the same source that is selling you the stock or other investment.

- ✔ Do your research first, before you rely on a brokerage report.

- ✔ Do your due diligence before you buy stocks, anyway. Look at the chap-ters in Part I and Part II to understand your need for diversification, risk tolerance, and so on.

- ✔ Verify the information provided with a trip to the library or a surf on the Net (see Appendix B).

Clint would be proud.

# Chapter 8

# Investing for Growth

. . . . . . . . . . . . . . . . . . . . . . . . . . . . . . . . . . . . . . . . . . . . . . .

## In This Chapter

▶ Defining growth stocks

▶ Figuring out how to choose growth stocks

▶ Looking at small-cap and other speculative investments

. . . . . . . . . . . . . . . . . . . . . . . . . . . . . . . . . . . . . . . . . . . . . . .

*W*hat's the number-one reason people invest in stocks? To grow their wealth. (This is also referred to as *capital appreciation.*) Yes, some people invest for income (in the form of dividends), but that's a different matter handled in Chapter 9. Investors seeking growth would rather see the money that could have been paid to them as dividends be reinvested in the company. In this way (hopefully), a greater gain is achieved by seeing the stock's price rise, or appreciate.

People interested in growing their wealth see stocks as one of the convenient ways to do it. Growth stocks tend to be riskier than other categories of stocks, but they offer excellent long-term prospects for making the big bucks. If you don't believe us, then just ask Warren Buffett, Jim Rogers, Peter Lynch, and other successful investors. Although someone like Warren Buffett is not considered to be a growth investor, his long-term, value-oriented approach has had a great track record, though his holdings have not been immune to recent market volatility. (*Value stocks* are stocks that are priced lower than the underlying value of the company and its assets — you can identify a value stock by analyzing the company's fundamentals and looking at key financial ratios, such as the price-to-earnings ratio. For more on the topic of ratios, see Appendix A.)

If you're the type of investor who has enough time to let somewhat risky stocks trend upward, or who has enough money so that a loss won't devastate you financially, then growth stocks are definitely for you. As they say, no guts, no glory. The challenge is to figure out which stocks will make you richer quicker.

Short of starting your own business, stock investing is the best way to profit from a business venture. We want to emphasize that to make money in stocks consistently over the long haul, you must remember that you're *investing* in a company. Buying the stock is just a means for you to participate in the company's success (or failure).

What does it matter that you think of stock investing as buying a *company* versus buying a *stock*? Invest in a stock only if you're just as excited about it as you would be if you were the CEO and in charge of running the company. If you're the sole owner of the company, do you act differently than one of a legion of obscure shareholders? Of course you do. As the owner of the company, you have a greater interest in the company. You have a strong desire to know how the enterprise is doing. As you invest in stocks, make believe you're the owner and take an active interest in the company's products, services, sales, earnings, and so on. This attitude and discipline can enhance your goals as a stock investor. This approach is especially important if your investment goal is growth.

# Understanding Growth Stocks

A stock is considered a *growth stock* when it's growing faster and higher than the overall stock market. Basically, a growth stock performs better than its peers in categories such as sales and earnings. Growth stocks also tend to have solid prospects for growth for the immediate future (from one to four years).

Over the years, a debate has continued in the financial community about growth investing versus value investing. Some people believe that growth and value are mutually exclusive. They maintain that large numbers of people buying stock with growth as the expectation tend to drive up the stock price relative to the company's current value. Growth investors, for example, aren't put off by price-to-earnings (P/E) ratios of 25, 30, or higher. Value investors, meanwhile, tend to be too nervous to buy a stock at those P/E ratio levels.

However, you most definitely *can* have both. A value-oriented approach to growth investing serves you best. Long-term-growth stock investors spend time analyzing the company's fundamentals to make sure the company's growth prospects lie on a solid foundation. But what if you have to choose between a growth stock and a value stock? Which do you choose? Seek value when you are buying the stock and analyze the company's prospects for growth. Growth includes, but is not limited to, the health and growth of the company's specific industry and the economy at large (which we discuss throughout this book).

The bottom line is that growth is much easier to achieve when you seek solid, value-oriented companies in growing industries. Chapter 17 explains how industries affect stock value.

Being a growth investor probably has the longest history of success compared to most other stock investing philosophies. The track record for those people who use growth investing — especially those who also place an emphasis on seeking value at the same time — is enviable. Benjamin Graham and Sir John Templeton are two of the more well-known practitioners. Each may have his own spin on the concepts, but both have successfully applied the basic principles of growth investing over many years.

# Analyzing Growth Stocks for the Very First Time

Although the information in the previous section can help you shrink your stock choices from thousands of stocks to maybe a few dozen or a few hundred (depending on how well the general stock market is doing), the purpose of this section is to help you cull the so-so growth stocks to unearth the go-go ones. It's time to dig deeper for the biggest potential winners. Keep in mind that you probably won't find a stock to satisfy all the criteria presented here. Just make sure that your selection meets as many criteria as realistically possible. But hey, if you do find a stock that meets all the criteria cited, *buy as much as you can*!

When choosing growth stocks, consider investing in a company only *if* it makes a profit and *if* you understand *how* it makes that profit and from *where* it generates sales. Part of your research means looking at the industry a company operates in (Chapter 17) and economic trends in general (Chapter 10).

## Making the right comparison

You have to measure the growth of a company *against* something to figure out whether it's a growth stock. Usually, you compare the growth of a company with growth from other companies in the same industry or with the stock market in general. In practical terms, when you measure the growth of a stock against the stock market, you're actually comparing it against a generally accepted benchmark such as a specific Standard & Poor's Canadian index (S&P/TSX), the Dow Jones Industrial Average (DJIA), or the Standard & Poor's 500 (S&P 500). For more on indexes, see Chapter 5.

If a company has an earnings growth of 15 percent per year over three years or more and the industry's average growth rate over the same time frame is 10 percent, then this stock qualifies as a growth stock.

A growth stock is called that not only because the company is growing but also because the company is performing well with some consistency. Having a single year where your earnings do well versus the S&P/TSX 60's or S&P 500's averages doesn't cut it. Growth must be consistently accomplished.

## Checking out a company's fundamentals

When you hear the word *fundamentals* in the world of stock investing, it refers to the company's financial condition and related data. When investors (especially value investors) do *fundamental analysis,* they look at the company's fundamentals — its balance sheet, income statement, cash flow, and other operational data along with external factors such as the company's market position, industry, and economic prospects. Essentially, the fundamentals indicate the company's financial condition. Chapters 12, 13, and 14 go into greater detail about analyzing a company's financial condition. However, the main numbers you want to look at include the following:

- ✔ **Sales:** Are the company's sales this year surpassing last year's? As a decent benchmark, you want to see this year's sales at least 10 percent higher than last year's. Although the figure may differ depending on the industry, 10 percent is a reasonable, general yardstick.

- ✔ **Earnings:** Are this year's earnings at least 10 percent higher than last year's? Earnings should grow at the same rate as sales (or, hopefully, at a better rate).

- ✔ **Debt:** Is the company's total debt for this year equal to or lower than the debt from the prior year? The death knell of many a company has been excessive debt.

A company's financial condition has more factors than we mention here, but these numbers are the most important. We also realize that using the 10-percent figure may seem like an oversimplification, but you don't need to complicate matters unnecessarily. We know someone's computerized financial model may come out to 9.675 percent, or maybe 11.07 percent, but keep it simple for now.

## Looking for leaders and megatrends

A strong company mixed with a growing industry is a common recipe for success. If you look at the history of stock investing, this point comes up constantly. Investors need to be on the alert for megatrends because they help ensure your success.

What is a megatrend? A *megatrend* is a major development that has huge implications for much (if not all) of society for a long time to come. Good examples are the advent of the Internet and the aging of Canada's population. Another trend is the green revolution that is sweeping across North America, Europe, and other parts of the world. These trends offer significant challenges and opportunities for the Canadian economy and all stock investors. Take the Internet, for example. Its full potential for economic and social application is *still* being developed. Millions are flocking to it for many reasons. And Statistics Canada data tell us that Canadians over age 55 will be the fastest-growing segment of our population during the next decade. How does the stock investor take advantage of a megatrend?

Over the last few years, two megatrends hit their stride: rising energy prices and an overheated housing market. As of 2009, these two issues remained major news items with tremendous ripple effects across the national economy. For the growth investor, a strategy became clear. Find value-oriented companies with solid fundamentals that are well positioned to benefit from these megatrends. Then sell! Investors who recognized these trends, invested, but did not sell their stock positions failed to actually realize those gains by cashing out. (See Chapters 19 and 20 to find out how to navigate strategically though up and down markets.)

Buy emerging-growth companies early on, not late in the game when they are no longer values. What can be the result? From 2003–08, many energy-related and housing-related stocks skyrocketed. As oil surpassed US$130 per barrel and gasoline hit CAN$1.40 a litre, most Canadian and foreign oil and oil-services companies saw their stocks go up 50 percent, 100 percent, and more. Housing-related stocks were even more impressive. In addition, companies that cater to these industries also prospered. Mortgage firms that were publicly traded also posted impressive gains.

## Considering a company with a strong niche

Companies that have established a strong niche are consistently profitable. Look for a company with one or more of these characteristics:

- ✔ **A strong brand:** Public companies such as McCain, Shoppers Drug Mart, Coca-Cola, and Microsoft come to mind. Yes, other companies out there can sell french fries, shampoo, pop, or software, but a business needs a lot more than a similar product to topple companies that have established an almost irrevocable identity with the public.

- ✔ **High barriers to entry:** Rogers Communications, Canadian National Railway Company, and Petro-Canada have set up tremendous distribution and delivery networks that competitors can't easily duplicate. High barriers give companies that are already established an important edge.

✔ **Research and development (R&D):** Companies such as Biovail and Merck spend a lot of money researching and developing new pharmaceutical products. This investment in the company's future becomes a new product with millions of consumers who become loyal purchasers, so the company's going to grow.

## *Noticing who's buying and/or recommending the stock*

You can invest in a great company and still see its stock go nowhere. Why? Because what makes the stock go up is *demand* — having more buyers than sellers. If you pick a stock for all the right reasons and the market notices the stock as well, that attention causes the stock price to climb. The things to watch for include the following:

✔ **Institutional buying:** Are mutual funds and pension plans buying up the stock you're looking at? If so, this type of buying power can exert tremendous upward pressure on the stock's price. Some resources and publications track institutional buying and how that affects any particular stock. (You can find these resources in Appendix B.) Frequently, when a mutual fund buys a stock, others soon follow. In spite of all the talk about independent research, a herd mentality still exists.

✔ **Analysts' attention:** Are analysts talking about the stock on the financial shows? As much as you should be skeptical about an analyst's recommendation (given the stock market debacle of a few years ago), it offers some positive reinforcement for your stock. Don't ever buy a stock solely on the basis of an analyst's recommendation. Just know that if you buy a stock based on your own research and analysts subsequently rave about it, your stock price is likely to go up. A single recommendation by an influential analyst can be enough to send a stock skyward.

✔ **Newsletter recommendations:** Independent researchers usually publish newsletters. If influential newsletters are touting your choice, that praise is also good for your stock. Although some great newsletters are out there (find them in Appendix B) and offer information that's as good as or better than the research departments of some brokerage firms, don't use a single tip to base your investment decision on. But it should make you feel good if the newsletters tout a stock that you've already chosen.

✔ **Consumer publications:** No, you won't find investment advice here. This one seems to come out of left field, but it's a source that you should notice. Publications such as *Consumer Reports* regularly look at products and services and rate them for consumer satisfaction. If a company's offerings are well received by consumers, that's a strong positive for the company. This kind of attention ultimately has a positive effect on that company's stock.

# *Learning investing lessons from history*

A growth stock isn't a creature like the Loch Ness monster — always talked about but rarely seen. Growth stocks have been part of the financial scene for nearly a century. Examples abound that offer rich information you can apply to today's stock market environment. Look at market winners over the past few decades, and ask yourself, "What made them profitable stocks?" The '70s were a tough, bearish decade for stocks, and the '80s and '90s were booming bull times. Being aware of the market environment and acting logically are as vital to successful stock investing as they are to any other pursuit. Over and over again, history gives you the formula for successful stock investing:

- ✔ Pick a company that has strong fundamentals, including signs such as rising sales and earnings with low debt. (See Chapter 12.)

- ✔ Be fully invested in stocks during a bull market, when prices are rising in the stock market and in the general economy. (See Chapter 16.)

- ✔ Make sure that the company is in a growing industry. (See Chapter 17.)

- ✔ During a bear market, switch more of your money out of growth stocks (such as technology) and into defensive stocks (such as utilities and health care).

- ✔ Monitor your stocks. Hold on to stocks that continue to grow, and sell those stocks that are declining.

# *Evaluating the management of a company*

The management of a company is crucial to its success. Before you buy stock in a company, you want to know that the company's management is doing a great job. But how do you do that? If you call up a company and ask, no one may even return your phone call. How do you know whether management is running the company properly? The best way is to check the numbers — the following sections tell you what to look at. If the company's management is running the business well, the ultimate result is a rising stock price.

### *Return on equity*

Although you can measure how well management is doing in several ways, you can get a quick snapshot of a management team's competence by checking the company's return on equity (ROE). You calculate the ROE simply by dividing earnings by equity. The resulting percentage gives you a good idea whether the company is using its equity (or net assets) efficiently and profitably.

Basically, the higher the percentage, the better; however, you can consider the ROE solid if the percentage is 10 percent or higher. Keep in mind that not all industries have identical ROEs.

To find out a company's earnings, check out the company's income statement. The *income statement* is a simple financial statement that expresses the equation sales minus expenses equals *net earnings* (or net income, or net profit). You can see an example of an income statement in Table 8-1. (We give more details on income statements in Chapter 12.)

| Table 8-1 | Snowbaby Inc. Income Statement | |
|---|---|---|
| | *2009 Income Statement* | *2010 Income Statement* |
| Sales | $82,000 | $90,000 |
| Expenses | –$75,000 | –$78,000 |
| Net earnings | $7,000 | $12,000 |

To find out a company's equity, check out that company's balance sheet. (See Chapters 12 and 14 for more details on balance sheets.) The balance sheet is actually a simple financial statement that illustrates total assets minus total liabilities equals *net equity*. For public stock companies, the net assets are called *shareholders' equity,* or simply "equity." Table 8-2 shows a balance sheet for Snowbaby Inc.

| Table 8-2 | Snowbaby Inc. Balance Sheet | |
|---|---|---|
| | *Balance Sheet for December 31, 2009* | *Balance Sheet for December 31, 2010* |
| Total assets (TA) | $55,000 | $65,000 |
| Total liabilities (TL) | –$20,000 | –$25,000 |
| Equity (TA less TL) | $35,000 | $40,000 |

Table 8-1 shows that Snowbaby's earnings went from $7,000 to $12,000. In Table 8-2, you can see that Snowbaby increased its equity from $35,000 to $40,000 in one year. The ROE for 2009 is 20 percent ($7,000 in earnings ÷ $35,000 in equity), which is a solid number. The following year, the ROE is 30 percent ($12,000 earnings ÷ $40,000 equity), another solid number.

# Protecting your downside

We become a Johnny-one-note on one topic: trailing stops. (See Chapter 21 for a full explanation of various defensive trading techniques.) *Trailing stops* are stop-losses that you regularly manage with the stock you invest in. We always advocate using them, especially if you're new to the game of buying growth stocks. Trailing stops can help you, no matter how good or bad the economy is (or how good or bad the stock you're investing in is).

Suppose you had invested in JDS Uniphase, a classic example of a phenomenal growth stock that went bad. In 2000 and 2001, when its stock peaked, investors were as happy as chocoholics at a Cadbury factory. Along with many investors who forgot that sound investing takes discipline and research, JDS Uniphase investors thought, "Downside risk? What downside risk?"

Here's an example of how a stop-loss order would have worked if you had invested in JDS Uniphase. Pretend you're back in 2000 and you buy JDS Uniphase at a split-adjusted price of $650 per share (we discuss stock splits in Chapter 15) and put in a stop-loss order with your broker at $600. (Remember to make it a *GTC*, or good-till-cancelled order. If you do, the stop-loss order stays on indefinitely.) As a general rule, we like to place the stop-loss order at 10 percent below the market value. As the stock goes up, you keep the stop-loss trailing upward like a tail. (Now you know why it's called a "trailing" stop; it trails the stock's price.) When JDS Uniphase hits $750, your stop-loss changes to, say, $700, and so on. Now what?

When JDS Uniphase starts its perilous descent, you get out at $700. The new price of $700 triggers the stop-loss, and the stock is automatically sold — you stopped the loss! Actually, in this case, you could call it a "stop and cash in the gain" order. Because you bought the stock at $650 and sold at $700, you pocket a respectable capital gain of $50 (7.5 percent appreciation). Now you safely step aside and watch the stock continue its plunge. Recently, it has been trading in single digits!

What if the market is doing well? Are trailing stops a good idea? Because these stops are placed below the stock price, you're not stopping the stock from rising upward indefinitely. All you're doing is protecting your investment from loss. That's discipline! The stock market of 2004 to 2007 was fairly good to stock investors because the bear market that started in 2000 took a break — at least until 2008 when another one started. During a bear market, trailing-stop strategies are critical because a potential decline in the stock price will become a greater risk.

## Equity and earnings growth

Two additional barometers of success are a company's growth in earnings and growth of equity. Look at the growth in earnings in Table 8-1. The earnings grew from $7,000 (in 2009) to $12,000 (in 2010), or a percentage increase of 71 percent ($12,000 – $7,000 = $5,000, and $5,000 @ds $7,000 = 71 percent), which is excellent. In Table 8-2, Snowbaby's equity grew by $5,000 (from $35,000 to $40,000), or 14 percent, which is very good — management is doing good things here.

### Insider buying

Watching management as it manages the business is important, but another indicator of how well the company is doing is to see whether management is buying stock in the company, as well. If a company is poised for growth, who knows better than management? And if management is buying up the company's stock en masse, then that's a great indicator of the stock's potential. See Chapter 15 for more details on insider trading.

## Making sure a company continues to do well

A company's financial situation does change, and you, as a diligent investor, need to continue to look at the numbers for as long as the stock is in your portfolio. You may have chosen a great stock from a great company with great numbers in 2009, but chances are pretty good the numbers have changed since then.

# Exploring Small-Caps and Speculative Stocks

Everyone wants to get in early on a hot new stock. Why not? You buy Shlobotky Inc. at $1 per share and hope it zooms to $98 before lunchtime. Who doesn't want to buy a stock that could become the next Biovail or Potash Corporation? This possibility is why investors are attracted to small-cap stocks.

*Small cap* (or small capitalization) is a reference to the company's market size. *Small-cap stocks* are stocks that have a market value under $1 billion. Investors may face more risk with small-cap stocks, but they also have the chance for greater gains.

Out of all the types of stocks, small-cap stocks continue to exhibit the greatest amount of growth. In the same way that a tree planted last year has more opportunity for growth than a mature 100-year-old redwood, small-caps have greater growth potential than established large-cap stocks. Of course, a small-cap company doesn't exhibit spectacular growth just because it's small. It grows when it does the right things, such as increasing sales and earnings by producing goods and services that customers want.

## Don't rush to buy IPO stock

When a company *goes public,* it means that it undergoes an initial public offering (IPO). The IPO is the process by which a private firm seeks the assistance of an investment banking firm to gain financing by issuing stock that is purchased by the public. IPOs generate a lot of excitement, and many investors consider the IPO to be that proverbial ground-floor opportunity. After all, some people find it appealing to get a stock before its price skyrockets — which it just may do when investors begin to flock to it.

Why *wouldn't* people find IPOs appealing? IPOs actually have a very poor track record of success in their first year. A recent study revealed that 60 percent of the time IPOs actually declined in price during the first 12 months. In other words, an IPO has a better than even chance of dropping in price.

The reason why so many IPOs fail at the outset is because insiders, such as original owners and senior executives of the now-public company, rush to sell their own newfound shares after the so-called lock-up period expires. This lock-up time frame is a period of a few months where insiders are prohibited by law from selling their shares. But when they're finally allowed to sell, the floodgates open and many executives sell many shares — usually at the same time. The downward pressure placed on their own stock, and possibly yours, is enormous.

The lesson for investors is that you're better off waiting to see how the stock and the company perform, and you're definitely better off waiting until a few months after the lock-up period has expired. Don't worry about missing that great opportunity; if it's a bona fide winner, you'll still do well after the IPO.

For every small company that becomes a Fortune 500 firm, hundreds of companies don't grow at all or go out of business. When you try to guess the next great stock before there's any evidence of growth, you're not investing — you're speculating. Have you heard that one before? (If not, flip to Chapter 2 for details.) Of course you have, and you'll hear it again. Don't get us wrong — there's nothing wrong with speculating. But it's important to *know* that you're speculating when you're doing it. If you're going to speculate in small stocks hoping for the next Research In Motion, then use the guidelines we present in the following sections to increase your chances of success.

## *Avoid IPOs, unless . . .*

Chapter 1 describes how initial public offerings (IPOs) represent the birth-place of public stocks, or the proverbial ground floor. Because a company's going public is frequently an unproven enterprise, investing in an IPO can be risky. It's even more risky when the company is small (revenues under $5 million). The two types of IPOs we describe below exemplify this point:

✔ **Startup IPO:** This is a company that didn't exist before the IPO. In other words, the entrepreneurs get together and create a business plan for an "idea." To get the financing they need for the company, they decide to go public immediately by approaching an investment banker. If the investment banker thinks that it's a good concept, the banker will seek funding (selling the stock to investors) via the IPO.

✔ **A large existing private company that decides to go public:** In many cases, the IPO is done for a company that already exists and is seeking expansion capital. The company may have been around for a long time as a smaller private concern, but it decides to seek funding through an IPO to grow even larger (or to fund a new product, promotional expenses, and so on).

Which of the two IPOs do you think is less risky? That's right! The large private company going public. Why? Because it's already a proven business, which is a safer bet than a brand-new startup. Some great examples of successful IPOs in recent years are the Canadian National Railway Company and Google (they were both established companies *before* they went public).

Great stocks started as small companies going public. You may be able to recount the stories of Research In Motion, Biovail, Dell, The Home Depot, and hundreds of other great successes. But do you remember an IPO by the company Lipschitz & Farquar? No? I didn't think so. It's among the majority of IPOs that don't succeed. For investors, the lesson is clear: Wait until a track record appears before you invest in a company. If you don't, you're simply rolling the dice (in other words, you're speculating, not investing!).

## *If it's a small-cap stock, make sure it's making money*

We emphasize two points when investing in stocks:

✔ Make sure that a company is established. (Being in business for at least three years is a good minimum.)

✔ Make sure that a company is profitable.

These points are especially important for investors in small stocks. Plenty of startup ventures lose money but hope to make a fortune down the road. A good example is a company in the biotechnology industry. Biotech and green technologies are exciting but esoteric areas, and at this early stage companies are finding it difficult to use the technologies in profitable ways. You may say, "But shouldn't I jump in now in anticipation of future profits?" You may get lucky, but understand that when you invest in unproven, small-cap stocks, you're speculating.

# Investing in small-cap stocks requires analysis

The only difference between a small-cap stock and a large-cap stock is a few zeros in their numbers and the fact that you need to do more research with small caps. Because of their size, small caps are riskier than large caps, so you offset the risk by accruing more information on yourself and the stock in question. Plenty of information is available on large-cap stocks because they're widely followed. Small-cap stocks don't get as much press, and fewer analysts issue reports on them. Here are a few points to keep in mind:

- ✔ **Understand your investment style.** Small-cap stocks may have more potential rewards, but they also carry more risk. No investor should devote a large portion of his capital to small-cap stocks. If you're considering retirement money, you're better off investing in large-cap stocks, exchange-traded funds (ETFs), investment-grade bonds, bank accounts, and mutual funds.

- ✔ **Check with SEDAR or EDGAROnline.** Get the financial reports for Canadian public companies through SEDAR (System for Electronic Document Analysis and Retrieval) at www.sedar.com. Get the financial reports that American-based companies must file with the U.S. Securities and Exchange Commission (SEC), such as its 10Ks and 10Qs (see Chapter 6 for more details), through EDGAROnline at www.freeedgar.com. Also, go to the SEC Web site at www.sec.gov to check its massive database of company filings at EDGAR (Electronic Data Gathering, Analysis, and Retrieval system).

- ✔ **Check other sources.** See whether brokers and independent research services, such as Value Line (www.valueline.com), follow the stock. If two or more different sources like the stock, it's worth further investigation. Check the resources in Appendix B for further sources of information before you invest.

# Chapter 9

# Investing for Income

*In This Chapter*

▶ Defining income stocks

▶ Selecting income stocks with a few criteria in mind

▶ Looking at some typical income stocks

*I*nvesting for income means investing in stocks that provide you with regular cash payments (dividends). Income stocks may not seem to offer stellar growth potential, but they're good for a steady infusion of cash. If you have a low tolerance for risk, or if your investment goal is anything less than long term, income stocks are your best bet. In this chapter, we explain the basics of income stocks, show you how to analyze income stocks with a few handy formulas, and describe several typical income stocks.

Getting your stock portfolio to yield more income is easier than you think. Many investors increase income using proven techniques such as covered call writing. Covered call writing is beyond the scope of this book, but we encourage you to find out more about this technique and whether it applies to your situation. Talk to your financial adviser or read up on it — it's covered more fully in *Stock Options For Dummies* by Alan R. Simon (Wiley).

# Understanding the Basics of Income Stocks

We certainly think that dividend-paying stocks are a great consideration for those investors seeking greater income in their portfolios. We especially like stocks with higher-than-average dividends (typically 4 percent or greater) that are known as *income stocks*. Income stocks take on a dual role in that they can appreciate but also provide regular income. The following sections take a closer look at dividends and income stocks.

## Getting a grip on dividends and dividend rates

When people talk about gaining income from stocks, they're usually talking about dividends. A *dividend* is nothing more than money paid out to the owner of stock. You purchase dividend stocks primarily for income — not for spectacular growth potential.

A dividend is quoted as an annual number but is usually paid on a quarterly basis. For example, if a stock pays a dividend of $4, you're probably paid $1 every quarter. If, in this example, you have 200 shares, you're paid $800 every year (if the dividend doesn't change during that period), or $200 per quarter. Getting that regular dividend cheque every three months (for as long as you hold the stock) can be a nice perk.

A good income stock has a higher-than-average dividend (typically 4 percent or higher).

Dividend rates aren't guaranteed — they can go up or down, or in some extreme cases the dividend can be discontinued. Fortunately, most companies that issue dividends continue them indefinitely and actually increase dividend payments from time to time. Historically, dividend increases have equalled (or exceeded) the rate of inflation.

## Recognizing who's well-suited for income stocks

What type of person is best suited to income stocks? Income stocks can be appropriate for many investors, but they're especially well-suited for the following individuals:

- ✔ **Conservative and novice investors:** Conservative investors like to see a slow-but-steady approach to growing their money while getting regular dividend cheques. Novice investors who want to start slowly also benefit from income stocks.

- ✔ **Retirees:** Growth investing (which we describe in Chapter 8) is best suited for long-term needs, while income investing is best suited to current needs. Retirees may want some growth in their portfolios, but they're more concerned with regular income that can keep pace with inflation.

## Checking out the advantages of income stocks

Income stocks tend to be among the least volatile of all stocks, and many investors view them as defensive stocks. *Defensive stocks* are stocks of companies that sell goods and services that are generally needed no matter what shape the economy is in. (Don't confuse defensive stocks with *defence stocks,* which specialize in goods and equipment for the military.) Food, beverage, and utility companies are great examples of defensive stocks. Even when the economy is experiencing tough times, people still need to eat, drink, and turn on the lights. Companies that offer relatively high dividends also tend to be large firms in established, stable industries.

Some industries in particular are known for high-dividend stocks. Utilities (such as electric, gas, and water), real estate, and the energy sector (oil and gas) are areas where you definitely find income stocks. In fact, Canadian stock markets represent a world-class selection of dividend-paying energy stocks. Yes, you can find high-dividend stocks in other industries, but you find a high concentration of them in these industries. For more details, see the sections highlighting these industries later in this chapter.

## Watching out for the disadvantages of income stocks

Before you say, "Income stocks are great! I'll get my chequebook and buy a batch right now," take a look at some potential disadvantages (ugh!). Income stocks do come with some fine print.

### What goes up . . .

Income stocks can go down as well as up, just as any stock can. Obviously, you don't mind your income stock going up in value, but it can go down just as easily. The factors that affect stocks in general — politics (Chapter 11), economic trends (Chapter 10), industry changes (Chapter 17), and so on — affect income stocks, too. Fortunately, income stocks don't get hit as hard as other stocks when the market is declining because high dividends tend to act as a support to the stock price. Therefore, income stocks' prices usually fall less dramatically than the prices of other stocks in a declining market.

### Interest-rate sensitivity

Income stocks can be sensitive to rising interest rates. When interest rates in Canada and the U.S. go up, other investments (such as corporate bonds, Canadian and U.S. Treasury securities, and GICs) are more attractive. When your income stock is yielding 4 percent and interest rates are going to 5 percent, 6 percent, or higher, you may think, "Hmm. Why settle for a 4-percent yield when I can get 5 percent or better elsewhere?" As more and more investors sell their low-yield stock, the prices for those stocks fall.

Another point to remember is that rising interest rates may hurt a company's financial strength. If a company has to pay more interest, this may affect the company's earnings, which in turn may affect the dividend.

Dividend-paying companies that are experiencing consistent, falling revenues tend to cut dividends. In this case, *consistent* means beyond just a year.

### Inflation eats into dividends

Although many companies raise their dividends on a regular basis, some don't. Or, if they do raise their dividends, the increases may be small. If income is your primary consideration, you want to be aware of this fact. If you're getting the same dividend year after year and this income is important to you, rising inflation becomes a problem. Say that you have XYZ stock at $10 per share with an annual dividend of 30 cents (the yield is 30 cents divided by $10, or 3 percent). If you have a yield of 3 percent two years in a row, how do you feel when inflation rises 6 percent one year and 7 percent the next year? Because inflation means that your costs are rising, inflation shrinks the value of the dividend income you receive.

As you can see, even conservative income investors can be confronted with different types of risk. (Chapters 4 and 16 cover the important topic of risk in much greater detail.) Fortunately, the rest of this chapter helps you carefully choose income stocks so that you can minimize these potential disadvantages.

### Don't forget the CRA

Another downside of income stocks is that the dividends from Canadian stocks are taxable as dividend income, subject to the *gross-up* adjustment and dividend tax credit. Dividends from foreign stocks are also taxable, but they don't have the same favourable gross-up and dividend-tax-credit treatments as Canadian dividends do. Either way, this means you have to report dividends as income to Canada Revenue Agency (CRA).

Dividend income is taxed at a higher level (especially for investors in the highest tax bracket) than the taxes attributable to capital gains, where only one-half of a capital gain is included in taxable income. For more information on the taxation of investment income, including capital gains, see Chapter 22.

## Playing it safe

If you're an investor seeking income and you're very nervous about potential risks with income stocks, here are some non-stock alternatives:

- **Treasury securities:** Issued by the federal government, these are considered the safest investments in the world. Canadian Treasury securities are sold to the public in order to pay off maturing debt and to raise the cash needed to operate the government. Three general types of treasury securities are sold in both Canada and the United States. Treasury bills (T-bills) mature in three months, six months, or one year. Treasury notes (Canada notes) are intermediate-term securities and mature in 2–10 years. Treasury bonds (Canada bonds) are long-term securities that have maturities ranging from 10–30 years. U.S. T-bills have much larger minimum purchase requirements than Canadian T-bills, which require minimums from $5,000 (for terms of 6–12 months)

up to $25,000 (for 30- to 60-day terms). A U.S.–denominated Canadian Treasury bill (guaranteed by the Canadian government) has a minimum requirement of US$100,000.

- **Bank certificates of deposit (CDs):** These investments are backed up (to a limit of $100,000) by the Canada Deposit Insurance Corporation (CDIC) and are very safe.

- **Guaranteed investment certificates (GICs):** Like CDs, GICs are safe and also guaranteed (again, up to a limit of $100,000) by the CDIC. They typically possess a shorter term and lower minimum investment amount than CDs.

- **Income mutual funds:** Many mutual funds, such as Canadian Treasury–bond mutual funds and corporate bond funds, are designed for income investors. They offer diversification and professional management, and you can usually invest minimal amounts.

# Analyzing Income Stocks

Look at income stocks in the same way you do growth stocks when assessing the financial strength of a company. Getting nice dividends comes to a screeching halt if the company can't afford to pay them. If your budget depends on dividend income, then monitoring the company's financial strength is that much more important. You can apply the same techniques for assessing the financial strength of growth stocks (see Chapter 8) to your assessment of income stocks.

## Understanding your needs first

You choose income stocks primarily because you want or need income now. As a secondary point, income stocks have the potential for steady, long-term appreciation. So if you're investing for retirement needs that won't occur for another 20 years, maybe income stocks aren't suitable for you — better to invest in growth stocks, because they're more likely to grow your money faster over your stated lengthy investment term.

## Minding your dividends and interest

Dividends are sometimes confused with interest. However, *dividends* are payouts to owners, but *interest* is a payment to a creditor. You, as a stock investor, are considered to be a part owner of the company you invest in and are entitled to dividends when they're issued. A Canadian chartered bank, on the other hand, considers you to be a creditor when you open an account. The bank borrows your money and then pays you interest on it.

If you're certain that you want income stocks, do a rough calculation to figure out how big a portion of your portfolio you want income stocks to occupy. Suppose you need $25,000 in investment income to satisfy your current financial needs. If you have bonds that give you $20,000 in interest income and you want the rest to come from dividends from income stocks, you need to choose stocks that pay you $5,000 in annual dividends. If you have $80,000 left to invest, you know that you need a portfolio of income stocks that provide $5,000 in dividend income, or a yield of 6.25 percent ($5,000 ÷ $80,000 = a yield of 6.25 percent).

Use the following table as a general guideline for understanding your need for income.

| *Item* | *Your Amounts* | *Sample Amounts* |
|---|---|---|
| **A. How much annual income do you need?** | | $10,000 |
| **B. What is the value of your portfolio (or money available for investment)?** | | $150,000 |
| **C. What is the yield necessary to achieve this income (item A ÷ item B)?** | | 6.7% |

With this simple table, you know that if you have $150,000 in income stocks yielding 6.7 percent, you receive an income of $10,000 — meeting your stated financial need. You may ask, "Why not just buy $150,000 in bonds or other investments that yield at least 6.7 percent?" Well, if you're satisfied with that $10,000 and inflation for the foreseeable future is zero, then you have a point. Unfortunately, inflation will probably be with us for a long time. Fortunately, the steady growth that income stocks provide is a benefit to you.

Every investor is different. If you're not sure about your current or future needs, your best choice is to consult with a financial planner.

## Checking out yield

Because income stocks pay out dividends — income — you need to assess which stocks can give you the highest income. How do you decide which stocks will pay the most money? The main thing to look for in choosing income stocks is *yield* (the percentage rate of return paid on a stock in the form of dividends). Looking at a stock's dividend yield is the quickest way to find out how much money you'll earn from a particular income stock versus other dividend-paying stocks (or even other investments such as a bank account). Table 9-1 illustrates this point. Dividend yield is calculated in the following way:

Dividend yield = dividend income ÷ stock investment

The next two sections use the information in Table 9-1 to compare the yields from different investments and to see how evaluating yield can help you choose the stock that will earn you the most money.

Don't stop scrutinizing stocks after you acquire them. You may have made a great choice that gives you a great dividend, but that doesn't mean the stock stays that way indefinitely. Monitor the company's progress for as long as it's in your portfolio. Use resources such as www.money.canoe.ca, www.bloomberg.com, and www.marketwatch.com (see Appendix B for more resources) to track your stock and to monitor how well that particular company continues to perform.

### Examining yield

Most people have no problem understanding yield when it comes to bank accounts. If one of us tells you that our guaranteed investment certificate (GIC) from the Caisse d'Epargne credit union (see Table 9-1) has an annual yield of 4 percent, you can easily figure out what the profit will be in one year. If $1,000 is deposited in that GIC account, a year later it will have $1,040 (slightly more if you include compounding). The GIC's market value in this example is the same as the deposit amount — $1,000. That makes it easy to calculate.

| Table 9-1 | | Comparing Yields | | |
|-----------|------|----------------------|----------------------------------------|----------------------------------------------------------------|
| *Investment* | *Type* | *Investment Amount* | *Annual Investment Income (dividend)* | *Yield (annual investment income ÷ investment amount)* |
| Smith Co. | Common stock | $20 per share | $1.00 per share | 5% |
| Jones Co. | Common stock | $30 per share | $1.50 per share | 5% |
| Caisse d-Epargne | Guaranteed Investment Certificate (GIC) | $1,000 deposit | $40 | 4% |

How about stocks? When you see a stock listed in the financial pages, the dividend yield is provided along with the stock's price and annual dividend. The dividend yield in the financial pages is always calculated as if you bought the stock on that given day. Just keep in mind that, based on supply and demand, stock prices change virtually every day (every minute!) that the market is open. Therefore, because the stock price changes every day, the yield changes as well. So, keep the following two things in mind when examining yield:

✔ **The yield listed in the financial pages may not represent the yield you're receiving.** What if you bought stock in Smith Co. (see Table 9-1) a month ago at $20 per share? With an annual dividend of $1, you know that your yield is 5 percent. But what if today Smith Co. is selling for $40 per share? If you look in the financial pages, the yield quoted is 2.5 percent. Gasp! Did the dividend get cut in half? No, not really. You're still getting 5 percent because you bought the stock at $20 rather than the current $40 price; the quoted yield is for investors who purchase Smith Co. today. Investors who buy Smith Co. stock today pay $40 and get the $1 dividend, and they're locked into the current yield of 2.5 percent. Although Smith Co. may have been a good income investment for you a month ago, it's not such a hot pick today because the price of the stock doubled — cutting the yield in half. Even though the dividend hasn't changed, the yield changed dramatically because of the stock's price change.

✔ **Stock price affects how good of an investment the stock may be.** Another way to look at yield is by looking at the amount of investment. Using Smith Co. in Table 9-1 as an example, if you buy, say, 100 shares when they are $20 per share, you pay only $2,000 (100 shares × $20 — leave out commissions to make the example simple). If, instead, you purchase the same stock later at $40 per share, your total investment amount is $4,000 (100 shares × $40). In either case, you get a total dividend income of $100 (100 shares × $1 dividend per share). From a yield perspective, which investment is yielding more — the $2,000 investment or the $4,000 investment? Of course, it's better to get the income ($100 in this case) with the smaller investment (a 5 percent yield is better than a 2.5 percent yield).

### Comparing yield between different stocks

All things being equal, choosing Smith Co. or Jones Co. is a coin toss (see Table 9-1). It's looking at your situation and each company's fundamentals and prospects that will sway you. What if Smith Co. is an auto stock (similar to General Motors) and Jones Co. is a utility serving the Vancouver area? Now what? Recently, the automotive industry struggled, but utilities were generally in much better shape. In this scenario, Smith Co.'s dividend would be in jeopardy, but Jones Co.'s dividend would be more secure. Another issue would be the payout ratio (see later in this chapter). Therefore, having the same yield is not the same as the same risk. Different companies have different risks associated with them.

## Checking the stock's payout ratio

You can use the *payout ratio* to figure out what percentage of a company's earnings is being paid out in the form of dividends. Keep in mind that companies pay dividends from their net earnings. Therefore, a company's earnings should always be higher than the dividends it pays out. Here's how to figure a payout ratio:

Dividend (per share) ÷ earnings (per share) = payout ratio

Say that the company CashFlow Now Inc. (CFN) has annual earnings of $1 million. (Remember that earnings are what you get when you subtract expenses from sales.) Total dividends are to be paid out of $500,000, and the company has 1 million outstanding shares. Using those numbers, you know that CFN has earnings per share (EPS) of $1 ($1 million in earnings ÷ 1 million shares) and that it pays an annual dividend of 50 cents per share ($500,000 ÷ 1 million shares). The dividend payout ratio is 50 percent (the 50-cent dividend = 50 percent of the $1 EPS). This number is a healthy dividend payout ratio because even if the company's earnings fall by 10 percent, or 20 percent, it still has plenty of room to pay dividends. People concerned about the safety of their dividend income should regularly watch the payout ratio. The maximum acceptable payout ratio should be 80 percent, and a good range is 50–70 percent. A payout ratio of 60 percent or lower is considered to be very safe.

When a company suffers significant financial difficulties, its ability to pay dividends is compromised. So if you need dividend income to help you pay your bills, you better be aware of the dividend payout ratio. Generally, a dividend payout ratio of 60 percent or less is safe. Obviously, the lower the percentage is, the safer the dividend.

## Diversifying your stocks

If most of your dividend income comes from stock in a single company or from a single industry, consider reallocating your investment to avoid having all your eggs in one basket. Concerns for diversification apply to income stocks as well as growth stocks. If all your income stocks are in the electric utility industry, then any problems in the electric utility industry are potential problems for your portfolio, as well. See Chapter 4 for more on diversification.

## Examining the company's bond rating

Bond rating? Huh? What's that got to do with dividend-paying stocks? Well, corporate bonds are like government bonds, except that they come with slightly better yields than government bonds. BCE, Air Canada, and EnCana Corporation are examples of Canadian issuers of corporate bonds. Corporate bonds must provide better yields because they are riskier than the government variety. Companies may go out of business; governments generally do not. The services of bond rating agencies are needed to help assess this credit risk.

Bond rating agencies, such as the Dominion Bond Rating Service (dbrs. com), and Standard & Poor's (www2.standardandpoors.com), which includes the former Canada Bond Rating Service, are there to help. Both have similar rating schemes. Ratings of AAA, AA, and A are considered to be *investment grade,* or of high quality. B and C ratings indicate poor, speculative, or default grades. Anything lower than that is considered to be very risky (these bonds are referred to as *junk bonds*). Both assess, among other things, whether a company will have enough money to pay its interest obligations as well as the full principal amounts at maturity.

A company's bond rating is very important to income-stock investors. The bond rating offers insight into the company's financial strength. To fully understand why this is important, consider the following ratings:

- **Good bond rating:** If the bond rating is good, this means that the company is strong enough to pay its obligations. These obligations include expenses, payments on debts, and dividends that are declared. If a bond rating agency gives the company a high rating (or if it raises the rating), that's a great sign for anyone holding the company's debt or receiving dividends.

- **Lowered bond rating:** If a bond rating agency lowers the rating of a bond, that means the company's financial strength is deteriorating — a red flag for anyone who owns the company's bonds or stock. A lower bond rating today may mean trouble for the dividend later on.

✔ **Bad bond rating:** If the bond rating isn't good, that means the company is having difficulty paying its obligations. If the company can't pay all its obligations, then it has to choose which ones to pay. More times than not, a financially troubled company chooses to cut dividends or (in a worst-case scenario) not pay dividends at all.

Just because a bond rating company issues a rating does not mean the rating is accurate. It is strictly an estimate. Look no further than all those U.S. banks that went under in 2009. Very few had a rating worse than BB! Right.

# Exploring Some Typical Income Stocks

Although virtually every industry has stocks that pay dividends, some industries have more dividend-paying stocks than others. You won't find too many dividend-paying income stocks in the computer or biotech industry! The reason is that these types of companies need a lot of money to finance expensive research and development (R&D) projects to create new products. Without R&D, the company can't create new products to fuel sales, growth, and future earnings. Computer technology, biotech, and other innovative industries are better for growth investors.

## Utilities

Utilities generate a large cash flow. (If you don't believe us, look at your gas and electric bills!) Cash flow includes money from income (sales of products and/or services) and other items (the selling of assets, for example). This cash flow is needed to cover things such as expenses, loan payments, and dividends. Utilities are considered to be the most common type of income stocks, and many investors have at least one in their portfolios. Investing in your own local utility isn't a bad idea. At least it makes paying the utility bill less painful.

Before you invest in a public utility, consider the following:

✔ **The utility company's financial condition:** Is the company making money, and are its sales and earnings growing from year to year? Make sure the utility's bonds are rated highly. We cover bond ratings in the "Examining the company's bond rating" section in this chapter.

✔ **The company's dividend payout ratio:** Because utilities tend to have a good cash flow, don't be too concerned if the ratio reaches 70 percent. Again, — from a safety point of view — the lower the rate, the better. See the "Checking the stock's payout ratio" section in this chapter.

✔ **The company's geographic location:** If the utility covers an area that's doing well and offers an increasing population base and business expansion, that bodes well for your stock.

## Real estate stocks and investment trusts

Real estate stocks are generally income-producing in nature because they have fairly stable and predictable cash flows. For example, Brookfield Asset Management and Brascan are two Canadian real estate companies that regularly declare dividends on their shares. In fact, Brascan has assets in both the real estate and power generation sectors.

Real estate investment trusts (REITs), on the other hand, make up a special breed of real estate "stock." A *REIT* is an investment that has the elements of both a stock and a *mutual fund* (a pool of money received from investors that's managed by an investment company). It's like a stock in that it's a company whose stock is publicly traded on the major stock exchanges. It has the usual features that you expect from a stock — it can be bought and sold easily through a broker, some income is passed on to investors, and so on.

A REIT resembles a mutual fund in that it doesn't make its money selling goods and services. And like a mutual fund, it makes money by buying, selling, and managing an investment portfolio — in the case of a REIT, the portfolio is full of real estate investments. It generates revenue from rents and property leases as any landlord does. In addition, some REITs own mortgages and gain income from the interest.

## Royalty (energy) trusts

In recent years, the oil and gas sector has generated much interest as people and businesses experience much higher energy prices. Due to a variety of bullish factors — such as increased international demand from China and other rapidly growing industrialized nations — oil and gas prices have zoomed to record highs. Some income investors have capitalized on this price increase by investing in energy stocks called resource (royalty) trusts.

*Resource trusts* are companies that hold assets such as oil-rich and/or gas-rich land and generate high fees from companies that seek access to these properties for exploration. The fees paid to the resource trusts are then disbursed as high dividends to their shareholders. By the second half of 2008, dividend-rich resource trusts sported yields in the 7–10 percent range. This range, if it can be sustained, is very enticing, given how low yields have been during the recent stock market and economic decline. You can research resource trusts in generally the same venues as regular stocks (see Appendix B).

# Chapter 10

# Getting a Grip on Economics

· · · · · · · · · · · · · · · · · · · · · · · · · · · · · · · · · · · · · · · · ·

*In This Chapter*

▶ Distinguishing between microeconomics and macroeconomics

▶ Boning up on key economic concepts

▶ Exploring the major schools of economic thought

▶ Keeping an eye on a couple of current economic issues

· · · · · · · · · · · · · · · · · · · · · · · · · · · · · · · · · · · · · · · · ·

"**S**tock prices have reached what looks like a permanently high plateau," said the celebrated economist Irving Fisher on October 17, 1929, shortly before history's most famous single-day stock market plunge. Nobody should have listened to Irving Fisher — not even Irving Fisher. He lost a tonne of money in the stock market and filed for bankruptcy at the start of the Great Depression. Sooooo . . . if you don't think understanding economics is important to your stock investing strategy, then by gum you'd be as wrong as Irving.

This chapter isn't full of economic gobbledygook; we won't beat you over the head with phrases like "inelastic demand aggregates" and "marginal statistical utility" (whatever that means). (You're breathing a sigh of relief, aren't you?) Presented properly, economics really is quite interesting. Understanding economics helps you make better decisions involving your investment choices. All of our successful stock picks were first grounded in commonsense, big-picture economics. Economics has also helped us avoid bad choices — Internet stocks in the late 1990s and mortgage and financial stocks during 2006–08 didn't make economic sense, and ultimately shareholders lost most (or all) of their money as stock prices sank into oblivion. Always ask yourself: "Does this stock pick make economic sense?" We find economics really fascinating, and we hope you find this chapter beneficial and, uh, tolerable.

Don't repeat the mistakes of the past! Be an informed stock investor. Some sources that can help you understand economics more fully include:

   ✔ American Institute for Economic Research: `www.aier.org`

   ✔ Canadian Economy Online: `www.canadianeconomy.gc.ca`

   ✔ Canadian Economics Association: `economics.ca`

✔ Conference Board of Canada: www.conferenceboard.ca

✔ Dismal Scientist: www.dismal.com

✔ Financial Sense: www.financialsense.com

✔ Foundation for Economic Education: www.fee.org

✔ The Mises Institute: www.mises.org

# Breaking Down Microeconomics versus Macroeconomics

You can divide the field of economics into two categories: microeconomics and macroeconomics. For stock investors,

✔ *Microeconomics* is looking at the economic small picture, such as the fundamentals of a company.

✔ *Macroeconomics* is looking at the economic big picture, such as the health of the general economy — in Canada, the U.S., and the whole world.

## Microeconomics

It may not always dawn on you that economics isn't about alien, arcane data and statistics. Economics is the rudimentary stuff of financial life such as sales, expenses, profit, debt, and so on. Your own household is the first and best example of microeconomics in action. If the money coming in is greater than the money going out, that's certainly good. If you have lots of debt (liabilities) and very little in the way of things you own (assets), then your net worth is negative (dead meat!) and the microeconomics of your household aren't good at all.

Much of this book covers microeconomics in terms of choosing your stock. After all, if you're going to put your hard-earned money in a stock, you have to familiarize yourself with the company represented by that stock. Is the company in good economic shape? You find out by checking the company's microeconomic indicators, such as its income statement (or the P&L), balance sheet, and cash flow. You find more information about these indicators in Chapter 12.

## Macroeconomics

If you're only familiar with the microeconomic and don't notice the big picture, you could see your portfolio crumble. Macroeconomics is an important part of your investment decision-making process because stocks aren't chosen in a vacuum. Even the best stocks in the world will go down if the economy is experiencing major problems. This is especially true for stocks of companies that offer products and services.

One of the most helpful macroeconomic indicators is the index of Leading Economic Indicators (LEI), which is an economic gauge that covers a broad array of statistics intended to estimate future economic activity in the U.S. It's calculated by the Conference Board (`www.conference-board.org`), and it's a useful gauge for all Canadian investors because it evaluates how the U.S. economy is progressing. As the U.S. economy goes so goes the Canadian economy, because we are very dependent on our free trade with the U.S. for our own economic prosperity.

A flaw with the analysis of the investing pundits on financial TV shows is that although they're usually very good at microeconomics, because of certain factors (a lack of education, bias, and so on), they aren't proficient in macroeconomics. They may tell you about a great stock in sector X, but they're missing what will hit that sector (and that stock) because of factors elsewhere in the economy. A good example is homebuilding stocks. In 2007, we noticed that a financial adviser extolled the virtues of a particular homebuilding company ("Great financials, great profit margin — this stock is a definite buy!"). However, the housing sector was about to be slammed by a huge wave of defaults and foreclosures because of mortgage problems and a slowing general economy. In the following months, that stock plummeted by 60 percent even though its microeconomic picture looked nice.

# Understanding Important Concepts in Economic Logic

In the following sections we discuss a few points you ought to be familiar with to keep yourself grounded with the right data and logic for your stock investing decisions.

## Supply and demand

Doing a chapter on economics without mentioning supply and demand is like doing a chapter on graceful aging without mentioning Tommy Hunter and Gordon Lightfoot. Supply and demand are the quintessential duo in the economic universe, and the more you understand how they work, the more successful your investment decisions will be.

Here are definitions for these two concepts (from our perspectives, of course):

- **Supply.** What's being offered or produced? How much is there? How desirable or necessary is it? Are there substitutes? How limited or plentiful is the supply in question? What factors affect supply, and do those factors affect it directly or indirectly?

- **Demand.** This refers to the market that will ultimately buy what's offered. Who are they? How many are they? Are they willing and able to buy? Are they individuals, small organizations, or large organizations? Do they merely want what's offered, or do they need it? What factors affect demand, and do those factors affect it directly or indirectly?

We count on supply and demand to tell us how well a product or service will sell. This in turn tells us whether the company providing the supply (again, product or service) has enough customers (demand) to be profitable and successful.

How do supply and demand relate to your investing decisions? Here's a simple example: A company sells medical equipment that's necessary for an aging population, and the aging population is a growing segment of Canadian society. Therefore, demand is strong and probably growing, so the stock of the company providing supply (the medical equipment) is probably a good bet. Another example is a company that produces fertilizer to allow for more efficient crop production at a time when world population is increasing, and land available for farming is becoming more scarce. The stock of a company like Potash or a competitor may be well-positioned to meet this demand in a profitable way.

Sometimes the laws of supply and demand can be overcome or temporarily suspended in the short term by something powerful such as Canadian government action (a good example is price controls, which we cover in Chapter 11). However, in the long term, supply and demand trump all.

## Wants and needs

One of our favourite definitions of economics is a very pithy one: "Economics is humanity dealing with scarcity." After all, to "economize" is to use resources wisely and to make choices about what to do with time, effort, and money. As humans, we know that resources (such as time, effort, and money) have to be used to voluntarily exchange with others to acquire goods and services that meet personal wants and needs (or both).

When times are good and we're doing well financially we're not that concerned about our needs, and we have a greater ability to address our wants, such as a new car or a better vacation. When times are good, we have an easier time with stock investing; many stocks tend to do well when times are good because more money flows toward both wants and needs.

But what if times are bad (or simply not as good)? When economic times are tough or uncertain, common sense kicks in for stock investors. Demand for products and services that people merely want but don't need is weak or negative. However, demand for those things that are needed in our lives (such as food or energy) makes them a safer choice for stock investors. In a bad economy, Canadian stock investors have to be even more selective.

As we write this, times remain very difficult, and the data tell us that 2010 and 2011 will still be economically hazardous and difficult for the Canadian, U.S., and world economies as a whole. Therefore, Canadian investors would be prudent to stick to investment choices tied to human needs.

## Dynamic analysis versus static analysis

Economics isn't about dry statistics; it's about human behaviour with incentives and disincentives. In other words, when it comes to economics, people behave in a way that usually suits their self-interest. For example, say you're driving down the highway and you notice two gas stations. Gas station A has gasoline at $1.10 per litre while gas station B has the same gas at $1.05. Which one is more profitable? All things being equal, gas station B (the one with the lower price) will make more money.

*Dynamic analysis* takes human behaviour into account, such as in our gasoline example. However, someone using *static analysis* would conclude that gas station A would be more profitable by assuming it would make an extra 5 cents per litre. If the world were a static place and if people were automatons, then the latter situation could possibly prove correct. But look . . . we're human! Everyone loves a bargain. Gas A is more expensive, so more people will buy gas B, resulting in higher profits for the lower-priced station.

Dynamic analysis takes into account how people or organizations act differently given incentives (such as discounts) or disincentives (such as sales taxes), while static analysis doesn't.

We're all faced with choices about what to do with our money. We're certain that you'd find the same product cheaper at a big box store than at a haughty boutique in downtown Montreal. Yet which one would make greater overall profits? Ask yourself how people would behave with the choices they face in the marketplace. Those companies that deliver with greater efficiency and value are a good bet for stock investing.

### Cause and effect

Cause and effect is an exercise in logic that stock investors should embrace. If something is a growing problem (or a growing opportunity), what is its possible cause? And, in turn, what effect will it have? The credit crisis of 2008 and 2009 is a great example of this. When U.S. banks were overburdened with debt and much of that debt was discovered to be low-quality (risky) debt, this situation caused several effects, among them major losses and potential bankruptcies. Wary investors see that too much debt in an uncertain economy can certainly cause some undesired effects. Individual companies suffer and their stock price goes down, which, of course, has a negative effect on your portfolio.

# Surveying a Few Schools of Economic Thought

Adhering to a particular economic philosophy can make you or break you as a stock investor. Be sure to discover which ones have withstood the test of time and which ones are the kiss of economic death. In the following sections, we introduce a few major schools of thought found in the world today.

Be sure to find which schools apply to the financial planners you work with and the resources you use — knowing a planner's school of thought can help you decide whether his general outlook is a fit with yours. If a financial planner isn't aware of the schools of thought — or answers "Keynesian" — it might indicate he doesn't fully understand how government policy and economics affect the stock-picking process.

### The Marx school

Frankly, the Marx school of economic thought (named after Karl Marx) makes us shudder. That's because in a communist country, the government runs everything. When the government runs everything, economic activity is controlled by a centralized, pervasive bureaucracy. And history has shown that such economies eventually collapse. Yugoslavia and the Soviet Union are examples; Cuba may be next to follow.

Part of the reason why centralized planning doesn't work is that no single bureaucrat or committee of bureaucrats has the ability to see and meet the complex and constantly changing wants and needs of millions of diverse individuals. Centralized planning of an economy eventually leads to misallocation of resources, and that has always led to intractable economic problems.

How does this relate to stocks? Marxist/socialist/communist economic thought is, at its core, antithetical to a healthy free market economy, which is necessary for stock investing. Stock investing requires a free market, one in which the functions of business (such as profit) can operate with minimal interference. Businesses must be allowed to be formed, and they must bear the burden of risk and reward. Poorly run businesses fail, while well-run companies are rewarded with profit (good for shareholders).

Although profit sometimes gets bad press, it is in fact the most necessary element of a successful economy. In other chapters of this book, you find out that profit is necessary for companies, but notice that we've extended that thought to the overall economy. Think about it for a moment. Profit is vital for economic growth. Profit is what makes an economy expand. Profit is an economic incentive missing from communist economies (and sorely missing from socialist ones). Profit is (and should be) a reward for innovation, risk, and the proper allocation of resources.

History has shown us conclusively that every country that has adopted a totalitarian, command-and-control economic model (communism, fascism, and so on) has ended in economic decline and abject failure. The bottom line is that Groucho Marx knows more about economics than Karl. Nuff said.

## *The Keynes school*

The economic philosophy of John Maynard Keynes (a British economist in the early 20th century) has been the dominant school of thought in Canadian and American politics and governmental economic policy matters for over a half-century. What a shame! What many don't realize is that, after decades of this policy being implemented, the long-term effect of Keynesian economics is now becoming evident.

Keynesian economics is an economic theory with the central idea that active government intervention in the marketplace and in monetary policy (managing the country's currency) is the best method of ensuring economic growth and stability. Believers in Keynesian economics think that it's the government's job to smooth out the ebbs and flows in the business cycle. In bad times, like now, intervention takes the form of increased spending by the government and tax cuts to stimulate the economy. In good times, the government intervenes by a reduction in spending and increases in taxes to curb potential inflation.

The problem is that the government intervention at the heart of Keynesian economics is now finally seen as the great flaw. The intervention actually causes the recessions, depressions, and artificial booms that it was originally supposed to remedy. The low-interest-rate policy that fuelled the recent housing boom in Canada and the U.S. comes to mind. Mindless lending practices in the U.S. also caused many American banks to collapse. As government continues to spend and allows total government debt to keep rising, the situation must eventually be addressed. When flaws in his theory were pointed out and shown to be a huge problem in the long run, Keynes was famously quoted as saying, "In the long run, we will all be dead." Well, he certainly is dead, but his ideas live on and continue to wreak havoc on our Canadian economy today. Government intervention, massive bailouts, economic dislocation, and rising inflation are being dealt with right now. (Another quote attributed to Keynes was, "It is better to be roughly right than precisely wrong." Looks like he has been precisely wrong, and it sure has been rough!)

What does Keynesian economics have to do with the stock market? This is the ideology that ends up causing artificial booms ("asset bubbles") and the resulting decline. Keynesian thinking is what drove the government (through the Federal Reserve and Bank of Canada) to increase liquidity (that is, increase the money supply and expand credit), which resulted in the bubbles that our society has witnessed in recent years. In the early stages of a bubble, everyone's happy as the value of their assets (such as stocks or real estate) rises and provides the illusion that has come to be known as "the wealth effect." Canadians felt wealthy in the late 1990s and mid-2000s when the stock market (especially tech, oil, and commodity stocks) went up dramatically. However, because bubbles are created by artificial means (the injection of credit), prices are bid up to unnatural levels and must ultimately come down. The stock market bubble popped in 2000 and again in early 2009, and millions of people lost trillions of dollars. As we write this, the latest bubble in credit and derivatives continues to deflate and wreak havoc on the stock market (especially financial stocks like banks and brokerage firms). Bubbles have become the visible legacy of the rampant credit and money expansion that resulted from applying Keynesian economics. (By the way, most politicians are Keynesians. Ha! Need we say more?)

## The Austrian school

Another school of economic thought for investors (anyone, actually) is the Austrian school. After 100 years of experience, the Austrian school has been proven consistently right.

The leading voice of this school was Ludwig von Mises, an Austrian economist in the early 20th century (now you know where the name of the school comes from!). He accurately forecast the Great Depression, the collapse of the Soviet Union, and other major economic events.

The Austrian school emphasizes free markets, limited government, private property rights, and a sound currency tied to the gold standard. This last point is important given what can happen when a government issues currency without limit — how this leads to currency debasement and, ultimately, collapse. In addition, the Austrian school provides research on how asset bubbles (such as the recent stock and housing market bubbles) form and the problems that can ensue when these bubbles cause booms and the inevitable bust.

How does this help you with stocks? About ten years ago, we recall reading an article about asset bubbles on www.mises.org, the site that showcases the work of Mises and other Austrian economists (such as Murray Rothbard and Henry Hazlitt). That article explained how the stock market was a bubble and why. Armed with this knowledge, we informed readers and clients about ways to protect against the stock market bubble. That forewarning saved many of our readers and clients from the bear market of 2000–02, and it was a concrete lesson in understanding (and applying) sound economic principles. Are you taking notes?

# Understanding Some Current Economic Issues Facing Stock Investors

As we told you earlier in this chapter, we won't provide an all-encompassing, extensive, voluminous coverage of economics, but we are committed to your investment success. The following are a few economic issues that you *must* be aware of in the coming months and years if you're intent on successful stock investing.

## Inflation

Inflation is an issue that could easily be lumped into the chapter on politics (Chapter 11, so you know) because it's as much a governmental phenomenon as it is an economic one. In modern economies, we use currencies (such as the dollar) to transact in our day-to-day lives. It's our medium of exchange; we use currencies to trade with so that we can obtain goods and services. The issuance of currency is a government matter; the central bank (in Canada it's the Bank of Canada; in the U.S. it's the Federal Reserve) issues the currency and manages its quantity (the money supply). When you hear the term "monetary policy," that's just the official way of saying that the Bank of Canada manages our official supply of money — the loonie as our national currency.

Since 2001, the Federal Reserve (and to a lesser extent the Bank of Canada) has been increasing the money supply at a very high rate. In recent years, much of this came in the form of credit that went into assets (such as stocks and real estate), but much of it has been (and is) going into the price of goods and services. This means that the result has been (and will be) high and higher prices.

Inflation is effectively a hidden tax that hurts most consumers, especially those on fixed incomes with limited means. Canadian stock investors should be aware of inflation and invest in ways that will benefit them. This is part of the reason why we repeatedly tell folks to invest in human need. As these prices go up, you need to be in the stocks of companies that will either benefit from inflation or (at the very least) not be hurt by it. Examples of human need include food, water, energy, commodities, and so on. Consider stocks in these necessary areas.

## Government intervention

Stock investing was actually an easy pursuit in the 1980s and the early 1990s. The market was generally unfettered, and economic logic was easy to apply. However, a major sea change has occurred during the past 10 to 15 years that has made stock investing more precarious, unpredictable, and hazardous. That sea change was driven by pronounced government intervention, which is akin to betting on a basketball game but finding out that the referees are interfering in the game. Government intervention comes in a variety of flavours, and it's usually an outgrowth of political considerations — so spend some time in Chapter 11, where we discuss the relationship between politics and stock investing in more detail.

### 9,000,000 percent inflation!

In a recent seminar, we asked students to name the top-performing stock market in the world from the previous year (from a nominal point of view). They blurted out "China," "Brazil," and other guesses, but they weren't even close. "Zimbabwe," we said to the puzzled class. That's right, a fairly obscure country in central Africa. Its stock market was up an astonishing 12,000 percent. Whew! Yet, the country is mired in poverty under an oppressive regime. How can that be? When socialist dictator Robert Mugabe took control of the country, he put in strict controls on the economy. Among those controls: Citizens couldn't have foreign accounts, couldn't buy gold or other alternative forms of money, and could only use the official currency, the Zimbabwean dollar. He then began to hyper-inflate the currency to initially benefit himself and his allies. After years of abuse, the inflation rate hit horrific levels. On paper, Zimbabwe had more multimillionaires per capita than any other nation even though most of the populace was destitute. By the summer of 2008, the inflation rate surpassed 9 million percent, as 40 billion Zimbabwean dollars equalled one U.S. dollar. Recently, the country's economic minister told the United Nations that the inflation rate was beyond calculation. Zimbabwe's fate regarding this extreme condition is yet to be clear. Stay tuned!

# Chapter 11

# Money, Mayhem, and Votes

*In This Chapter*

▶ Looking at the effects of politics and government on stocks

▶ Checking out a few handy political resources

*P*olitics can be infuriating, disruptive, meddlesome, corrupting, and harmful. Don't let that fool you — it does have its bad side, too! Even if politics doesn't amuse or interest you, you can't ignore it. If you aren't careful, it can wreak havoc on your portfolio. Politics wields great influence on the economic and social environment, which affects how companies succeed or fail. This success or failure in turn either helps or hurts your stock's price. After all, a stock is merely a reflection of what the underlying company has to deal with — including the positive or negative impact of political decisions made. Politics (manifested in taxes, regulations, price controls, capital controls, and other government actions) can make or break a company or industry quicker than any other external force.

What Canadians (especially government policy makers) must understand is that a new tax, law, regulation, or government action has a *macro* effect on a stock, an industry, or even an entire economic system, whereas a company has a *micro* effect on an economy. The following gives you a simple snapshot of these effects:

> Politics → policy → economy → industry → company → stock → stock investor

Now, this chapter doesn't moralize about politics or advocate a political point of view; after all, this book is about stock investing. In general, policies can be good or bad regardless of their effect on the economy — some policies are enacted to achieve greater purposes even if they kick you in the wallet. However, in the context of this chapter, politics is covered from a cause-and-effect perspective: How does politics affect prosperity in general and stock investing in particular?

A proficient stock investor can't — must not — look at stocks as though they exist in a vacuum. Our favourite example of this rule is the idea of fish in a Great Lake. You can have a great fish (your stock) among a whole school of fish (the stock market) in a wonderful lake (the economy). But what if the lake gets polluted (bad policy)? What happens to the fish? Politics controls the lake and can make it hospitable — or dangerous — for the participants. You get the point. The example may sound too simple, yet it isn't. So many people — political committees, corporate managers, bureaucrats, and politicians — still get this picture so wrong time and time again, to the detriment of the economy and stock investors. Heck, we don't mind if they get it wrong with *their* money, but their actions make it tough for *your* money.

Although the two inexorably get intertwined, we do what we can to treat politics and economics as separate issues. Economics gets its own spotlight in Chapter 10.

# Tying Together Politics and Stocks

The campaigns heat up. Liberals, Conservatives, and smaller parties vie for your attention and subsequent votes. All sorts of political viewpoints enter into the battlefield of ideas. But after all is said and done, Canadian voters make their decisions. Election Day brings a new slate of politicians into office, and they in turn joust and debate on new rules and programs in the legislative halls of Parliament. Before and after election time, Canadian investors must keep a watchful eye on the proceedings. In the following sections, we explain some basic political concepts that relate to stock investing.

Our discussion in this chapter is not restricted to Canadian politics. In fact, in this highly interconnected world economy, it is not even restricted to North American politics. As long as a company operates in another country, it will be affected by the politics of that country. Ultimately, the effect of this interconnectedness trickles down to the company, stock, and individual stock investor level!

## Seeing the general effects of politics on stock investing

For stock investors, politics manifests itself as a major factor in investment-making decisions in ways shown in Table 11-1.

| Table 11-1 | Politics and Investing |
|---|---|
| *Possible Legislation* | *Effect on Investing* |
| Taxes | Will a new tax affect a particular stock (industry or economy)? Generally, more or higher taxes ultimately have a negative impact on stock investing. Income taxes and capital gains taxes are good examples. |
| Laws | Will Parliament (or, in some instances, provincial legislatures) pass a law that will have a negative impact on a stock, the industry, or the economy? Price controls — laws that set the price of a product, service, or commodity — are examples of negative laws. |
| Regulations | Will a new (or existing) regulation have a negative (or positive) effect on the stock of your choice? Generally, more or tougher regulations have a negative impact on stocks. |
| Government spending and debt | If government agencies spend too much or misallocate resources, they may create greater burdens on society, which in turn will be bearish for the economy and the stock market. |
| Money supply | The money supply — the dollars you use — is controlled by the Bank of Canada. How can money supply affect stocks? Big time! Increasing or decreasing the money supply results in either an inflationary or a deflationary environment, which can help or hurt the economy, specific industries, and stock picks. |
| Interest rates | The Bank of Canada (and the Federal Reserve in the U.S.) has crucial influence here. It can raise or lower key interest rates that in turn can have an effect on the entire economy and the stock market. When interest rates go up, it makes credit more expensive for companies. When interest rates go down, companies can get cheaper credit, which can be better for profits — if that debt is used carefully. |

*(continued)*

**Table 11-1** *(continued)*

| Possible Legislation | Effect on Investing |
| --- | --- |
| Government bailouts | This occurs when the government intervenes directly and uses either tax money, borrowed money, or printed money to bail out a troubled enterprise. This is a negative to the overall economy because funds are diverted by force from the healthier private economy to an ailing enterprise. |
| | The Canadian government's bailout of General Motors in Oshawa is a recent example of a very high-cost handout. The U.S. government's bailout of Chrysler, AIG, and a plethora of financial institutions are but some examples of scores of bailouts that have occurred south of our border. No one is even sure whether these interventions will work in the long run. |

When many of the factors in Table 11-1 work in tandem, they can have a magnified effect that can have tremendous consequences for your stock portfolio. Alert investors keep a constant vigil when the legislature is open for business, and they adjust their portfolios accordingly.

## Ascertaining the political climate

The bottom line is that you ignore political realities at your own (economic) risk. To be and stay aware, ask yourself the following questions about the stock of each company in which you invest:

- What laws will directly affect my stock investment adversely?

- Will any laws affect the company's industry?

- Will any current or prospective laws affect the company's sources of revenue?

- Will any current or prospective laws affect the company's expenses or supplies?

- Am I staying informed about political and economic issues that may possibly have a negative impact on my investment?

- Will such things as excessive regulations, price controls, or new taxes have a negative impact on my stock's industry?

# The seeds of financial disaster sown in the last decade

As we write this book, the financial headlines blare away about the trillion-dollar financial and credit catastrophes unfolding on Wall Street. Colossal U.S. government-sponsored enterprises such as Fannie Mae and Freddie Mac have collapsed, and shareholders have been wiped out. Large financial entities such as AIG and Merrill Lynch have been rocked by multibillion-dollar losses. Although Canada's banks are more secure, we have our share of problems in other areas, as evidenced by GM's trials in Oshawa and the mothballing of expensive oil sands projects in Alberta. When the U.S. sneezes, the rest of the world, including Canada, is affected. Politicians and pundits give indignant speeches about the failures of capitalism. But what really happened?

Politically popular policies and regulations enacted by the federal government in Canada and especially in the U.S. during the late 1990s and the early part of this decade laid the groundwork for today's massive financial mess. The Federal Reserve in 2001 lowered interest rates to artificially low levels, removed lending standards (to boost home ownership), greatly increased the money supply, and expanded credit on a massive scale. This fuelled a historic mortgage boom that created the housing bubble in the U.S. Trillions in mortgage money was loaned out, much of it to home buyers of *very* questionable credit quality. These subprime mortgages were repackaged as bonds and sold to financial entities on Wall Street and across the globe. When the mortgages went bad, financial entities lost billions.

In Canada, the national bank also lowered interest rates to follow the beat of the U.S. drums, but our banking standards were more stringent. As a result, there were few foreclosures and other related financial distresses here. Yet, to the extent that Canadians held U.S. stocks, we too were very much affected as investors. That is why so many Canadians have seen our investment portfolios drop over the last few years.

Now, politicians rail about what government should do, but what they don't understand is that the root of the problem is what government *did* do, years before. The lesson is that political/government intervention can unleash unintended consequences that can destroy a company whose stock you own.

Here's an example: Canadian oil and gas service and exploration companies benefited from the global need for more energy supplies. But investment opportunities didn't stop there. As oil and gas supplies became costly and problematic, alternative energy sources gained national attention. Specifically, the debate was rekindled on wind power, solar power, and other exciting new technologies, such as fuel cells. As traditional sources of energy (crude oil) became more expensive, alternative sources of energy became more economically viable. Canadian investors who anticipated the new interest in alternative energy sought companies to invest in that would logically benefit. With winds of change at their back due to public acceptance of innovative energy technologies, Canadian investors can take renewed notice of alternative energy options

## Distinguishing between nonsystemic and systemic effects

Politics can affect your investments in two basic ways: nonsystemic and systemic.

- ✔ *Nonsystemic* means that the system isn't affected but a particular participant is affected.
- ✔ *Systemic* means that all the players in the system are affected.

In this case, the system is the economy at large. Politics imposes itself (through taxes, laws, regulations, and so on) and has an undue influence on all the members of that system.

### Nonsystemic

Say you decide to buy stock in a company called Hockey Sticks Unlimited Inc. (HSU). You believe that the market for hockey sticks has great potential and that HSU stands to grow substantially. How can politics affect HSU?

What if Canadian politicians believe that HSU is too big and that it controls too much of the hockey stick industry? Maybe they view HSU as a monopoly and want the federal government to step in to shrink HSU's reach and influence for the benefit of competition and Canadian consumers. Maybe the government believes that HSU engages in unfair or predatory business practices and that it's in violation of antitrust (or antimonopoly) laws. If the Canadian government acts against HSU, the action is a nonsystemic issue: The action is directed toward the participant (in this case, HSU) and not the hockey stick industry in general.

What happens if you're an investor in HSU? Does your stock investment suffer as a result of government action directed against the company? Let's just say the stock price will be tipped and end up lost in the stands.

### Systemic

This time, imagine that Canadian politicians want to target the Canadian golf industry for intervention because they maintain that golf should be free or close to free for all to participate in and that a law must be passed to make it accessible to all, especially those people who can't afford to play. So to remedy the situation, the following law is enacted: "Law #67590305598002 declares that from this day forward, all Canadian golf courses must charge only one dollar for any golfer who chooses to participate."

That law sounds great to any golfer. But what are the unintended effects when such a law becomes reality? Many people agree with the sentiment of the law, but what about the cause-and-effect aspects of it? Obviously, all things being equal, golf courses will be forced to close. Staying in business is uneconomical if their costs are higher than their income. If they can't charge any more than a dollar, how can they possibly stay open? Ultimately (and ironically), no one can play golf.

What happens to investors of a specific golf-related company that operates in Canada? If the world of golf shrinks, demand for that company's product or service shrinks as well. The value of this company's stock will certainly be stuck in a sand trap.

Examples of politics creating systemic problems are endless, but you get the point.

## Understanding price controls

Stock investors should be very wary of price controls, which are a great example of regulation. It is something that is not here yet, but that we as Canadians experienced in the late seventies. A *price control* is a fixed price on a particular product, commodity, or service mandated by the government.

Price controls have been tried continuously throughout history, and they've continuously been removed because they ultimately do more harm than good. It's easy to see why. Say you run a business that sells chairs, and a law is passed that states, "From this point onward, chairs can be sold only for $10." If all your costs stay constant at $9 or less, the regulation isn't that bad. However, price controls put two dynamics in motion:

- First, the artificially lower price encourages consumption — more people buy chairs.
- Second, production is discouraged. What company wants to make chairs if it can't sell them for a decent profit?

What happens to the company with a fixed sales price (in this example, $10) and rising costs? Profits shrink, and depending on how long the price controls are in effect, the company eventually experiences losses. The chair producer is eventually driven out of business. The chair-building industry shrinks, and the result is a chair shortage. Profits (and jobs) soon vanish. So what happens if you own stock in a company that builds chairs? Well, when you hear which way the stock price is going, you better be sitting down (if, of course, you have a chair).

Many economists are warning that as the U.S. government continues to print money to finance its stimulus packages and huge debt levels, the risk of inflation will soar. If inflation does occur, vote-hungry politicians will be very tempted to implement price controls in certain industry segments, especially those most prone to inflationary pressures such as oil and food. At its worst, you may even see wage controls. In fact, the Ontario government came very close to reneging on its promise to increase the minimum wage, and only stopped because it realized that this was wage control in disguise. The Liberals did not wish to be the first to enter into the icy and choppy waters of wage and price controls!

# Poking into Political Resources

Ignoring what's going on in the world of politics is like sleepwalking near the Grand Canyon — a bad idea! You have to be aware of what's going on. Governmental data, reports, and political rumblings are important clues to the kind of environment that's unfolding for the economy and financial markets. Do your research with the following resources so you can stay a step ahead in your stock-picking strategies.

## Government reports to watch for

The best analysts look at economic reports from both private and government sources. The following sections list some reports and statistics issued by the government that are worth checking out. For private reports on the economy, investors can turn to sources such as the American Institute for Economic Research (www.aier.org) and Moody's (www.economy.com). In Canada, the *National Post* and *The Globe and Mail* routinely list the release dates of key domestic economic reports in their business pages. Also check out RBC Economics Research (www.rbc.com/economics) and click the Releases Calendar icon in the Tools section.

### GDP

*Gross domestic product* (GDP), which measures a nation's total output of goods and services for the quarter, is considered the broadest measure of economic activity. Although GDP is measured in dollars, it's usually quoted as a percentage. You typically hear a news report that says something like, "The economy grew by 2.5 percent last quarter." Because GDP is an important overall barometer of the Canadian economy, the key thing to remember is that it should be a positive number. The report on the GDP is released quarterly by Statistics Canada (www.statcan.gc.ca) for Canadian economic performance. Specifically, type in the search term "Canadian Economic Observer" in Statistics Canada's home page to take you to its flagship publication for Canadian economic statistics, including GDP. For quarterly reports on the U.S. GDP, check out the U.S. Department of Commerce (www.commerce.gov).

Regularly monitor the GDP along with economic data that relate directly to your stock portfolio. The following list gives some general guidelines for evaluating GDP:

- ✔ **Over 3 percent:** This number indicates strong growth and bodes well for stocks. At 5 percent or higher, the economy is sizzling!

- ✔ **1 to 3 percent:** This figure indicates moderate growth and can occur either as the economy is rebounding from a recession or as it's slowing down from a previously strong period.

- ✔ **0 percent or negative (as low as –3 percent):** This number isn't good and indicates the economy is either not growing or is actually shrinking a bit. A negative GDP is considered *recessionary* (meaning that the economy's growth is receding).

- ✔ **Under –3 percent:** A GDP this low indicates a very difficult period for the economy. A GDP under –3 percent, especially for two or more quarters, indicates a serious recession or possibly a depression.

Looking at a single quarter isn't that useful. Track the GDP over many quarters to see which way the general economy is trending. When you look at the GDP for a particular quarter of a year, ask yourself whether it's better (or worse) than the quarter before. If it's better (or worse), then ask yourself to what extent it has changed. Is it dramatically better (or worse) than the quarter before? Is the economy showing steady growth, or is it slowing? If several quarters show solid growth, the overall economy is generally bullish.

Traditionally, if two or more consecutive quarters show negative growth (economic output is shrinking), the economy is considered to be in a recession. A recession can be a painful necessity; it usually occurs when the economy can't absorb the total amount of goods being produced because of excess production. A bear market in stocks usually accompanies a recession.

The GDP is just a rough estimate at best. It can't possibly calculate all the factors that go into economic growth. For example, crime has a negative effect on economic growth, but it's not reflected in the GDP. Still, most economists agree that the GDP provides a snapshot of the overall economy's progress.

### Unemployment

The Labour Force Survey is provided by Statistics Canada (www.statcan.gc.ca) and Human Resources and Skills Development Canada (www.hrsdc.gc.ca). (In the U.S., it's provided by the Bureau of Labor Statistics — www.bls.gov.) This information gives investors a snapshot of the health and productivity of the economy.

### The Consumer Price Index

The Consumer Price Index (CPI) is a statistic that tracks the prices of a representative basket of goods and services on a monthly basis. This statistic, which is also computed by Statistics Canada (and the Bureau of Labor Statistics in the U.S.), is meant to track price inflation. Investors should pay attention to the CPI, because a low-inflation environment is good for stocks (and bonds, too) while high inflation is generally more favourable for sectors such as commodities and precious metals.

## Web sites to surf

To find out about new laws being passed or about proposed legislation in Canada, go to the Department of Justice Canada's Web site (laws.justice. gc.ca). For a look at upcoming laws in the U.S., check out Congress and what's going on at its primary Web sites: the U.S. House of Representatives (www.house.gov) and the U.S. Senate (www.senate.gov).

You also may want to check out THOMAS, a service provided by the U.S. Library of Congress, at http://thomas.loc.gov. THOMAS is a search engine that helps you find any piece of U.S. legislation, either by bill number or keyword. This search engine is an excellent way to find out whether an industry is being targeted for increased regulation or deregulation. In the late 1980s, real estate was hit hard when the government passed new regulations and tax rules (related stocks went down). When the telecom industry was deregulated in the mid-1990s, the industry grew dramatically (related stocks went up). While there are no resources like THOMAS in Canada, a simple Google search, or even a visit or call to the local legal library of a university, may be of some help.

Turn to the following sources for economic data:

- ✔ For Canada:
  - Conference Board of Canada, www.conferenceboard.ca
  - Bank of Canada, www.bankofcanada.ca
  - The Canadian Taxpayers Federation, www.taxpayer.com
- ✔ For the U.S.:
  - Conference Board, www.conferenceboard.org
  - U.S. Department of Commerce, www.doc.gov
  - The Federal Reserve, www.federalreserve.gov
  - Free Lunch, www.freelunch.com

You can find more resources in Appendix B. The more knowledge you pick up about how politics and government actions can help (or harm) an investment, the better you'll be at growing (and protecting) your wealth.

# Part III
# Picking the Winners

The 5th Wave                                    By Rich Tennant

"I take it your stocks are still trading high on the 'yawn index.'"

# In this part . . .

To be an effective stock investor, you need to know where to go to get key information about a company's financial health. After you find this information, you have to know what it means — and be able to see how some companies try to make their numbers look better than they really are. This part equips you with this knowledge. We cover some of the many risks faced by the companies you invest in or are thinking of investing in — and how you, as a smart stock investor, can assess those risks. We also give you insights on the importance of analyzing industries before investing, and we present some exciting emerging-sector opportunities that you may wish to pursue.

# Chapter 12

# Financial-Statement Boot Camp

*In This Chapter*

▶ Paging through an income statement

▶ Taking a snapshot of assets and liabilities — the balance sheet

▶ Assessing cash flows

▶ Using ratios to put the numbers into perspective

*I*n this chapter, we introduce you to financial statements — key performance indicators for any publicly traded company (and for any other organization, for that matter). We discuss the fact that a company's income statement, balance sheet, and cash-flow statement provide you with a big-picture view of its financial health.

In this chapter, we dig deep into some of the main *line items* that make up each financial statement. These are the elements or components of financial statements that can have an important story to tell. We admit that accounting may not be the most exciting subject, so we will stick to what you really need to know to be effective as an investor. However, make no mistake that in this economic environment getting a good read on a company's fiscal condition is critical.

## Reading the Income Statement

It comes as no surprise to you that business and economic activity are undertaken with the idea of generating a profit. Because we're not writing an essay on political economy, we don't go into the details of why that is or isn't a good idea. We'll leave that to others.

*Profit* is simply the gross revenue of an enterprise, less the cost of producing that income, over a defined period of time. So much is made these days of earnings and earnings reports. Do you hear much about a company's cash balance, accumulated depreciation, or owner's equity on Canada's Business News Network or CNBC's *Mad Money* and other financial shows? Does everyone salivate four times a year for asset season?

Earnings are *the* driving force and key indicator of a company's progress and success. If earnings are growing, the financial press doesn't worry much about the other stuff. Conversely, serve up a couple of double faults on the earnings front, and everybody's all over asset impairment, write-offs, debt, weak cash positions, and the like.

Long-term stock price appreciation is based on the growth of a company's asset base and the owner's equity in that base. If a company is generating cash, and particularly if it earns it at a growing rate, that's a good thing. As Warren Buffett says, "If the business does well, the stock always follows." (We'd add from our own experience that it *almost* always follows — in the stock market, as with life, no guarantees apply.)

We discuss other earnings measures, such as free cash flow and EBITDA, later in this chapter. The point is that you can measure income in many ways. Each reveals an important aspect of business performance, both for determining the value of the company and for comparing companies.

## Revenues

*Revenues* are the monies a company is owed for providing goods or services to another party. In large companies, revenue recognition can be very complicated, and is one area that unethical managers like to manipulate. Revenue is also referred to as the *top line*.

In smaller companies, sales and revenues are straightforward. They represent accounting dollars generated for business products sold or services performed. (Remember, with accrual accounting it doesn't matter whether the company has been paid yet. If a sale meets accounting tests for recognition, the sale is put on the books even if the cash is received later.)

In many businesses, such as transportation or utilities, the top line may be called *revenues,* but it's the same thing. Occasionally, you will see an allowance for returns included that reduces the sales figure. If not, you can usually safely assume that returns have already been factored out and reduced the sales figure.

## Cost of sales

A company's income statement shows how profitable a company's core operations are by indicating the revenue generated from sales of a product or service and then deducting the costs associated with the company's products or services. *Cost of sales* (COS) or *cost of goods sold* (COGS) relates directly to the sale of products or services. For manufacturers, this figure includes labour expenses, material costs, and overhead costs (for example, the portion of electricity costs that relates directly to the products sold). COS or COGS for companies selling goods is technically the beginning inventory, plus the cost of goods purchased or manufactured during some period, minus the ending inventory.

When a company uses the terms *costs* and *expenses* in its financial statements, what it really could be trying to say is that costs are incurred to produce products or render services and expenses are all the other stuff, like paying office rent and support staff.

COS is an important driver of business success. For all but a few companies with high intellectual property or service content, COS is the largest eater of the revenue pie. For example, the physical COS of Microsoft is tiny with respect to revenue, whereas a grocery store like Loblaws or a discount retailer like Zellers may see COS in the 70- to 80-percent range. Apples-to-apples comparisons are critical to effective analysis.

## Gross margin

*Gross margin,* or *gross profit,* is the difference between a company's total sales and its cost of sales. It is the basic economic output of the business before additional overhead, marketing, and financing costs enter the picture. Gross profit takes on added meaning when taken as a percentage. This percentage — and trends in the percentage — speaks volumes for the health and direction of the business.

## Selling, general, and administrative (SG&A)

A section of every income statement itemizes a series of expenses called *operating expenses.* These are the expenses other than COS, and other than interest and taxes. SG&A expense is one of these operating expenses.

*SG&A expenses* are operating costs associated with making sales, running the business, keeping headquarters, marketing, data processing, and administrating operations. These expenses are indirect in nature. No matter the business, any company incurs indirect costs, or the costs of doing business that aren't *directly* related to producing and selling individual units of product or service. Some call it "overhead"; however, SG&A expenses go a little beyond the traditional definition of overhead, and some overhead items we've seen are usually allocated to direct costs, or COS.

Many investors use SG&A as a barometer of management effectiveness — a solid management team keeps SG&A expenses in check. SG&A can mushroom into a vast slush fund and an internal corporate pork barrel that can easily get out of control. Be alert for excessive SG&A; the more the company keeps (in executive salaries, for example), the less the shareholder gets (in stock price growth and dividends). Like gross margin, looking at SG&A as a percentage is best.

## Research and development (R&D)

This type of operating expense is common and essential in pharmaceutical and technology companies, which need to make ongoing investments in future products. R&D can also be rife with abuse; if a company wastes money, it can easily hide it in the R&D category. Because these investments occur long before products are produced, and because many of them never pan out into saleable products, companies are allowed by accounting rules to record most research and development (R&D) costs as a period expense.

Also note that companies without a significant R&D effort may not report it in a separate line. And in some financial statements, R&D is called *product development.*

## Depreciation and amortization

Depreciation and amortization represent the accountant's assignment of the operating cost of a long-lived asset to specific business periods, or its estimated useful life. *Depreciation* is used when referring to physical fixed assets, and *amortization* is used when referring to intangible assets (such as goodwill, patents, and so forth). Some of you Canadian oil and mining investing bugs may run into the term *depletion:* a cost recovery for the exhaustion of natural resource assets.

In our experience, depreciation and amortization (operating) expenses show up in a wide variety of ways on the earnings statement. Sometimes you'll see a specific line in financial statements for depreciation expenses, especially for capital-intensive businesses.

## Reserves

*Reserves* are operating expenses, or charges, taken in anticipation of events that are likely to negatively affect financial results. Reserves can be set aside to cushion companies from things such as doubtful accounts receivable or other bad debts. Reserves are sometimes taken during the good years and used in unprofitable years to smooth out the earnings numbers and make a company's operations seem more consistent than they really are.

# Interest and taxes

Interest and taxes are the corporate world's equivalent of the proverbial sure things. So, not surprisingly, space is reserved for them on the earnings statement.

Companies invariably have some form of interest income or interest expense, and usually they have both. *Interest income* comes primarily from cash and short-term investments reflected on the balance sheet. *Interest expense* comes, again not surprisingly, from short- and long-term debt balances. Interest reporting is usually done as a *net interest* — that is, by combining interest income and expense into a net figure.

Taxes are quite complicated, just as they are for individuals, and the details go beyond the scope of this book. Normally an income-tax provision is recorded as a single line item on the earnings statement, although this consists of myriad federal, provincial, and local taxes put together.

You don't need to pay too much attention to taxes, but in today's economic climate you absolutely have to keep an eye on interest expenses. This is especially true for companies with high debt loads. These companies may be unable to make their debt payments (principal and/or interest), and may not be able to refinance their debt either. Such companies are at great risk of bankruptcy — just ask GM.

# Income from continuing operations

What results from netting out (deducting) interest and taxes from operating income is *income from continuing operations*. From this figure, you can get a good picture of company performance, not only from an operating perspective but also from a financial one. A close look at interest costs tells you, for instance, whether operating success (operating income) comes at a financial price (high interest expense). If operating income is low or declining and financing cost (interest) is large or increasing, look out below!

Income from continuing operations tells shareholders, in totality, what their investment return is after everyone, including the Canada Revenue Agency, is paid. Income from continuing operations is a good indicator of total business performance, but be aware of truly extraordinary events driving expenses or income.

## A bit of EBITDA

Some companies and financial analysts like to use *EBITDA,* or *earnings before interest, taxes, depreciation, and amortization,* as their business-health barometer. EBITDA fans consider it the truest indicator of operating success. EBITDA measures operating cash generated before interest charges (not from operations) are applied and before taxes and non-cash depreciation and amortization. In a sense, EBITDA is operating income before accountants, bankers, and governments take their share. EBITDA is sometimes looked at as a liquidity measure: positive-EBITDA companies can service their debt, but negative-EBITDA companies must borrow more.

Although the desire for so-called pure business measures makes EBITDA compelling,

many investors look at EBITDA as a dangerous shell game. Sooner or later, a company must replace assets. A business can't proceed on the assumption that its assets will last forever, which is the assumption that is made when depreciation and amortization are factored out. Ironically, this is especially true for the technology businesses that favour this measure but sit on top of some of the most rapidly depreciating assets! And as for interest and taxes, they're facts of business life. Who are we kidding, anyway? Watch out for glowing announcements of positive EBITDA when accompanied by losses on the earnings statement.

## Extraordinary items

*Extraordinary items* on an earnings statement are, according to accounting rules, to be tied to events that are atypical, irregular, and non-recurring. *Atypical* events aren't related to the usual activities of the business, and seldom occur. *Non-recurring* events aren't expected to occur again.

Extraordinary items commonly result from business closures (discontinued operations) or major restatements due to changes in accounting rules. They may result from debt restructurings or other complex financial transactions. They may result from layoffs and other employee transactions. Extraordinary items generally are *not* supposed to include asset write-downs (such as receivables, inventory, or intangibles), foreign currency gains or losses, or divestitures. They're not the elements described in our section about special items.

Our advice to you is to watch for extraordinary expenses that aren't so extraordinary. For example, companies that routinely have some kind of write-off every year or reporting period aren't doing as well as the investing community is being led to believe. If earnings are consistently $1 a share each quarter, with a consistent $4 write-off each year, the true value generated by the business is closer to zero than to four.

Also, *realized gains or losses* on investments are non-recurring items and ought to be segregated on the income statement if significant in amount. Some companies may try to create the impression that these are regular income sources by excluding them from extraordinary, unusual, or special items.

# Impairments, investments, and other write-downs

When the value of an asset changes significantly in the eyes of management, a company can elect to take a write-down recognizing the change. The *write-down* shows up as a decrease in asset value on the balance sheet for the asset category involved and (usually) as a one-time operating expense somewhere on the earnings statement. The rules for when and how to take these write-downs are, shall we say, flexible. The rules for writing down investment losses are particularly complex and beyond the scope of this book. The good news is that write-downs are normally reported as a separate line and are well documented in the notes.

For you as a stock investor, knowing the detail or amount may not be as important as knowing the pattern. Are these write-downs really one-time adjustments, or does the company continually overinvest in unproductive assets? Are companies quick to recognize mistakes, or do they push the financial impact of mistakes into the financial statements of future periods, toward ultimate fiscal oblivion? Write-down behaviour provides insight into management behaviour and effectiveness as well as overall business consistency — and should not be ignored. We discuss how companies may try to manipulate earnings through special items in Chapter 13. Common special items include restructuring charges, discontinued operations, and pension losses, and these are discussed below.

## Restructuring charges

*Restructuring charges* from continuing operations are those expenses — such as employee layoffs, maintenance, or early lease terminations — that are incurred when a company closes down or mothballs facilities, or writes off impaired assets. Because these assets would have been used up in the process of creating operating revenues, charges for restructuring these assets are usually factored into the calculation of net income. Massive employee layoffs and plant closings, like we still see today, may indicate that the company does not expect future business activity to support current employee levels or the operation of plants, machinery, and equipment. Restructuring charges include real cash expenses, not just allocations of expense.

Some companies take what is called the *big bath*. They write off as much as they can now so that future earnings will look better through higher reported profits. Be mindful of manipulation in this area, one we revisit in Chapter 14.

### Discontinued operations

When a company ceases part of its operations, it has to report current results, but separately from operating results. This reporting enables investors to make better comparisons from period to period and creates a fairer representation of results.

### Pension tension

After years of volatile and declining stock markets, many large pension plans are underfunded. Companies are now reporting pension losses instead of the gains they were accustomed to. These losses show up in a variety of forms, including special charges to earnings, cash flow, or equity, depending on the type of plan and the accounting rules involved. Although pension shortfalls may not be an immediate liquidity concern, they are often too large for investors to ignore. Keep an eye on pension expenses.

## Net income

Sales less COS, less operating expenses, less interest and taxes, less or plus extraordinaries and special items, give you a company's *net income* (sometimes referred to as *net earnings,* or *income attributable to common shareholders,* or some similar phrase). Net income represents the final net earnings result of the business on an accounting — not necessarily a cash — basis.

Net earnings are usually divided by the number of shares outstanding to arrive at *earnings per share* — the common barometer seen in nearly all financial reports. Most analysts and investors focus on *diluted* earnings per share, which figure in outstanding employee stock options and other equity grants beyond the actual shares outstanding.

# The Balance Sheet

The *balance sheet* can be a great indicator of the financial condition of a business. It is a snapshot of assets, liabilities, and what's left over at a point in time. It tells you about where the company has been and how well it did getting there.

Many investors and business analysts look closely for the following information in a balance sheet:

✔ The absolute and relative size of the numbers

✔ The makeup of assets, liabilities, and owner's equity

✔ Trends

✔ Valuation (assessing whether stated values reflect actual values)

Each of these examinations is done with an eye toward what the figure should be for a company in that line of business. A company such as Tim Hortons, which has frequent, small cash sales, shouldn't have a large accounts receivable balance. A retailer like The Bay should have sizeable inventories, but they shouldn't be out of line for the industry and for the company's category. A semiconductor manufacturer like Tundra has a large amount of capital equipment but should depreciate it aggressively to account for rapid technological change.

To determine whether balance-sheet numbers are in line, most analysts apply certain ratios to the numbers. Ratios serve to draw comparisons among companies, and among companies and their industry. By doing so, analysts detect whether a company's performance is better or worse than peers in its industry. Key ratios are presented and discussed in Appendix A.

## Cash and cash equivalents

For most businesses, cash is the best type of asset to have. With cash, no question exists about its value: Cash is cash! *Cash equivalents* are essentially cash. They're short-term marketable securities, such as GICs and term deposits, with little to no price risk that can be converted to cash at a moment's notice.

Value investors, in particular, like cash. Cash is security, and it forms the strongest part of the safety net that value investors seek. You should question a cash balance only if it appears excessive against the needs of the business. Also, take a look at the notes to the financial statements to make sure the marketable securities have not lost significant value and that they are, in fact, cash equivalents. Should a company put any extra cash to work in an investment or acquisition that might return more than the 3 or 4 percent it would get in a bank? And why isn't it being returned to shareholders as a dividend? Most companies don't retain that much cash, but occasionally it can become a red flag.

*Accounts receivable* represent funds that are owed to the business for products delivered or services performed. As individuals, everyone likes to be owed money — until we're owed *too much* money. The same attitude applies to corporations.

The type of industry that a company operates in dictates the amount of accounts receivable. Obviously a small-sale retailer such as Tim Hortons operates mostly on cash — you don't give them an IOU for those maple-dip donuts, do you? Most companies that sell directly to consumers have few accounts receivable.

Contrast this with companies that sell to other companies (business-to-business) or to distributors or retailers in the supply chain. Most of this business is done *on account,* meaning that first goods or services are delivered, and then invoices are sent. The billing process creates an accounts receivable that goes away only when the customer pays the bill. So suppliers to other businesses or distribution and sales channels often have significant accounts receivable.

How much of a company's asset base should be made up of accounts receivable? Current thinking suggests that cash businesses such as Tim Hortons have 5 percent or less of their asset base in accounts receivable. Traditional retailers and other business-to-consumer companies have 20 to 30 percent or more in receivables if they provide credit to customers through their own credit cards. Equipment manufacturers and other business-to-business companies sometimes carry receivables of 50 percent or more of their total assets.

For most business-to-business industries, accounts receivable are a part of doing business and, in a sense, a *cost* of doing business (cash is forgone to give the customer time to pay). The question is, "How much commitment to accounts receivable is necessary to support the business?" Be keenly aware of situations in which companies aren't collecting on their bills or are using accounts receivable to create credit incentives for otherwise questionable customers to buy their product.

To assign value to accounts receivable, pay attention to the following factors:

- ✔ **Size of accounts receivable relative to sales and other assets:** Is a company extending itself too much to sustain or grow the business? Industry comparisons and common sense dictate the answer.

- ✔ **Trends in accounts receivable:** Is a company continually owed more and more money, with potentially greater and greater exposure to non-payment? Look at a company's accounts-receivable history and compare the numbers to its sales figures.

> ✔ **Quality of accounts receivable:** Typically, most companies collect on more than 95 percent of their accounts-receivable balances, and thus they're almost as good as cash. But if accounts-receivable balances grow, and particularly if large reserves show up on the income statement (marked as "allowance for doubtful accounts" or some such), this is a red signal flare that no investor should miss.

Some financial statements show notes receivable as a separate balance-sheet item under current assets. *Notes receivable* are essentially a special form of accounts receivable — a promissory note for a significant amount that's extended to a specific firm for a specific reason. For the most part, notes receivable should be treated as normal accounts receivable, but it might be worth a quick glance at the note-holder and the terms of the note to spot anything unusual.

# Inventory

Inventory can be a critical, make-or-break asset, and it factors in company valuation. Companies live and die by their ability to effectively manage inventory.

*Inventory* is all valued material procured by a business and resold, with or without added value, to a customer. *Retail inventory* consists of goods bought, warehoused, and sold through stores. *Manufacturing inventory* consists of raw material, work in process, and finished goods awaiting shipment.

For most companies, the key to successfully managing inventory is to match it as closely as possible to sales. That is, the faster that procured inventory can be processed and sold, the better. Money tied up in inventory is money that can't be invested elsewhere in the business — this is referred to as an *opportunity cost* of doing business.

Valuing inventory can be challenging. Companies don't provide much information about their inventories. The most information you'll normally get is a breakdown of how much inventory there was at the beginning of the year, how much inventory was purchased (or manufactured) during the year, and how much was left over at the end of the year. Little else is known about what those inventories really are, or about their real value. A warehouse of outdated computer processors probably carries a book inventory value, but the computers aren't worth much on the market.

Inventory valuation is further affected by accounting methods employed by a firm. The method affects both balance-sheet carrying value and cost recognition on the income statement.

You need to appraise inventory balances for economic value and efficiency of use. Look at the size of the asset in an absolute sense and relative to the size and sales of the business. Look for trends, favourable and unfavourable, in inventory balances. Apply the inventory ratio analyses we discuss in Appendix A. Look at competitors and industry standards. Where possible, look at inventory quality and past track records for inventory obsolescence and resulting write-offs. And then be conservative. It often makes sense to assign a value of 50 to 75 percent, sometimes less, to inventory values appearing on a balance sheet. The auditors could easily have dropped the ball when they counted and valued a client company's inventory!

## Fixed assets

The balance sheet entry called *property, plant, and equipment* (PP&E) is pretty clear from the name. It refers to the fixed assets — land, buildings, machinery, fixtures, office and computer equipment, and similar items — owned by the firm for productive use. Depending on the industry, this line item may have a different name. Retail stores like Zellers, for example, don't have plants.

Valuation of PP&E can vary widely. The key to understanding PP&E value is to understand depreciation. *Depreciation* is an amount subtracted each year by accountants from an asset purchase price for normal wear and tear and technological obsolescence. Depreciation methods are discussed further later in this section, but for now all you need to know is that depreciation can affect underlying asset values substantially. Of course, the value of property, plant, and equipment can vary a lot by what it is, where it is, and how it's used. These factors, in turn, vary by industry and things specific to the company itself, such as its location.

Although most PP&E items are subject to depreciation charges, land is not. Is the value of land overstated on the books? Hardly. Land is normally carried at purchase, or acquisition, value. This affords a unique value-investing opportunity. Land purchased in the 1940s or 1950s is often worth much more today than it was back then, but it is seldom reflected in the books. There may be some real hidden gems lurking below the balance sheets of forestry, mining, and certain old-line industrial corporations.

Accountants have a variety of accepted methods for assigning depreciation dollars at their disposal. A detailed discussion of depreciation and depreciation methods is accounting stuff that's well beyond the scope of this book. But you may find it useful to recognize two major groupings of methods for assigning depreciation dollars: accelerated and straight-line depreciation.

The choice of depreciation methods is important. *Accelerated depreciation* allows greater deductions in the earlier years of the life of an asset, resulting in the most conservative PP&E asset valuations. It also results in the most conservative view of earnings and allows more room for future net earnings growth because you can assume that a greater portion of asset depreciation is behind you.

But some companies may deliberately prop up current earnings by employing *straight-line depreciation* methods, which spread the costs evenly over the life of an asset. Watch for companies switching over to straight-line from accelerated methods. Depreciation methods are disclosed in the notes section of the statements.

Depreciation is an accounting — not a cash — expense. No cheque is cut for depreciation. Instead, the cheque is cut when the asset is purchased. Depreciation is the leading difference between stated earnings and cash flows, and it can mean the difference between survival and failure for a company recording net income losses. Cash flow, unburdened by depreciation, may still be positive. But look out below. Cash consumed to keep a losing business afloat may not be available the next time a key piece of equipment needs to be replaced. Reporting methods that downplay depreciation or ignore it altogether, such as the *pro forma* reporting craze, indicate trouble. For more info on this issue, see Chapter 13.

# *Investments*

Besides buying marketable securities that are easy to sell, many companies commit surplus cash to more substantial long-term investments. These company investments can serve many purposes: to achieve returns as any other investor would, to participate in the growth of a related or unrelated industry, or to eventually obtain control of another company. Long-term investments are harder to dispose of than marketable securities, but they can be very profitable during the holding period. Favourable tax treatment of Canadian dividends and gains makes investing in other Canadian companies more attractive still.

Investments can be valued in many ways, but ultimately they all boil down to historical cost or market valuation. Watch out for declining fair values and particularly for large *gross unrealized losses* — future write-offs and asset value impairment loom large. Gauge the size of investments on the balance sheet, look for details, and understand management's intent in making the investments.

## Intangible assets

Asset valuation gets *really* fun for Canadian investors, and especially for value investors, when the discussion turns to intangibles, also sometimes referred to as *soft* assets. *Intangibles* are non-physical assets that are critical in acquiring and maintaining sales and producing a competitive edge. Intangibles include patents, copyrights, franchises, brand names, and trademarks. Also included is the all-encompassing *goodwill* often acquired when buying (and overpaying for) other companies. Goodwill is the premium paid over and above the net asset value (tangible and intangible assets minus liabilities) of a company. Such premiums are paid for various reasons, like to outbid another company in a takeover battle, or as a gesture of confidence in the future of the acquirer.

Placing a financial value on these ethereal and nebulous brand-related assets is difficult, but accountants seem to be able to pull it off. If a historical cost exists, accountants may carry the intangible at that cost. This is often the case with goodwill from company acquisitions or mergers.

The key to assessing intangible assets is to understand their carrying value and the amortization technique. Intangible assets should all be amortized, because patents expire, brand value may be diluted, and so forth. Goodwill from acquisitions most certainly — at least for now — must be amortized. Like depreciation, valuation depends heavily on the method of amortization. Basically the same choice is available between straight-line and accelerated amortization, and the chosen method is disclosed somewhere in the financial-statement notes (refer to "Fixed assets," earlier in this chapter for the difference between accelerated and straight-line methods).

Intangibles are subject to a great deal of discretion in their accounting, and their sources and form can be numerous and highly variable from one company to the next. Cast a skeptical eye on large goodwill accounts in particular, especially if a company seems reluctant to write them off.

But with the advent of modern technology and marketing, the ideas of intellectual capital and brand equity are part of a company's value and cannot simply be ignored. In fact, for some companies, these intangibles may represent their greatest value. What is the value of the Coca-Cola Company without the brand name? Or the value of Microsoft without its lock on PC operating-system design? Such brands and locks often ultimately produce the best profit streams and best value. Contemporary stock investors need a clear understanding of intangible assets and should not just dismiss them in an offhand way.

# Payables

Almost everyone, individuals or corporations, has *payables,* defined as money owed to others for products purchased or services rendered. The liability is created when the service or product arrives; a cash payment follows later to discharge the liability. Nearly all companies maintain a regular balance of current accounts payable, interest payable, and the like.

If payment is received in advance, as with a deposit, the unearned portion is tracked as a liability. Sometimes *contingent liabilities* may be recorded, as in warranty claims expected to be paid but not yet actualized.

You can do little with current liabilities except subtract them out from intrinsic company value. But also realize that current liabilities aren't necessarily a bad thing and that they can result in higher effective returns on ownership capital with relatively low cost and risk.

# Long-term liabilities

Long-term corporate liabilities are really no different than those in personal finance: They represent contracted commitments to pay back a sum of money over time, with interest. For the individual, they come in the form of loans and mortgages; for the corporation, they occur more often in the form of tradable notes and bonds. The result, however, is the same in both cases.

As for short-term liabilities, you don't need to look too closely at the amount or quality of these liabilities. Trends can be important, however. Relying increasingly on long-term debt may be a sign of trouble, especially these days. The company may not be making ends meet and may be having trouble raising capital in these tight credit markets, which is never a good sign.

In addition, a company that's constantly changing, restructuring, or otherwise tinkering with long-term debt may be sending tacit signals of trouble. The company may be seeking concessions from lenders behind the scenes. In any event, attention paid to this kind of activity diverts attention from the core business, which is not a good thing and should be a warning flag for value investors.

Excessive use of debt signals potential danger if things don't turn out the way a company expects them to. Leverage is a good thing when things are going a company's way. Debt financing can be used to produce more product for more markets — and, thus, more profit and, in the end, a bigger business. Return to owners is proportionately higher: Their investment stays the same while the returns grow. But as everyone knows, this can work the other way.

Stock investors don't like surprises, and a company with uncertain prospects and a lot of debt is very risky.

Again, factor in liabilities as a negative factor in company and stock valuation and look for unfavourable trends or the excessive use of long-term debt. Generally, liabilities don't require the close study that you might give to assets.

## Owner's equity

Because you're contemplating making an investment in a company, isn't owner's equity the most important balance-sheet item? You and other investors are, in essence, either directly or indirectly contributing capital. This capital is in turn converted into an asset *and then* in turn converted into revenue and profit to produce a return to the owner. You're making a decision to allocate capital to a company that, for its part, tries to do the best job allocating capital to opportunities that produce the best return.

*Owner's equity,* or *book value,* is the sum of paid-in capital and retained earnings — assets (which can be valued and reported with a degree of latitude) minus liabilities (which occur at face value). Thus, book-value reporting is done with a degree of latitude. Value investors talk about three different book value measures:

- ✔ **Book value as owner's equity:** Total book assets minus liabilities
- ✔ **Tangible book value:** Total book value minus all or part of intangibles
- ✔ **Book value per share:** Accounting book value divided by the number of common shares outstanding

All three of these measures crop up in value-investing discussions and papers. Be alert, because sometimes they're used interchangeably.

Like liabilities, the equity portion of the balance sheet is critical to a company's functioning, but it really requires relatively little scrutiny on your part. We take you on a short tour but avoid the tedious discussions of classes of stock, par value, and the like that befuddle so many readers of financial stories. For this discussion, owner's equity consists of two things: paid-in capital — a fancy term for stock — and retained earnings.

### Paid-in capital

*Paid-in capital* represents the total value paid into the company by its owners — its shareholders. It gets a little complicated with the discussion of par value and additional paid-in capital. Total paid-in capital represents capital actually paid into the company at initial or subsequent company stock sales and has nothing to do with market price or market value. In and of itself, you need pay little attention to this item.

### Retained earnings

*Retained earnings* are profits from past operating periods that are retained or reinvested in the business. Technically speaking, company profits belong to the shareholders, but it becomes management's option to decide whether to actually pay them out. Typically, managers think that they can invest the money more effectively than their shareholders. Stock investors of all stripes are betting that they're right!

So long as a company's business is viable, shareholders probably want to see retained earnings as high as possible, and growing. It's a capital allocation game — the earnings are better suited to that company's purpose than anywhere else. By investing in the company, you've already decided that, so you may as well keep your money on the table.

So generally when it comes to retained earnings, more is better — especially if accompanied by a reasonable dividend policy in which management *is* sharing some of the spoils with the owners. On the other hand, watch for rapidly declining or, worse, negative retained-earnings balances. Negative retained earnings are almost a sure sign of trouble, usually brought on by asset values declining faster than expected, excessive debt, an overinflated stock offering price, or a combination of the three. As a value investor, you should view negative retained earnings as another bright-red signal flare.

# The Statement of Cash Flows

Earlier, we mentioned the difference in timing between certain accounting transactions and related cash collections and disbursements. Build it and ship it this month and then record the revenue, even though cash payments may not arrive until months later. Buy and pay for a million-dollar machine today, but expense it over its production life through depreciation. Amortize a patent and never write a cheque at all.

These transactions and a host of others create differences between accounting earnings and cash measures of business activity. A business needs cash to operate. A business generating positive cash flow is much healthier than one that's bleeding cash and borrowing to stay afloat. Because of non-cash items, earnings statements don't give a complete cash picture. So stock investors look for a statement of cash flows as a standard part of the financial-statement package.

Sometimes the statement of cash flows is called *sources and uses of funds* or something similar. Accountants use the terms *funds* and *cash* interchangeably.

The statement of cash flows tracks cash obtained in, or used in, three separate kinds of business activity: operating, investing, and financing. It also tracks dividends paid to shareholders. It is a very important piece of the financial-statement puzzle.

## Cash flow from operations

Similar to operating income, *cash flow from operations* tells you what cash is generated from, or *provided by,* normal business operation and what cash is consumed by, or *used for,* the business. ("Provided by" and "used for" are the terms used on the cash-flow statement.) Net income from continuing operations is thus the starting point.

To the net income, add (or subtract) the *adjustments to reconcile net income to operating cash flow.* Here is where you *add back* depreciation and amortization dollars; that is, dollars that came out of accounting income but had no corresponding cash payment. So far, so good.

Next comes *cash provided by (used for) current assets and current liabilities.* If this is familiar territory and you understand how increases in current assets and liabilities affect cash, it makes sense to you that an inventory increase consumed some cash. Increases in liabilities *provide* cash. Decreases in liabilities *use* cash. (This concept is easier to grasp: It's a single cash transaction to pay a bill.) Increases in current assets (other than cash) *use* cash. Decreases in assets (as in a net decrease in inventory) *provide* cash.

## Cash flow from investing activities

Cash flow from operations tells what cash was generated in the normal course of business and by changes in current asset and liability (working capital) accounts on the balance sheet. But what about cash used to invest in the business? Or used to invest in other businesses? What about cash acquired by selling investments in other businesses? The second section of the statement of cash flow provides this information.

For most growing companies, cash flow from operations should absolutely be positive, but cash flow from investing activities is often negative. Why? Is this okay? Yes, because growing companies need more physical investments — property, plant, and equipment (PP&E) — to sustain growth. Generally, negative cash flows in PP&E suggest that the company is satisfied with its growth plan and feels that funds must be invested elsewhere for a maximum investment return.

## "Free" cash flow

Free cash flow sounds like what we all want in our lives, eh? Positive cash flow, and it's free! Free cash flow is a good indication of what a company really has left over after meeting obligations, and thus the flow could theoretically return to shareholders.

*Free cash flow* is defined as net after-tax earnings, plus depreciation and amortization and other non-cash items, minus capital expenditures, minus (or plus) changes in working capital (current assets and liabilities).

Earn income, pay for the costs of doing business, and then what's left over is yours to keep as an owner. Pretty simple. Free cash flow is a much more realistic long-term view of business success and potential owner proceeds than EBITDA (which doesn't factor out as many cash costs). Many investors, especially value investors, use free cash flow as the basis for calculating intrinsic value.

## Cash flow from financing activities

*Investing activities* tell what a firm does with cash to increase or decrease fixed assets and assets not directly related to operations. *Financing activities* tell where a firm has obtained capital in the form of cash to fund the business. Proceeds from the sale of company shares or bonds (long-term debt) are a *source* of cash. If a company pays off a bond issue or buys back its own stock, that's a *use* of cash for financing.

A consistent cash flow from financing activities indicates excessive dependence on credit or equity markets. Typically, this figure oscillates between negative and positive. A big negative spike reflects a big bond issue or stock sale. In such a case, check to see if the resulting cash is used for investments in the business (probably okay) or to make up for a shortfall in operating cash flow (probably not okay). If the generated cash flows straight to the cash balance, you should wonder why a company is selling shares or increasing debt just to increase cash, although often the reasons are difficult to know. Perhaps an acquisition? Perhaps something more troubling?

# Introducing Ratio Analysis

Financial statements often contain an overwhelming amount of information and numbers. As a result, financial analysts and accountants have developed ratios to help them tease out the story behind the numbers. Ratio analysis can help you put things in proper context. They measure the financial health of a company from year to year, or quarter to quarter. A company's overall financial health is driven by factors like profitability, debt load, and operating efficiency. Ratios exist to specifically measure these and other factors.

We explore ratios in more detail in Appendix A. In the meantime, we just want you to take heart and not be overwhelmed by all the numbers. Many of the investment Web sites we introduce to you in Appendix B and elsewhere in this book also publish key ratios that you can (and should) use to compare one company to another. This way, you don't have to physically line up companies' financial statements beside each other to compare their relative performance.

Why compare the ratios of one company to another, or to an industry-average ratio? When a company's ratios differ from those of similar companies or industry averages, they can serve as early-warning signals of problems — or opportunities. Even without inter-company comparisons, ratios provide you with a lens to bring into clearer focus the information that comes from reams of financial statements. Ratios explain the relationship between two or more numbers, thus providing you with scale and context. Used properly, ratios tell a powerful overall story about the financial condition of a company.

# Chapter 13

# Silly Income-Statement Tricks

• • • • • • • • • • • • • • • • • • • • • • • • • • • • • • • • • • • • • • • • • • • •

*In This Chapter*

▶ Introducing creative accounting (sounds like a good thing, but it's not)

▶ Revealing revenue overstatement

▶ Exposing how companies hide expenses

▶ Exploring how companies use stock options without cost

▶ Understanding how companies smooth income with reserves

▶ Looking out for the amazing disappearing tax asset

▶ Finding out about pro forma accounting and disclosure

• • • • • • • • • • • • • • • • • • • • • • • • • • • • • • • • • • • • • • • • • • • •

**S**tock investors must see beyond the obvious when reviewing financial statements. All too many companies are quick to use *aggressive accounting* techniques that make their financial statements look better than they really are. Nortel, Enron, and WorldCom quickly come to mind. Aggressive accounting refers to recognizing revenue too quickly, and expenses too slowly. It also means overestimating asset values, and underestimating or hiding liabilities.

Acting as a company watchdog isn't enough for you as a stock investor. You should be a forensic investor, acting more like a bloodhound sniffing out indicators of *window dressing* (another term that describes aggressive accounting), or even fraud. You, as a smart investor, have to look under the hood at some important details in the financial statements. You also have to see how financial-statement messages relate to the broader issues facing the company to be able to spot inconsistencies and aggressive accounting.

Most Canadian stock investors are reluctant to review financial statements and related footnotes because of their complexity. It's not fun. This is understandable, because a thorough knowledge of the financial statements of a company of any size can require lots of time and effort. However, by using an efficient approach — which we outline in this chapter — you can quickly glean the key information about a company's financial condition. You can determine a fairer representation of its current state and future prospects by focusing on certain indicators of aggressive accounting.

If the message conveyed by financial statements is bad, some companies will be tempted to use creative accounting techniques to hide damaging information or to provide a twisted and distorted picture of their financial condition. This chapter shows you how companies may try to do this, with a focus on the income statement. We also show you how to spot aggressive accounting and assess its impact. (Keep in mind that accounting transactions don't affect just the income statement or just the balance sheet. When a transaction affects one financial statement, it eventually impacts the other.) Therefore, approach financial statements, and the companies they represent, with a healthy skepticism and be alert to window dressing.

## How Did All This Start?

Recent reports of high-profile company failures, such as those noted above, have put the spotlight on aggressive accounting. Investors and analysts have renewed the call for audited financial statements that show a fair picture of a company's financial performance and position. The main purpose of an audit is to ensure that the financial statements fairly present the company's financial condition and that they comply with generally accepted accounting principles (GAAP).

However, some auditors were not doing their job, which was to provide an objective opinion on financial statements. They gave clean bills of health to some very sick companies. Analysts fared no better; many were too busy giving buy recommendations on those very same troubled companies. The stage was set for a great big fall that even Humpty Dumpty could not duplicate.

Stock investors expect a company to provide meaningful disclosure about where it has been, where it is, and (to a certain extent) where it is going. Without solid financial statements, the value of the company in investors' eyes may diminish, and they will lose confidence in the company. Companies without solid results are easily tempted into using aggressive accounting.

The problem of creative accounting is not a new one. Even today, the market remains unforgiving of companies that miss their estimates. Seeing a public company fail to meet its so-called estimate numbers by mere pennies and watching it lose more than 5 percent of its stock value in one day is not uncommon. Pressures to make the numbers may result in a company taking part in a certain amount of earnings manipulation — the subject of this chapter.

How are earnings manipulated? We present details in this chapter about some of the common methods of window dressing that are used to boost current-year earnings or smooth out income. The following points introduce you to several of these methods:

✔ Recording revenue before it is earned

✔ Creating fictitious revenue

✔ Boosting profits with non-recurring transactions

✔ Shifting current expenses to a later period

✔ Shifting future expenses to an earlier period

How can you tell from a bird's-eye view that a company may be heading for trouble? Broad indicators include

✔ **Earnings-trend problems:** One of the most significant indicators of window dressing is a downward trend in earnings. Companies disclose earnings for the last two to three years in the annual report, so they don't focus just on one year's net income.

✔ **Reduced and inconsistent cash flow:** Management can exploit the leeway provided by GAAP in several ways to create the illusion of increased earnings. We discuss some key window-dressing approaches in this chapter. You can use the cash-flow statement to verify the validity of earnings. If net income is moving up while cash flow from operations is falling, something may be out of order.

✔ **Excessive debt:** Debt load is a critical factor in determining whether a company can survive these difficult times. Companies saddled with too much debt lack the financial flexibility to respond to emergencies or take advantage of opportunities. Investors should pay special attention to a company's debt-to-equity ratio and the total debt-to-shareholders' or debt-to-owners' equity. (We discuss ratios in Appendix A.) The level of shareholders' or owners' equity on the statements should exceed the amount of debt by a significant amount; debt payments should be easily serviced.

✔ **Overstated inventories and receivables:** Accounts receivable and inventory ratios reveal a lot, and they're also discussed in Appendix A. Customers may not be paying their bills, or the company may be stuck with aging merchandise. Liquidity problems will eventually arise. Overstated inventories and receivables are often at the heart of window dressing, or even corporate fraud, and can hurt future profits. Trends over time are also important here. (We discuss accounts-receivable and inventory issues in Chapter 14.)

✔ **Auditor-switching:** Auditor dismissals and the financial condition of a company can be interdependent. Firms in the midst of financial distress switch auditors more often than healthy companies do.

# Revealing Revenue Manipulation

Companies sometimes try to boost earnings by manipulating the recognition of revenue. They recognize it before a sale is actually complete, before the product or service is delivered to a customer, or at a time when the customer still has substantial options to terminate, void, or delay the sale. Companies may be tempted to speed revenue recognition — or to simply create it!

## Accelerating sales

Companies often negotiate special payment terms and other incentives to entice customers to shift next fiscal year's first-quarter purchases into the current fiscal year's income statement. The existence of big bonuses for sales staff provides added incentive to meet current-year sales targets. Moving (or *stuffing*) large amounts of inventory onto the shoulders of retailers and distributors also avoids having excess inventory in company warehouses, which costs money.

Be mindful that although accelerating revenue in the current year may improve profitability this year, the ultimate result is a sales decline showing up on the following year's first-quarter income statement. Management may conveniently explain this away as a "seasonal trend."

## Paying with cash, credit card, or stock?

Beyond the above loan arrangements, it sometimes happens that companies accept a customer's stock as consideration for goods and services sold. Companies occasionally buy stakes in other companies to help influence future product sales or to cultivate strategic relationships. Be mindful of this uncommon but very risky practice.

## Creating revenue out of thin air

Revenues can also be created. Yup. Created — without a bona fide sales transaction. Companies that are audacious enough to do this can artificially swap services and book them as sales. At the same time, the buyer classifies the swap as capital outlays on the balance sheet. In accounting-speak, the income statement gets a revenue credit (good) and the balance sheet gets a debit (also good).

Similar sleight of hand can be found in the practice of booking as revenues customers' questionable contractual obligations — which may never be collected. This violates the GAAP principle of booking revenues only when collection is likely and the amount of revenue is determinable. Under these scenarios, no cash is exchanged or received, but accounting earnings are artificially increased, and assets are inflated.

## Moving revenue in mysterious ways

Some companies are so fixated on the top line that they distort the way revenue is presented on the income statement. Analysts and stock investors place a lot of emphasis on revenue growth, so the incentive is there for companies to window-dress revenues.

### Gross and net

Several companies, especially those in the Internet sector, book revenues that actually belong to someone else! Some travel Web site operators and online auction sites have a revenue figure that represents the aggregate value of all products and services sold or brokered. They don't net out the portion of those revenues that belong to the actual service providers represented on their site. Such an accounting practice is also disturbing because many analysts and investors still value stocks, in part, on the basis of revenue growth. They rely on accurate top lines!

### Coupon clipping

Coupon promotions are common techniques used by retailers — especially Internet e-tailers — that wish to promote higher sales volumes. Most companies that engage in window dressing exclude the value of promotional giveaways when booking revenue. They have found a more exciting approach.

Assume for a moment that someone buys a music CD for $30 and uses a $10 coupon to make the purchase. Under GAAP, just $20 of revenue ought to be booked. But some retailers would book $30 in revenue and then charge the $10 in promotional costs to marketing expenses. This may result in artificially higher sales and gross margin, better top-line comments from financial analysts, and an inflated share price. Can you spell "distortion"?

# Hiding Expenses: Capitalizing Costs

You can turn a garden variety of what should be expenses into assets by depreciating and amortizing capital assets (resources that last over one year) more slowly than otherwise required under the principle of reasonableness (in other words, by easing it slowly into expenses). With certain costs incurred, management can judgmentally overestimate a period of useful benefit to longer than one year. That would let management justify recording part of it on the balance sheet (as an asset) instead of on the income statement (as an expense).

## Small fry

One example of capitalizing expenses is paying for computer peripheral equipment or office supplies and then spreading the costs over three or more years. These types of expenses rarely benefit periods longer than a year or two and should probably be expensed when incurred, depending on the circumstances. Another example is advertising, where accounting standards state that advertising expenses should not be capitalized. GAAP is also specific about start-up costs (like store pre-opening costs) and states that these should be expensed instead of capitalized. Be alert to a series of smaller costs that have not been deducted on the income statement and that show up on the balance sheet. It may indicate that management is not shy to use aggressive accounting in more significant areas, as well.

## Big fry

On a larger scale, some companies set up associated companies to perform R&D work for them. The original company gets to avoid expensing potentially massive research costs by having the associated company assume the R&D costs (and related revenue). After this type of accounting sleight of hand, the cost of R&D essentially disappears from the books.

R&D can also be manipulated the other way, to help a company take a special charge against income. (Special charges to write off assets are discussed in Chapter 14.) Briefly, when assets are acquired in a business combination, they may be assigned their fair values. The acquirer of R&D-related assets accounts for the transaction by judgmentally determining these assets have "future uses." R&D assets are then capitalized, and all others are expensed when the deal closes. So it's somewhat easy to justify expensing these R&D costs.

## Related-party transactions

A *related party* is one that can exercise control or significant influence over the management or operating policies of another party. A problem can arise, for instance, if dealings take place with non-public companies that are controlled by management. In some cases, these non-public companies can get saddled with expenses in order for the public company to look great.

Canadian stock investors need to take a closer look at these invisible enterprises that might be propping up a firm. The notes to financial statements disclose the nature, extent, amount, and timing of related-party transactions during the year.

# *Sussing Out Stock Options*

You have to be vigilant in assessing the negative effects of stock options. The negative effects happen in the form of the dilution of shares and, thus, your stake in the company. When more shares are issued due to someone exercising options, the share of profits and equity that applies to you gets dwindled down.

Alan Greenspan (former chairperson of the U.S. Federal Reserve) and his successor, Ben Bernanke, mentioned this issue; economist Peter Schiff has talked about it for years. Will the economy, investment community, shareholders, and companies themselves be better served with a requirement that the economic value of stock options be expensed on financial statements?

## *How options work*

An option gives an employee the right, but not the obligation, to buy a share of stock in the future at a predetermined price. The more the price of the stock goes up, the more valuable the right becomes. Options give employees a stake in their company's future. They also give a young (or established) company the chance and ability to grow; the company can use its scarce cash funds for growth, not for compensation expenses.

## *What to watch for*

Upcoming accounting rules under IFRS — international financial reporting standards that are to come into full force in 2012 — provide that the market value of an option is required to be expensed on a U.S. or Canadian public company's income statement. Until then, a company can opt not to do this. If it opts out, a public company is still required to report its earnings per share on the income statement on a basic basis and on a diluted basis. *Diluted* reporting takes into account the potential reduction in the ownership of existing shareholders due to the granting and exercising of options. Many market experts believe that the failure to expense stock options has introduced a significant distortion in reported earnings that has grown with the increasing prevalence of this form of compensation.

Admittedly, nothing's nefarious about encouraging stock ownership among employees. But those who call for change argue that stock-option compensation causes company management to focus on driving up the stock price in the short term to provide continuing value for their option programs. These actions aren't focused on growing long-term shareholder wealth. Canadian stock investors need to keep an eye on the extent, timing, and reasonableness of stock options in a company.

Expensing option costs helps to present a more accurate and conservative picture of a company's financial performance. Several North American surveys found that many companies would have seen reported earnings trimmed by as much as 200 percent had stock-option expenses been recognized on their income statements. It's a big enchilada of an issue!

Executives may be tempted to grant options *before* good news is released to the public. Be wary of this very real risk!

# Reviewing Reserves

Some companies use unrealistic assumptions to estimate certain liabilities. In doing so, they hide accruals in cookie jars during the good times and reach into them as needed in the bad times. Management can smooth income to show consistency, or a desired trend that investors like to see.

Companies will build up reserves on the balance sheet (as temporary offsets to assets) during highly profitable periods for things such as

- Insurance losses
- Lawsuits
- Loan losses
- Product and service warranty costs
- Sales returns and service guarantees

A company builds reserves for these items by booking an expense each period, thus offsetting the expense by increasing a reserve liability on the balance sheet.

Think of reserve liabilities as the company saying, "I don't know how much in insurance losses and product returns pertains to this year's sales, but I do know that it will be something. So I'll book an expense on the income statement (in the amount of the estimated liability) and offset this with a liability on the balance sheet that may occur and will have to be paid off sometime in the future." When the actual loss occurs, the payment then reduces the reserve liability, not the income statement.

The opportunity to manipulate earnings comes in the form of guessing how much has to be written off as expenses, regardless of actual write-offs. In other words, reserves are judgmentally determined amounts, so a company wishing to raise profits may manipulate the reserves to accomplish this. It's not too difficult for management to justify a change in reserves to the auditor. This may simply be based on a change in the business environment. But it could also be a blatant attempt by management to channel profits to the income statement.

# Taking On Tax Losses

With the economy in major doldrums over the last few years, many companies suffered losses. This often qualified them for tax credits to be received in a future tax period. Many companies recognize this as a special item (revenue) on the income statement in the current year to boost the bottom line. A tax asset is also booked on the balance sheet.

Invariably, after a year or so, window dressers make the tax asset (tax credit receivable) disappear — the company reevaluates the likelihood of actually qualifying for the credit and determines that it stands no chance of collecting from CRA. The tax asset gets written off, a special charge is created (in the year a company would prefer to see a charge), and the investor is left with even more distorted financial statements.

# Pro Forma Performance

If normal accounting manipulation — the type performed within GAAP rules — wasn't enough to ruin your stock-investing day, consider the latest trend in window dressing: the pro forma earnings statement. Pro forma reports have become almost a public-relations alternative to the classic GAAP earnings statement.

## Picky, picky

Responding in part to investor and analyst pressure and in part to a fairly loose (to date) compliance environment, companies started using pro forma reporting as a press-friendly reporting alternative.

Actually, *pro forma* has been in the accounting vocabulary for a long time. Pro forma statements were originally used as "unofficial" statements designed to project — not report — company performance. Companies planning to go public or merge with another company issued a pro forma set of statements to give an investor a clue as to what forward-looking statements might look like. But no longer are pro forma statements limited to special situations, as today's press-friendly financial reporting sometimes does an end run right around GAAP.

With pro forma reporting, companies can spin their business pretty much as they please. They include certain things but leave out other things — such as supposed unusual and nonrecurring expenses — that they consider irrelevant to assessing performance. From your perspective as a stock investor, pro forma reporting not only undermines statement quality but also makes it difficult to compare one company to another.

Pro forma is really an extension of the EBITDA reporting concept made popular in the 1980s (see Chapter 12). Although EBITDA made numbers look better than they were by excluding financing costs and asset recovery, at least the application of EBITDA was consistent from one company to the next.

Companies routinely omit option costs, investment gains and losses, asset impairment or write-downs, goodwill amortization, and other non-cash items. In that these expenses are non-cash, value investors can wink and turn their heads a little — for a while. But we've occasionally seen some very real cash expenses, such as interest expense, get written out of the pro forma. Bad form!

## The good news is . . .

Although companies can release to the public pretty much any pro forma report they please, there's a catch: They must also provide GAAP-compliant numbers in releases and submit full GAAP-compliant reports to regulators. So you have the pro forma reports, good enough for many investors and reflective of how companies want to see themselves. You also have GAAP financial statements. But you must dig deeper to understand the difference between the pro forma and GAAP — and why the company wants to maintain that difference.

From a stock-investing perspective, pro forma reports are obviously dangerous in their concealment of long-term asset recovery and similar expenses. In addition, they make it difficult to compare one company to another — each company reports different things, and companies may report differently from one period to the next. Sorting out these differences can be very time consuming.

We never said that basing stock investing on financial statements was easy.

# Chapter 14

# Silly Balance-Sheet Tricks

· · · · · · · · · · · · · · · · · · · · · · · · · · · · · · · · · · · · · · · · · · · · · · · · · ·

## In This Chapter

▶ Playing with payouts

▶ Manipulating inventory

▶ Writing off acquisitions

▶ Claiming massive losses

▶ Transferring debt away from the balance sheet

▶ Considering the impact of pension plans

▶ Identifying the tricks of the trade

· · · · · · · · · · · · · · · · · · · · · · · · · · · · · · · · · · · · · · · · · · · · · · · · · ·

*W*hat with all the media hype about earnings estimates and revenue forecasts, you'd think the balance sheet was an annoying add-on to the financial statements. However, many in the accounting world believe that the balance sheet ought to be the prime focus for anyone who analyzes financial statements. Perhaps the tide is finally turning.

Think about how most Canadians view their finances. To many, their job is like an income statement — it's the main source of revenue that goes on to pay living expenses. Their bank account is like a balance sheet — it's a reflection of what's been saved and what is owed to others. If someone loses his or her job, and if the economy stays in a prolonged downturn, what becomes more important? The balance sheet, of course. How much is in the savings account until another job comes along? Is the cash in that account enough to meet mortgage and credit card payments?

Clearly, both the income statement and the balance sheet are important. It's just that they paint pictures that are of different importance to different investors. If you seek value, you'll tend to focus on balance sheets. If you're a growth and momentum investor, you'll likely throw caution to the wind and prioritize those revenue-growing companies that may return 5 percent tomorrow.

Regardless whether your focus is on the income statement or the balance sheet, the balance sheet is still important. It's also another area that management may be tempted to manipulate.

# Accounts Receivable: Allowing for Returned Stuff

When the values of *customer-receivable balances* (what customers still owe a company at any given point in time) are in doubt — and most to a certain extent are — management sets up a provision called the *allowance for doubtful accounts*. It does this by expensing the amount of the reserve to the income statement and creating a corresponding liability on the balance sheet. The liability offsets the accounts-receivable balance. The allowance for doubtful accounts is intended to smooth out the income statement impact of bad debts. Instead of charging accounts-receivable losses to the income statement as they occur, which could cause wild swings in income, companies charge a stable amount of bad-debts expense to the income statement each period. Later, when a specific customer's account is actually identified for writing off, the allowance account gets charged, not the expense account on the income statement.

In practice, the allowance for doubtful accounts (a reserve) is an area that involves considerable judgment on management's part and is therefore susceptible to manipulation to boost earnings. At the end of the day, however, the exact amount of actual future bad debts is always unknown.

## Message to auditor: It's the economy, stupid!

A company wishing to squeeze a bit more income into its income-statement earnings may reduce the annual expense slightly to put an upward slant on earnings. This wouldn't be an exorbitant reduction in bad-debt expense, but rather a subtle shift. When the auditors with the green visors and thick glasses come in at the end of the year, the finance people with the Hugo Boss suits will justify their rationale for the allowance account. But that rationale could be a change from reserving 100 percent of doubtful customers' balances to reserving only 40 percent. They may come up with and convey a slick justification — like a "recovering economy" — to believe that 60 percent or more of the balances will probably be collected.

## Red flags and other signs

Stock investors can spot red flags with the allowance account only if sufficient detailed information is available. For example, you can examine the relationship between the allowance for doubtful accounts and gross receivables (adding back the allowance for doubtful accounts to net receivables).

Has the allowance as a percentage of gross receivables declined over the years? If so, that could be a sign of manipulation (the company has not maintained adequate allowances). It could also simply mean an improved collection of receivables. Check out the notes to financial statements, which may provide a breakout of the allowance for doubtful accounts and gross accounts receivable.

If sufficient detail is provided in the income statement, you may be able to spot red flags by analyzing the bad-debt expense (as percentage of sales) trend. Look for significant reduction in the debt-expense percentage from year to year. If the bad-debt expense percentage reduces significantly, try to assess the reason for the reduction. This may be difficult to do, but if you spot window dressing elsewhere chances are good that it's happening in this area, too.

# Increasing Profits through Inventories

Inventory is another area ripe for aggressive accounting. Under GAAP, the last-in, first-out (LIFO) method of accounting for inventory charges the most current prices of inventory to the cost of sales on the income statement. During these recent years of gradually rising prices, the value companies assign to the cost of sales has been higher because the sales of pricier inventory have been transferred into their cost-of-sales figures. In addition, keep in mind that industries exist that sell increasingly costly goods. Oil, pharmaceutical, and many mining companies still stand to benefit from window dressing their inventories because prices in those sectors never seem to come down or stop rising. We also discuss the impact of inventory in Chapter 12.

If a company wishes to increase its cash flow (by reducing taxes paid due to lower taxable income), it can use the LIFO method of accounting (assuming rising prices) for inventory. It will manage its inventory levels to keep the cost of sales higher. The lower the ending inventory (the less inventory placed in the balance sheet), the lower the net and taxable income. Voila, less taxes to CRA!

One way to increase profits is through the reserve for inventory obsolescence, which is similar to the allowance for doubtful receivable accounts. It, too, is used to smooth out the net-income impact of writing off old, mouldy, obsolete inventory. Typically, amounts are properly and gradually written off each quarter (which increases the reserve for inventory obsolescence on the balance sheet), instead of irregularly and suddenly recording the write-down to the income statement when the inventory is deemed obsolete. That's good accounting practice. But any company seeking to boost profits may revisit the account reserved for inventory obsolescence to determine whether they can justify reducing the allowance — thus increasing the bottom line.

Auditors will review the validity and reasonableness of inventory reserves and any changes to inventory accounting policy to detect any manipulation. But in this area, you'll never get close enough to see anything unusual for yourself. This is an example of how much reliance all stock investors place on the work of external auditors.

# Making Acquisitions Look So Good

Entire industries continue to get rattled and changed through consolidations, acquisitions, and spin-offs. Look no further than the auto sector to see how fast and furiously changes can happen in an industry! Some acquirers, particularly those using stock as an acquisition currency, use crazy market conditions as an opportunity to engage in very aggressive accounting for acquisitions. What did they do?

In the allocation of the purchase price, they classified a large portion of the acquisition price as *in-process* research and development. In-process R&D can be written off as a one-time charge, or *big bath*. This has the effect of removing any future earnings drag.

Also be very wary of pre-merger charges. Instead of doing the dirty work of recording those costs on the income statement, some companies compel the company they're acquiring to take a hit, taking as many charges against income as feasible right before the deal closes. This is a clever idea because the target company is poised to be acquired — the terms of the deal are set, so it's not concerned about what its own shareholders will say. The acquiring company gets a head start using a basket of acquired assets that have been devalued but are still very productive. A reduction in the future amount depreciated each year appears in the income statement.

# Special Charges and More Big Baths

Many companies that have experienced horrible results choose to take all their lumps at one time. This restructuring — or big-bath accounting — involves claiming massive chunks of losses in the income statement with a corresponding write-down on the balance sheet of an asset, usually an intangible like goodwill.

Canadian investors witness this phenomenon with mining companies that find out the commodity reserves they thought they had underground did not really exist. At the end of the day, the company is saying that a company it overpaid for in the past no longer has much value, and it's writing off the goodwill asset associated with the acquisition on an accelerated basis.

From the viewpoint of an investor nothing is inherently insidious about big-bath accounting, because it doesn't inflate profits. But it *is* an embarrassment and a disgrace to a company. So why do companies still do it?

Jim the forward-looking chief financial officer looks into his crystal ball and sees that if more value is written off than should be, future net income figures will look better. He muses, "Okay, my company looks bad now — but if I run a big bath, income will look great tomorrow. Book it, Danno!" That makes it really, really difficult for stock investors to properly value his company or to compare it meaningfully with other companies in the same industry. Distortions are large and confusing to unravel. Even Olly would admit to Stan that it's a fine mess they're in.

So what can you do in a case like this? Look for areas where special charges may occur. Restructuring charges can cover lots of types of expenses, but common signs include

- ✔ Closing physical facilities

- ✔ Laying off employees and paying severance costs (treated the same as closing facilities)

- ✔ Selling, closing, or exiting a business (discontinued operations)

- ✔ Increasing reserves for litigation (if you have a hard time finding facts about litigation, be on the alert for nasty legal surprises)

- ✔ Writing off goodwill or current assets (as described in this chapter)

Companies overstate special charges for other reasons, too. Management hopes that analysts will look beyond a one-time loss and focus only on future earnings, as many do.

As a stock investor, always be skeptical about special charges. Try as best you can to assess the impact with the information you have. If it appears that the write-offs are blatant, be wary of investing in that company. After all, it has already proven that it's capable of making very big mistakes.

# Hiding Liabilities: Off-Balance-Sheet Obligations

Some companies hide bad things like excessive debt by transferring it away from the balance sheet. Where does this debt go? Quite often it will be to a special-purpose entity such as an affiliated company or partnership. Companies may push accounting rules to the outer limits and say that their debt doesn't, by the letter of accounting law, meet the definition of debt to be disclosed as a liability. Instead, these companies disclose complex agreements entered into that not even seasoned analysts can understand without benefit of a flowchart! This lack of full and understandable information challenges you to find out what the company must pay in order to fulfill its debt and other obligations.

Four tactics, including the type described above, warrant further mention here. Each has the potential to hide the extent of a company's liabilities (and assets) through complex transactions that may also hide the substance of a company's financial position. We'll start with the relatively easy ones.

## Leasing transactions

If you rent your home, you don't own it. If you own your home, it's an asset, but any mortgage is a liability. Same with companies. A synthetic lease lets a company consider a purchase of property as a lease but gives it the tax advantages of ownership. An arm's-length (unrelated) company technically owns the property, usually a financial institution that really doesn't wish to bother operating it. Debt is used to finance the property, and the company has to pay it off. To be able to justify this off-balance-sheet accounting, the lease term has to be short — no more than seven years. If interest rates rise or values drop, the company can land into trouble. Sure, the lease is disclosed in a footnote, but few notice it (and if they did, even fewer can understand it).

To illustrate, take a company that owns aircraft and finances the planes with debt. You would expect it to report an asset (the aircraft) and a liability (the debt). Under existing GAAP (in most jurisdictions, including Canada and the U.S.), a company that operates assets under a short-term operating lease reports neither the asset nor the liability. Imagine a balance sheet that shows an airline without any aircraft. Would you consider that to be a faithful representation of the substance of the transaction? No, neither would we. As we write this book, accounting standards–setters continue to debate this matter.

## Securitization transactions

A company that transfers certain assets (like loans or notes receivable) through a securitization transaction may be able to recognize the transaction as a sale of assets — removing the assets receivable from its balance sheet. *Securitization* refers to the process of aggregating similar financial instruments, such as loans or mortgages, into a security to be sold on the open market. Companies do this to generate cash quicker and to improve their bottom line on the income statement.

Some securitizations are appropriately accounted for as sales. But many others continue to expose the transferring company to significant risks of devaluation still inherent in the transferred assets, which should not have been removed. Again, management's judgment was allowed to come into play. But was it good judgment?

## Commitments and contingencies

A *contingent liability* is one that is difficult to quantify, or one that may or may not come to pass. It's a potential claim for which any liability depends on a future event or circumstance. Examples include outstanding lawsuits, special contract obligations, or debt covenants (terms and conditions that must be upheld).

When evaluating a bank stock, look under the management discussion and analysis (MD&A) section of the annual report for discussion about credit risk. In the footnotes, look for discussion about commitments, contingencies, and pledged assets. Determine roughly how big the potential impact can be if some of these commitments turn into reality.

## Creation of unconsolidated or special-purpose entities (SPEs)

Under GAAP, a company transferring assets and liabilities to a subsidiary company must consolidate that subsidiary in the parent company's financial statements. However, in some cases, the transferor may be able to elude the requirement to consolidate.

A *special-purpose entity* (SPE) allows sponsor/originator companies bearing most of the SPE's debt risk to keep that debt off the consolidated balance sheet under U.S. GAAP. In Canada and elsewhere, the rules are somewhat similar. The majority of SPEs in the world are perfectly legitimate, and some financing and tax benefits also exist. But keep in mind that the primary motivation of having SPEs is often to achieve off-balance-sheet financing.

U.S. and Canadian accounting standards require companies to more clearly disclose their involvement with an SPE — including providing more information about the nature and amount of the associated risks. This enhanced information must be included in the footnotes of a company's annual report. Read those footnotes carefully if you ever see them. Run a what-if scenario to see what would happen if those liabilities came to life in the way that Frankenstein's monster did.

# Pension Plans

Most public companies have pension plans for employees, and corresponding obligations to adequately fund those plans. If any deficiency exists in the amount that's contributed to the plan, the company ultimately has to fund the shortfall. Cash infusions would dig into the company's cash balances and could potentially impair its ability to do the things it wants to.

During these tough economic times this is an important issue. Many companies still fail to adjust downward the assumptions underpinning their pension plans, such as the returns the plans would generate in upcoming years. Some pension plans are still based on assumptions that their investment funds will grow at a very strong pace, when in fact recent returns have remained closer to zero than anything else.

## Accounting impact, too

In addition to a cash-flow impact, pension plans also provide an accounting impact. Pension-plan returns are determined for the company annually. If the actual gain on the plan is less than the predicted gains, GAAP requires that a loss be booked on the income statement. To get around reporting the loss, or the full extent of it, companies may pressure actuaries (they're the guys that make even accountants look cool) to use favourable assumptions about returns, mortality rates, retirement dates, and so on in an effort to window-dress the impact on the bottom line.

This type of accounting manipulation occurs for companies with *defined-benefit pension plans*. A defined-benefit plan sets required retirement income for a future period, and the employer then funds the plan to ensure that the future pension obligation is met. Management often gets away with this because pension accounting is a nebulous task at best.

For investors, it's very difficult to understand the intricacies of pension plans. But many analysts say that determining the exact impact on earnings and evaluating how much cash will be spent to prop up ailing plans is nearly impossible anyway. Pension accounting is based on several estimates and forecasts, and many are not publicly disclosed. But the question has to remain in the back of your mind: How long will it be before the company has to pay the piper?

Keep in mind, however, that one bad year may not throw pension accounting out of kilter. Bad years tend to be offset with good years over the long term. But when you see four consecutive years of poor returns, problems can't wait to arise.

## Oh, and one more thing . . .

Shortfalls and asset returns aren't the only areas of manipulation. Actuaries use discount rates to calculate the present value of future pension liabilities. They're intended to be based on long-term bond yields. In many cases, however, discount rates remain far too high and make liabilities look far too low. That implies that not only do some companies overestimate how much money their plans will generate, but they also probably underestimate their liabilities, too.

# Tricks of the Trade: Other Things to Watch Out For

Companies make their balance sheets look better than they really are in other ways, too. Some companies cloud bad news; others twist accounting rules to suit their needs. Many companies use fancy business words that are accurate but that only one percent of the population really understands. In this section, we show you how they do all this.

## Smoke and mirrors

When you read company financial statements, be alert to companies that put the spotlight in the annual report on only their great accomplishments. While they duly follow accounting rules and disclose the more nasty items — such as litigation against the company, or dependence on only a few customers — they bury this information behind the good news.

The smoke-and-mirrors ruse is also prevalent in press releases of quarterly financial results. The spin is almost always positive, despite the fact that the numbers may actually be saying otherwise. Audit committees and external auditors don't currently vet press releases, so you, the stock investor, are on your own to dissect the press release for validity.

## And materiality rabbits, too

Many accountants started out wanting to be magicians. When they saw that they couldn't do tricks with cards, they went to bean-counting school. Their best trick was the ability to say that one plus one is equal to "anything you want it to be." Even true magicians were impressed.

For you, the stock investor, accounting manipulation is not entertaining at all. It's more akin to a bad horror show, really. Be careful when you hear the word *materiality,* a concept that many companies misuse. They may intentionally allow accounting errors to slip through within a defined percentage ceiling. This is actually justified in auditing speak if, and only if, the effect on profit is too small to matter to a reader of the financial statement.

When auditors question management about these violations of GAAP, they may answer dryly, "It doesn't matter. It's immaterial." Sometimes, the auditors will accept this. Materiality is based on considerable judgment. No clear-cut line shows where it starts and where it ends. It requires consideration of the potential impact on a stock investor's decision.

## Buzzwords and other warning signs

Several phrases and buzzwords tend to strike fear into stock investors' hearts. *Going concern* is one of those phrases, and it's a biggie. Going concern reflects the idea that a company will continue to operate indefinitely and will not go out of business and liquidate its assets. This is the basis of most accounting rules. For example, you don't book a receivable if the company is not likely to be around tomorrow. For the going-concern assumption to apply, the company must be able to generate or raise enough funds to stay in business. If auditors suspect a going-concern problem, they're compelled to report it in an auditor's report. If you see this, exit stage left!

Changing auditors is another thing you don't want to see happen. Sure, there may be a very good and benign reason for this. But quite frequently, it's because management and the auditor can't agree on a significant accounting issue. If the auditor digs in, he may get fired. Alternately, if an auditor suspects management fraud and wishes to disassociate herself from the company, she can resign. Either way, it reflects poorly on management. Be very suspicious when this happens and don't take the words of investor-relations people at face value.

A CEO pursuing "other interests" may be akin to a captain not wanting to stay behind on a sinking ship. CEOs perched high on their masts have clear views of the horizon. When they see that big tidal wave coming, they may call in the helicopter and put on their golden parachutes. Alternately, Captain Crook may have simply faced a mutiny and is walking the gangplank — at night, to save face. If he's lucky, Jonah's whale is lurking below to save him!

And footnotes, oh boring footnotes. But not to management! No siree, Bob. This is where management will bury much of the bad stuff. Footnotes are more effective than warm milk in putting you to sleep, or than raw onions in creating tears of boredom. But ignore these and you risk investment peril. And dealing with the bad stuff in footnotes can be more challenging than a game of I Spy. Just ask the external auditors of Enron. Oops, we forgot, they ceased to exist after botching that audit. Enron did, after all, have some fancy footnotes.

Recent Canadian and U.S. GAAP changes brought about by regulators and accounting standards–setters have improved the transparency of financial statements and have remedied — but not totally prohibited — a handful of the creative accounting techniques discussed in this book. More developments in the world according to GAAP will further curtail manipulative accounting techniques. Tightening GAAP is good for stock investors, but it is not the only answer to this problem.

People still question the rigour of audits. Yet, is it possible that too much reliance is placed on the auditors to uncover fraudulent practices of creative accounting? After all, audits provide reasonable assurance, not guarantees, of problem-free accounts. So auditors ought to be considered watchdogs, and not bloodhounds, in the realm of validating financial reporting.

A clear need for cultural change in the analyst community exists as well. Earnings estimates should not be a focal point; nor should brokerage houses underwrite new issues of securities of companies they also provide analyst opinions on. Analysts should penalize those companies that rely on accounting trickery rather than fairness and full disclosure.

# Chapter 15

# Looking at What the Insiders Do: Corporate Hijinks

· · · · · · · · · · · · · · · · · · · · · · · · · · · · · · · · · · · · ·

### In This Chapter

▶ Figuring out how to track insider trading

▶ Examining insider buying and selling

▶ Understanding the reasons for corporate buybacks

▶ Getting a handle on stock splits

· · · · · · · · · · · · · · · · · · · · · · · · · · · · · · · · · · · · ·

*I*magine you're boarding a cruise ship, ready to enjoy a hard-earned vacation. As you merrily walk up the plank, you notice that the ship's captain and crew are charging out of the vessel, flailing their arms, and screaming at the top of their lungs — some are even jumping into the water below. So here's a quiz: Would you get on that ship? You get double credit if you can also explain why (or why not). And what does this scenario have to do with stock investing, anyway? Well, plenty. The behaviour of the people who are in charge of the boat gives you important clues about the near-term prospects for that boat. Similarly, the actions of company insiders can provide important clues about the near-term prospects for their company.

*Company insiders* are individuals who are key managers or investors in a company. Insiders may be the president of the company, the treasurer, or another managing officer. An insider can be someone who owns a large stake in the company, or someone on the board of directors. In any case, insiders usually have a bird's-eye view of what's going on with the company. They have a good idea of how well (or how poorly) the company is doing.

Keep tabs on what insiders are doing, because their buy/sell transactions have a strong correlation to the near-term movement of their company's stock. However, don't buy or sell stock only because you heard that some insider did it. Use the information about insider trading to confirm your own good sense in buying or selling stock. Insider trading can be a great precursor to a significant move that you can profit from if you know what to look for. Many shrewd investors have made their profits (or have avoided losses) by tracking insider activity.

# Tracking Insider Trading

Fortunately, we live in an age of disclosure. Insiders who buy or sell the stock of companies listed on a U.S. exchange must file reports that document their trading activity with the U.S. Securities and Exchange Commission (SEC), which then makes the documents available to the public. You can also access similar trading activity records filed with the Canadian Securities Administrators (CSA) for companies listed on a Canadian exchange.

## U.S. insider trading information

You can view the public documents of companies listed on a U.S. exchange either at the SEC office or at the SEC Web site, which maintains the EDGAROnline database (`www.freeedgar.com` or `www.edgar-online.com`). Just click on the Search Filings button. Some of the most useful documents you can view there include the following:

- **Form 3:** This form is the initial statement that insiders provide, and they must file it within ten days of obtaining insider status. Insiders file this report even if they haven't made a purchase yet; the report establishes an insider's status.

- **Form 4:** This is the document that shows an insider's activity. For example, Form 4 would include information about a change in the insider's position as shareholder — how many shares the person has bought and sold, or other relevant changes. Any activity in a particular month must be reported on Form 4 by the tenth day of the following month. For example, if an insider sells stock during January, the SEC must get the report by February 10.

- **Form 5:** This annual report covers transactions that are small and not required to be reported on Form 4. Transactions may include minor, internal transfers of stock, or other transactions.

- **Form 144:** This form serves as an insider's public declaration of his or her intention to sell *restricted stock* — stock that is received from the company as compensation, stock that is awarded, or stock that is bought as a term of employment. Insiders must hold restricted stock for at least one year before they can sell it. When insiders decide to sell, they file Form 144 and then must sell the stock within 90 days, or else they must submit a new Form 144. Insiders must file the form on or before the stock's sale date. When a sale is finalized, insiders are then required to file Form 4.

The SEC has enacted the *short-swing profit rule* to protect the investing public. This rule prevents insiders from quickly buying the same stock that they just sold at a profit. An insider must wait at least six months before buying the stock again. The SEC created this rule to prevent insiders from using their privileged knowledge to make an unfair profit while the investing public can't react fast enough. The rule is also true if an insider sells stock. An insider can't sell it at a higher price within a six-month period.

## Canadian insider trading information

Canadian insider trading information isn't presented in the same format as is U.S. insider trading activity. In the U.S., insiders complete forms. In Canada, we have just a listing, or table, of key insider trading information:

✔ Who traded shares?

✔ What was the person's relationship to the company?

✔ How many shares were traded?

✔ At what price were the shares traded?

✔ What class of shares was traded?

✔ When did the trades occur?

✔ Where does the person reside?

You can access the public documents of companies listed on a Canadian exchange at the System for Electronic Disclosure by Insiders (SEDI) Web site at www.sedi.ca. This site is maintained by the CSA.

Here's how you can launch a query from the SEDI Web site:

1. Click the "Access public filings" link. A new screen appears.

2. Click the "View summary reports" link. You are taken to a new page with specific search instructions listed at the top. Near the bottom of the same page, you are given four options for insider trading searches:

   • **Insider transaction detail filters:** These allow you to refine your search for even more precise results.

   • **Issuer event history:** Responding to your search criteria, the system provides a list and description of events (like annual meetings, special votes for mergers, new board members, and so on) for a Canadian company.

- **Insider information by issuer:** This search will list all insiders and their holdings.

- **Weekly summary:** This option provides you with all recent insider trading information for a Canadian company, or issuer (of stock).

Select the bread-and-butter weekly summary option. The other three options require you to input more detailed criteria pertaining to insider trade activity. Check out the SEDI Web site for even more detail on how these filters can help you.

You can download reports (as PDF files) for one-, two-, and three-week periods. These insider activity summaries are presented alphabetically by company name.

In SEDI, you can also click the "View insider information" link to search by insider, or click the "View issuer information" link to view the details of the insiders of an *issuer,* or company.

# Looking at Insider Transactions

The classic phrase "Actions speak louder than words" should have been coined for insider trading. Insiders are in the know, and keeping a watchful eye on their transactions — both buying and selling their company's stock — can provide you with very useful investing information. Analyzing insider buying versus insider selling can be as different as night and day: Insider buying is simple, but insider selling can be complicated. In the following sections, we present both sides of insider trading.

## Learning from insider buying

Insider buying is usually an unambiguous signal indicating how an insider feels about his or her company. After all, the primary reason why all investors buy stock is because they expect it to do well. If one insider is buying stock, it's generally not a monumental event. But if several or more insiders are buying, those purchases should certainly catch your attention.

Insider buying is generally a positive omen and beneficial for the stock's price. Also, when insiders buy stock, less stock is available to the public. If the investing public meets this decreased supply with increased demand, the stock price then rises. Keep these factors in mind when analyzing insider buying:

✔ **Identify who's buying the stock.** The CEO is buying 5,000 shares. Is that reason enough for you to jump in? Maybe. After all, the CEO certainly knows how well the company is doing. But what if that CEO is just starting her new position? What if before this purchase she had no stock in the company at all? Maybe the stock is part of her employment package.

The fact that a new company executive is making her first stock purchase isn't as strong a signal urging you to buy as the fact that a long-time CEO is doubling her holdings. Also, if large numbers of insiders are buying, that sends a stronger signal than if a single insider is buying.

✔ **See how much is being bought.** In the example in the previous bullet point, the CEO bought 5,000 shares, which is a lot of stock no matter how you count it. But is it enough buying for you to base an investment decision on? Maybe, but a closer look may reveal more. If she already owned 1 million shares at the time of the purchase, then buying 5,000 additional shares wouldn't be such an exciting indicator of a pending stock rise. In this case, 5,000 shares is a small incremental move and doesn't offer much to get excited about.

But what if this particular insider has owned only 5,000 shares for the past three years and is now buying 1 million shares? Now that should arouse your interest! Usually, a massive purchase tells you that a particular insider has strong feelings about the company's prospects and, thus, she's making a huge increase in her share of stock ownership. Still, a purchase of 1 million shares by the CEO isn't as strong a signal as ten insiders buying 100,000 shares each would be. Again, if only one person is buying, it may or may not be a strong indication of an impending rise. However, if lots of people are buying, consider this activity to be a fantastic indicator.

An insider purchase of any kind is a positive sign. But it's always more significant when a greater number of insiders are making purchases. "The more the merrier!" is a good rule for judging insider buying. All these individuals have their own unique perspectives on the company and its prospects for the foreseeable future.

✔ **Notice the timing of the purchase.** The timing of insider stock purchases is important, as well. If we tell you that five insiders bought stock at various points last year, you may murmur, "Hmm . . ." But if we tell you that all five people bought substantial chunks of stock at the same time, and they did it right before earnings season, this should make you reply, "*Hmmmmm!*"

# *Picking up tips from insider selling*

Insider buying either bodes well for the stock or is at worst a neutral event. Insider stock buying is rarely a negative event. But how about insider selling? When an insider sells stock, the event can either be neutral or negative. Insider selling is usually a little tougher to figure out because insiders may have many different motivations to sell stock that have nothing to do with the company's future prospects. (Read on for a list of some common reasons.) Just because the president of the company is selling 5,000 shares from his personal portfolio, it doesn't necessarily mean you should sell, too.

Insiders may sell their stock for a couple of reasons: They may think that the company won't be doing well in the near future — a negative sign for you — or they may simply need the money for a variety of personal reasons that have nothing to do with the company's potential. Some typical reasons why insiders may sell stock include these:

- **To diversify their holdings:** If an insider's portfolio is heavily weighted with one company's stock, a financial adviser may suggest that he balance his portfolio by selling some of that company's stock and then purchasing other securities.

- **To finance personal emergencies:** Sometimes an insider needs money for medical, legal, or family reasons.

- **To buy a home or to make another major purchase:** An insider may need the money to make a down payment, or perhaps to buy something outright without having to take out a loan.

How do you go about investigating the details regarding insider stock selling? Although insiders must report their pertinent stock sales and purchases to regulators, the information isn't always immediately revealing. As a general rule, consider the following questions when analyzing insider selling:

- **How many insiders are selling?** If only one insider is selling, that single transaction doesn't give you enough information to act on. However, if many insiders are selling, view this as a red flag. Check out any news or information that is currently available. Web sites such as www.stockhouse.com, www.sec.gov, finance.yahoo.com, and finance.yahoo.ca can help you get that information (along with the other resources in Appendix B).

- **Are the sales showing a pattern or unusual activity?** If one insider sold some stock last month, that sale alone isn't that significant an event. However, if ten insiders have each made multiple sales in the past few months, those sales are cause for concern. See whether any new developments at the company are potentially negative. If massive insider selling has recently occurred and you don't know why, consider putting a stop-loss order on your stock immediately. (We cover stop-loss orders in Chapter 21.)

✔ **How much stock is being sold?** If a CEO sells 5,000 shares of stock but still retains 100,000 shares, that's not a big deal. But if the CEO sells all or most of his holdings, that's a possible negative sign. Check to see whether other company executives have also sold stock.

✔ **Do outside events or analyst reports seem coincidental with the sale of the stock?** Sometimes, an influential analyst may issue a report warning about a company's prospects. If the company's management pooh-poohs the report but most of them are bailing out anyway (selling their stock), you may want to do the same. Frequently, when insiders know that damaging information is forthcoming, they sell the stock before it takes a dip.

Similarly, if the company's management issues positive public statements or reports that are contradictory to their own behaviour (they're selling their stock holdings), the SEC may investigate to see whether the company is doing anything that may require issuing a penalty. The SEC regularly tracks insider sales.

# Considering Corporate Stock Buybacks

When you read the financial pages or watch the financial shows on television, you sometimes hear that a company is buying its own stock. The announcement may be something like, "SuperBucks Corp. has announced that it will spend $2 billion to buy back its own stock." Why would a company do that, and what does that mean to you if you own the stock or are considering buying it?

When companies buy back their own stock, they're generally indicating that they believe their stock is undervalued and that it has the potential to rise. If a company shows strong fundamentals (for example, a good financial condition and increasing sales and earnings) and it's buying more of its own stock, it's worth investigating — and may make a great addition to your portfolio.

Just because a company announces a stock buyback doesn't always mean that one will happen. The announcement itself is meant to stir interest in the stock and cause the price to rise. The stock buyback may be only an opportunity for insiders to sell stock, or it may be needed for executive compensation — recruiting and retaining competent management is a positive use of money.

If you see that a company is buying back its stock while most of the insiders are selling their personal shares, that's not a good sign. It may not necessarily be a bad sign, but it's not a positive sign. Play it safe and invest elsewhere.

The following sections present some common reasons why a company may buy back its shares from investors as well as some ideas on the negative effects of stock buybacks.

## *Boosting earnings per share*

By simply buying back its own shares from shareholders, a company can increase its earnings per share (see Appendix A for more on earnings per share) without actually earning extra money. Sound like a magician's trick? Well, it is, kind of. A corporate stock buyback is a financial sleight of hand that investors should be aware of. Here's how it works: Noware Earnings Inc. (NEI) has 10 million shares outstanding, and it's expected to net earnings of $10 million for the fourth quarter. NEI's earnings per share (EPS) would be $1 per share. So far, so good. But what happens if NEI buys 2 million of its own shares? The total of shares outstanding shrinks to 8 million. The new EPS becomes $1.25 — the stock buyback artificially boosts the earnings per share by 25 percent!

The important point to remember about stock buybacks is that actual company earnings don't change — no fundamental changes occur in company management or operations — so the increase in EPS can be misleading if you are unaware of the buyback and its impact. But the marketplace can be obsessive about earnings, and, because earnings are the lifeblood of any company, an earnings boost — even if it's cosmetic — can also boost the stock price.

If you watch a company's price-to-earnings ratio (see Appendix A), you know that increased earnings usually mean an eventual increase in the stock price. Additionally, a stock buyback affects supply and demand. With less available stock in the market, demand necessarily sends the stock price upward.

Whenever a company makes a major purchase, such as buying back its own stock, think about how the company is paying for it and whether it seems like a good use of the company's purchasing power. In general, companies buy their stock for the same reasons any investor buys stock — they believe the stock is a good investment and will appreciate in time. Companies generally pay for a stock buyback in one of two basic ways: funds from operations or borrowed money. Both methods have a downside. For more details, see the section "Exploring the downside of buybacks" in this chapter.

## *Beating back a takeover bid*

Suppose you read in the financial pages that Company X is attempting a hostile takeover of Company Z. A hostile takeover doesn't mean that Company X sent storm troopers armed with mace to Company Z's headquarters to trounce its management. All a *hostile takeover* means is that X wants to buy enough shares of Z's stock to effectively control Z, and Z is unhappy about being owned or controlled by X. Because the buying and selling of stock is done in a public market or exchange, companies can buy each other's stock. Sometimes the target company prefers not to be acquired, in which case it may buy back shares of its own stock to give it a measure of protection against unwanted moves by interested companies.

# Exploring the downside of buybacks

As beneficial as stock buybacks can be, they have to be paid for, and this expense has consequences. If a company pays for the stock with funds from operations, it may have a negative effect on the company's ability to finance current and future operations. When a company uses funds from operations for the stock buyback, less money is available for other activities, such as upgrading technology or research and development. In general, any misuse of money affects a company's ability to grow its sales and earnings — two measures that need to maintain upward mobility in order to keep stock prices rising.

A company faces great danger when it uses debt to finance a stock buyback. If the company uses borrowed funds, it has less borrowing power for other uses (such as upgrading technology or making other improvements). In addition, the company has to pay back the borrowed funds with costly interest, thus lowering earnings figures. In today's tight capital markets, corporate debt attracts very high interest rates.

Stock Splits: Nothing to Go Bananas OverFrequently, management teams decide to do a stock split. A *stock split* is the exchange of existing shares of stock for new shares from the same company. Stock splits don't increase or decrease the capitalization of the company. They just change the number of shares available in the market and the per-share price.

In a typical stock split, a company may announce that it will do a 2-for-1 split. For example, a company may have 10 million shares outstanding, with a market price of $40 each. In a 2-for-1 split, the company then has 20 million shares (the share total doubles), but the market price is adjusted to $20 (the share price is halved). Companies do other splits, such as a 3-for-2 or 4-for-1, but 2-for-1 is the most common split.

Why do companies split their stock? Usually, management believes the stock's price is too high, thus possibly discouraging investors from purchasing it. The stock split is a strategy to stir interest in the stock, and this increased interest frequently results in a rise in the stock's price. In today's stock market, stock splits are few and far between.

Qualifying for a stock split is similar to qualifying to receive a dividend — you must be listed as a shareholder as of the date of record. (For information on the date of record, see Chapter 6.)

A stock split is technically a neutral event because the ultimate market value of the company's stock doesn't change as a result of the split. The following sections present the two most basic types of splits: ordinary and reverse stock splits.

## Ordinary stock splits

*Ordinary stock splits* — when the number of stock shares increases — are the ones we usually hear about. (For example, a 2-for-1 stock split doubles the number of shares.) If you own 100 shares of Dublin Inc. stock (at $60 per share) and the company announces a stock split, what happens? If you own the stock in certificate form, you receive in the mail a stock certificate for 100 shares of Dublin Inc. Now, before you cheer over how your money just doubled, check the stock's new price. Each share is adjusted to a $30 value. However, you now own 200 shares.

Not all stock is in certificate form. Stocks held in a brokerage account are recorded in book-entry form. Most stock, in fact, is in book-entry form. A company issues stock certificates only when necessary or when the investor requests it. If you keep the stock in your brokerage account, check with your broker for the new share total to make sure you're credited with the new number of shares after the stock split.

A stock split is primarily a neutral event, so why does a company bother to do it? The most common reason is that management believes the stock is too expensive, so it wants to lower the stock price to make the stock more afford-able and, therefore, more attractive to new investors. Studies have shown that stock splits frequently precede a rise in the stock price. Although stock splits are considered a non-event in and of themselves, many stock experts see them as bullish signals because of the interest they generate among the investing public.

## Reverse stock splits

A *reverse stock split* usually occurs when a company's management wants to raise the price of its stock. Just as ordinary splits can occur when manage-ment believes the price is too expensive, a reverse stock split means the company feels the stock's price is too cheap. If a stock's price looks too low, this may discourage interest by individual or institutional investors (such as mutual funds). Management wants to drum up more interest in the stock for the benefit of shareholders (some of whom are probably insiders).

The company may also do a reverse split to decrease costs. When you have to send an annual report and other correspondence regularly to all the share-holders, the mailings can get a little pricey, especially when you have lots of investors who have only a few shares each. A reverse split helps to consoli-date the shares to lower overall management costs.

A reverse split can best be explained with an example. TuCheep Inc. (TCI) is selling at $2 per share on the Nasdaq. At that rock-bottom price, the investing public may ignore the stock. So TCI announces a 10-for-1 reverse stock split. Now what? If an existing shareholder had 100 shares at $2 (the old shares), the shareholder now owns 10 shares at $20.

Technically, a reverse split is considered a neutral event. However, just as investors may infer positive expectations from an ordinary stock split, they may have negative expectations from a reverse split, because a reverse split tends to occur for negative reasons.

If, in the event of a reverse stock split, you have an odd number of shares, the company doesn't produce a fractional share. Instead, you get a cheque for the cash equivalent. For example, if you have 51 shares and the company announces a 2-for-1 reverse split, the odds are they'll give you 25 shares and a cash payout for the odd share (or fractional share).

Keep good records about your stock splits in case you need to calculate capital gains for tax purposes. (See Chapter 22 for tax information.)

# Chapter 16

# Five Minutes for Misconduct

*In This Chapter*

▶ Understanding how the board of directors controls risk

▶ Considering the impact of ethical lapses

▶ Watching a company's reputation tank

▶ Facing technological risk

*I*n this brief chapter, we consider a critical area that investors disregard at their peril — corporate "tone at the top." In other words, as a stock investor, you have to keep an eye out for companies lacking strong board of director governance, or strong corporate management and accounting controls. You need to be wary of reported instances of corporate fraud, or suspected or confirmed "favours" stemming from conflicts of interest. All can lead to significant losses of cash and other assets — for both a company and its investors.

Another critical area we discuss in this chapter relates to privacy and piracy risks. A breach of privacy or an incidence of piracy may not be a company's fault, but it may cause a serious exposure that can hurt the company's core business. If you invest in a tax software company, for example, you definitely do not want to read about rampant piracy of its products. Even worse, you don't want to find out that your online tax filing with the Canada Revenue Agency — and the loads of confidential information in it — can be intercepted by a hacker on the Internet.

In this chapter, we show you that staying tuned to media reports, press releases, and auditor's reports are important ways to get bad corporate behaviour and other risks on your investment radar screen. Ideally, you should evaluate these risks before you invest. You want to stay away from companies with poor track records in these very important areas.

# Ruin at the Top: Corporate Governance Risk

Good corporate control starts at the top. If the control at the top is poor, you can bet dollars to donuts that a culture of poor controls will trickle down to other areas of the company. Poor corporate governance creates a pervasive risk that's referred to as *corporate governance risk*. This risk area merits a close look from any stock investor. The recent meltdowns at Bear Stearns, Lehman Brothers, and Citigroup made those companies poster children for poor corporate governance, greed, and an array of other ills.

## The role of the board of directors

To understand what represents good corporate governance, it helps to review the role of the board of directors (BOD) of a public company. The BOD is responsible to the shareholders for overseeing the management of the company and for the good stewardship and safekeeping of its assets. How does the BOD do this?

The BOD is responsible to set in place the company's systems of internal control and to arrange for a review of their efficiency and effectiveness. Management control systems are designed to manage, rather than eliminate, the risk of failure to achieve corporate business objectives. These corporate objectives centre on efficient and effective operations, good reporting of results, and compliance to laws, regulations, and policies.

If Canada's Potash Corporation wants to remain a low-cost provider of agricultural fertilizer with fast delivery to international customers, it will set checks and balances to help it achieve this. These checks may include state-of-the-art extraction facilities, precise reporting of production costs, and forward arrangements with customs brokers. Potash Corporation also has to comply with Saskatchewan's health and safety laws to ensure its employees are safe in what can be a dangerous mining environment. For all companies, watch out for any poor press about high production costs or safety lapses. They aren't the only indicators of a company's tone at the top, but they are good ones.

## How the BOD manages risks

A BOD reviews the efficiency and effectiveness of systems of management control through a process of analyzing corporate strategy; major projects, investments, or divestments to be undertaken; and external- and internal-audit work plans and resulting reports. Many BODs have delegated the oversight of risk to duly created sub-committees of the board, including risk-management committees.

# Senior management's role in good governance: Rolling up the sleeves

The BOD manages risks through an *oversight* of corporate governance practices. It sets the tone. It ensures that all the management-control ducks are in a row. But the BOD does not make day-to-day decisions. Its members don't really have to roll up their sleeves — that's the job of senior management.

Because corporate governance is, by definition, a company's strategic response to risk, that response is made through decision makers — senior management. You can tell if management promotes good basic corporate governance by spotting the following:

- **Strategic planning:** Does senior management — through press releases, shareholder meetings, or the annual report — demonstrate that it is developing strategic plans and objectives to fulfill the organization's purpose? This purpose may include market leadership, customer-service excellence, and similar high-level objectives.

- **Leadership:** Has management communicated, via the annual report or other communiqués, the organization's purpose in a *vision statement*? If a company lacks vision and doesn't know where it's going on its journey, it's like a rudderless ship. A vision statement evokes a strong image of the reality made possible by accomplishing the company's mission. (A *mission statement* tells you why you are beginning a journey.)

- **Organization design:** Has management established a company structure that makes it run efficiently and effectively? This includes having the right number and location of plants, offices, and staff.

- **Risk management:** Does management demonstrate an awareness of its risks in its annual report? Is it putting assets at risk to achieve the organization's objectives?

- **Assurance:** Does management provide feedback to shareholders on the efficiency and effectiveness of its governance and internal control processes? This includes publishing the external auditor's management letter (on internal controls), even if the company doesn't have to.

# Management's role in controlling risk

Before looking at other risks, we want to suggest that you not seek out companies that eliminate risk altogether. Risk is an *opportunity* to companies, and companies take advantage of opportunities to make money. Each risk also has a different impact and likelihood, and each must be handled and viewed differently. The risk of a flood destroying a plant is remote, but the impact to operations is likely huge. So, transferring this risk to an insurance company is the way to go. The risk of fraud in a company that sells home security systems has to be avoided at all costs. Such a company will make sure that it screens employees, has good cash control, and has other checks and balances in place to avoid this risk to reputation as much as possible.

As a stock investor, the annual report you get includes a brief discussion of risks. This is likely to be found in the management discussion and analysis (MD&A) section of the annual report. A good discussion of risks includes the steps taken to manage risks. How a company handles its risks will help you better assess whether you've invested in a high-risk company or one with fewer potential potholes. Look for evidence (in the annual report or even by calling the company's risk executive) of the following risk-management techniques:

- **Avoiding risk:** Does the company occasionally redesign business processes or its physical infrastructure to avoid particular risks? For example, did the last fire scare result in fire emergency training, new sprinkler systems, and so on?

- **Diversifying risk exposure:** Does management spread certain risks among numerous assets or processes to reduce the overall risk of loss or impairment? For example, is sensitive and important backup medical data kept in an off-site data storage facility?

- **Controlling risky situations:** Are activities designed to prevent, detect, or contain adverse events, or to promote positive outcomes? For instance, are employees who handle hazardous materials supported by proper prevention training, backup staff, and properly functioning equipment?

- **Sharing risk:** Does management share a portion of the risk through a contract with another party, such as an insurance company?

- **Transferring risk:** Has management distributed certain risks to another party through contract, such as outsourcing payroll duties or computer maintenance?

- **Accepting some risks:** Does management allow minor risks to exist to avoid spending more time and money on managing these risks than the potential damage warrants?

When evaluating overall corporate governance risk, consider *strategic risk* — a risk that exists when bad business decisions are made, the implementation of decisions is poor, or a lack of responsiveness to industry changes is apparent. Make sure that when you invest in a company, you understand what it does, why it's doing it, and how the company will get it done.

## Back to the BOD

When looking for danger signs in a company's board of directors that'll make smart stock investors think twice, observe in the annual report or press releases whether the

- ✔ Board is large (difficult to reach decisions)
- ✔ Chairperson and chief executive are the same person (potential conflict of interest)
- ✔ Chief executive appoints outside directors (potential conflicts of interest)
- ✔ Outside directors are overly busy because they serve on many other boards (efforts spread too thin)
- ✔ Outside directors are over the age of 70 (stale view of company)
- ✔ Outside directors have business dealings with the company (potential conflicts of interest)

# Misbehavin': Ethical Risk

Several types of risk stem from failures in the ethical conduct of a company's management or of other employees. Although good corporate governance at the BOD level helps to mitigate ethical problems, the risk of questionable or illegal acts is inherent in all companies.

## Fraud

*Fraud* occurs when deception causes a monetary loss to a company. The lie may be a payroll clerk who creates a fictitious person on the payroll, and the monetary loss may be caused by the clerk impersonating that fictitious person to cash the fake employee's payroll cheque. Fraud can also arise from an intentional misrepresentation to a company's suppliers and customers. Examples of these fraud risks include theft, bid rigging, bribery, kickback schemes, and customer abuse (such as overbilling).

If the fraud is significant, you should be able to spot its existence in the notes to the financial statements dealing with litigation. If the fraud is material (serious dollars are involved), under Canadian securities law a company must also disclose it in a public filing with SEDAR (www.sedar.com; we discuss SEDAR in Chapter 6). The media will almost certainly jump on that story. Otherwise, fraud is usually an internal matter that's seldom self-disclosed to the public because of the damage that can be caused to a company's reputation. If a company doesn't have to disclose something like this, it won't. As an investor, just take a quick look at the litigation footnotes to see if any trend exists.

## Conflict of interest

There may be instances of *conflicts of interest* where BOD members, management, or employees personally benefit from their positions in the organization. The allegations surrounding Hollinger Inc. and its founder and active board member Conrad Black — that Black and other senior executives received hundreds of millions of dollars in unauthorized payments — immediately come to mind. Or imagine Manny the manager, who compels the company he works for to buy goods or services from another company that he has a financial interest in. Manny's behaviour, if left unchecked, can lead him to even worse offences such as fraud.

In some cases of conflicts of interest — maybe even in a company you invest in — damages have to be paid, and the resultant negative publicity can harm a company's reputation and share price. Again, it's difficult to spot conflicts of interest because they are typically internal and very private matters. But if governance at the top is poor, invariably a trickle-down effect occurs throughout the company. E-mail or phone your investor-relations contact to see if the company has a code of conduct that is communicated to all employees. Companies with policies about conflicts of interest have a lower risk of related fraud. As an investor, you may not be able to detect fraud that was already uncovered by the company. But you can see whether the company has policies in place to try to *prevent* fraud from happening in the first place!

## A Bad Rep: Reputational Risk

Reputational risk is what you get when things go really wrong with corporate governance, management controls, and ethical breaches. Reputation is the corporate brand, and it's an extremely important attribute for any company to protect and grow. Reputation is also more than just image. *Image* is the immediate perception of a company, but reputation is the stakeholders' collective social memory of the company and its activities. Negative publicity regarding a company's business practices, whether true or not, will more than likely cause the customer base to decline, costly lawsuits to be filed, and many other headaches to arise.

Any company that fails to deliver on the expectations of its *stakeholders* — shareholders, customers, regulators, employees, and the larger community — risks experiencing a rapid drop in its share price. It's vital that everyone employed by, or associated with, the company you invest in (such as a BOD member) acts with the highest level of integrity and professionalism in all that he or she does.

One way you can spot reputational risk rearing its head is by reading media stories about a company and then following up by checking the press releases the company issues in response. Is a negative article just a case of media sensationalism, or does the story ring true? In other situations, the negative impact of a bad corporate reputation just creeps up on a company, and before you know it, the stock is down 30 percent over the course of a year. You never knew that, one by one, customers started to exit stage left. The key here is to never underestimate the negative impact of reputational risk.

When a company's reputation gets called into question by the court of public opinion, the punishment — a steep drop in share price — is much worse than the crime. An accused company is found guilty well before it has a chance to prove its innocence to shareholders.

# Information and Technology Risks

With information technology comes great benefits. Operations speed up, and costs often go down. But technology can also present some risks.

## Piracy

Many people are simply unaware that copying software without a valid licence is piracy and, therefore, against the law. By copying software at work, they're putting their employers at risk for charges of software piracy. Coming under investigation for software piracy can seriously damage a business's reputation, potentially causing a loss in market share due to poor customer perception.

Piracy of technology can also work the other way, where another company infringes on the patent owned by the company you invested in. You see a lot of this in the technology, biotechnology, and pharmaceutical industries. These are R&D-intensive industries, with lots of ideas floating around that are ripe for someone else to steal. One example of online piracy is called peer-to-peer file sharing through something called "torrents." File sharing in this way is very commonplace and especially hurts companies in the audio, video, publishing, and other electronic data-intensive industries. Although torrents are illegal, they are rampant because they represent a free or low-cost way to get intellectual property. They are here to stay and are a clear and present danger to many companies. Be alert to piracy of all forms by scanning press releases.

## Privacy

We can think of few things as destructive to the reputation of a company than the inadvertent release of confidential and sensitive information to a third party. We often hear stories about personal medical information being hacked and sold to interested parties. Sometimes, sensitive corporate information even gets posted on a Web site or blog! A few years ago, a Microsoft employee began *blogging* (posting comments on a personal Web log, or blog) about some of the unfair practices he perceived to exist at the company. Microsoft was not thrilled, and a nasty legal battle ensued. The bottom line is that the e-business boom has created concerns about the security of personal information that's collected and used over the Internet, making privacy risk management a corporate priority.

Businesses must protect the large amounts of personal information exchanged in the transactions that move business. Company stakeholders are concerned about how their information is used and secured, what controls are in place to correct erroneous information, and with whom this information will be shared. Such information can include a person's name, contact information, age, occupation, salary, marital status, financial status, religious affiliation, nationality, credit card numbers, identity card numbers, medical records, and employment records. Can you imagine how you would feel if a company lost track of your personal records?

Any semblance of poor controls in this area means that customers may choose to do business elsewhere. Any failure by management to respond to privacy issues and risks can result in adverse consequences that range from loss of market to regulatory sanctions, loss of information flow, costly litigation, or damage to reputation.

As a stock investor, determine whether a corporate privacy policy exists. Check out the company Web site for insights. How is privacy managed? What privacy failures have occurred in the industry, and what are consumer protection groups and privacy advocates saying about the issues?

# Chapter 17

# Analyzing Industries

. . . . . . . . . . . . . . . . . . . . . . . . . . . . . . . . . . . . . . . . . . . . . . . . .

*In This Chapter*

▶ Selecting industries by asking a few important questions

▶ Keeping an eye on four major industries

. . . . . . . . . . . . . . . . . . . . . . . . . . . . . . . . . . . . . . . . . . . . . . . . .

Suppose you have to bet your entire nest egg on a one-kilometre race. All you need to do is select a winning group. Your choices are the following:

Group A: Thoroughbred race horses

Group B: Overweight Elvis impersonators

Group C: Lethargic snails

This isn't a trick question, and you have one minute to answer. Notice that we didn't ask you to pick a single winner out of a giant mush of horses, Elvii, and snails; we only asked you to pick the winning group in the race. The obvious answer is the thoroughbred race horses (and no, they weren't ridden by the overweight Elvis impersonators, because that would take away from the eloquent point being made). In this example, even the slowest member of group A easily outdistances the fastest member of either group B or C.

Industries, like groups A, B, and C in our example, aren't equal, and life isn't fair. After all, if life were fair, Elvis would be alive and the impersonators wouldn't exist. Fortunately, picking stocks doesn't have to be as difficult as picking a winning racehorse. The basic point is that it's easier to pick a successful stock from a group of winners (a growing, vibrant industry). Understanding industries only enhances your stock-picking strategy.

A successful, long-term investor looks at the industry just as carefully as he looks at the individual stock. Luckily, choosing a winning industry to invest in is easier than choosing individual stocks, as you find out in this chapter. We know some investors who can pick a winning stock in a losing industry, and we also know investors who've chosen a losing stock in a winning industry (the former is far outnumbered by the latter). Just think how well you do when you choose a great stock in a great industry! Of course, if you repeatedly choose bad stocks in bad industries, you may as well get out of the stock market altogether (maybe your calling is instead to be a celebrity impersonator!).

# Interrogating the Industries

Your common sense is an important tool in choosing industries with winning stocks. The following sections explore some of the most important questions to ask yourself when you're choosing an industry.

Keep in mind that an industry isn't the same as a sector. Even some market pros use the two words almost interchangeably. A *sector* is basically a "mega-industry," or a broader group of interrelated industries. For example, pharmaceuticals and cosmetic surgery are each an industry, but both are part of the larger healthcare sector. An *industry* is typically a category of business that performs a precise activity (such as manufacturing computer chips, or trucking). Not all industries in a sector perform equally in the same market conditions. See Chapter 18 for details on some interesting sectors.

## Which category does the industry fall into?

Most industries can neatly be placed in one of two categories: cyclical and defensive. In a rough way, these categories generally translate into what society wants and what it needs. Society buys what it *wants* when times are good and holds off when times are bad. It buys what it *needs* in both good and bad times. A want is a "like to have," and a need is a "must have." Kapish?

### Cyclical industries

*Cyclical industries* are industries whose fortunes rise and fall with the economy's rise and fall. In other words, if the economy is doing well and the stock market is doing well, consumers and investors are confident and tend to spend and invest more money than usual, so cyclical industries tend to do well. Real estate, computer semiconductors, and automobiles are great examples of cyclical industries.

Your own situation offers some common-sense insight into the concept of cyclical industries. Think about your behaviour as a consumer and you get a revealing clue into the thinking of millions of consumers. When you (and millions of other Canadians) feel good about your career, your finances, and your future, you have a greater tendency to buy more (and more expensive) stuff. When people feel financially strong, they're more apt to buy a new house or car or make some other large financial commitment. Also, people take on more debt because they feel confident they can pay it back. In light of this behaviour, what industries do you think would do well?

The same point holds for business spending. When businesses think that economic times are good and foresee continuing good times, they tend to spend more money on large purchases such as new equipment or technology. They think that when they're doing well and are flush with financial success, it's a good idea to reinvest that money in the business to increase future success.

### Defensive industries

*Defensive industries* are industries that produce goods and services that are needed no matter what's happening in the economy. Your common sense kicks in here, too. What do you buy even when times are tough? Think about what millions of people buy no matter how bad the economy gets. A good example is food — people still need to eat regardless of good or bad times. Other examples of defensive industries are utilities and healthcare.

In bad economic times, defensive stocks tend to do better than cyclical stocks. However, when times are good, cyclical stocks tend to do better than defensive stocks. Defensive stocks don't do as well in good times because people don't eat twice as much or use up more electricity.

So how do defensive stocks grow? Their growth generally relies on two factors:

- **Population growth:** As more and more consumers are born, more people become available to buy essential goods and services.

- **New markets:** A company can grow by seeking out new groups of consumers to buy its products and services. Coca-Cola, for example, found new markets in Asia during the 1990s. As communist regimes fell from power and more societies embraced a free market and consumer goods, the company sold more beverages, and its stock soared.

One way to invest in a particular industry is to take advantage of exchange-traded funds (ETFs), which have become very popular in recent years. ETFs are structured much like mutual funds but are fixed portfolios that trade like a stock. If you find a winning industry but you can't find a winning stock (or don't want to bother with the necessary research), then ETFs are a great consideration. You can find out more about ETFs at Globefund.com (go to www.globefund.com and click the ETF Centre link).

# Is the industry growing?

The question may seem obvious, but you still need to ask it before you purchase stock. The saying "the trend is your friend" applies when choosing an industry in which to invest, as long as the trend is an upward one. If you look at three different stocks that are equal in every significant way but you find that stock A is in an industry growing 15 percent per year while the other two stocks are in industries that have either little growth or are shrinking, which stock would you choose?

Sometimes the stock of a financially unsound or poorly run company goes up dramatically because the industry it's in is very exciting to the public. The most obvious example is Internet stocks from 1998–2000. Stocks such as Pets.com shot up to incredible heights because investors thought the Internet was the place to be. Sooner or later, however, the measure of a successful company is its ability to be profitable (Pets.com went bankrupt in 2000). Serious investors look at the company's fundamentals (see Chapter 12 to find out how to do this) and the prospects for the industry's growth before settling on a particular stock.

To judge how well an industry is doing, various information sources monitor all the major industries and measure their progress. The more reliable sources for industry information include the following:

- MarketWatch (www.marketwatch.com)
- *Financial Post* (www.financialpost.com)
- *Report On Business* (www.theglobeandmail.com/report-on-business)
- Standard & Poor's (www.standardpoor.com)
- Hoover's (www.hoovers.com)
- Yahoo! Finance (http://finance.yahoo.com)
- *The Wall Street Journal* (www.wsj.com)

The preceding sources generally give you in-depth information about the major industries. Visit their Web sites to read their current research and articles along with links to relevant sites for more details. For example, *The Globe and Mail's Report on Business* site has an Industry News tab. Click it and you'll see an Industry Sections area listing specific industries. Examples of specific industries are mining, agriculture, forest products, and energy, oil, and gas. These Web sites are updated daily, and publish indexes for all the major sectors and industries so that you can get a useful snapshot of how well an industry is doing.

Standard & Poor's (S&P) Industry Survey is an especially excellent source of information on U.S. industries. Besides ranking and comparing industries and informing you about their current prospects, the survey also lists the top companies by size, sales, earnings, and other key information. We like that each industry is covered in a few pages, so you get the critical information you need without reading a novel.

# Are the industry's products or services in demand?

Look at the products and services that an industry provides. Do they look like things society will continue to want? Are there products and services on the horizon that could replace them? Does the industry face a danger of potential obsolescence?

When evaluating future demand, look for a *sunrise industry* — one that's new or emerging or has promising appeal for the future. Good examples of sunrise industries in recent years are green technology, alternative energy, and biotech and Internet companies. In contrast, a *sunset industry* is one that's either declining or has little potential for growth. For example, you probably shouldn't invest in the videocassette manufacturing industry as demand for DVDs and other alternatives increases. Owning stock in a strong, profitable company in a sunrise industry is often the most desirable choice.

Current research unveils the following megatrends:

- **The aging of Canada:** More senior citizens than ever before will be living in Canada. Because of this fact, financial and healthcare services will prosper.

- **Advances in high technology:** Internet, telecom, medical, and biotechnology innovations will continue. Internet 2.0 refers to the buildout of — and massive investment in — an even more robust Internet infrastructure.

- **Increasing need for basic materials:** As society advances here and in the rest of the world, building blocks such as metals and other precious commodities will be in demand.

- **Security concerns:** Terrorism and other international tensions mean more attention for national defence, border security, and related matters.

- **Energy challenges:** Traditional and nontraditional sources of energy (solar, fuel cells, and so on) will demand society's attention as it faces shrinking supplies of the world's available cheap crude oil.

# What does the industry's growth rely on?

An industry doesn't exist in a vacuum. External factors weigh heavily on its ability to survive and thrive. Does the industry rely on an established megatrend? Then it will probably be strong for a while. Does it rely on factors that are losing relevance? Then it may begin to decline soon. Technological and demographic changes are other factors that may contribute to an industry's growth or fall.

Perhaps the industry offers great new medical products for senior citizens. What are the prospects for growth? The greying of the population is an established megatrend. As millions of Canadians climb past age 50, profitable opportunities await companies that are prepared to cater to them.

## Is the industry dependent on another industry?

This twist on the prior question is a reminder that industries frequently are intertwined and can become codependent. When one industry suffers, you may find it helpful to understand which industries will subsequently suffer. The reverse can also be true — when one industry is doing well, other industries may reap the benefits.

In either case, if the stock you choose is in an industry that's highly dependent on other industries, you should know about it. If you're considering stocks of vacation-resort companies and you see the headlines blaring, "Airlines losing money as public stops flying," what do you do? This type of question forces you to think logically and consider cause and effect. Logic and common sense are powerful tools that frequently trump all the number-crunching activity performed by analysts.

## What are the leading companies in the industry?

After you've chosen the industry, what types of companies do you want to invest in? You can choose from two basic types:

- ✔ **Established leaders:** These companies are considered industry leaders or have a large share of the market. Investing in these companies is the safer way to go; what better choice for novice investors than companies that have already proven themselves?

- ✔ **Innovators:** If the industry is hot and you want to be more aggressive in your approach, investigate companies that offer new products, patents, or technologies. These companies are probably smaller but have a greater potential for growth in a proven industry.

# Is the industry a target of government action?

You need to know if the government is targeting an industry, because intervention by politicians and bureaucrats (rightly or wrongly) can have an impact on an industry's economic situation. For example, would you invest in a tobacco company now that the government has issued all its regulations and warnings?

Investors need to take heed when political "noise" starts coming out about a particular industry. An industry can be hurt either by direct government intervention or by the threat of it. Intervention can take the form of lawsuits, investigations, taxes, regulations, or sometimes an outright ban. In any case, being on the wrong end of government intervention is the greatest external threat to a company's survival.

Sometimes, government action helps an industry. Generally, beneficial action takes two forms:

- **Deregulation and/or tax decreases:** Parliament sometimes reduces burdens on an industry. In May 1984, the Canadian federal government deregulated Canadian airlines, an action that caused a boom in travel for Canadians. The airline industry subsequently experienced tremendous growth because more people flew than ever before. This increase in the number of North American airline passengers spurred growth for the lodging and resort industries. Likewise, telecom deregulation in the mid-1990s in Canada and the U.S. helped that industry to boom.

- **Direct funding:** Government has the power to steer taxpayer money toward business as well. In recent years, federal and provincial governments have provided tax credits and other incentives for alternative energy such as solar power. The government of Canada and many provincial governments also provide "efficient energy use" rebates and tax incentives for Canadians who, for example, switch to more efficient furnaces.

# Outlining Key Industries

Not all industries go up and down in tandem. Indeed, at any given time, some industry is successful no matter what's happening with the general economy. In fact, Canadian stock investors have made a lot of money simply by choosing an industry that benefits from economic trends.

For example, the Canadian economy was in bad shape during the 1970s. It was a period of *stagflation* — low growth, high unemployment, and high inflation. This decade was the worst time for the economy since the Great Depression; most industries (and therefore most stocks) were having tough times. But some industries did well — in fact, some flourished. Real estate and precious metals, for example, performed well in this environment. Because the inflation rate soared into double digits, inflationary hedges such as gold and silver did very well. During the '70s, gold skyrocketed from $35 an ounce to $850 an ounce over the course of the decade. Silver went from under $2 to over $50 in the same period. What do you think happened to stocks of gold and silver mining companies? That's right — they skyrocketed as well. Gold stocks gave Canadian investors spectacular returns.

In the 1980s, the economy was rejuvenated when taxes were cut, regulations were decreased, and inflation fell. Most industries did well, but even in a growing economy some industries struggle. Examples of industries that struggled during that time include precious metals and energy stocks.

Now fast forward to 2010. Think about the industries that have recently struggled and those that have performed well during the past few years. The stocks of many Canadian companies involved in energy, agriculture, and general commodities have done very well. In the same time frame, industries like airlines, housing, and U.S. financials (such as banks and brokerage firms) have had a very rough time. Choosing the right industries (or avoiding the wrong ones) has always been a major factor in successful stock picking.

In the following sections, we list some of the largest industries you can invest in and provide tips on how to tell when they're doing well . . . and not so well. (To research these industries, use the resources mentioned earlier in this chapter, as well as those listed in Appendix B.)

## Moving in: Real estate

We include real estate as a key industry because it's a cyclical *bellwether industry* — one that has a great effect on many other industries that may be dependent on it. Real estate is looked at as a key component of economic health because so many other industries — including building materials, mortgages, household appliances, and contract labour services — are tied to it. A booming real estate industry bodes well for much of the Canadian economy.

Housing starts are one way to measure real estate activity. This data is an important leading indicator of health in the industry. Housing starts indicate new construction, which means more business for related industries.

Keep an eye on the Canadian and U.S. real estate industries for negative news that could be bearish for the economy and the stock market. Because real estate is purchased with mortgage money, investors and analysts watch the mortgage market for trouble signs such as rising delinquencies and foreclosures. These statistics serve as a warning for general economic weakness.

The North American real estate mania hit its zenith during 2006–07. A *mania* is typically the final (and craziest) part of a mature bull market. In a mania, the prices of the assets experiencing the bull market (such as stock or real estate) skyrocket to extreme levels, which entice more and more investors to jump in, causing prices to rise even further. It gets to the point where seemingly everyone thinks that it's easy to get rich by buying this particular asset, and almost no one notices that the market has become unsustainable. After prices are exhausted and start to level off, investor excitement dies down, and then investors try to exit by selling their holdings to realize some profit. As more and more sell off their holdings, demand decreases while supply increases. The mania dissipates and the bear market appears. This is definitely what happened to real estate in 2008–09, when the industry fell on hard times as the housing bubble popped.

## Driving it home: Automotive

Cars are big-ticket items and are another barometer of people's economic well-being — people buy new cars when they're doing well financially. When sales of cars are up, it's usually a positive indicator for the economy.

Conversely, trouble in the auto industry is a red flag for trouble in the general economy. (Just ask GM, which both you and your taxpaying neighbours to the south now actually own part of!) One red flag is that an increase in auto repossessions and car loan delinquencies translates to a warning about general economic weakness. During 2007–09, some major difficulty definitely showed up in the auto industry as GM and Chrysler experienced financial troubles. (Ford was in better shape.) When the auto industry struggles, other industries tied to it also struggle. These include consumer credit and numerous manufacturing subcategories that cater to the auto industry (such as base metals and electrical components).

## Talking tech: Computers and related electronics

In recent years, technology stocks have become very popular with investors. Indeed, technology is a great sector, and its impact on the economy's present and future success can't be underestimated. The share price of technology companies can rise substantially because investors buy shares based on expectations — today's untested, unproven companies may become the Googles and Apples of tomorrow.

In spite of the sector's potential, companies can still fail if customers don't embrace their products. Even in technology stocks, you still must apply the rules and guidelines about financially successful companies that we discuss throughout this book. Pick the best in a growing industry and you'll succeed over the long haul. But because technology still hasn't recovered from its recent bear market, weakness in the industry means that investors need to be very picky and cautious.

## Banking on it: Financials

Banking and financial services are an intrinsic part of any economy. Debt is the most telling sign of this industry for investors. If a company's debt is growing faster than the economy, you need to watch how that debt impacts stocks and mutual funds. If debt gets out of control, it can be disastrous for the economy. As credit specialists point out, the amount of debt and debt-related securities recently reached historic and troublesome levels. As this book goes to press, U.S. financial stocks have experienced a tough market as debt and defaults on debt (like subprime debt) have become headline news. (In Canada, our banks are in much better shape. Yet they have still suffered in the stock market, because recessions don't treat banks very well, even the more solid ones.) Because this is a multi-trillion-dollar issue and it weighs heavily across the economic landscape, problems will persist well into the future. Canadian investors should remain wary and selective.

# Chapter 18

# Emerging-Sector Opportunities

- - - - - - - - - - - - - - - - - - - - - - - - - - - - - - - - - - - -

## In This Chapter

▶ Checking out bullish opportunities

▶ Understanding your bearish opportunities

▶ Getting investment pointers for your unique situation

- - - - - - - - - - - - - - - - - - - - - - - - - - - - - - - - - - - -

*W*e're thrilled to include this chapter in this 3rd edition of *Stock Investing For Canadians For Dummies*. Had you read this chapter in the previous edition and acted accordingly, you could have made a fortune (we kid you not). So we think it has earned an encore. A lot of this book is fundamentally about making your own decisions and doing your own research, but you know what — if we can save you some time and effort, why not? You can thank us later. Anyway, it's time to make you privy to what our research tells us are unfolding megatrends that offer the greatest potential rewards (or risks) for stock investors. As usual, and as we indicate in Chapter 17, your stock investing actions must be tempered by existing industry conditions, which are in turn driven by the economy and other factors.

Moving forward, only a handful of changes in your portfolio over the past four decades would have made you tremendously rich. Had you put your money into natural resources (such as gold, silver, and oil) at the beginning of the 1970s and stayed put until the end of the decade, you would have made a fortune. Then, had you cashed in and switched to Japanese stocks in 1980 and held them for the rest of the decade, you would have made another fortune. Then, had you switched in 1990 to U.S. stocks for the entire decade, you would have made yet another fortune. What if you had cashed in your stocks in 2000? Well, for starters, you would have avoided huge losses in the down bear market. How about being bullish? What looks like a strong bull market for this decade?

By and large, the latter part of this decade and perhaps the beginning of the next one seems to parallel the '70s. The general realm of natural resources, something Canada has in abundance, looks to be the primary bull market for this decade. Why? First, look at what this decade has in common with the '70s:

- ✔ Problems with energy (rising costs, supply disruptions, and so on)

- ✔ Rising inflation (as the dollar, loonie, and other world currencies are increased in supply, something the U.S. Federal Reserve and the Bank of Canada already did and will continue to do for a while)

- ✔ International conflict (Iraq, Afghanistan, Iran, North Korea, and so on)

- ✔ Sluggish or recessionary Canadian and world economies

- ✔ Rising prices for essential natural resources (grains, metals, energy, lumber, and so on)

However, this decade has more to consider, including the following:

- ✔ Debt, debt, and more debt. Canada has increased its debt burden in 2009 to the tune of over $800 billion dollars. The U.S. debt is $76 trillion as of July 2009, five times its gross domestic product (GDP) total of $15 trillion. The U.S. is now the world's largest debtor nation.

- ✔ The U.S. as a major importer (versus being an exporter in the '70s)

- ✔ Canada as an export-dependent nation at a time when the U.S. and world economies are suffering, and not always buying what we're selling

- ✔ China, Russia, Brazil, and India as major economic competitors (and consumers of resources)

- ✔ The threat of terrorism affecting North America within its borders

- ✔ $550+ trillion worth of derivatives (almost 20 times larger than the world's total GDP)! Many of these derivatives, which are complicated investment vehicles, are nebulous and ultra-risky.

- ✔ Annual Canadian Old Age Security and universal healthcare costs in the tens of billions of dollars. Rising retirement and healthcare costs began in 2008 as the oldest baby boomers started to retire at age 62, and will escalate in 2011 and beyond as many turn 65.

This list isn't comprehensive (due to space limitations). The preceding points are enough to make you understand that this investing environment has changed dramatically, and you need to refocus your overall game plan to keep your money growing. It also makes you want to race off to Gilligan's island!

You'll see two types of opportunities in this chapter: bullish and bearish. We think you would also benefit from reading Chapter 17 on industries — if we can't help you find the winning stocks, then by golly we can at least show you what potential problem areas to stay away from.

# Bullish Opportunities

Being bullish (or going "long") is the natural inclination for most investors. It's an easy concept — buy low, sell high. No rocket science there. The following sections don't identify every bullish opportunity, but they do cover the most obvious ones (at least to us).

In the examples in the following sections, we reference time frames of several years. Why? You would have seen these stocks dip by 10 or 20 percent or more over a given short time frame such as a few weeks or a few months. But investing wisely means that time ultimately will get the stock price to higher ground, especially if you ride the megatrends.

As you research this area for places to help your investments grow, let us just mention two words that should guide you along the way: human need. As long as most (or even all) of your portfolio is geared toward those goods and services the public will need no matter how good or bad the economy is, you should do well in the long run. Remember, not *want*, but *need* — it's a safer bet in the coming years.

## Commodities

Two countries that figure to have a mega-impact on the world in the near future are China and India. In the past ten years, these countries have put their economies on the fast track. Consider the following:

- They've generally turned away from socialism and a command economy and have turned to a free market or more capitalistic system.

- Industrialization, privatization, and profit incentives have ignited tremendous booms in these countries.

- Both nations' populations have continued to grow, with nearly 3 billion people combined.

What do these facts mean for stock investors? Somebody has to sell China and India what they need. China, for example, has a voracious appetite for natural resources like building materials, energy, copper, grain, and so on. Canada is a treasure trove of these commodities. Companies that have provided these needed goods and services do very well. Take, for example, Agrium (AGU). You could have bought AGU in 2005 for about $20 per share. As of August 2009, AGU hit $40 for a nice gain of 100 percent (not including dividends). (In 2008 Agrium actually hit $100, but corrected after the start of the Great Recession. The key lesson here is that good stocks stay good even in recessions.) In that same time frame, the S&P 500 and TSX were up by only about 4 to 5 percent (basically flat for three years).

Of course, China and India are only a part of the world's emerging markets, but they're certainly the most important to North Americans (in terms of economic impact). They are indeed megatrends that will either help (or hurt) your portfolio. In the coming years, demand will likely continue to be strong, and investors will see the obvious positive implications for solid companies that meet this demand.

To find out more, check out the resources in Appendix A, such as Jim Rogers's book entitled *Hot Commodities*. You can also conduct research at sites such as www.futuresource.com, or the commodities section of the *National Post* (www.nationalpost.com).

## Oil and gas

As we write this, high-double-digit prices for oil and near $1-per-litre gas have become startling realities. Recent headlines suggest that the costs of energy are a major challenge for the Canadian and world economies. For decades, North American society has benefited from cheap oil, but global supply and demand (among other things) have caught up with us. A barrel of oil has gone from $67 in August 2005 to $85 only four years later. Gasoline has experienced a similar rise. Higher energy prices due to increased consumption are here to stay. If you're going to pay more for energy, you may as well benefit.

As energy prices have risen strongly over the past few years, how have stocks fared? The general stock market (as represented by the Dow Jones Industrial Average and the S&P 500 index) didn't do much from 2005 to mid-2008. How about energy stocks? For an example, look at Suncor (SU), a major Canadian oil exploration company whose fortunes are certainly tied to the energy market. Here's a company that you could have bought in late 2005 for about $20 per share. How has SU fared during this time frame? Despite pulling back from a high of over $100 in 2007, its stock is at $42 as of August 2009 for a solid gain of over 100 percent.

The bottom line is that Canadian stock investors will either have to consider energy in their investment strategies or risk having energy prices steamroll over their potential gains. Investment opportunities are plentiful in companies that provide, sell, distribute, or explore energy. But you may want to consider energy alternatives as well. Canada, the U.S., and the rest of the world will be forced to turn to alternative energy sources in the coming years. As conventional oil and gas become scarce, North Americans will look into gaining energy from sources such as wind, solar, fuel cell technologies, and Canada's oil sands, among others. (See the next section for more about alternative energy.)

As you read this chapter, you may not be sure about what particular company you should invest in. If that's the case, why not consider a convenient way to invest in an entire industry or sector? A good consideration is an exchange-traded fund (ETF). Buying an ETF is like buying a whole portfolio of stocks as if it were a single stock. An example is an ETF with the symbol XLE. XLE has a cross-section of the largest public oil and gas companies, such as Exxon Mobil, Chevron, and others. To find out more about ETFs, go to the American Stock Exchange (www.amex.com) or *Financial Post* (www.financialpost.com) for all the details.

## Alternative energy

Because a traditional energy source like oil has its supply issues (oil's days are numbered), it makes sense to anticipate what's next on the horizon that can logically fulfill Canada's energy needs. These changes must happen, and Canadian stock investors should benefit from what will be a historic shift into alternative energy. Alternative energy includes (but isn't limited to) nuclear energy, solar, wind, fuel cell, geothermal, and ocean currents. You can now find many stocks and ETFs that are among the myriad choices for investors to gain exposure in a sector as it becomes more and more prominent in the coming months and years. Check out Appendix B for general resources to help you research this great sector.

## Gold and other precious metals

Over the ages, gold has come to be synonymous with wealth. In modern times, gold has become known as an inflation hedge and investment insurance, especially during times of inflation and geopolitical uncertainty. After being in a 20-year bear market (from its high of $850 in 1980 to its low of $252 in 2000), gold is in a powerful bull market. Aggressive investors should be investigating Canadian and other gold stocks and ETFs. Why now?

According to many (if not most) gold market analysts, such as Bill Murphy of the Gold Anti-Trust Action Committee (www.gata.org), as well as sites that specialize in the gold market, like www.lemetropolecafe.com, www.gold-eagle.com, and www.kitco.com, the fundamentals for gold are more bullish than ever. In recent years, demand has begun to significantly exceed supply. The shortfall has been filled from gold sales by central banks. Because of continued and growing demand in Canada, the U.S., and abroad (most notably Russia, India, and China), total worldwide annual demand is outstripping supply by anywhere from 1,000 to 2,000 tons (depending on whose estimates you believe). Juxtapose this demand with current economic conditions (such as the declining value of the dollar and other paper currencies) and geopolitical instability, and you can see that gold and gold-related investments (such as quality gold stocks and ETFs) show bullish potential.

Because gold does well in an inflationary environment, understanding inflation itself is important. Inflation isn't the price of things going up; it's the value of the currency going down. The reason it goes down in value is primarily because the government can print money at will (the money supply). When you significantly increase the money supply, you create a bullish environment for hard assets such as gold. (For more about inflation, see Chapter 10.)

Gold analysts such as Bill Murphy, Doug Casey, Jay Taylor, James Sinclair, and many others accurately forecast that the price of gold would hit four figures (it did in March 2008) and that the current environment sees gold zigzagging to new highs in the coming years. If that's the case, Canadian and other gold-mining stocks and ETFs will perform fantastically well (not unlike their heyday in the late 1970s). For conservative investors, consider the large, established mining firms such as Newmont Mining (NEM), Barrick Gold (ABX), Goldcorp Inc (G), and Agnico-Eagle (AEM). For the more daring, consider junior mining stocks. Do your research using the Web sites mentioned in this section.

As an additional note, the general precious metals market is strong and is a good consideration for solid gains because of the current inflationary environment. We think that silver and even uranium (for energy) offer Canadian investors good opportunities. To find out more, check out *Precious Metals Investing For Dummies* (Wiley).

## Healthcare

We're sure you've heard much about the "greying" of Canada. This phrase obviously represents a firm megatrend in place. For stock investors, this megatrend is a purely demographic play, and the numbers are with them. The number of Canadians over the age of 50, and especially those considered senior citizens, represents the fastest growing segment of Canadian society. The same megatrend is in place in all corners of the world (especially Europe). As more and more people move into this category, the idea that companies that serve this segment will also prosper becomes a no-brainer. Well-managed companies that run nursing homes and eldercare services will see their stocks rise.

Be careful about which healthcare firms you select, because this sector includes stocks that are defensive and also some that are cyclical. Companies that sell expensive equipment (such as CAT scans or MRI technology) may not do that well in an economic downturn because hospitals and other healthcare facilities may not want to upgrade or replace their equipment. Therefore, healthcare companies that sell big-ticket items can be considered cyclical. On the other hand, businesses that sell necessary items like medicine and bandages (such as pharmaceuticals and drug retailers) can be considered defensive. People who need medicine (such as Aspirin or antacids) will buy it no matter how bad the economy is. In fact, people will probably buy even more Aspirin and antacids in bad economic times.

Also be wary of political trends as they affect healthcare. The U.S. may be slowly lurching toward socialized medicine. If this possibility develops, turn your bullish expectations into bearish ones. History (and experience) tells us that a government takeover of an industry like healthcare spells danger for investors (and patients, too).

To find out more about healthcare opportunities, check out the industry and main stocks by using the resources in Appendix B.

## Defending the nation

The horrific events of September 11, 2001, remind the world how vulnerable we are as a free and open society. It has been a brave new world ever since. People watch their TV screens and listen to their radios to discover that terrorism's wretched tentacles reach across the globe. The most obvious way the country can respond is to increase security at home while deploying forces across the world to combat terrorists and tangle with the countries that support them. Foes of the U.S. and their allies aren't singular nations that are easily defined, fought, and defeated within a few months or a few years. Instead, they're implacable and virulent, and they're spread out over many countries.

In addition to terrorism, geopolitical developments pose potential problems. Russia, China, and Iran are among the hot spots that will continue to challenge Americans and even Canadians economically as well as militarily.

As the U.S. continues to retool its military and seek ways to monitor, track, and attack terrorists, defence companies that sell certain products and services will benefit. For publications that do a great job informing investors and speculators regarding the war economy, check out the U.S. & World Early Warning Report (www.chaostan.com).

# A Bearish Outlook

Stocks are versatile in that you can make money even when they go down in value. Techniques range from using put options to going short, or doing a short sale of stock. (See Chapter 21 regarding going short, and find out more about put options at www.cboe.com.) For traditional investors, the more appropriate strategy is first and foremost to avoid or minimize losses. Making money betting that a stock will fall is closer to speculating than actual investing. So all we want is that investors see the pitfalls and act accordingly. The following sections offer cautionary alerts to keep you away from troubled areas in the economy (or find speculative opportunities to short stocks).

The Dow Jones Industrial Average (DJIA) hit a high of 11,722 in January 2000 and, after seven roller-coaster years, hit an all-time high of 14,164.53 on October 9, 2007. (As we write this, the DJIA is about 8,300.) As you can see, the general market since January 2000 has been mediocre. Although some stock groups have grown quite well, stocks in general have struggled, and some sectors have done rather poorly. Choosing the right sector is critical for your stock investing success going forward. That's because the global economy is still in a mess.

## Avoiding consumer discretionary sectors

When the economy is struggling or contracting and people are concerned about their financial situation, some sectors will undoubtedly suffer. If you have money tied up in stocks attached to companies in these sectors, you may suffer as well. In today's economic environment, we would generally avoid sectors such as "consumer discretionary," which refers to companies that sell products or services that people may want but usually don't need. In other words, when consumers (both individuals and organizations) have to make hard choices on tighter budgets, the first areas of spending that will logically shrink are those goods and services that simply aren't that necessary in people's daily lives.

Here's an example: In trying times, those who typically eat at fancy, expensive restaurants will cut back. Maybe they'll eat at fast food places or simply opt for good ol' home cooking. Multiply this choice by millions of consumers and you see that high-end restaurants (and their stocks, if they're public companies) will see their fortunes sink. Your logic and common sense are very useful here.

# A warning on real estate

In the second edition of this book, we warned you to stay away from housing because it became an enormous (and dangerous) bubble during 2002–06. It has since sunk into its own depression in the U.S., and into the doldrums in Canada. Although buying opportunities are plenty and sellers are having a difficult time, our warning on housing and the general real estate market (of course, all stocks associated with this sector) is still on. Be very cautious here and wait for a rebound. "But," you may ask, "isn't the worst over? Isn't 2009 the bottom?" Possibly, but just understand that more credit problems still hang over the market.

Some recent industry data indicate that during 2007, one out of every seven American homes purchased was underwater as of mid-2009. In other words, one out of every seven homeowners has a mortgage more valuable than the property purchased! Yikes! That means that some homebuyer out there has, say, a $250,000 mortgage on a property that has seen its market price decline to less than $250,000. How many homeowners will keep paying a mortgage that's worth more than the property itself, especially if times are tough and people are struggling or have lost a job?

In Canada, the problem is less pronounced. For one thing, Canadians cannot just walk away from a mortgage like Americans can because Canadian law says the mortgage debt follows the owner of the house, not just the house. Yet, markets such as Toronto, Calgary, and Vancouver have certainly seen price declines recently.

The fortunes of the U.S. housing market can affect you as a stock investor if you've chosen stocks that are impacted by the U.S. real estate industry.

In addition, think about *mortgage resets,* a U.S. housing market phenomenon. What does that mean? During the middle of this decade (2004–07), many people purchased property with adjustable-rate mortgages (ARMs). These ARMs typically had an introductory period with a low fixed monthly payment during the first few years and then were adjusted higher afterward. Many folks got into ARMs with the expectation that real estate would continue rising and that they'd be able to handle the new (higher) monthly payments later. These ARMs became ticking time bombs. Many of them hit unprepared homeowners and forced quick sales, which made real estate prices drop as sales outnumbered purchases and the U.S. inventory of available homes for sale ballooned to record levels. And the ARMs aren't finished — many more are due to be adjusted during 2009–11.

You can see that the real estate industry, with the ARMs issues and record levels of defaults and foreclosures, will need more time to heal and get back on a growth path. For Canadian stock investors, the point is obvious. Stocks related to real estate such as homebuilders, property developers, construction firms, and mortgage companies are too speculative at this point. Wait until the coast is clear.

To find out more about what's going on with this sector, check out www.realtor.com and www.realestatetopsites.com. The Canadian Real Estate Association (www.crea.ca) has data, including informative podcasts, on the national real estate market.

## The great credit monster

Too much debt means that someone will get hurt. The unprecedented explosion in debt may, especially in the U.S., have given the North American economy a huge boost in the late 1990s, but debt now poses great dangers for the rest of this decade. This massive debt problem is obviously tied to real estate. However, it goes much further. Individuals, companies, and government agencies are carrying too much debt for comfort. It's not just mortgage debt; it's also consumer, business, government, and margin debt. With total debt now in the vicinity of more than $45 trillion, saying that a lot of this debt won't be repaid is probably a safe bet. Individual and institutional defaults will rock the economy and the financial markets. Bankruptcy is (and will continue to be) a huge issue.

Debt will (and does) weigh heavily on stocks, either directly or indirectly. Because every type of debt is now at record levels, no one is truly immune. Say you have a retail stock of a company that has no debt whatsoever. Are you immune? Not really, because consumer debt (credit cards, personal loans, and so on) is at an all-time high. If consumer spending declines, the retailer's sales go down, its profits shrink, and ultimately, its stock goes down.

Exposure to debt is quite pervasive. Check your RRSP, your bond funds, and your RRIF status. Why? Remember those mortgages we talk about earlier in this chapter? Banks and mortgage companies issued trillions of dollars' worth of those mortgages in recent years, but after the mortgages were issued, they were sold to other financial institutions, even a few Canadian banks. The lion's share of mortgages was sold to the most obvious buyers, the U.S. Federal National Mortgage Association (FNM) and the U.S. Federal Mortgage Assurance Corporation (FRE). These giant, American government-sponsored entities are usually referred to as "Fannie Mae" and "Freddie Mac." They were taken over in 2008 by the federal government because of gross mismanagement and overindebtedness (in the trillions!). Hmm . . . there goes that alarmist robot with the flailing arms again.

In Canada, we did not have risky ARM banking products to peddle. Yet, the world's problems became our problems, and our own national debt levels have soared as a result. For example, the federal government had to support its own significant auto and other manufacturing sectors, and also wanted to create employment by building more infrastructure like roads and bridges.

That cost money — and lots of it. To execute this plan the Canadian government recently announced a $22 billion stimulus package — with an attendant deficit of $50 billion, just for 2009. For 2009, the national debt cracked $500 billion. The cost of servicing this debt is about 30 percent of all government spending. That's why debt matters!

What's a stock investor to do?

- ✔ Well, remember that first commandment to avoid or minimize losses? Make sure you review your portfolio and sell stocks that may get pulverized by the credit monster. That includes many U.S. banks and any brokerage firm.

- ✔ Make sure the companies themselves have no debt, low debt, or at least manageable debt. (Check their financial reports; see Chapter 12 for more details.)

- ✔ For the venturesome, seek shorting opportunities in those companies most exposed to the dangers of debt. (For more information on shorting, go to Chapter 21.)

## Cyclical stocks

Another type of stock that we think you should be cautious about is cyclical stocks. Heavy equipment, automobiles, and technology tend to be cyclical and are very susceptible to downturns in the general economy. Conversely, cyclical stocks do very well when the economy is growing or on an upswing (hence the label).

As individuals and corporations get squeezed with more debt and less disposable income, hard choices need to be made. Ultimately, the result is that people buy fewer big-ticket items. That means a company selling those items ends up selling less and earning less profit. This loss of profit, in turn, makes that company's stock go down.

Firms that experience lagging sales often turn to aggressive discounting. Recently, General Motors Corporation (GM) and Ford Motor Company (F) offered employee discount sales to the public. Both companies have been experiencing plunging sales and profits and ballooning debt in recent years. Unfortunately, that was a token gesture at best. Both companies filed for bankruptcy in 2009.

In a struggling recessionary economy, investing in cyclical stocks is like sunbathing on an anthill and using jam instead of sunblock — not a pretty picture.

# Geographic regions: Stalled economic engines

One interesting way to look at stock investing opportunities is through a geographic lens. Perhaps you wish to throw your support behind an emerging nation that you believe will soon thrive economically, and proceed to invest in the stock of a company that operates in that country. If everything works out well, you'll find your investment success to be rewarding from a financial perspective. However, emerging nations have not escaped the claws of the recent and generally worldwide recession. As a result, we urge you to invest cautiously in companies that operate in these countries. However, after the world economy recovers, stock investors would do well to know a bit more about the more promising nations we discuss in this section.

## China

If you recently bought a household product and checked to see where it was manufactured, you very likely saw a "Made in China" label. China is in the news a lot more often than it used to be, and today's news about China has more to do with the economy and business, and less to do with political unrest and corruption. Yup, China is a waking giant that is touching the lives of all Canadians in one way or another.

China's stock market is now the third biggest in Asia, and China's now a member of the World Trade Organization (WTO), a powerful group of countries with lots of economic and political clout. To add to China's attractiveness as a stock investing destination, government policies have become much friendlier to investors than they were only a few years ago. Scandals and rural political unrest still abound, but this time the government is being a bit less heavy-handed in its efforts to minimize it. A lot of risk still exists in China, so for now just keep an eye on it. At best, we recommend only small nibbles of conservative and better known Chinese stocks.

## India

Stock investors who set their sights on India may find some undervalued businesses that have seen the market value of their shares plummet after the global recession. India deserves consideration because it is still experiencing a positive transformation in its business and financial markets. In fact, India is currently the fourth largest economy in terms of purchasing power. It's also the ninth most industrialized country in the world, and it continues to have a progressive economy. This progress is thanks in the most part to smart political and economic reforms undertaken in the '90s.

As we implied with China, only a small fraction of your portfolio should be considered for investment in Indian stocks. But even a small investment targeted in the right area can produce big returns.

TECHNICAL STUFF

# How shares trade in China

Publicly traded Chinese companies can list their shares on certain global equity markets in addition to, or instead of, being listed on the major Chinese stock exchanges (Shanghai and Shenzhen). Also, some companies are listed on only one of the mainland Chinese exchanges. Almost anything goes with regard to how and where Chinese shares may be listed.

Four types of shares are listed in China:

✔ *State shares* are held on behalf of the Chinese state and are prohibited from being traded on an open equity market.

✔ *Legal-person shares* (also known as "C" shares) are shares of a company owned by another company or institution with a legal-person status. The foreign trading of legal-person shares is also prohibited.

✔ *Individual shares* (also known as "A" shares) can be traded and owned only by Chinese citizens, and they are traded only in China's domestic markets.

✔ *Foreign-capital shares* (known as "B" shares, or overseas-listed shares) can

be traded by Canadians and others who are foreign to the Chinese mainland. "B" shares are traded in the stock exchanges of mainland China. Many Chinese companies issue both A shares and B shares.

Another class of shares, called "H" shares, is listed on the Hong Kong Stock Exchange. These Chinese company shares are sometimes also listed as ADRs on U.S. stock exchanges. An ADR (American depository receipt) is a negotiable certificate issued by a U.S. bank that represents a specific number of shares (or a single share) in a foreign stock that's traded on a U.S. exchange. ADRs are expressed only in U.S. dollars, and a U.S. financial institution operating in Hong Kong holds the underlying security. (ADRs are also available for other nations foreign to the U.S.) ADRs serve to reduce the administrative costs that would otherwise accumulate on each transaction.

By the way, in Hong Kong, the best stocks are referred to as "red chips." For Chinese people, the colour red exemplifies good fortune!

## Latin America

Latin America is a group of countries that includes Mexico, Chile, Brazil, Argentina, and Venezuela. Although we speak of them as a group here, you must view each country's business, economic, and political climate separately. This distinction should be made because as a *group,* and over the last few decades, Latin America's macroeconomic performance has been subpar. There's a track record of slow responses to economic and political crises.

Since a couple of decades ago, this region has been touted as a great growth market for North American companies because of the availability of cheap labour and a hunger for consumer goods. However, this potential has never been fulfilled in a significant way. Argentina is still struggling with an economic slowdown, Mexico devalued its currency over a decade ago, Brazil has a socialist president who is leery of foreign investment and still has loads of debt, and Venezuela has an ultra-nationalistic leader at its helm.

---

## Bombay Stock Exchange

The Bombay Stock Exchange is about 125 years old, and it's Asia's largest exchange. The Sensex 30 is India's best-known stock market index. Think of it as the Indian equivalent to the Dow Jones Industrial Average, or an S&P/TSX index.

---

Your broker will have information about the nuts and bolts of trading shares in public companies operating in any of these countries (see Chapter 21 for more about placing orders to buy and sell stocks).

# Important Considerations for Bulls and Bears

We don't presume that stocks go straight up or that they zigzag upward indefinitely. Your due diligence is necessary for your success. Make sure that you're investing appropriately for your situation. If you're 35, heading into your peak earning years, want to ride a home-run stock, and understand the risks, then go ahead and speculate with that small-cap gold-mining stock or the solar power technology junior stock.

But if you're more risk averse or your situation is screaming out loud for you to be conservative, then don't speculate. Go instead with a more diversified portfolio of large-cap stocks or get the ETF for that particular sector. And don't forget the trailing stop-loss strategy (see Chapter 21). 'Nuff said.

For those people who want to make money by going short in those sectors that look bearish, again take a deep breath and remember what's appropriate. Conservative investors simply avoid the risky areas. Aggressive investors or speculators may want to deploy profitable bearish strategies (with a portion of their investable funds). Here are some highlights for all of you.

## Conservative and bullish

Being conservative and bullish is proper when you're in (or near) retirement, have a family to support, or live in a very large shoe with so many kids that you don't know what to do. After you choose a promising sector, just select large-cap companies that are financially strong, are generating cash and profits, have low debt, and are market leaders. This entire book shows you how to do just that.

However, you may not like the idea of buying stocks directly. In that case, consider either sector mutual funds or ETFs. That way you can choose the industry and effectively buy a basket of the top stocks in that area. ETFs have been a hot item lately, and we think they're a great choice for most investors because they offer some huge advantages over mutual funds. For example, you can put stop-loss orders on them or borrow against them in your stock portfolio. Check with your financial adviser to see whether ETFs are appropriate for you.

## Aggressive and bullish

If you're aggressive and bullish, you want to buy stocks directly. For real growth potential, look at mid caps or small caps. Remember that you're speculating, so you understand the downside risk but are willing to tolerate it because the upside potential can reward you so handsomely. Few things in the investment world give you a better gain than a supercharged stock in a hot sector.

## Conservative and bearish

For many (if not most) investors, making money on a falling market isn't generally a good idea. Doing so takes a lot of expertise and risk tolerance. Really, for conservative investors, the key word is safety. Analyze your portfolio with an adviser you trust and sell the potentially troubled stocks. If you're not sure what to do on a particular stock, then (at the very least) put in stop-loss orders and make them GTC (good-till-cancelled; see Chapter 21 for details). As odd as it sounds, sometimes losing less than others makes you come out ahead if you play it right.

For example, look at the bear market that hit North American markets in the mid-1970s. In 1974–75, the stock market fell 45 percent. Stocks didn't recover until 1982. If you had a stock that was at $100, it would have fallen to $55 and not returned to $100 until seven or eight years later. Whew! Sometimes just burying your money in the backyard sounds like genius. What if you had a stop-loss at $90? You would have gotten out with a minimal loss and could have reinvested the money elsewhere (such as in bonds or CDs) and looked much brighter than your neighbour feverishly digging for money in his backyard.

## Aggressive and bearish

Being aggressive in a bearish market isn't for the faint of heart. However, this is where the quickest fortunes have been made by some of history's greatest investors. Going short can make you great money when the market is bearish, but it can sink you if you're wrong. We rarely tell our clients and students to short a stock, because it can backfire. Yes, ways to go short with less risk are out there, but we prefer to buy put options.

Put options are a way to make money with limited risk when you essentially make a bet that an investment (such as stocks) will go down. Obviously, options go beyond the scope of this book, but at least let us give you some direction, because an appropriate options strategy exists for most stock portfolios. You can find great (free) tutorials on using options at Web sites such as the Chicago Board Options Exchange (www.cboe.com) and the Options Industry Council (www.888options.com).

# Part IV
# Investment Strategies

The 5th Wave                    By Rich Tennant

"Growth stock? Income stock? I say we stick the money in the ground like always, and then feed this guy to the sharks."

# In this part . . .

**S**uccessful stock investing is more than choosing a particular stock — it's also how you go about doing it. Successful investors go beyond merely picking good stocks and watching the financial news. They implement trading techniques and investment strategies that help them either minimize losses or maximize gains (hopefully both). The chapters in this part introduce some of the most effective investing techniques and describe some smart ways to hold onto more of your profits when tax time rolls around.

# Chapter 19

# Choosing between Investing and Trading

. . . . . . . . . . . . . . . . . . . . . . . . . . . . . . . . . . . . . . . . . . . . . . . . . . . . . . . . . . . . . . . . . . . . . . . . . . . . . . . .

*In This Chapter*

▶ Understanding the differences between investing and trading

▶ Checking out the tools of stock trading

▶ Sticking to important rules for safe trading

. . . . . . . . . . . . . . . . . . . . . . . . . . . . . . . . . . . . . . . . . . . . . . . . . . . . . . . . . . . . . . . . . . . . . . . . . . . . . . . .

*Y*ou may have heard about stock trading and wondered how it compares to stock investing. Rest assured that trading and investing are two different animals. Trading can be advantageous when you're looking to profit from short-term swings in the market due to volatility. During our still unpredictable economic times, trading in and out of stocks over shorter time frames may be very appropriate. However, trading can be dangerous because the market's short-term movements can be quite pronounced. If you think the market will go up in the short term, and it goes down instead, you can lose loads of cash in one fell swoop.

The only reason we're including trading in this book is because you, dear reader, should get some do's and don'ts in this short-term venture. If you're going to trade stocks, you should have some guidelines to keep the downside to a minimum. We explain what you need to know in this chapter.

## The Differences between Investing and Trading

Stock investing and stock trading may sound similar, but they're actually pretty different:

✔ Investing looks primarily at fundamentals (earnings, sales, industry outlook, and so on), which tend to be long-term drivers of stock prices. The long-term investor waits out the zigzags as long as the bullish outlook and the general uptrend are intact. The good part is that investing involves fewer transaction costs. The bad part is that sometimes the stock can correct (go down temporarily) or have periods of flat performance, which the long-term Canadian investor has to patiently tolerate.

✔ In trading, much more activity takes place during a range of a few days, weeks, or months. Traders may dump losers immediately and cash out winners to lock in some profit before the next dip in price. Trading can mean more costs due to frequent commissions and short-term taxable gains. For trading, the fundamentals are either not a factor or at best a secondary or minor factor because short-term movements in a stock price are more geared to momentum and sentiment, which is reflected in the data found in charts along with price and volume statistics.

The following sections give you the full scoop on the differences between investing and trading.

## The time factor

When we first started investing in stocks, it was easy to delineate what was *short term, intermediate term,* and *long term:*

✔ Short term was less than one year.

✔ Intermediate term was usually one to three years or one to five years, depending on your personal outlook.

✔ Long term was beyond that time frame.

In recent years, however, investors have become very impatient. For some investors, short term is now measured in days, intermediate term in weeks, and long term in months. In the old days, investors were akin to cooks using the crock pot; today, they use the microwave. But these people are actually traders, not investors. If an investment does well, they sell it immediately and move on to (hopefully) another profitable investment. If the investment is down, they sell it immediately and move on to (hopefully) greener pastures elsewhere.

There's no such thing as a three-month investment when it comes to stocks. Stocks require time for the marketplace to discover them. Sometimes great stocks see their prices move very little because the market (again, millions of individual and institutional investors) hasn't noticed them yet. In trading, on the other hand, you jump in and out relatively quickly. Typical trades occur over the span of a few days or a few weeks. Of course, if a position you take on grows more profitable and your expectations are positive, you can stay in longer. But many experienced traders won't tempt fate and stay in too long; a reversal of fortune can always occur, so don't be shy about cashing out and taking a profit.

# The psychology factor

In investing, you can be very analytical. You can look at a stock and its fundamentals and then at the prospects for the stock's industry and the general economy, and you can make a good choice knowing that you're not worried about the price going up or down a few percentage points in the next few days or weeks. If you've done your homework, your stock will eventually go up and do well over the long haul.

Trading is different. Trading involves looking at stocks that have the ability to move quickly, regardless of the direction. The reason is that seasoned traders want to make money quickly and capitalize on crowd psychology. It matters little whether investors are bidding up or down; the trader is primarily looking for a stock with momentum.

# Checking out an example

The stock investor takes the long view and stays patient and focused. As we try to stress throughout this book, investing should be measured in years, and the stock's *fundamentals* (a company's profits, sales, industry, and so on) are the foundation. A patient and successful investor holds on as the stock zigzags upward. When the inevitable correction occurs, a successful investor either just waits it out or takes that moment as a buying opportunity and adds shares to her holdings. In a bullish (up) outlook, the investor expects the stock to generally trend upward. If the investor expects a stock to have a downward path, then obviously she simply avoids it.

The stock trader sees things differently. The trader may indeed be just as bullish on a particular stock but also bet on the occasional pullback or correction that's typical of most stocks. The trader may buy 100 shares of a stock and keep it as a core holding, but also make different bets on its price movement.

For an example, take a look at the chart in Figure 19-1. This is a chart of Zig Zag Corporation (ZZC), and it's helpful in showing you how investing and trading behave differently during the same time frame.

An investor would have bought ZZC stock in 2007 and held on. As long as the fundamentals don't change, the investor just "buys right and sits tight." Although some traders may smirk at such a simple strategy, it's a time-tested approach. Look at billionaire Warren Buffett for a great example of this. He has been known to hold stocks for decades. Many investors (and traders, too) envy his extraordinary success, but relatively few try to emulate it. Patience and discipline aren't always popular or fashionable in investing, but a patient, disciplined approach has generally proven to be superior to many trading systems that tell you to jump in and jump out. However, because markets have been more volatile this last decade than in almost all previous decades, trading cannot be dismissed as a viable approach to make money on stocks.

Going back to Figure 19-1, how would successful traders have performed with ZZC? The trader may start off as an investor and make that initial investment in the stock. As time passes, the trader would be watching technical indicators to time an entry or exit point. A *technical indicator* is a result of a mathematical calculation based on prices and the volume of trading, typically displayed as a chart. (See the "Technical analysis" section in this chapter.)

Stock traders typically use options (such as calls and puts) because they're cheap and can provide a magnified move with the underlying stock. In other words, options are a form of leverage, meaning that the price swing can be greater (up or down) than the move in the underlying stock. If a stock moves up 10 percent, then an option (in this case a call option) could go up 20 percent or more. Of course, if the stock goes down 10 percent, then that same option could easily go down 20 percent or more.

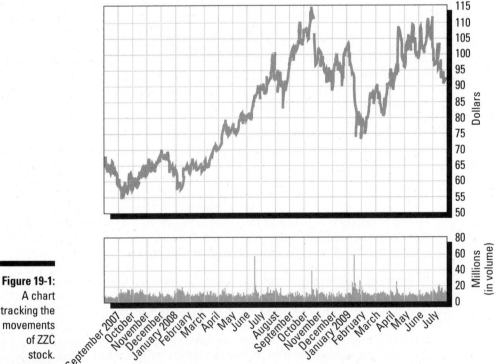

**Figure 19-1:**
A chart tracking the movements of ZZC stock.

What are call and put options?

- ✔ A *call option* is a bet that a particular stock (or exchange-traded fund) will go up during the life of the option.

- ✔ A *put option* is a bet that a particular stock (or exchange-traded fund) will go down during the life of the option.

Think of the following (very rough) rule of thumb:

- ✔ If the stock goes up 10 percent, a call option on that stock could go up 20 percent. Of course, a put option on that same stock would lose 20 percent (or more).

- ✔ If the stock goes down 10 percent, a call option could go down 20 percent. Of course, a put option on that same stock would gain 20 percent (or more).

- ✔ If the stock stays flat or neutral, both the call and put options would start to lose value because options have a finite life and can potentially be worthless by the time they expire.

Referring back to Figure 19-1, the Canadian stock trader may have seen his stock rise during October and November 2007 from about $55 per share to $70. Technical indicators may have flashed that the stock is overbought. Some traders would have cashed in and sat with the cash, waiting for the next opportunity. Other traders would have kept the stock but cashed in any call options that were purchased before that time frame for a nice profit. The money from cashing out the sale of the call options would sit waiting for the next entry point. Perhaps the trader would then use the money to purchase put options, betting that a correction was soon due. Then you see the huge move up by ZZC starting at about $55 in December 2007 and hitting $115 in October 2008 before correcting in a zigzag fashion down to about $73 in January 2009.

Had the trader employed both calls and puts, he would have had plenty of opportunities for profit. During the summer of 2008, the call options would have been profitable and could have been cashed out. In that scenario, a call option could easily reward the astute trader with triple-percentage gains. Of course, the puts in the same time frame would have greatly lost value. Heading into the September 2008–January 2009 period, the bearish strategies would have paid off because put options would rise in value as the underlying asset (in this case the stock of ZZC) declined.

As you can see, the successful trader must diligently monitor his positions and frequently enter more than one position on the same stock to try to capitalize on the stock's movements. Whenever you take opposing positions on the same security, you're doing a form of hedging. Hedging takes into consideration the idea that the market can easily go against you, which is an especially likely scenario if the market is volatile. In that case, why not profit from the move?

Keep in mind that any profits are offset by any losses from options that lose value (or expire worthless) and by transaction costs.

Scores of books have been written about options, so we won't go into great detail here. But to get familiar with options — especially if short-term speculating or trading greatly interests you — start with *Stock Options For Dummies* by Alan R. Simon and *Trading Options For Dummies* by George A. Fontanills, both published by Wiley.

# Tools of the Canadian Trader

As you can judge from the example we provide earlier in this chapter, successful trading requires lots of diligent attention. Because stocks can go all over the place, the Canadian trader uses various tools to determine entry and exit points. We cover some of those tools and strategies in the following sections.

## Technical analysis

The most common tool of short-term speculators and traders is technical analysis. *Technical analysis* looks at the recent price movements and volume of trading for particular securities and commodities. The price movements are depicted on charts, so "charting a security" is a common practice among those who use technical analysis.

The technical analyst uses some useful short-term indicators, including

- ✔ *Moving averages* to gauge the general trend for a particular stock. Typical moving averages are the 10-day, 20-day, 50-day, and 200-day averages. Stocks that stay above these averages tend to be bullish, while stocks that keep falling below these averages tend to be bearish.

- ✔ *Relative strength indicators (RSI)* to see if a stock is considered oversold or overbought. A technical analyst sees an oversold stock as a buying opportunity and an overbought stock as a selling opportunity.

Technical analysis is a complex topic, and we just can't do it justice in this solitary chapter. We don't mean to shortchange it, as it's worthy of study for serious traders. We mention it here because traders should be aware of it, regardless of how extensively they use it. We strongly recommend that serious traders do some extensive research on the topic. Consider starting your research with *Technical Analysis For Dummies* by Barbara Rockefeller (Wiley).

As most longtime readers probably know by now, we're not ardent fans of technical analysis. Don't get us wrong; we respect it as a short-term trading tool. It can be remarkably useful over a period of a few weeks or months. However, it's not that useful for long-term investing. Yes, you can use it to maximize an entry or exit point, but over the long haul, a company's fundamentals are the primary drivers of the stock's price. When you look at the pantheon of consistently successful investors in history, it's no accident that most of them use fundamental analysis and are into some form of value investing.

## Brokerage orders

Because trading in the market's short-term gyrations can be a fast-moving activity, it pays to get proficient with brokerage orders and trading triggers to help you manage your trading portfolio and take advantage of the market's swift moves.

The moment after a diligent trader buys a stock or an option, she'll enter her next order very quickly — often even before the stock has made a major move. For example, if she buys a stock for $50 at 10 a.m. on a weekday morning, she may enter a stop-loss order at, say, $45 at 11 a.m. and simultaneously put in a sell order at $60. That way she can limit the loss to $5 per share and maybe catch a $10 profit on the upside. These moves are possible now due to the sophisticated technology that most brokers have on their Web sites.

That's just an example of what you can do with brokerage orders. Find out more about brokerage orders and trade triggers in Chapter 21.

## Advisory services

You don't have to go it alone with your trading strategies — the world is filled with advisory services, newsletters, and Web sites that cater to the art and science of short-term trading. Some notable ones that we respect include Elliott Wave International (www.elliottwave.com) and Stock Trading Canada (www.stocktradingcanada.ca). A monthly publication that covers the realm of trading is *Stock, Futures and Options* magazine (www.sfomag.com). Of course, you can do your own diligent research at the library and on the Internet (check Appendix B for resources).

# The Basic Rules of Trading

If you're going to trade, adhere to some golden rules to help you maximize your success (or at least minimize potential losses):

- **Don't commit all your cash at once:** In a fast-moving market, opportunities come up all the time. Try to keep some cash on hand to take advantage of those opportunities.

- **Have a plan:** Try to have predetermined points at which you cut losses or take profits.

- **Taking profits is not a sin:** Sometimes, a bird in the hand is worth two in the bush. Markets can reverse fairly quickly. If you have a stock position sitting there with a fat profit, it can't hurt to take the profit. This gives you cash for the next opportunity.

- **Discover hedging techniques:** Just because you're bullish doesn't mean that you can't also put on a bearish position. Hedging techniques protect you when the market moves against you.

- **Find out which events move markets:** Research the Canadian market and discover what types of events tend to move it (either up or down). Do the same for foreign stock markets, especially the U.S. stock market. Serious short-term traders keep one eye on their positions and the other on what's going on in the world. Keep informed by regularly reading financial publications and Web sites (see Appendix B for resources).

- **Check the stock's trading history:** Charts and related data tell you how a particular stock has moved in recent weeks, months, and years. Do you see any seasonality or reliable patterns that may help you judge future movements?

- **Use stop-loss and limit orders:** Using trade orders is an integral part of the trader's overall strategy. Find out more in Chapter 21.

- **Use discipline and patience versus emotion and panic:** Part of the human equation in the world of financial markets is that fear and greed can become an irrational, short-term driver of prices. Instead of joining the crowd, watch them to give you an advantage in assessing a stock's price movements. Stick with your plan and use discipline and patience.

- **Minimize transaction costs:** Keep in mind that because trading is typically active and short term, transaction costs are significant. Active trading can mean lots of brokerage commissions, even in this age of Internet-based brokerage firms. Therefore, traders should shop around for brokerage firms that charge low commissions for those who trade frequently ($9.99 per trade is typical for Canadian discount brokerages, which you can check out in Appendix B).

✔ **Understand the beta of a stock:** The volatility of a stock is an important consideration for traders. The more volatile a stock is, the greater its ups and downs are. Therefore, traders should regularly check the stock's beta. *Beta* is a statistical measure of how volatile a particular stock is relative to a market standard (such as the S&P 500 index).

How is it measured? The S&P 500 (for example) is given a beta of 1. A stock with a beta of 2 is considered twice as volatile as the index. In other words, if the index falls by 10 percent, the stock in question has the potential of falling by 20 percent. A stock with a beta of 0.5 is considered to be half as volatile as the index. In other words, if the index falls by 10 percent, that low-beta stock would be expected to fall only 5 percent.

Traders looking for fast (and hopefully profitable) movement look for high-beta opportunities. A stock's beta can be found on various financial Web sites (see resources in Appendix B).

✔ **Read and learn from top traders:** Last (but not least), learn from the great ones out there, such as the legendary Jesse Livermore. You can read all about his trading exploits in the book *Reminiscences of a Stock Operator* by Edwin Lefevre (Wiley).

Because trading can be very risky, you need to know as much as you can. Don't use your rent money or retirement money, and for crying out loud, don't break open your kid's piggy bank. Trading should be done only with *risk capital* (money that, if lost, doesn't hurt your lifestyle). And don't forget the advice from the immortal Will Rogers: "Don't gamble; take all your savings and buy some good stock and hold it till it goes up, then sell it. If it don't go up, don't buy it."

# Chapter 20

# Selecting a Strategy That's Just Right for You

. . . . . . . . . . . . . . . . . . . . . . . . . . . . . . . . . . . . . . . . . . . . . .

## In This Chapter

▶ Basing your investing strategy on your needs and time frame

▶ Deciding where and how to allocate your assets

▶ Recognizing when to unload your stocks

. . . . . . . . . . . . . . . . . . . . . . . . . . . . . . . . . . . . . . . . . . . . . .

**S**tocks are a means to an end. What end are you seeking? Look at stocks as tools for wealth building. Sometimes they're great tools, and sometimes they're awful. The results you get depend on your approach. Some stocks are appropriate for a conservative approach; others are more suitable for an aggressive approach. Sometimes stocks aren't a good idea at all. Golly! A stock investing book that suggests that stocks aren't always the answer! That's like a teenager saying, "Dad, I respectfully decline your generous offer of money for my weekend trip, and I'd be glad to mow the lawn."

In this chapter, we help you select a stock-investing strategy based on your personal circumstances and the amount of money you have to invest. We also provide tips on when to sell your stocks.

## Laying Out Your Plans

A senior citizen in one of our investment seminars wanted to be more aggressive with his portfolio, and his broker was more than happy to cater to his desire for growth stocks. Of course, stocks got clobbered in the volatile bear market of 2000–02, and yes, he did lose lots of money. However, we soon discovered that even after the losses, he still had a substantial stock portfolio valued at over $1 million. He had more than enough to ensure a comfortable retirement. He sought aggressive growth even though it was really unnecessary for his situation. If anything, the aggressive strategy could have put his portfolio (and hence his retirement) in jeopardy.

Growth is desirable even in your twilight years because inflation can eat away at a fixed-income portfolio. But different rates of growth exist, and the type you choose should be commensurate with your unique situation and financial needs. Notice that we say "needs," not "wants." These perspectives are entirely different. You may *want* to invest in aggressive stocks regardless of their suitability (after all, it's your money), but your financial situation may dictate that you *need* to take another approach. Just understand the difference.

Stocks can play a role in all sorts of investment strategies, but in this chapter we discuss only a few well-known approaches. Keep in mind that your stock-investing strategy can change based on the major changes in your life and the lifestyle that you lead, such as the ones we present in the following sections.

## Living the bachelor life: Young single with no dependants

If you're young (age 20–40) and single, with no children or other dependants, being more aggressive with your stock selection is fine (as long as you don't use your rent money for investments). The reasoning is that if you do make riskier choices and they backfire, individuals dependent on you won't get hurt. In addition, if you're in this category you can usually bounce back a lot easier over the long term even if you have financial challenges or if a bear (down) market hits your stocks.

Consider a mix of small-cap, mid-cap, and large-cap stocks in growth industries (see Chapter 1 for an explanation of small cap, mid cap, and large cap; we provide information on industries in Chapter 17). Invest some of your money in five to seven stocks and the remainder in growth-stock mutual funds. You can revise your investment allocations along the way as the general economy and/or your personal situation changes (like when you finally say "I do" to the love of your life).

## Going together like a horse and carriage: Married with children

Married couples with children must follow a more conservative investing strategy, regardless of whether one spouse works or both spouses work. Children change the picture drastically (believe us; we each have them — and the baggy eyes to prove it). You need more stable growth in your portfolio (and unbreakable furniture in your home).

Consider a mix of large-cap growth stocks and dividend-paying defensive stocks. (See Chapter 9 for more on defensive stocks.) Invest some of your money in five to seven stocks and the remainder in growth and income mutual funds. Of course, you can tweak your allocations along the way according to changes in the general economic conditions or your personal situation. Consider setting aside money for postsecondary education in a growth-oriented mutual fund and in other vehicles such as savings bonds (as early as possible).

## Getting ready for retirement: Over 40 and either single or married

Whether you're over 40 and single or over 40 and married — and if married, whether one or both of you work — start to slowly convert your portfolio from aggressive growth to conservative growth. Shift more of your money out of individual stocks and into less-volatile investments such as balanced funds, Canada Savings Bonds, and GICs.

Devote some time and effort (with a financial planner if necessary) to calculating what your potential financial needs will be at retirement time. This step is critical in helping you decide what age to target for financial independence. (What's that? I can stop working?! Yee-ha!)

Consider five to seven large-cap stocks that are predominantly dividend-paying defensive stocks in stable and needed industries (such as utilities, food and beverage, and so on). Put some of your investment money in balanced mutual funds. Don't invest all your money — keep about 10 to 15 percent of it in something very secure, such as short term Canada Savings Bonds and bank vehicles (savings accounts and GICs). Keep savings in at least two separate institutions if possible to be diversified in today's uncertain economy. Remember that you can revise your allocations in the future as necessary.

## Kicking back in the hammock: Already retired

If you're retired, you're probably in your 60s or older. Safe, reliable income and wealth preservation form the crux of your investment strategy. Some growth-oriented investments are okay as long as they're conservative and don't jeopardize your need for income. At one time, financial planners told their retired clients to replace growth-oriented investments with safe income-oriented investments. However, times have changed as senior citizens live longer than ever before.

Issues such as longevity and inflation (steadily increasing costs of living) mean that today's (and tomorrow's) retirees need growth in their portfolios. To be safe, make sure that 5–20 percent of your retirement portfolio has some growth-oriented securities such as stocks to make sure you continue meeting your financial needs as the years pass. Perform an annual review to see whether the stock allocation needs to be adjusted.

Consider a mix of large-cap stocks dominated by dividend-paying defensive stocks in stable industries. Spread your money over three to six stocks, balanced mutual funds, and short-term investment-grade bond funds. Have a portion of your money in savings bonds and bank investments. You need to monitor and tweak your investment portfolio along the way to account for changes in either the general economic environment or your lifestyle needs.

# Allocating Your Assets

Asset allocation is really an attempt to properly implement the concept of diversification — the key to safety and stability. *Diversification* is the inclusion in your portfolio of different (and frequently offsetting) investments to shield your wealth from most types of current risk while planning for future growth. To achieve proper diversification, you need to analyze your entire portfolio to look for glaring weaknesses or vulnerable areas. We don't discuss your total investment plan here — only the stock portion.

Canadian investors frequently believe that having different stocks in different industries constitutes proper diversification. Well . . . not quite. Stocks in closely related industries tend to be affected (in differing degrees) by the same economic events, government policies, and so on. It's best to invest in stocks across different sectors. A *sector* is essentially a group of related industries; water, gas, and electric services are industries, but together they (plus a few other industries) make up the utilities sector. For more on analyzing industries to pick winning stocks, see Chapter 17.

Earlier in this chapter we talk about some basics for investing depending on your lifestyle, but how do you know how much you need to invest to meet your financial goals? In the following sections, we present some typical amounts most typical investors can (and should) devote to stock investing.

## Investors with less than $10,000

If you have $10,000 or less to allocate to stocks, you may want to consider a mutual fund rather than individual stocks because that sum of money may not be enough to properly diversify. But if you're going to invest a sum that small, consider allocating it equally into two to four stocks in two different sectors that look strong for the foreseeable future. For small investors, consider sectors that are defensive in nature (such as food and utilities).

Because $10,000 or less is a small sum in the world of stock investing, you may have to purchase in odd lots. (*Odd lots* usually mean 99 shares or fewer. A block of 100 shares is considered a *round lot,* and 200 shares would be considered two round lots.) Say you're buying four stocks, and all of them are priced at $50 per share. Obviously, your $10,000 won't buy you 100 shares of each. You may have to consider investing $2,500 in each stock, which means that you end up buying only 50 shares of each stock (not including commissions).

Try to avoid the temptation of getting into initial public offerings (IPOs; see Chapter 8), penny stocks, and other speculative issues. Participation in them may cost little (stock prices are often under $10 per share and can be under $1), but the risk exposure is too high for inexperienced investors. If you can't buy 100 shares of a large-cap stock, consider buying fewer shares, because commissions are still relatively low. In general, it's safer to buy 50 shares of a large, established company than the same amount in a smaller, riskier company.

## Investors with $10,000 to $50,000

If you have between $10,000 and $50,000 to invest, you have more breathing space for diversification. Consider buying four to six stocks in two or three different sectors. If you're the cautious type, defensive stocks will do. For growth investors, seek the industries in those sectors that have proven growth. This approach gets you off to a good start, and the section "Knowing When to Sell" in this chapter can help you maintain your portfolio by changing your strategy when necessary.

Does diversification mean that you shouldn't, under any circumstances, have all your stocks in one sector? It depends on you. For example, if you've worked all your life in a particular field and you're knowledgeable and comfortable with the sector, having a greater exposure is okay because your greater personal expertise offsets the risk. If you worked in retail for 20 years and know the industry inside and out, you probably know more about the good, the bad, and the ugly of the retail sector than most Bay Street analysts. Use your insight for more profitability. You still shouldn't invest all your money in that single sector, however, because diversification is still vital.

## Investors with $50,000 or more

If you have $50,000 or more to invest, have no more than five to ten stocks in two or three different sectors. It's difficult to thoroughly track more than two or three sectors and do it successfully — best to keep it simple. For example, Warren Buffett, considered the greatest stock market investor of all time, invests only in businesses that he understands. If that strategy works for billionaire investors, then, by golly, it can't be that bad for smaller investors.

We suggest investing in no more than seven to ten stocks, because there is such a thing as overdiversification. The more stocks you have, the tougher it is to keep track of them. Owning more stocks means you need to do more research, read more annual reports and news articles, and follow the business news of more companies. Even in the best of times, you need to regularly monitor your stocks because successful investing requires diligent effort.

Consider whether to hire a personal money manager (a person who manages investment portfolios for a fee). If you have $50,000 to $100,000 or more, doing so may make sense. Get a referral from a financial planner and carefully weigh the benefits against the costs. Here are some points to consider:

- **Make sure the money manager has a philosophy and an approach that you agree with.** Ask her to give you a copy of her written investment philosophy. How does she feel about small-cap stocks versus large caps, or income investing versus growth investing?

- **Find out whether you're comfortable with how the money manager selects stocks.** Is he a value investor or a growth investor? Is he aggressive or conservative? Does he analyze a stock based on its fundamentals (sales, earnings, book value, and so on), or does he use stock price charts?

- **Ask the money manager to explain her strategy.** A good way to evaluate the success (or failure) of the money manager's strategy is to ask her for her past recommendations. Did she pick more winners than losers?

- **Ask the money manager to describe his economic philosophy.** Is it Keynesian, Austrian, or some other school of thought? Yes, it does matter; Chapter 10 gives you some details about this.

# Knowing When to Sell

The act of buying stock is relatively easy. However, the act of selling stock can be an agonizing decision for investors. But it's agonizing only in two instances: when you've made money with your stock and when you've lost it. That about covers it. It sounds like a bad joke, but it's not that far from the truth.

The idea of selling stock when it has appreciated (the stock price has increased in value) comes with the following concerns:

- **Tax implications:** This concern is a good reason to consider selling. See Chapter 22 for information about how selling stocks under given circumstances can affect your taxes.

- **Emotional baggage:** "That stock was in our family for years." Believe it or not, investors cite this personal reason (or one of a dozen other personal reasons) for agonizing over the sale of an appreciated stock.

The following is a list of issues investors should be aware of when they're selling a stock that has lost money:

- ✔ **Tax benefits:** This issue is a good reason to consider selling a stock. See Chapter 22 for more on timing your stock sales to minimize your Canada Revenue Agency tax burden.

- ✔ **Pride:** "If I sell, I'll have to admit I was wrong" (followed by silent sobbing). So what? The best investors in history have made bad investments (some that have been quite embarrassing, in fact). Losing a little pride is cheaper than losing your money.

- ✔ **Doubt:** "If I sell my stock now, it may rebound later." Frequently, when an investor buys a stock at $50 and it goes to $40, the investor believes that if he sells, the stock will make an immediate rebound and go to $60, and then he'll be kicking himself. That may happen, but more often than not the stock price goes lower.

- ✔ **Separation anxiety:** "But I've had this stock so long that it's become a part of me." People hang onto a losing stock for all sorts of illogical reasons. Being married to a person is great; being married to a stock is ludicrous. If a stock isn't helping your goals, then it's hurting your goals.

People have plenty more reasons to agonize over the sale of a bad stock, but you can learn to handle the stock sale in a disciplined manner.

You have only two reasons to consider selling a stock, regardless of whether the stock price has gone up or down:

- ✔ **You need the money.** Obviously, if you need the money for a bona fide reason — such as paying off debt, wiping out a tax bill, or buying a home — then you need the money. This reason is easy to see. After all, regardless of investment or tax considerations, stocks are there to serve you. We hope you do some financial planning so that you don't need to sell your stocks for these types of expenses, but you can't avoid unexpected expenditures.

- ✔ **The stock ceases to perform as you desire.** If the stock isn't serving your wealth-building goals or fulfilling your investment objectives, it's time to get rid of it and move on to the next stock. Just as soon as you get a stiff upper lip and resolve to unload this losing stock, a little voice saying, "If I sell my stock now, it may rebound later," starts to haunt you. So you hang onto the stock, but then — bam! — before you know it, you lose more money.

Selling a stock shouldn't require a psychologist, but it does require discipline, which is why we're big proponents of trailing stops (see Chapter 21 for more on stop orders). Trailing stops take the agony out of selling the stock. All else being equal, you shouldn't sell a winning stock. If it's doing well, why sell it? Keep it as long as possible. But if it stops being a winning stock, sell it. If you don't know how or when to sell it, then apply a stop-loss order at 5 or 10 percent below the market value and let the market action take its course.

# Chapter 21

# Understanding Brokerage Orders and Trading Techniques

### In This Chapter

▶ Looking at different types of brokerage orders

▶ Trading on margin to maximize profits

▶ Making sense of going short

*I*nvestment success isn't just about picking rising stocks; it's also about how you go about doing it. Frequently, investors think that good stock picking means doing your homework and then making that buy (or sell). However, you can take it a step further to maximize profits (or minimize losses). As a stock investor, you can take advantage of techniques and services available through your standard brokerage account. (See Chapter 7 for more on brokerage accounts.) This chapter presents some of the best ways you can use these powerful techniques — useful whether you're buying or selling stock. In fact, if you retain nothing more from this chapter than the concept of *trailing stops* (see the section "Trailing stops"), you'll have gotten your money's worth. (Really!)

Just before the most recent, low-interest-rate-fuelled stock market bubble popped, we warned our readers that a bear market was on the way. All the data warned us about it, and undoubtedly it seemed like a time for caution. Canadian stock investors didn't necessarily have to believe us, but they could have (at the very least) used trailing stops and other techniques to ensure greater investing success. Investors who used stop-loss orders avoided the carnage of trillions of dollars in stock losses. In this chapter, we show you how to use these techniques to maximize your investing profit.

# Checking Out Brokerage Orders

Orders you place with your stockbroker fit neatly into three categories:

- ✔ Time-related orders
- ✔ Condition-related orders
- ✔ Advanced orders

At the very least, get familiar with the first two types of orders. They're easy to implement, and they're invaluable tools for wealth building and (more importantly) wealth saving! Advanced orders usually are combinations of the first two types.

Using a combination of orders helps you fine-tune your strategy so that you can maintain greater control over your investments. Speak with your broker about the different types of orders you can use to maximize the gains (or minimize the losses) from your stock investing activities. You also can read the broker's policies on stock orders at the brokerage Web site.

## On the clock: Time-related orders

Time-related orders mean just that; the order has a time limit. Typically, you use these orders in conjunction with conditional orders. The two most common time-related orders are day orders and good-till-cancelled (GTC) orders.

### Day order

A *day order* is an order to buy a stock that expires at the end of that particular trading day. If you tell your broker, "Buy BYOB Inc. at $37.50 and make it a day order," you mean that you want to purchase the stock at $37.50. But if the stock doesn't hit that price, your order expires at the end of the trading day unfilled. Why would you place such an order? Maybe BYOB is trading at $39, but you don't want to buy it at that price because you don't believe the stock is worth it. Consequently, you have no problem not getting the stock that day.

When would you use day orders? It depends on your preferences and personal circumstances. We don't use day orders too often because few events cause us to say, "Gee, we'll just try to buy or sell between now and the end of today's trading action." However, you may feel that you don't want a specified order to linger beyond today's market action. Perhaps you want to test a price. ("I want to get rid of stock A at $39 to make a quick profit, but it's currently trading at $37.50. However, I may change my mind tomorrow.") A day order is the perfect strategy to use in this case.

If you make any trade and don't specify time with the order, most (if not all) brokers automatically treat it as a day order.

### Good-till-cancelled (GTC)

A good-till-cancelled (GTC) order is the most commonly requested order by investors. Although GTC orders are time-related, they're always tied to a condition, such as when the stock achieves a certain price. The GTC order means just what it says: The order stays in effect until it's transacted or until the investor cancels it. Although the order implies that it can run indefinitely, most Canadian brokers have a limit of 30 or 60 days (or more). By that time, either the broker cancels the order or contacts you to see whether you want to extend it. Ask about your broker's particular policy.

A GTC order is usually coupled with conditional or condition-related orders. For example, say you want to buy ASAP Corp. stock but you don't want to buy it at the current price of $48 per share. You've done your homework on the stock, including looking at the stock's price-to-earnings ratio, price-to-book ratio, and so on (see Appendix A for more on ratios). So you say, "Hey, this stock isn't worth $48 per share. I'd only buy it at $36 per share." You think the stock would make a good addition to your portfolio, but not at the current market price. (It's overpriced or overvalued, according to your analysis.) How should you proceed? Your best bet is to ask your broker to do a "GTC order at $36." This request means that your broker will buy the shares if and when they hit the $36 mark (or until you cancel the order). Just make sure your account has the funds available to complete the transaction.

GTC orders are very useful, so become familiar with your broker's policy on them. While you're at it, ask whether any fees apply. Many brokers don't charge for GTC orders because, if they happen to result in a buy (or sell) order, they generate a normal commission just as any stock transaction does. Other brokers may charge a small fee.

To be successful with GTC orders, you need to know the following information:

- ✔ **When you want to buy:** People have had a tendency to rush into buying a stock without giving some thought to what they could do to get more for their money. Some Canadians don't realize that the stock market can be a place for bargain-hunting consumers. If you're ready to buy a quality pair of socks for $16 in a department store but the sales clerk says that those same socks are going on sale tomorrow for only $8, what would you do — assuming that you're a cost-conscious consumer? Unless you're barefoot, you're probably better off waiting. The same point holds true with stocks.

  Say you want to buy SOX Inc. at $26, but it's currently trading at $30. You think that $30 is too expensive, but you're happy to buy the stock at $26 or lower. However, you have no idea whether the stock will move to your desired price today, tomorrow, next week, or even next month (or maybe never). In this case, a GTC order is appropriate.

✔ **When you want to sell:** What if you bought some socks at a department store and then you discovered that they have holes (darn it!)? Wouldn't you want to get rid of them? Of course you would. If a stock's price starts to unravel, you want to be able to get rid of it, as well.

Perhaps you already own SOX (at $25, for instance) but are concerned that market conditions may drive the price lower. You're not certain which way the stock will move in the coming days and weeks. In this case, a GTC order to sell the stock at a specified price is a suitable strategy. Because the stock price is $25, you may want to place a GTC order to sell it if it falls to $22.50 to prevent further losses. Again, in this example, GTC is the time frame, and it accompanies a condition (sell when the stock hits $22.50).

## At your command: Condition-related orders

A condition-related order means that the order is executed only when a certain condition is met. Conditional orders enhance your ability to buy stocks at a lower price, to sell at a better price, or to minimize potential losses. When stock markets become bearish or uncertain, conditional orders are highly recommended. A good example of a conditional order is a *limit order*. A limit order may say, "Buy Mojeski Corp. at $45." But if Mojeski Corp. isn't at $45 (this price is the condition), the order isn't executed.

### Market orders

When you buy stock, the simplest type of order is a *market order* — an order to buy or sell a stock at the market's current best available price. It doesn't get any more basic than that.

Here's an example: Kowalski Inc. is available at the market price of $10. When you call up your broker and instruct him to buy 100 shares "at the market," he'll implement the order for your account, and you pay $1,000 plus commission.

We say "current best available price" because the stock's price is constantly moving, and catching the best price can be a function of the broker's ability to process the stock purchase. For very active stocks, the price change can happen within seconds. It's not unheard of to have three brokers simultaneously place orders for the same stocks and get three different prices because of differences in the brokers' capabilities. (Some computers are faster than others.)

The advantage of a market order is that the transaction is processed immediately, and you get your stock without worrying about whether it hits a particular price. For example, if you buy Kowalski Inc. with a market order, you know that by the end of that phone call (or Web site visit) you're assured of getting the stock. The disadvantage of a market order is that you can't control the price that you pay for the stock. Whether you're buying or selling your shares, you may not realize the exact price you expect (especially if you're buying a volatile stock — usually unpredictable because it has low trading volumes).

Market orders get finalized in the chronological order in which they're placed. Your price may change because the orders ahead of you in line caused the stock price to rise or fall based on the latest events.

### Stop orders (also known as stop-loss orders)

A *stop order* (or *stop-loss order,* if you own the stock) is a condition-related order that instructs the broker to sell a particular stock only when the stock reaches a particular price. It acts like a trigger, and the stop order converts to a market order to sell the stock immediately.

The stop-loss order isn't designed to take advantage of small, short-term moves in the stock's price. It's meant to help you protect the bulk of your money when the market turns against your stock investment in a sudden manner.

Say that your Kowalski Inc. stock rises to $20 per share, and you seek to protect your investment against a possible future market decline. A stop-loss order at $18 triggers your broker to sell the stock immediately if it falls to the $18 mark. In this example, if the stock suddenly drops to $17, it still triggers the stop-loss order, but the finalized sale price is $17. In a volatile market, you may not be able to sell at your precise stop-loss price. However, because the order automatically gets converted into a market order, the sale will be done, and you prevent further declines in the stock.

The main benefit of a stop-loss order is that it prevents a major decline in a stock that you own. It's a form of discipline that's important in investing because it minimizes potential losses. You may find it agonizing to sell a stock that has fallen. If you don't sell, however, your stock may continue to plummet as you keep holding on while hoping for a rebound in the price.

Most investors set a stop-loss amount at about 10 percent below the market value of a stock. This percentage gives the stock some room to fluctuate, which most stocks tend to do on a day-to-day basis.

### Trailing stops

Trailing stops are an important technique in wealth preservation for seasoned stock investors, and they can be one of your key strategies in using stop-loss orders. A *trailing stop* is a stop-loss order that an investor actively manages by moving it up along with the stock's market price. The stop-loss order "trails" the stock price upward. As the stop-loss goes upward, it protects more and more of the stock's value from declining.

A real-life example may be the best way to help you understand trailing stops. Say you bought a stock at $25 per share. As soon as you finished buying it, you immediately told your broker to put a stop-loss order at $22 and to make it a good-till-cancelled (GTC) order. Think of what you did. In effect, you placed an ongoing safety net under your stock. The stock can go as high as the sky, but if it should fall, the stock's price triggers a market order at $22. Your stock is automatically sold, minimizing your loss.

If your stock goes to $50 per share in a few months, you can call your broker, cancel the former stop-loss order at $22, and replace it with a new (higher) stop-loss order. You simply say, "Please put a new stop-loss order at $45 and make it a GTC order." This higher stop-loss price protects not only your original investment of $20 but also a big chunk of your profit, as well. As time goes by and the stock price climbs, you can continue to raise the stop-loss price and add GTC provisions. Now you know why it's called a trailing stop: It trails the stock price upward like a giant tail. All along the way, it protects more and more of your growing investment without limiting its upward movement.

William O'Neill, publisher and founder of *Investor's Business Daily,* advocates setting a trailing stop of 8 percent below your purchase price. That's his preference. Some investors who invest in very volatile stocks may put in trailing stops of 20 or 25 percent. Is a stop-loss order desirable or advisable in every situation? No. It depends on your level of experience, your investment goals, and the market environment. Still, stop-loss orders are appropriate in most cases, especially if the market seems uncertain (or if you do!).

A trailing stop is a stop-loss order that you actively manage. The stop-loss order is good-till-cancelled (GTC), and it constantly trails the stock's price as it moves up. To successfully implement trailing stops, keep the following points in mind:

- ✓ **Remember that brokers usually don't place trailing stops for you automatically.** In fact, they won't (or shouldn't) place any type of order without your consent. Deciding on the type of order to place is your responsibility. You can raise, lower, or cancel a trailing-stop order at will, but you need to monitor your investment when substantial moves occur to respond to the movement appropriately.

✓ **Change the stop-loss order when the stock price moves significantly.** Hopefully, you won't call your broker every time the stock moves 50 cents. Change the stop-loss order when the stock price moves about 10 percent. When you initially purchase the stock (say at $90 per share), request that the broker place the stop-loss order at $81. When the stock moves to $100, cancel the $81 stop-loss order and replace it at $90. When the stock's price moves to $110, change the stop-loss order to $99, and so on.

✓ **Understand your broker's policy on GTC orders.** If your broker usually lets GTC orders expire after 30 or 60 days, be aware of it. You don't want to risk a sudden drop in your stock's price without the stop-loss order protection. If your broker's time limit is 60 days, note this so that you can renew the order for additional time.

✓ **Monitor your stock.** A trailing stop isn't a set-it-and-forget-it technique. Monitoring your investment is critical. Of course, if your investment falls, the stop-loss order prevents further loss. Should the stock price rise substantially, remember to adjust your trailing stop accordingly. Keep raising the safety net as the stock continues to rise. Part of monitoring the stock is knowing the beta, which you can read more about in the next section.

### Using beta measurement

To be a successful investor, you need to understand the volatility of the particular stock you invest in. In stock market parlance, this volatility is also called the beta of a stock. *Beta* is a quantitative measure of the volatility of a given stock (and mutual funds and portfolios, too) relative to the overall market, usually the S&P 500 Index. (For more information on U.S. and Canadian indexes, see Chapter 5.) Beta specifically measures the performance movement of a stock as the S&P moves 1 percent up or down. A beta measurement above 1 is more volatile than the overall market, while a beta below 1 is less volatile. Some stocks are relatively stable in their price movements; others jump around.

Because beta measures how volatile or unstable the stock's price is, it tends to be uttered in the same breath as "risk" — more volatility indicates more risk. Similarly, less volatility tends to mean less risk.

Table 21-1 shows some sample betas of well-known U.S. and Canadian companies (as of July 2009).

| Table 21-1 | | Looking at Well-Known Betas |
|---|---|---|
| *Company* | *Beta* | *Comments* |
| Tim Hortons (THI.TO) | 0.85 | A bit less volatile than the Canadian market. If the S&P/TSX Composite Index moves 10%, Tim Hortons only moves 8.5%. |
| Advanced Micro Devices (AMD) | 1.72 | Almost two times more volatile than the U.S. market — typical for technology stocks. |
| Public Service Enterprise Group (PEG) | 0.57 | Statistically considered much less volatile than the market. |

You can find a company's beta at Web sites that usually provide a lot of financial information, such as Nasdaq's Web site (www.nasdaq.com) or Yahoo! Finance (finance.yahoo.ca).

The beta is useful to know because it gives you a general idea of the stock's trading range. If a stock is currently priced at $50 and it typically trades in the $48–$52 range, a trailing stop at $49 doesn't make sense. In this case, your stock will probably be sold the same day you initiate the stop-loss order. If your stock is a volatile growth stock that could swing up and down by 10 percent, you should more logically set your stop-loss order at 15 percent below that day's price.

The stock of a large-cap company in a mature industry tends to have a low beta — one close to the overall market. Small- and mid-cap stocks in new or emerging industries tend to have greater volatility in their day-to-day price fluctuations; hence, they tend to have a high beta. (You can find out more about large-, small-, and mid-cap stocks in Chapter 1.)

### Limit orders

A *limit order* is a very precise condition-related order, implying that a limit exists either on the buy or the sell side of the transaction. You want to buy (or sell) only at a specified price or better. Period. Limit orders work well for you if you're buying the stock, but they may not be good for you if you're selling the stock. Here's how it works in both instances:

✔ **When you're buying:** Just because you like a particular company and you want its stock, it doesn't mean you're willing to pay the current market price. Maybe you want to buy Kowalski Inc., but the current market price of $20 per share isn't acceptable to you. You prefer to buy it at $16 because you think this price reflects its true market value. So what do you do? You tell your broker, "Buy Kowalski with a limit order at $16." You also have to specify whether it's a day order (good for the day) or a GTC order (which we discuss in its own section earlier in this chapter).

What happens if the stock experiences great volatility? What if it drops to $16.01 and then suddenly drops again to $15.95 on the next move? Actually, nothing happens, you may be dismayed to hear. Because your order was limited to $16, it can be transacted only at $16, no more or less. The only way for this particular trade to occur is if the stock rises back to $16. However, if the price keeps dropping, then your limit order isn't transacted and it may expire or be cancelled.

On the other hand, many brokers, including TD Waterhouse, interpret the limit order as "Buy at this specific price or better." Presumably, if your limit order is to buy the stock at $10, you'll be just as happy if your broker buys that stock for you at $9.95. This way, if you don't get exactly $10 because the stock's price was volatile, you'll still get the stock at a lower price. Speak to your particular broker to be clear about their meaning of limit order.

✔ **When you're selling:** Limit orders are activated only when a stock hits a specific price. If you buy Kowalski Inc. at $20 and you worry about a decline in the share price, you may decide to put in a limit order at $18. If you watch the news and hear that Kowalski's price is dropping, you may sigh and say, "I sure am glad that I put in that limit order at $18!" However, in a volatile market, the share price may leapfrog over your specified price. It could go from $18.01 to $17.99 and then continue its descent. Because the stock price never hit $18 on the mark, it isn't sold. You may be sitting at home satisfied (mistakenly) that you played it smart while your stock plummets to $15, or $10, or worse! This is why having a stop-loss order in place is best.

## The joys of technology: Advanced orders

Brokers have added sophisticated capabilities to the existing repertoire of orders that are available for stock investors. One example is *advanced orders,* which provide investors with a way to use a combination of orders for more sophisticated trades. An example of an advanced order is something like,

"Only sell stock B, and if it sells, use the proceeds to buy stock D." You get the idea. Check with your broker for details on this service. Examples of advanced orders include the following:

- ✔ **One order cancels another order:** This happens when you enter two orders simultaneously with the condition that if one order is executed, the second order is automatically cancelled.

- ✔ **One order triggers another order:** Here you submit an order, and if that order is filled another order is automatically submitted. Many brokers have different names for these types of orders, so ask them if they can provide such an order.

Other types of advanced orders are available, but you get the picture. Talk to your brokerage firm and find out what's available in your particular account. Investors need to know that today's technology allows them to have more power and control over the implementation of buying and selling transactions.

# Pass the Margin, Please

*Margin* means buying securities, such as stocks, by using funds that you borrow from your broker. Buying stock on margin is similar to buying a condominium with a mortgage. If you buy a condominium at the purchase price of $100,000 and put 10 percent down, your equity (the part you own) is $10,000 and you borrow the remaining $90,000 with a mortgage. If the value of the condo rises to $120,000 and you sell (for simplicity's sake, we don't include closing costs in this example), you will have obviously made a profit of $20,000. The $20,000 gain on the property represents a gain of 20 percent on the purchase price of $100,000, but because your real investment was $10,000 (the down payment), your gain effectively works out to 200 percent (a gain of $20,000 on your initial investment of $10,000).

Buying on margin is an example of using leverage to maximize your gain when prices rise. *Leverage* is simply using borrowed money to increase your profit. This type of leverage is great in a favourable (bull) market, but it works against you in an unfavourable (bear) market. Say that a $100,000 condominium you purchase with a $90,000 mortgage falls in value to $80,000 (property values can decrease rapidly during economic hard times). Your outstanding debt of $90,000 exceeds the value of the property. Because you owe more than you own, you have a negative net worth. Leverage is a double-edged sword.

## Examining marginal outcomes

Suppose you think that the stock for the company Mergatroid Inc., currently at $40 per share, will go up in value. You want to buy 100 shares, but you have only $2,000. What can you do? If you're intent on buying 100 shares (versus simply buying the 50 shares that you have the cash for), you can borrow the additional $2,000 from your broker on margin. If you do that, what are the potential outcomes?

### If the stock price goes up

This is the best outcome for you. If Mergatroid goes to $50 per share, your investment will be worth $5,000 and your outstanding margin loan will be $2,000. If you sell, the total proceeds will pay off the loan and leave you with $3,000. Because your initial investment was $2,000, your profit is a solid 50 percent, because ultimately your $2,000 principal amount generated a $1,000 profit. (For the sake of this example, we leave out any charges such as commissions and interest paid on the margin loan.) However, if you pay the entire $4,000 up front — without the margin loan — your $4,000 investment will generate a profit of $1,000, or 25 percent. Using margin, you double the return on your money.

Leverage, when used properly, is very profitable. However, it is still debt, so understand that you must pay it off eventually.

### If the stock price fails to rise

If the stock goes nowhere, you still have to pay interest on that margin loan. If the stock pays dividends, this money can defray some of the cost of the margin loan. In other words, dividends can help you pay off what you borrow from the broker.

Having the stock neither rise nor fall may seem like a neutral situation, but you pay interest on your margin loan with each passing day. For this reason, margin trading can be a good consideration for conservative investors only if the stock pays a high dividend. Many times, a high dividend from $4,000 worth of stock can exceed the margin interest you have to pay on the $2,000 (50 percent) you borrow from the broker to buy that stock.

### If the stock price goes down

If the stock price falls, buying on margin can work against you. What if Mergatroid goes to $38 per share? The market value of 100 shares will be $3,800, but your equity will shrink to only $1,800 because you have to pay back your $2,000 margin loan. You're not exactly looking at a disaster at this point, but you'd better be careful, because the margin loan exceeds 50 percent of your stock investment. If it goes any lower, you may get the notorious *margin call,* when the broker actually contacts you to ask you to restore the ratio between the margin loan and the value of the securities. See the following section for information about appropriate debt-to-equity ratios.

# *Maintaining your balance*

When you purchase stock on margin, you must maintain a balanced ratio of margin debt to equity of at least 50 percent. If the debt portion exceeds this limit, you'll be required to restore the ratio by depositing either more stock or more cash into your brokerage account. The additional stock you deposit can be stock that's transferred from another account.

If, for example, Mergatroid falls to $28 per share, the margin loan portion exceeds 50 percent of the equity value in that stock — in this case, the market value of your stock is $2,800, but the margin loan is still at $2,000. The margin loan is a worrisome 71 percent of the market value ($2,000 ÷ $2,800 = 71 percent). Expect to get a call from your broker to put more securities or cash into the account to restore the 50-percent balance.

If you can't come up with more stock, other securities, or cash, the next step is to sell stock from the account and then to use the proceeds to pay off the margin loan. For you, it means realizing a capital loss — you lost money on your investment.

Margin, as you can see, can escalate your profits (on the upside), but magnify your losses (on the downside). If your stock plummets drastically, you can end up with a margin loan that exceeds the market value of the stock that you used the loan to purchase. In the bear market of 2000, many people were hurt by stock losses, and a large number of these losses were made worse because people didn't manage the responsibilities involved with margin trading.

If you buy stock on margin, use a disciplined approach. Be extra careful when using leverage, such as a margin loan, because it can backfire. Keep the following points in mind:

- ✔ **Have ample reserves of cash or marginable securities in your account.** Try to keep the margin ratio at 35 percent or less to minimize the chance of a margin call.

- ✔ **Consider using margin to buy stock in large companies that have a relatively stable price and pay a good dividend (if you're a beginner).** Some people buy income stocks that have dividend yields that exceed the margin interest rate, meaning that the stock ends up paying for its own margin loan. Just remember those stop orders.

- ✔ **Monitor your stocks constantly.** If the market turns against you, the result will be especially painful if you use margin.

- ✔ **Have a payback plan for your margin debt.** Margin loans against your investments mean that you're paying interest. Your ultimate goal is to make money, and paying interest eats into your profits.

# Going Short and Coming Out Ahead

The vast majority of stock investors are familiar with buying stock, holding on to it for a while, and hoping its value goes up. This kind of thinking is called *going long,* and investors who go long are considered to be *long on stocks.* Going long essentially means that you're bullish and seeking your profits from rising prices. However, astute investors also profit in the market when stock prices fall. *Going short* (also called *shorting a stock, selling short,* or *doing a short sale*) on a stock is a common technique for profiting from a stock price decline. Investors have made big profits during bear markets by going short. A short sale is a bet that a particular stock will go down.

To go short, you have to be deemed (by your broker) creditworthy — your account needs to be approved for short selling. When you're approved for margin trading, you're probably all set to sell short, too. Speak to your broker (or check for this information on the broker's Web site) about limitations in your account regarding going short.

Because going short on stocks carries greater risks than going long, we strongly advise beginning investors to avoid shorting stocks until they become more seasoned.

Most people easily understand making money by going long. It boils down to "Buy low and sell high." Piece of cake. Going short means making money by selling high and then buying low. Huh? Thinking in reverse is not a piece of cake. Although thinking of this stock adage in reverse may be challenging, the mechanics of going short are really very simple. Consider an example that uses a fictitious company called DOA Inc. As a stock, DOA ($50 per share) is looking pretty sickly. It has lots of debt and plummeting sales and earnings, and the news is out that DOA's industry (commercial real estate) will face hard times for the foreseeable future. This situation describes a stock that is an ideal candidate for shorting. The future may be bleak for DOA, but promising for savvy investors.

You must understand brokerage rules before you conduct short selling. The broker must approve you for it, and you must meet the minimum collateral requirement, which is typically 50 percent of the shorted stock's market value. If the stock generates dividends, those are paid to the owner of the stock, not to the person who is borrowing it to go short. (See the next section, "Setting up a short sale," to see how this technique works.) Check with your broker for complete details and review the resources in Appendix B.

## Setting up a short sale

This section explains how to go short. Say you believe that DOA is the right stock to short — you're pretty sure its price is going to fall. With DOA at $50, you instruct your broker to "Go short 100 shares on DOA." (It doesn't have to be 100 shares; we're just using that as an example.) Now, here's what happens next:

1. **Your broker borrows 100 shares of DOA stock, either from his own inventory or from another client or broker.**

   That's right. The stock can be borrowed from a client, no permission necessary. The broker guarantees the transaction, and the client/owner of the stock never has to be informed about it, because she never loses legal and beneficial right to the stock. You borrow 100 shares, and you'll return 100 shares when it's time to complete the transaction.

2. **Your broker then sells the stock and gives you the money.**

   Your account is credited with $5,000 (100 shares × $50) in cash — the money gained from selling the borrowed stock. This cash acts like a loan on which you're going to have to pay interest.

3. **You use the $5,000 for a little while.**

   Your broker has deposited the $5,000 into your account. You can use this money to buy other investments.

4. **You buy the stock back and return it to its rightful owner.**

   When it's time to close, or cover, the transaction (either you want to close it or the owner of the shares wants to sell the shares, so you have to give them back), you must return the number of shares you borrowed (in this case, it was 100 shares). If you buy back the 100 shares at $40 per share (remember that you shorted this particular stock because you were sure its price was going to fall) and these 100 shares are returned to their owner, you make a $1,000 profit. (To keep the example tidy, we don't include brokerage commissions.) By selling short, you made money when the stock price fell!

## Oops! Going short when prices grow taller

We bet you guessed there was a flip side to the wonderful profitability of selling short. Presume that you were wrong about DOA and that the stock price rises from the ashes as it goes from $50 to $87. Now what? You still have to return the 100 shares you borrowed. With the stock's price at $87, you have to buy the stock for $8,700 (100 shares at the new, higher price of $87). Ouch! How do you pay for it? Well, you have that original $5,000 in your account from when you initially went short on the stock. But where do you get the other $3,700 ($8,700 less the original $5,000)? You guessed it — your pocket! You have to cough up the difference. If the stock continues to rise, that's a lot of coughing.

How much money do you lose if the stock goes to $100 or more? A heck of a lot. As a matter of fact, there's theoretically no limit to how much you can lose. That's why going short can be riskier than going long. With going long, the most you can lose is 100 percent of your money. However, with going short, you can lose more than 100 percent of the money you invested. Yikes!

Because the potential for loss is unlimited when you short a stock, we suggest that you use a stop order (also called a *buy-stop order*) to minimize the damage. Better yet, make it a good-till-cancelled order, which we discuss earlier in this chapter. You can set the stop order at a given price, and if the stock hits that price, you buy the stock back so that you can return it to its owner before the price rises even higher. You still lose money, but you limit your losses.

## Feeling the squeeze

If you go short on a stock, remember that, sooner or later, you have to buy that stock back so that you can return it to its owner. What happens when a lot of people are short on a particular stock and its price starts to rise? All those short sellers will be scrambling to buy the stock back so that they can close their transactions before they lose too much money. This mass buying quickens the pace of the stock's ascent and puts a squeeze (called a *short squeeze*) on the investors who had been shorting the stock.

Earlier in the chapter, we explain that your broker can borrow stock from another client so that you can go short on it. What happens when that client wants to sell the stock in her account — the stock that you borrowed and is no longer in her account? When that happens, your broker asks you to return the borrowed stock. That's when you feel the squeeze — you have to buy the stock back at the current price.

Going short can be a great manoeuvre in a declining (bear) market, but it can be brutal if the stock price goes up. If you're a beginner, stay away from short selling until you have enough experience (and money) to risk it.

# Chapter 22

# Keeping More of Your Money from the Taxman

*In This Chapter*

▶ Investigating how interest income is taxed

▶ Determining dividend taxes and credits

▶ Understanding stock dividends and splits

▶ Considering capital gains and losses

▶ Exploring the taxation of oil, gas, and mineral investments

▶ Investigating how mutual funds are taxed

▶ Getting REITs right

▶ Figuring out strategies to avoid, reduce, split, or defer taxes

▶ Saving through TFSAs

*H*ow much tax does investment income draw? Yup, you guessed it — it depends! (We hate it when people say that, too!)

Different forms of income attract different levels of taxation. For example, relative to other types of investment income, interest income draws the most punishing tax. Things get a bit better with dividend income, where the Canada Revenue Agency (CRA) taxes you but may also give you a tax credit to cushion the blow. With capital gains, the CRA hits you with only a partial blow — only a fraction of your gains or losses is included in, or deducted from, your income. And then there's the other investment-related stuff, like real estate investment trusts, which add more murkiness to the CRA's arsenal of rules. Hey, without the smoke and mirrors, tax accountants would starve!

We explore these and other tax-related issues in this chapter. Before cutting into the nitty-gritty stuff, however, we set the stage with an overview that will help you deal more easily with the many tax rules associated with investment income. Knowing the tax rules for investment income is a critical first step in tax planning, if your objective is to minimize your taxes. We trust that at the end of this chapter, you'll realize what we have come to realize — most of the rules, and their associated tax planning tips, are more manageable than they look!

# Interest Income

Interest income is taxable *in full* in the year in which it's received. No deductions or credits are associated with interest income. Bank accounts, GICs, term deposits, mortgages receivable, and bonds are some of the financial instruments out there that produce interest income.

The CRA wants your interest income so much that, for interest income on compound-interest obligations obtained in 1990 or later (for example, Canada Savings Bonds), interest has to be reported on an annual accrual basis from the investment's anniversary date. That means you report it as though you have received interest even if you haven't. Providers of investment vehicles (like banks that provide GICs) are required by law to send their clients annual information slips (T5, Statement of Investment Income) reporting interest, dividends, and other forms of investment income.

For interest on investments obtained before 1990 and after 1981, interest income can be reported in several ways at the investor's option. If you hold such older investments, a brief refresher on these options never hurts. Interest can be

 - Accrued and reported annually.

 - Recognized as received.

 - Reported as it becomes receivable. This is interest that you fully earned, and you have a legal right to claim it.

 - Accrued and reported on a triennial basis from the date of acquisition. This means that interest on compounding investments needs to be reported only once every three years, starting at the year of acquisition. If you don't choose one of the other options, this is the method the CRA applies.

You can use different options for different investments, but you have to apply your choices consistently from year to year. Of course, if an interest-bearing investment is held within your RRSP, the tax on the interest earned is deferred until the time you withdraw it. We'll discuss RRSP strategy, and some important recent changes in RRSP rules, later in this chapter.

The CRA dictates that investments of a similar nature must report their income in a similar manner. For instance, if you report interest on a Canada Savings Bond on an annual accrual basis, you should report all your government bonds in like manner.

Some interest-bearing investments have their own unique reporting methods. These investments include annuity contracts, investments bought at a discount to face value, stripped bonds, Canada Savings Bonds, and indexed debt obligations. Consider these nuances when making investment and tax planning decisions; they can have a major impact on your taxes payable. Check out these and other current tax law requirements at the CRA's Web site (www. cra-arc.gc.ca).

# Dividend Income

Compared to interest income, any dividends you receive from a Canadian corporation are subject to preferential tax rates. Dividends received are taxed at a lower rate because of the availability of a dividend tax credit. This dividend tax credit is available to you because the corporation has already paid tax on the earnings when it distributed them as dividends to you. In this way, the CRA guards against double taxation.

However, not all tax credits are created equal. The CRA says that "eligible dividends" received by taxable individuals resident in Canada — that would be you — are grossed up (an arbitrary CRA "adjustment") by 45 percent, and that the dividend tax credit relating to such eligible dividends be 19 percent. Non-eligible dividends (those that are not designated as "eligible" on a T5 tax slip or otherwise) would be grossed up by 25 percent with a dividend tax credit of 13.3334 percent. The net tax effect for you is that eligible dividends attract a 14.5-percent federal tax rate at the highest level of income, and the non-eligible dividends attract about a 19-percent federal tax rate at the highest level of income.

Essentially, an eligible dividend is any taxable dividend paid after 2005 to a resident of Canada by a Canadian corporation that is designated by that corporation to be an eligible dividend. If dividends from Canadian and foreign corporations were received inside your RRSP, tax on this income is deferred. When you finally withdraw money from your RRSP, it will be fully taxable as regular income. That's because inside RRSPs investment income loses its nature and comes in only one flavour — high-tax vanilla. Inside RRSPs, you also lose the tax advantage of applying any tax credit. Again, we deal with RRSP strategies later in this chapter.

Provinces now have their own dividend tax credit, similar to the federal credit. Previously, provincial tax was calculated as a simple percentage of the federal tax after the federal dividend tax credit was applied.

# Stock Dividends and Splits

A *stock dividend* is a dividend that a corporation pays by issuing shares instead of cash. Stock dividends are generally considered to be ordinary taxable dividends and are treated as such. The amount of the dividend you include in taxable income — your share of the increase in paid-up capital — also represents the cost of your new shares for future sales as well as capital gain or loss calculations.

*Stock splits* — where you get more shares without any change in the total dollar value of those shares — are not taxable. You gained or lost nothing from an economic or a tax standpoint.

When you get your T3 (Statement of Trust Income Allocations and Designations) or T5 tax slip showing your annual dividend income (including any stock dividend values), you'll see boxes that contain both the actual dividends and the taxable amount of dividends paid. Be careful to include only the taxable amount of dividends on your tax return.

If your spouse has low income, you are claiming him or her as a dependant, and he or she earns dividends eligible for the gross-up and dividend tax credit, consider transferring those dividends to yourself and then including them in your income. The tax benefits associated with dividends are more valuable in your hands (in your higher tax bracket) than in your spouse's hands.

# Capital Gains and Losses

A *capital gain* occurs when you sell or otherwise dispose of a capital property for more than you paid for it — technically, the CRA refers to this cost as the *adjusted cost base* because it may sometimes require you to adjust your original cost. However, we'll keep things simple and leave special rules about costs out of the picture for now. Just keep in mind that capital gains are reduced by any disposition costs incurred, such as brokers' commissions.

Unlike ordinary income such as salary or interest, only 50 percent of the capital gain that you make outside of your RRSP is included in your taxable income. This is called a *taxable capital gain,* and this portion of the total capital gain is taxed in the year of the sale. If you suffer a *capital loss* — where your costs exceed your proceeds — the 50-percent allowable portion must first be used to offset any taxable capital gains that may exist in the same year. Any unused allowable capital allowance can be carried back up to three years, or carried forward indefinitely, but only to reduce any future taxable capital gains.

Keep in mind that just because you didn't receive any proceeds from a sale, that doesn't always mean you have no capital gain or loss to report. A special scenario can play out when you gift shares or other capital property to family members. In such cases, the CRA may deem you to have received fair-market-value consideration at the time of the gift (or a sale for less than fair market value). The amount of cash actually changing hands is irrelevant to the CRA.

## Capital-gains deduction

If you own shares in a qualifying small business corporation (SBC) you may be able to claim a $750,000 ($500,000 for dispositions occurring before March 19, 2007) capital gains exemption when those shares are sold. At a 50-percent inclusion rate, this translates into a very large taxable amount (or benefit, depending on how you view it). But your claim of this special deduction may be reduced by past capital gains deduction claims or by allowable business investment losses and other adjustments. A detailed discussion of this area is beyond the scope of this book. If you have SBC shares, we recommend you seek professional advice from a tax adviser when you're ready to sell or transfer them.

## Superficial losses

The CRA has certain rules concerning superficial losses. A *superficial loss* occurs if you execute a transaction (like a sale or other transfer of investments) that creates a loss while you, or a related person, keep or quickly regain control of the same (or identical) property that created the loss in the first place. The CRA applies the superficial loss provision beginning 30 days before and ending 30 days after the disposition of a property. In other words, no fancy footwork (such as the manipulation of the timing or ownership of losses) is permitted a month before or after the sale.

## Reserves

If the sale of a property results in a capital gain and a portion of the sale's proceeds is not due until after the year's end, you may claim a *reasonable reserve* for the unrealized part of that gain. However, you can't wait forever. At least one-fifth of the capital gain must be included in your taxable income every year, unless it stems from the sale of shares in an SBC to your children. In that case, a minimum one-tenth of the capital gain must be included in your income each year. We recommend that you seek professional tax advice whenever dealing with complex areas such as SBC shares and reserves.

# Oil, Gas, and Mineral Stock Investments

The CRA offers tax incentives to encourage Canadians to invest capital to aid the exploration and development of oil, gas, and minerals. These incentives are provided through limited partnerships, flow-through shares, joint ventures, and royalty trust units. By going through these risky avenues, you may be able to deduct certain exploration expenses.

Joint ventures and limited partnerships are a lot alike, except for the fact that at-risk rules don't apply to the former. *Flow-through shares* enable companies to forgo certain income tax deductions that they could have claimed and to pass them on to investors — the deductions flow through to you. (Because many junior exploration companies can't generate a regular taxable income, they aren't able to use their tax deductions, anyway.) Flow-through-share investor deductions typically lower the cost base of the shares to nil. This decrease can ultimately result in a tax-preferential capital gain when the shares are sold.

Furthermore, the government also provides tax incentives regarding the availability of flow-through shares for Canadian investors in certain renewable-energy and energy conservation projects. This applies to eligible Canadian conservation expenses incurred after 2002 concerning flow-through share agreements entered into after July 26, 2002. In this way, the government makes these shares more attractive for people to buy.

Check out the suitability of these tax-advantaged, but risky, mechanisms with your investment or tax adviser before proceeding. Also check out the CRA Web site at `www.cra-arc.gc.ca/tx/bsnss/tpcs/fts-paa/nvstr/ menu-eng.html` to learn more about these investment options. As you can see, the rules are tight, complex, and well beyond the scope of this book.

As an added incentive to seek professional advice when your tax situation gets complicated, you can deduct fees (but not commissions) for advice you get about the purchase, sale, and administration of shares and certain other securities. But those fees have to be paid to professionals whose main business is managing such investments.

# Mutual Funds

If you hold stocks indirectly through mutual funds outside of an RRSP, taxation depends on whether you acquire a share of a mutual fund corporation or a unit of a mutual fund trust (like a REIT, which we discuss in the next section). With both, you may receive distributions during the year. With a mutual fund corporation, these distributions are either capital gains dividends — which are treated the same as capital gains, with only 50 percent included in income — or taxable dividends. A mutual fund trust allocates its income to the unitholders, who then report the income as capital gains, dividends, foreign income, or other income. Regardless of source, when you sell units of mutual fund trusts or shares of mutual fund corporations you may realize a capital gain. Again, the beneficial tax treatment of capital gains and dividends is lost if they are received within an RRSP.

Funds often reinvest distributions to unitholders as new shares of the fund. Here, although you don't see the cash, you'll still be taxed on the income distributed. That's why you may have received a tax slip even though you saw no cash. Track the reinvestments well, because they will increase your adjusted cost base and therefore reduce any capital gains when you sell the investment.

# The Tax-Wise REIT

A real estate investment trust (REIT) is essentially a closed-end mutual fund trust. The number of investors is limited. Each year, the trust earns rental income and, sometimes, capital gains. However, these items are taxed at the unitholder level, and most of the cash generated by the REIT is distributed to you, the unitholder. Because REITs can deduct depreciation (a non-cash expense), the REIT's income that's passed on and taxed at the unitholder level is less than the cash that you actually receive.

The bottom line from a tax perspective is that a certain percentage of the distributions you get from a REIT will escape from being included in your current year's taxable income. All you do in the current year is reduce your REIT's tax cost base by a simply calculated amount. You realize a capital gain (on a lower adjusted cost base) when the units are sold. Tax deferral is a key benefit of REITs. Another tax benefit is that when you do sell your REIT units, only 50 percent of any capital gain is included in your taxable income.

Here's another way of viewing the taxation of REITs:

- **Receiving your distributions:** On a quarterly or monthly basis, you will be paid an actual cash distribution based on your REIT's income. At the end of every calendar year, you will get a further distribution of cash that represents any realized capital gains and other income.

- **Allocating your income:** After the end of the year, you will also receive a T3 Supplementary form. (You get a T3 instead of a T5 because a REIT is a mutual fund trust for the purposes of the *Income Tax Act*.) The T3 Supplementary shows you, among other things, your allocation of taxable income and taxable capital gains for the year. These figures are the ones to include as part of your taxable income for the year. If you sell your units before the end of the calendar year, you'll still get a T3 from your formerly held REIT representing the part of the year when you received distributions.

> ✔ **Reducing your adjusted cost base:** To the extent that the sum total of *distributions* received exceeds your *taxable income* allocation for the year, your REIT unit–adjusted cost base is reduced.

Check with your tax adviser to see about the tax impact of REITs and other income trusts.

# Deferred-Income Tax Shelters and Plans

Deferred-income plans like RRSPs are designed to let you earn investment income and, at the same time, *defer* paying tax for as long as the investments and income stay inside the plan. RRSPs even go a step further and provide a tax deduction, within CRA limits, for the contributions you make. The following sections explore RRSPs and other deferred-income plans. You'll learn how you can use these plans strategically to maximize your investment returns. But before you can implement tax strategy and planning in this area, you first have to understand how these plans actually work.

## Registered Retirement Savings Plans (RRSPs)

*RRSPs* are registered savings plans that let you contribute cash or eligible investments for future use — usually for retirement. Eligible investments include stocks, mutual funds, shares of small business corporations, bonds, income trusts, exchange-traded funds, royalty units, partnership units, investment-grade gold and silver bullion and coins, and others that are beyond the scope of this book. You cannot hold precious metals that are not investment grade, commodity futures, gems, land, employee stock options, and some other excluded items.

You can open several different RRSP accounts, and you can passively or actively invest in each one in different ways with different investments, such as GICs, stocks, or mutual funds.

Because RRSP contributions lower your taxable income, you save tax immediately. Keep in mind, however, that RRSP withdrawals trigger an income inclusion for the year — even if the full amount withdrawn is reinstated into the plan later in that same year. Also bear in mind that while you can pay RRSP–related administrative fees outside of your plan, they aren't tax-deductible.

### RRSP contribution limits

Your RRSP contribution limit is 18 percent of your prior year's *earned income,* less the prior year's pension adjustment reported on your annual T4 (Statement of Remuneration Paid). If you have any additional past-service pension adjustments, they are also deducted. The contribution limit is also adjusted for total pension adjustment reversals (PARs) made. PARs reinstate lost contribution room if you left your employer's Registered Pension Plan (RPP) and/or deferred profit-sharing plan before retirement.

### Earned income limits

*Earned income* includes:

- Alimony or separation allowances received
- Disability pensions under the Canada Pension Plan (CPP) or Quebec Pension Plan (QPP)
- Employee profit-sharing plan allocations
- Employment earnings (net of union dues and eligible employment expenses)
- Net income from self-employment and partnerships
- Net rental income
- Research grants (net of related expenses)
- Royalties
- Supplementary unemployment benefit plan payments (not Employment Insurance, or EI)

But earned income is reduced by:

- Current-year losses from self-employment or an active partnership
- Current-year rental losses
- Deductible alimony and maintenance payments.

Only one significant disadvantage is associated with receiving dividends compared to a fully taxed salary or interest income. In the context of the earned income calculation that determines your RRSP contribution room, dividends aren't deemed by the CRA to be earned income. Therefore, they don't create RRSP contribution room for you.

### Dollar limits

For 2009 and 2010, the maximum RRSP deduction limits are $21,000 and $22,000, respectively. The CRA Web site (which you should check from time to time) states that, "if you did not use all of your RRSP deduction limit for the years 1991–2008, you can carry forward the unused amount to 2009."

Check out the notice of assessment you receive from the CRA after filing your prior year's tax return to find your RRSP contribution limits for the current tax year. This assessment guides your contribution limit calculation in the most precise way possible. Contributions have to be made within 60 days of the calendar year-end to be deductible for the previous tax year. Also remember that contributions to your RRSP can be made up to and including the year in which you turn 71 years old.

### Spousal Registered Retirement Savings Plans

Many investors have their own RRSP and also open a spouse or common-law partner's RRSP, subject to limits of deductible amounts. Spousal contributions are deemed by the CRA to be the recipient spouse/common-law partner's property. Spousal contributions reduce the contributor's RRSP limit, but they don't impact the recipient spouse's contribution limits for his or her own RRSP.

Your spousal RRSP contribution has no immediate added tax benefit over and above contributing toward your personal RRSP. But your tax savings could be large in the future, because spousal RRSP contributions can provide you and your spouse with the opportunity to balance out retirement income and reduce your combined future taxes. Withdrawals by a spouse in retirement could be non-taxable, or taxed at much lower rates than if all the savings were being drawn by only one spouse. Be mindful, however, that withdrawals from a spousal plan might be taxable in your hands if spousal contributions were made in either the year of the withdrawal or within the two preceding years. Spousal RRSP contributions can be made until the end of the year in which the spouse or common-law partner turns 71 years old.

### Self-directed RRSPs

Self-directed RRSPs are popular with Canadians who wish to hold and manage individual stocks in their RRSP. Another reason many stock investors set up a self-directed RRSP is to capitalize on the recent removal of all foreign-content limits (the same as for non–self-directed RRSPs) by exploring stocks traded on stock exchanges outside of Canada while still getting a tax deduction.

A self-directed RRSP provides a greater selection of investment options than a regular RRSP. That's the key difference between the two choices. They are available through discount and full-service brokerage firms. These plans are designed for Canadians who wish to personally control and manage the assets residing in their plan. Like for non–self-directed RRSPs, the annual administration fee and commissions that you pay aren't tax deductible.

The list of what you can throw into a self-directed RRSP plan, over and above stocks, includes the following:

- ✔ Bank deposit accounts and investment certificates
- ✔ Federal, provincial, and municipal bonds and debentures (debt instruments that pay interest)
- ✔ Mortgages and mortgage-backed securities
- ✔ Mutual funds
- ✔ Rights and warrants of corporations listed on Canadian stock exchanges
- ✔ Savings bonds
- ✔ Treasury bills

No restriction exists on foreign property holdings within an RRSP. Check out the CRA's Web site (`www.cra-arc.gc.ca`) for current information on the tax treatment of foreign property investments.

### Retirement allowances

You can transfer retiring allowances (like severance packages and accumulated attendance credits) directly into your RRSP, subject to certain limits and rules. For years of service from 1989 to 1995, inclusive, the contribution limit is $2,000 per year of service. For those years before 1989, an additional $1,500 can be contributed (for a potential total of $3,500 per year) for each year of service that you didn't have a pension plan. For years of service from 1996 and on, no additional bump contributions are permitted. Also, you can't carry forward these unused RRSP contributions to future periods.

### Locked-in RRSPs

When employees leave their workplaces, they may have a choice of either receiving a pension at retirement or transferring the commuted value of their pensions to another plan. Under strict Canadian law, the commuted value cannot be immediately paid out directly to the individual. Instead, the transferred commuted (actuarially calculated) value is either placed directly into another company pension plan or placed in a *locked-in retirement account* (LIRA), also referred to as a *locked-in RRSP*. Both are essentially the same thing.

With a regular RRSP, you can make a withdrawal at any time. With a locked-in RRSP, early withdrawals cannot typically be made. Furthermore, when you retire as early as age 55, or as late as age 71, the locked-in RRSP cash can be applied to purchase a life annuity or a life income fund (ask your tax adviser if one of these is a route you should consider). You may not be able to transfer funds into a RRIF (discussed in the next section). However, Ontario and other residents are now an exception and may be able to transfer the proceeds of locked-in RRSPs into a locked-in RRIF. This is another complex area beyond the scope of this book, so discuss it with your tax adviser when appropriate.

# Registered Retirement Income Funds (RRIFs)

You have to terminate your RRSP(s) by the end of the year in which you turn 71 years old. When the time comes, you can choose from three options:

- **Withdraw the RRSP funds.** The total of lump-sum cash withdrawn is included in your annual income.

- **Transfer your RRSP into a RRIF.** A RRIF is like an RRSP because the RRIF's funds and income earned stay untaxed until they are withdrawn. You can exercise management control over investment decisions. However, you must withdraw a minimum amount from the plan each year, based on your age or the age of a younger spouse or common-law partner. The minimum amount to be withdrawn increases each year until age 94. At that time, the amounts become set at 20 percent annually until the plan is depleted.

- **Buy an annuity providing a regular income for a set period of time.** This may include your lifetime, the combined lifetimes of you and your spouse or common-law partner, a set period, or a combination of these time frames. The choices are wide open. No part of the RRSP will be taxed immediately on this type of transfer. The tax kicks in when the annuity payments begin to be received.

Take note that you can withdraw amounts over and above the minimum, although any excess amounts withdrawn will also become taxable in that year.

# Registered Education Savings Plans (RESPs)

Registered Education Savings Plans (RESPs) are special plans that help you save for your child's education. You can invest your RESP in a stock, mutual fund, GIC, or just about any other investment; your financial institution can guide you through the details.

You can also tailor your RESP for growth potential, interest income, or a balance between the two. We recommend the balanced approach. It may be a good idea for Canadian investors to add a few growth stocks to their RESP plans. However, we recommend that no more than 25 percent of a RESP's holdings be represented by stocks. The balance should be income oriented. Educational savings are far too important to be placed at undue risk.

The lack of restrictions on foreign content allows you to take full advantage of the growth potential of international stock markets. Although the other rules behind RESPs are beyond the scope of this book, we will provide you with some more essentials:

- You can invest up to a lifetime maximum of $50,000 per child.

- Under a family plan, you can designate as many beneficiaries to the plan as you want.

- Contributions are not tax deductible to you but funds may be withdrawn tax-free at any time you wish.

- The income within the RESP grows on a tax-sheltered basis and is paid out as an Educational Assistance Payment (EAP) to qualifying beneficiaries who pay the tax themselves (meaning that in most cases there will be little or no tax to pay).

- Universities, community colleges, vocational and technical colleges, and universities outside Canada qualify.

- Beneficiaries have to attend an accredited post-secondary institution on a full-time basis.

- The program must be no less than three consecutive weeks (13 weeks if the educational institution is outside Canada) with at least ten course hours per week.

- Part-time students will be permitted to access up to $2,500 of their income and grants for each semester. Students will be required to be enrolled in a qualifying education program for at least 12 hours a month, in a course with a duration of at least three consecutive weeks.

- If the designated beneficiary does not pursue postsecondary education, another eligible beneficiary can be designated.

## Invest inside or outside your RRSP?

At the outset of this chapter, we point out that the money you make on your investments draws different effective rates of tax, depending on the type of income you receive from the investment. Income you generate from your investments held outside of your RRSP will be taxed differently if it's interest income, dividends, or capital gains. But the variables and choices don't end there.

You can choose to earn investment income either inside or outside of an RRSP — each option has different tax implications and other consequences. This is where it pays to understand the tax treatment of various sources of investment income. This knowledge will make it easier to decide which investments should be in a tax-advantaged plan such as an RRSP, and which investments should be held outside of an RRSP. No one-size-fits-all formula applies here — only rules that can be carefully plugged into your personal financial objectives!

## Perspectives on the RRSP debate

A popular view is that it may not be best to keep investments that generate interest income outside of your RRSP because interest income is more heavily taxed. If you hold investments inside your RRSP, your interest returns will be higher because your income is temporarily sheltered from tax. But capital gains and dividends, on the other hand, are taxed at preferential rates. You may want to hold investments generating capital gains and dividends outside of your RRSP.

No one right answer applies; everyone has different personal and financial objectives. But seeking the advice of a financial or tax planner will likely help you to arrive at the best decision.

## *There's a catch*

If you have an RRSP or other tax shelter, you have a few obligations. You are required to identify any tax-sheltered investment deductions and to disclose the shelter identification number on your tax return. The folks who sold you their tax shelter products should provide you with the required filing forms and associated details, like the amount of the deduction.

Also be aware that you face a number of special rules regarding tax-shelter deductions, which can result in alternative minimum tax (AMT) or expose you to *at-risk rules,* where you are not allowed to write off more than the cost base of your investment.

Apart from this, your deductions for interest expenses will also be restricted if certain loans are deemed by the CRA to be limited-recourse debt. *Limited-recourse* rules require that funds must be borrowed with bona fide arrangements in place to repay the principal back within 10 years. It can't be a make believe — or phantom — loan, with no intention to repay it within a reasonable time period. Interest must be payable on a regular basis, at interest rates greater than or equal to those prescribed by the CRA. You have to be at full risk for the loan. Also, if you have limited-recourse debt, it's not included in the cost base of your investment. This can potentially set the stage for high taxable capital gains.

## *Tax-Free Savings Accounts*

Canadian stock investors now have another way to save on taxes. With the Tax-Free Savings Account (TFSA), you can put money aside in eligible investments and any growth in value is tax-free. You can use the funds from a TFSA to buy a new car, start a business, or take a holiday vacation. All Canadians can participate.

# Investigating the TFSA rules

If you're Canadian, a resident, and 18 years or older, you can save up to $5,000 every year in a TFSA. The 2009 contribution limit for each qualified person is $5,000. (Periodically check in with your financial institution to see if future TFSA limits are scheduled to rise.) In the meantime, any unused contribution room for 2009 can be carried forward and added to your 2010 TFSA contribution limit. Also, any withdrawals made in 2009 will create additional contribution room for 2010.

Your contributions aren't deductible for income tax purposes. However, the investment income earned in your TFSA, including any capital gains, is not taxed even when you withdraw proceeds from the TFSA.

Another advantage of a TFSA is that income earned in a TFSA does not penalize you in terms of your eligibility for federal income-tested benefits and credits. You can even give money to your spouse to invest in his or her TFSA.

# Comparing TFSAs to RRSPs

Although an RRSP is geared to your retirement, a TFSA is open for just about any use. Both allow you to accumulate wealth tax-free within the plan. However, RRSP contributions are tax deductible and can reduce your income tax up front; TFSA contributions, on the other hand, are not tax deductible. Also, RRSP withdrawals are added to your income and taxed at rates in place at that time. TFSA withdrawals are not included in your income, so they are essentially tax-free.

More details are available at www.tfsa.gc.ca; the site also includes a Tax-Free Savings Account calculator that allows you to estimate TFSA savings amounts.

# Part V
# The Part of Tens

The 5th Wave                    By Rich Tennant

## In this part . . .

This wouldn't be a *For Dummies* book if we didn't include a Part of Tens. Here, you find quick-reference lists of many of the most basic stock investing concepts and practices. We explain how to profit before others do, describe methods for protecting those profits, tell you about investing red flags, and show you how to handle investing challenges and opportunities. Check the information in this part when you don't have time to read the denser parts of the book, or when you just need a quick refresher on what to do before, after, and even during your stock investing pursuits.

# Chapter 23

# Ten Ways to Profit Before the Crowd Does

*In This Chapter*
▶ Noting good reports from the media and stock analysts
▶ Looking at higher earnings
▶ Observing industries, megatrends, and politics
▶ Checking in on insider buying and institutional investing

*I*f you find a stock that has all ten points listed in this chapter going for it, back up the truck and load up! Don't forget to tell us about it! Well . . . you don't need all ten of these points to give you the flashing buy signal, but the more, the better.

## Use Your Instincts

Look at the world around you. Remember that you're a daily participant in the economy. Your savvy consumer instincts tell you much about what goods and services are great . . . or not so great. What do you like? What products do you see flying off the shelves? Do you see anything that throngs of fellow Canadian consumers are lining up around the block to buy? One of the greatest investors of our time, Peter Lynch, used to go with his wife to various stores and consumer outlets. He watched how consumers responded to what was offered. Whatever he found that was popular became a subject of research, which led to great stock picks for the Fidelity Magellan Fund, a stock mutual fund that he managed very successfully for years.

# Take Notice of Praise from Consumer Groups

A company is only as good as the profit it generates, and the profit it generates is only as good as the revenues it generates. The revenues are based on whether customers are accepting (and shelling out money for) the company's products or services. Therefore, if what the company offers is popular with consumers, that bodes well for profits and, ultimately, higher stock prices.

When you're ready to invest in stocks, look for high consumer satisfaction. Review consumer publications and Web sites such as Consumer Reports (www.consumerreports.org) and read the surveys and consumer feedback information. Good publicity and word-of-mouth consumer satisfaction are things that Canadian investors should be aware of. Stock-picking expert Lynch sees this popularity with consumers as very valuable information. He likes to see what consumers buy because that's where the company's success starts.

# Check Out Powerful Demographics

If you know that a company generates lots of profit from the teenage market and you find out that the teenage market is going to expand by 10 percent per year for the foreseeable future, what would you do? Exactly — you'd buy that company's stock. If a company has strong fundamentals and appealing products or services and its market is expanding, that company has a winning combination.

Stay alert to growing trends in society. How are demographics changing? Which sectors of the population are growing or shrinking? What shifts are expected in society in terms of age or ethnicity? Check out the data freely available at the Statistics Canada Web site (www.statcan.gc.ca).

A market that's growing in size isn't an indicator all by itself (in fact, no indicator gives you the green light all by itself), but it should alert you to do some research. The fact that a strong company sees improving demographic shifts (translation: more potential customers) in its marketplace is a big plus.

# Look for a Rise in Earnings

If a company earned $1 per share for the past three years and its earnings are now $1.20 per share (a 20 percent increase), consider this increase a positive harbinger. As the saying goes, "Earnings drive the market," so you need to pay attention to a company's profitability. The more a company makes, the greater the chance that its stock price will increase.

Some people wonder whether to invest in a company that was losing money and then finally turns a profit. Perhaps you're considering the stock of a company involved in new, untested technology. Our advice is to be careful in this situation. In such a case, predicting whether a second year of profits will show up is hard, but of course, that's what investors are hoping.

For the serious investor, a track record of positive earnings is important. Several years of earnings (especially growing earnings) are crucial in the decision-making process. As earnings rise, make sure the growth is at a rate of 10 percent or higher.

Say you're looking at the stock Buckets-o-Cash Inc. (BOC). BOC had earnings of $1 per share in 2007, $1.10 in 2008, and $1.21 in 2009. First, you can see that the company is a profitable enterprise. Second (and more important), you can see that the earnings grew 10 percent each year. The fact that earnings grew consistently year after year is important because it indicates the company is being managed well. Effective company management has a very positive effect on the stock price as the market notices the company's progress.

Growing earnings are important for another reason — inflation. If a company earns $1 per share in each year, that's better than earning less or losing money. But inflation erodes money's purchasing power. If earnings stay constant, the company's ability to grow decreases because the value of its money declines as a result of inflation.

Check out Chapter 12 for an introduction to the importance of earnings.

# Analyze Industries

Become a regular and informed watcher of a specific industry that shows great promise. Being aware of an industry's progress and its promising potential is a great starting point to find a great stock before the rest of the crowd does. Start reading the trade magazines (ask your librarian for help), regularly peruse the industry's Web sites, and (if possible) attend trade shows and conferences. It's easier to find a good stock this way than trying to scan the thousands of companies that span the entire economy. For more on analyzing industries, check out Chapter 17.

# Stay Aware of Positive Publicity for Industries

When the media report that a company is doing well financially or that its products and services are being well-received by both the media and the market, that news lets you know that the company's stock may be going places. This positive publicity ties in nicely with the point made earlier in this chapter about consumer acceptance for the company's products and services.

Positive press and consumer acceptance are important because they mean the company is doing what's necessary to please its customers. The positive media coverage also may attract new customers to the company. Gaining customers means more sales and more earnings, which translates into a higher stock price. You can find corporate publicity articles at Web sites such as Canada NewsWire (www.newswire.ca); you can also track the industries at Industry Canada (www.ic.gc.ca).

# Watch Megatrends

Watching the news and reading the headlines for megatrends (a trend that affects an entire country or major subsections of it) isn't just an activity to pass the time. It's a profitable pursuit because noticing what society at large is doing is a great early warning system. This is one of our favourite ways to pick winning stocks. We've even done some of the work for you (you can thank us later): take a look at emerging-sector opportunities in Chapter 18.

# Keep Track of Politics

The storm clouds or pending sunshine in today's political sphere can mean lots of rain or lots of light in the markets the following day. Stock markets tend to be reactive to positive or negative scuttlebutt in the world of politics. Politicians get a lot of coverage, especially during election season, which gives the stock investor an idea of what's coming down the pike. When politicians of all stripes start talking about, say, the need to be environmentally sensitive and how industry should go green, that tells you something (like that you should invest in eco-friendly companies). When politicians get elected and their agenda becomes obvious (raise taxes, increase regulations, provide incentives for activity X, and so on), those actions deserve further investigation for investment potential.

Keep a regular eye on popular publications and Web sites that delve into the world of Canadian and international politics. Visit Web sites such as www. ctv.ca/news and www.cnn.com regularly. Some financial publications, such as *The Kiplinger Letter* (www.kiplinger.com), also make a point of watching U.S. political trends. A Canadian alternative is *This Magazine* (this.org/magazine) which is focused on Canadian politics, social trends, and more. Flip to Chapter 11 for more on the effect of politics on stock investing.

# Recognize Heavy Insider or Corporate Buying

Company insiders (such as the CEO and the treasurer) know more about the company's health than anyone else. If insiders are buying stock by the boatload, these purchases are certainly a positive sign for investors. Chapter 15 thoroughly covers insider trading, but we highlight the main points here. Insiders can do one of two things:

- **Buy stock for themselves:** If individuals such as the CEO or the treasurer are buying stocks for their personal portfolios, you can assume that they think the stock is a good investment.

- **Buy stock as a corporate decision:** A corporation buying its own stock is usually considered a positive move. The corporation may see its own stock as a good investment. Additionally, corporate stock buying reduces the number of shares available in the market, potentially pushing the stock price higher.

All things being equal, either of these situations will have a positive impact on the stock price. Odds are you won't see a stampede of insiders buying the stock in a day or week, but you may see it over a period of months. This is generally true simply because each insider has different circumstances, and insider buying is usually done on an individual basis. An accumulation of purchases tells you that members of the management team believe so strongly that the company will do well that they're willing to put their own money at risk.

# Follow Institutional Investors

You can generally break down the market into two basic groups: retail and institutional. Retail is you, me, and millions of other individuals. The institutional group includes mutual funds like London Life's mutual fund segment, hedge funds, pensions like the giant Ontario Teachers' Pension Plan, and other large entities. These large entities aren't just private, corporate organizations — they now include governmental entities such as the newly formed sovereign wealth funds that are becoming direct participants in the markets. Sovereign wealth funds are government investment pools, funded by foreign currency reserves but administered separately from currency reserves for profit. Institutional investors can have a big impact on markets because they can move millions (sometimes even billions) of dollars in and out of markets.

To find out more about the actions of institutional investors, use resources such as Institutional Investor News (`www.iinews.com`), search engines on the Internet, and resources in Appendix B to get started.

# Chapter 24

# Ten Ways to Protect Your Stock Market Profits

*In This Chapter*

▶ Using long-term investing strategies

▶ Considering orders, triggers, and options

▶ Selling your stocks if you absolutely must

*W*hew! When you see the headlines out there, you tend to think that your money is like a balloon in a room full of porcupines — headed for trouble. Fortunately, successful stock investing (or just plain avoiding losses) isn't that difficult to accomplish, even in a crazy market. This chapter lists some things to keep in mind when you want to be defensive about your hard-earned stock market profits.

## Accrue Cash

Always try to have some extra cash on the sideline no matter how tempted you are to be 100 percent fully invested. You never know when buying opportunities may show up, especially in stocks you already own. Being in cash is its own form of diversification away from market risk.

## Spread Your Money across Several Stocks

You should never have too much tied to a single stock because it's way too risky. Spread your money elsewhere. As a general rule of thumb, you shouldn't have more than 15 percent of your financial assets tied to a single company.

# Buy More of a Down (Yet Solid) Stock

Gadzooks! Your stock just went down like a lemming off a cliff! What a rotten day in the market. Now what do you do? Well, if you've chosen well (profitable company, good industry, and so on), then why not buy more? If you bought a solid, profitable stock at $44, then why not pick some up at $33? That way you can dollar-cost average a bit and end up with a better cost basis. When the inevitable rebound in the stock price occurs, you're looking pretty smart.

# Apply Long-Term Logic

Even if you've done your homework and chosen well, you may still find yourself scratching your head and saying, "Holy Moly! My stock just went down. What the heck happened?!" It's happened to us many times. You may make what you think is the greatest choice in stock market history and still see the price decline. What's a prudent investor to do? Believe it or not, wait. Wait? Yes . . . wait. Markets move in irrational ways in the short term, but rationality finally kicks in after a longer time horizon (such as 12, 18, or 24 months or longer).

Common sense takes over regarding a stock price over a protracted period. Long term, good choices go up and bad choices go down. Sooner or later, market participants (millions of both big and small investors) finally notice good companies and invest accordingly.

# Use the Almighty Stop-Loss Order

Getting jittery about the market? What's happening with your stock? Keep in mind that success with your stocks isn't just based on what you invest in — it's also based on how you invest. The stop-loss order is a perennial standby, and you should reach for it as often as the police commissioner reaches for the superhero hotline.

A *stop-loss order* is simply a conditional order that you put in with your brokerage firm on a stock you hold in your account. If the stock is at, say, $50 per share, you can put a stop-loss order in at $45 so that if your stock falls and hits $45, it's automatically sold. Keep in mind that a stop-loss order is also a time-related order; you can stipulate that it can be a *day order* or a *good-till-cancelled* (GTC) order. The day order expires at the end of trading that day, while the GTC order expires at a much later time (determined by the broker). Find out more about stop-loss orders in Chapter 21.

# Use the Almighty Trailing-Stop Order

The *trailing-stop order* is a nice variation on the stop-loss order that we discuss in the preceding section. This order takes the stop-loss order a step further by making it move upward with the stock but not budging on the down side. In other words, the stop loss trails the stock's price upward but won't adjust downward. You set the trailing stop at a percentage (or dollar amount) below the stock price.

For example, say your stock is at $50; you can set the trailing stop at 10 percent below and make it a GTC order. If the stock falls to $45 (which is 10 percent below $50), it's then automatically sold to prevent further losses. But if the stock rises to, say, $60, the trailing stop adjusts upward and would then be at $54 (10 percent below the stock's new price). Should the stock reverse and then fall, the trailing stop stays put at $54 and a sell order is then triggered. At that point you've protected 100 percent of your original investment ($50 per share) and the $4 profit, too. Find out more about trailing stops in Chapter 21.

# Set Up Broker Triggers

Don't be gun-shy about *broker triggers* (like that pun?). These are just orders and/or e-mail alerts that brokers use to help their customers navigate the market environment. Is some news hitting your stock or its particular industry? Triggers act like an early warning system when certain events and conditions occur so that you can act on them (by buying or selling your stock). Many brokerage firms have Web sites that allow you to customize your orders. In addition, Web sites such as www.marketwatch.com and www.bloomberg.com can e-mail you news alerts on stocks and market news. You can find out more about broker orders (such as trade triggers) in Chapter 21.

# Consider the Put Option

A *put option* is a speculative vehicle that helps you make money when you bet on an investment (such as a stock) going down. Put options are beyond the scope of this book, but that doesn't mean we can't whet your appetite about something we feel is a good alternative to simply watching your investment decrease. The type of put option we want to mention is referred to as a *protective put*.

Many people buy puts when they're betting (and hoping) that a particular stock will go down. Of course, if you own that particular stock, you certainly aren't hoping that it goes down, but you can get a protective put as a form of insurance in case the stock does decline. In this case you buy a put on your own stock. If the stock goes down (temporarily), your protective put goes up. You can then hold on to the stock and sell the put option at a profit. The profit you make on the put can offset (wholly or partially) the temporary decline in the stock.

# Check Out the Covered Call Option

Writing covered call options is a good way to generate income from an existing stock in your portfolio. Simply stated, a *covered call option* is a vehicle that gives you a chance to make money from stocks in your brokerage account. It's an ultra safe way to generate more income — as much as 10 percent, 15 percent, or more — from your stock position.

Covered call options are beyond the scope of this book, but we recommend that you look into them, as they can be a safe wealth-building feature, even in portfolios that are temporarily down. You can find excellent tutorials and beginners' information on both covered call options and protective puts (the topic of the preceding section) at places such as the Chicago Board Options Exchange (www.cboe.com) and the Options Industry Council (www.888options.com). For more on options in general, see *Stock Options For Dummies* by Alan R. Simon and *Futures & Options For Dummies* by Joe Duarte (both published by Wiley).

# When All Else Fails, Sell

The most successful investors in history have taken their lumps. As the old adage goes, "Keep your winners and sell your losers." You sell losers to minimize the downside. It's easier to recoup a 10 percent or 20 percent loss in your portfolio on the whole than it is to recoup a huge loss in a particular stock. In addition, for what it's worth, the losses are usually tax-deductible, which can at least help minimize the pain at tax time. (See Chapter 22 for details on handling taxes.)

# Chapter 25

# Ten Red Flags for Stock Investors

*In This Chapter*

▶ Seeing a slowdown in earnings and sales

▶ Keeping an eye out for high debt or low bond ratings

▶ Staying aware of industry or political troubles

▶ Spotting questionable accounting practices

*H*ave you ever watched a movie and noticed that one of the characters coughs excessively throughout the entire film? To us, that's a dead giveaway the character is a goner. Or maybe you've seen a movie in which a bit character annoys a crime boss, so right away you know that it's time for him to "sleep with the fishes." Stocks aren't that different. If you're alert, you can recognize some definite signs that your investment may be ready to kick the bucket.

Let the tips in this chapter serve as a symptoms checklist on your stock investment. This chapter helps you catch your stock as it starts to cough so that you can get out before it sleeps with the fishes. (We just can't help you with mixed metaphors.)

## Earnings Slow Down or Head South

Profit is the lifeblood of a company. Of course, the opposite is true as well — lack of profit is a sign of a company's poor financial health. Watch the earnings. Are they increasing or not? If they aren't, find out why. Keep in mind that if the general economy is experiencing a recession, stagnant earnings are still better than robust losses — everything is relative. Earnings slowdowns for a company may very well be a temporary phenomenon. If a firm's earnings are holding up better than its competitors or the market in general, you don't need to be alarmed.

Nonetheless, a company's earnings are its most important measure of success. Keep an eye on the company's P/E ratio (see Appendix A for details on this ratio). It could change negatively (go up) as a result of one of two basic scenarios:

- ✔ The stock price goes up as earnings barely budge.
- ✔ The stock price doesn't move, yet earnings drop.

Both of these scenarios result in a rising P/E ratio that ultimately has a negative effect on the stock price.

A P/E ratio that's lower than industry competitors' P/E ratios makes a company's stock a favourable investment.

Don't buy the argument that "Although the company has losses, its sales are exploding." This argument is a variation of "The company may be losing money, but it'll make it up on volume." For example, say that Sweet Patootee Inc. (SPI) had sales of $1 billion in 2009 and that the firm expects sales to be $1.5 billion in 2010, projecting an increase of 50 percent. But what if SPI's earnings were $200 million in 2009 and the company actually expects a loss for 2010? The business wouldn't succeed, because sales without earnings aren't enough — the company needs to make a profit. Remember that if you put your money in the stock of a company that's losing money today with hopes that it will become profitable tomorrow, you're not investing, you're speculating.

# Sales Slow Down

Before you invest in a company, make sure that sales are strong and rising. If sales start to decline, that downward motion ultimately affects earnings (see the previous section). Although a firm's earnings may go safely up and down, sales should consistently rise. If they cease to rise, a variety of reasons may be to blame. First, the situation may be temporary because the economy in general is having tough times. However, it may be more serious. Perhaps the company is having marketing problems, or a competitor is eating away at its market share. Or maybe a new technology is replacing its products and services. In any case, falling sales raise a red flag you shouldn't ignore.

By the way, when we talk sales, we're talking about the sales of what the company usually offers (its products or services). Sometimes a company may sell something other than what it normally offers (such as equipment, real estate, or a subdivision of its business), and this sale may make the total sales number temporarily blip upward. Watch for this because it can fool your perception of the company's financial strength. Maybe the unusual sale is due to financial or cash flow problems that the company's experiencing. The bottom line is to simply check it out.

# Debt Is Too High or Unsustainable

Excessive debt is the kiss of death for a struggling company. During 2000–02, many Canadian companies that experts thought were invincible went bankrupt. During 2008–09 many prominent businesses struggled with high debt, including brokerage firms (longtime Wall Street powerhouses Bear Stearns and Lehman Brothers collapsed into bankruptcy in early 2008), large regional U.S. banks, and that old standby General Motors. It's getting so that stock investing is riskier than hang gliding in a hurricane!

Be aware of a company's debt and solvency. Chapter 12 and Appendix A can help you read and understand a company's financial data so that you can make an informed decision about buying or selling its stock.

# Analysts Are Exuberant Despite Logic

Too often, analysts give glowing praise to stocks that any logical person with some modest financial acumen would avoid like the plague. Why is this? In many instances, the analysts have, alas, a dark motive (or something not so dark such as . . . ugh . . . stupidity). In any case, remember that analysts are employed by firms that earn hefty investment banking fees from the very companies that these analysts tout. In that situation, issuing a less-than-complete or less-than-accurate report can be easy.

In fact, be extremely wary of analysts' views, especially the analysts who make positive recommendations even when the company in question has worrisome features, such as no income and tremendous debt. It seems like a paradox: Sell a stock when all the pros say to buy it? How can that be? The merits of any stock should speak for themselves. When a company is losing money, all the great recommendations in the world can't reverse its fortunes.

Also, keep in mind that if everybody is buying a particular stock — the current analysts' favourite — who's left to buy it? When the stock turns out to be a dud, you aren't able to sell it because all the other suckers already own it (thanks to analysts' recommendations). And if they already own it, they're probably already aware of the company's flaws. What happens then? You got it: More and more people end up selling it. When more people are selling than buying a stock, its price declines.

# Insider Selling

Heavy insider selling is to a stock what garlic, sunrises, and holy water are to vampires: an almost certain sign of doom! If you notice that increasing numbers of insiders (such as a company's president, treasurer, or vice president of finance) are selling their stock holdings, you can consider it a red flag. In recent years, massive insider selling has become a telltale sign of a company's imminent fall from grace. After all, who better to know the company's prospects for success (or lack thereof) than its high-level management? What management does (selling stock, for example) speaks louder than what management says. (Do you hear that loud and persistent coughing again?) For more information on insider trading, see Chapter 15.

# A Bond Rating Cut

It may seem odd, but the prospects for a company's bonds are an indicator of the prospects for the company's stock. Many firms issue bonds so they can borrow money to fund operations or new ventures. These corporate bonds are usually rated by major bond-rating agencies such as Standard & Poor's. These agencies issue a rating on the bond with this question in mind: "Does the issuer of the bond (the company) have the financial wherewithal to pay back the bond principal and interest in full according to the terms of the bond indenture (the bond agreement)?"

If a company is rated as financially strong, the bond-rating agency will issue a high bond rating (such as AAA or AA). If the agency's view of the company is generally negative, the bond rating for the company will be lower (such as BBB or lower). When a company's bonds are downgraded it's definitely a red flag for investors. Check out Chapter 9 for more information on bond ratings. Also be wary of the fact that these agencies often operate in a conflict of interest scenario. In other words, to drum up and maintain business, they may issue a better rating than the client company being rated deserves. It keeps their clients happy!

# Increased Negative Coverage

You may easily recognize unfavourable reports of a company's stock as a sign to unload that stock. Or you may be a contrarian and see bad press as an opportunity to scoop up some shares of a company victimized by negative reporting. In any case, take the negative reports as a signal to further investigate the merits of holding on to the stock or as a sign for selling it so that you can make room in your portfolio for a more promising stock choice.

# Industry Problems

Sometimes, being a strong company doesn't matter if that company's industry is having problems. If the industry is in trouble, the company's decline probably isn't that far behind. Tighten up those trailing stops (see Chapter 21 to find out how).

Also, try to be aware of industries that are intimately related to the industry of a company's stock you own or are considering buying. Very often, problems in one industry can affect or spread to a related industry. For example, plummeting auto sales may have a negative effect on prospects for auto parts or auto services companies. To find out more about industries, check out Chapter 17.

# Political Problems

Political considerations are always a factor in investing. Be it taxes, regulations, or other government actions, politics can easily break a company and sink its stock. If your company's stock is sensitive to political developments, be aware of potential political pitfalls. Reading *The Globe and Mail* and the *Wall Street Journal* and regularly viewing major financial Web sites like www. bnn.ca and www.bloomberg.com can help you stay informed. (We give you lists of sources in Appendix B.)

In recent years, drug and tobacco stocks in general suffered because of prevailing political attitudes. Also, the prices of certain stocks in particular (Microsoft in the late 1990s comes to mind) have dropped drastically because the companies were targets of government actions for such reasons as antitrust concerns and public safety issues. To find out more about political considerations affecting stocks, go to Chapter 11.

# Funny Accounting: No Laughing Here!

Throughout this book, we discuss the topic of accounting as an important way to see how well (or how poorly) a company is doing. Understanding a company's balance sheet and income statement and making a simple comparison of these documents over a period of several years can give you great insights into the company's prospects. You don't have to be an accountant to grasp key concepts. Livent is a perfect example of how you can avoid a stock investing disaster with some rudimentary knowledge of accounting. We discuss window dressing (spotting the use of illegal or highly questionable accounting tricks) in Chapters 13 and 14. Livent used several of those tricks (like inappropriately deferring expenses and accelerating revenues at the same time).

Another classic example is Enron. Despite the fact that Enron hid many of its financial problems from public view, the information that was available made the message clear: "Danger Will Robinson! Houston, we have a problem!" If investors had done some simple homework, they would have plainly seen the following revealing points over a year and a half before the collapse:

- **Enron's price-to-earnings (P/E) ratio hit 90 in 2000.** This stratospheric P/E kept most value investors (including ourselves) away.

- **Its price-to-book (P/B) ratio hit 12.** For investors, this ratio means that the market value of the company, compared to the company's book value (also called *accounting value*), was 12 to 1 — for every $12 of market value, investors were getting only $1 in book value. When you consider that a P/B ratio of 3 or 4 is considered nosebleed territory for value investors, you can see that Enron's P/B ratio was screaming, "Watch out below!"

- **The price-to-sales (P/S) ratio hit an incredible 22.** This ratio means that investors paid $22 in market value for every $1 of sales the company generated. When a P/S of 5 or 10 is considered too high, 22 is nosebleed territory!

We found this information in public filings that anyone could have seen. To understand these points more fully (along with other equally incisive and lucid accounting and financial points), and to discover how to use the information to avoid similar mistakes in the future, see Chapters 13 and 14 and Appendix A.

# Chapter 26

# Ten Challenges and Opportunities for Stock Investors

. . . . . . . . . . . . . . . . . . . . . . . . . . . . . . . . . . . . . . . . . . . . . . . . . . .

## In This Chapter

▶ Understanding the most pressing concerns for stock investors

▶ Recognizing other markets that can affect stocks

▶ Spotting hidden opportunities with new economic megatrends

. . . . . . . . . . . . . . . . . . . . . . . . . . . . . . . . . . . . . . . . . . . . . . . . . . .

*O*ver the years, we've found that the easiest way to make money with stocks (or to avoid losing money with stocks) is to simply be aware of the economic environment in which they operate. Stocks can be the best (or worst) investment depending on the economic/political environment. Many economic challenges face the stock market, including what's happening with government policy, societal trends, and national/international geopolitical conditions. In this chapter, we discuss the most important issues or megatrends that can affect you and your loved ones, as well as your stock investments.

 You need to be aware of the big picture by regularly checking in with great Web sites such as Financial Sense (www.financialsense.com), Free-Market News Network (www.freemarketnews.com), and the Mises Institute (www.mises.org). See Appendix B for more resources.

## Debt, Debt, and More Debt

In June 2009, the U.S. gross domestic product (GDP) surpassed the $14 trillion mark. Great! However, the total level of debt in the country surpassed $43 trillion. Ugh . . . NOT great. What has kept the U.S. economy afloat and "growing" during the past eight to ten years is massive and pervasive debt that must be dealt with. Debt in just about every category is at record levels, including mortgage, consumer, margin, corporate, and government debt. The problem is that this debt must be either paid off or wiped out through bankruptcy. In 2009, you saw financial catastrophes with debt gone bad in the U.S. banking and brokerage industries. Canada was spared a banking catastrophe but still felt the ill effects of a damaging recession. The Canadian government also had to increase its debt load to stimulate the domestic economy, but by nowhere near the magnitude and increments underlying the U.S. stimulus plans.

Make sure you're dealing with your debt level now. Reduce it as much as possible, and make sure you're analyzing your stocks in the same light. Companies that carry too much debt are at great risk. If a company sinks, your stock will follow. If the company goes into bankruptcy, your stock's value will be vapourized.

# Derivatives

*Derivatives* are the largest financial market in the world. As of June 2009, the total dollar value exceeds $475 trillion. It easily dwarfs the world economy. Easily! Now, you don't have to understand them, but you should be aware of what could go wrong if a derivatives problem occurs. Companies such as Bear Stearns and AIG imploded very quickly, primarily because of tragic errors in their derivatives portfolios. We would love to explain derivatives more fully, but it would take a whole chapter by itself. If you want a detailed explanation, sources such as www.wikipedia.com and www.investopedia.com do a fairly good job. Derivatives "accidents" have dotted the financial landscape over the past 10 to 15 years, and they had (and will have) the potential to do major damage to the stock market.

There's no use fretting about derivatives. While you're at it, you may as well worry about meteors and minority governments. Just take a common-sense approach to protect your portfolio as you grow your wealth. Stay away from firms that have large derivatives positions (typically banks and brokerage firms). Look into diversifying, trailing stops, and the other strategies discussed in this book and in the resources cited.

# Real Estate

Real estate is one challenge the experts warned you about during 2004–05. By the time you read this, everyone will realize that the North American real estate industry is down dramatically from its former bubble highs, and in the U.S. in particular it's languishing with record levels of foreclosures and unsold inventories of property (as of mid-2009). If you're tempted to jump in, tread carefully, because a full, healthy recovery in a slow-moving market like real estate tends to take a long time. You're better off waiting until the data from the industry become more positive.

The message to you at this point is clear: Make sure you have your mortgage under control and your debt at a manageable level. Make sure the real estate industry is showing signs of solid recovery before you buy any stock of any related companies.

Some early signs of a recovery are at least three consecutive quarters of rising building permits and a steady shrinkage of the national inventory of unsold real estate, among others. A good site for real estate is www.realtor.ca.

# Inflation

Inflation may soon become a major economic trend to watch. If it does materialize in a big way, you'll want to be poised to defend yourself against it, and even benefit from it.

The reason why high (and rising) inflation is now a worldwide risk is because most major countries are increasing their money supply at double-digit gangbuster levels. At the same time, however, the increase in money supply is being counteracted by deflation, which is mainly caused by unemployment and stagnant economic activity. The jury is still out as to the extent and timing of inflationary pressure, but you'll definitely want to be prepared for major inflation if and when it comes.

Reassess your portfolio and avoid companies that may be hurt by rising inflation (such as mortgage companies and other fixed-debt securities). Consider shifting more of your portfolio to companies that benefit from inflation (or at least aren't hurt by it), such as those in the food, materials, energy, and precious metals sectors.

# Pensions and Unfunded Liabilities

In 2009, the first wave of the 84 million Canadian and American baby boomers retire. The problem is that pensions for these folks will likely fall short. The latest data show that many pensions are underfunded, and many future retirees are in for a rude awakening.

In addition, Social Security and Medicare in the U.S. (and Old Age Security, the Canada Pension Plan, and universal health care benefits in Canada) are certain to be gigantic challenges during the next few decades. As of July 2009, the total liabilities for these mammoth programs exceed $52 trillion in the U.S. and $67 billion in Canada. That's not a typo; it's a combined liability. Current beneficiaries likely will not be affected, but anyone under 65 certainly will be. Let's face it: We're living longer than ever before, and we need to be more proactive about our personal responsibility in our senior years.

The message is clear: People need to save and invest more to fill in the financial gaps that seem to be inevitable. Stocks are a wealth-building tool that's well-suited for long-term needs such as your retirement concerns. Start now, because the future has a way of sneaking up on you faster than you think.

# The Growth of Government

Every economy has two components: private (consumers and producers) and public (government). No matter how you slice it, government is supported (think taxes) by the private sector. The total combined budget for federal, provincial, and local governments in Canada is $235 billion; in the U.S., it exceeds $6 trillion as of July 2009. The trend is for larger and more activist government, which entails higher overall taxes, increased regulations, and other government growth (inflation, spending, and so on). History tells us that this isn't a positive trend and that it can weigh very heavily on the finances of the private sector (translation: the stock market goes down). What's an investor to do?

We repeat the message from throughout this book: Stick to stocks from companies whose products or services address basic human needs, and understand the good, the bad, and the ugly of government and its effect on the economy and financial markets (Chapters 10 and 11 are good places to start).

# Recession/Depression

Recessions and depressions are actually a tie-in to the point in the previous section — they're symptoms of excessive government growth and intervention. In any event, Canadians and Americans have been trying to fend off a recession throughout much of 2009. We think that struggling economic times will still be evident when you read these words.

In rough economic times, the best stocks are defensive (food, beverage, utilities, and so on), because people buy these things no matter how good or bad the economy is. Cyclical stocks will get beaten down, so it may be a good idea to shop around for real values after the economy turns around. Meanwhile, deploy protective strategies with your money, and play it safe with solid, financially sound companies.

# Commodities

In many respects, this decade resembles the 1970s. Stocks were having a dreadful time as inflation, the energy crisis, and international tensions escalated. However, it was a great time to invest in energy, precious metals, and commodities. Gold and silver hit all-time highs by the end of the 1970s. Stock investors who scooped up shares of companies in these specific industries racked up tremendous gains.

The lesson for investors to understand is that conditions in this decade offer opportunities in natural resources that mirror the late 1970s. In addition, China and India are growing, and they'll need more commodities (grains, base metals, energy, water, and so on) for their expanding economies and populations. As demand continues to outpace supply, the stocks of Canadian companies in particular that provide products and services in natural resources will shine.

# Energy

Oil hit a recent high of $147 per barrel in early summer 2008. Although the price corrected (it was at approximately $70 as of mid-August 2009), the world's appetite for energy (oil, gas, and so on) has caused prices to hit record highs, and the coming years promise more demand. The energy markets are experiencing a sea change that makes current conditions different and far more serious than in recent decades.

For stock investors, this at least means the chance to grow your money both directly (energy companies, obviously) and indirectly (alternate energy companies). If you want your wealth to grow, you need to understand the impact that energy has on your portfolio. (See Chapter 18 for more on emerging-sector opportunities.)

# Dangers from Left Field

Gee, after being beaten up by the previous nine points, what else do you need? This reminds us of the episode of *Get Smart* where the arch villain says, "You've been whipped, beaten, and tortured, but the picnic is over!" (We still use that great line at parties.) In any case, we hope we've impressed upon you that it's a brave new world fraught with dangers for the clueless but filled with wealth-building opportunities for the clued-in. The fact is that no one knows what will hit our economy and society from out of the blue. Events such as 9/11, the tsunami in Asia, and Hurricane Katrina certainly tell us that the world has unseen perils for us and our prosperity. Terrorism and other factors will have an impact. Fortunately, you can make changes — even slight changes — that can protect or grow your wealth.

Whether you're talking about healthcare stocks that boom in response to new health threats or concerns (such as the H1N1 virus) or stocks of companies that prosper because of national security issues, your stock investing program can survive and thrive. Stay informed, and understand that successful stock investing doesn't happen in a vacuum.

# Part VI
# Appendixes

The 5th Wave                    By Rich Tennant

"Sell."

# In this part . . .

Check out the appendixes for resources that aid you in making informed investment decisions. In Appendix A, we explain financial ratios. These important numbers help you better determine whether to invest in a particular company's stock. In Appendix B, we offer you a treasure trove of resources.

# Appendix A

# Financial Ratios

$C$onsidering how many financial catastrophes have occurred in recent years (and continue to occur in the current headlines), doing your homework regarding the financial health of your stock choices is more important than ever. This appendix should be your go-to section when you find stocks that you're considering for your portfolio. It lists the most common ratios that investors should be aware of and use. A solid company doesn't have to pass all these ratio tests with flying colours, but at a minimum it should comfortably pass the ones regarding profitability and solvency:

✔ **Profitability:** Is the company making money? Is it making more or less than it did in the prior period? Are sales growing? Are profits growing?

You can answer these questions by looking at the following ratios:

- • Return on equity

- • Return on assets

- • Common size ratio (income statement)

✔ **Solvency:** Is the company keeping debts and other liabilities under control? Are the company's assets growing? Is the company's net equity (or net worth or shareholders' equity) growing?

You can answer these questions by looking at the following ratios:

- • Quick ratio

- • Debt to net equity

- • Working capital

While you examine ratios, keep these points in mind:

✔ Not every company and/or industry is the same. A ratio that seems dubious in one industry may be just fine in another. Investigate and check out the norms in that particular industry. (See Chapter 17 for details on analyzing industries.)

✔ A single ratio isn't enough on which to base your investment decision. Look at several ratios covering the major aspects of the company's finances.

✔ Look at two or more years of the company's numbers to judge whether the most recent ratio is better, worse, or unchanged from the previous year's ratio. Ratios can give you early warning signs regarding the company's prospects. (See Chapter 12 for details on two important documents that list a company's numbers — the balance sheet and the income statement.)

# Liquidity Ratios

*Liquidity* is the ability to quickly turn assets into cash. Liquid assets are simply assets that are easy to convert to cash. Real estate, for example, is certainly an asset, but it's not liquid because converting it to cash could take weeks, months, or even years. Current assets such as chequing accounts, savings accounts, marketable securities, accounts receivable, and inventory are much easier to sell or convert to cash in a short period of time.

Paying bills or immediate debt takes liquidity. Liquidity ratios help you understand a company's ability to pay its current liabilities. The most common liquidity ratios are the current ratio and the quick ratio; the numbers to calculate them are located on the balance sheet.

## Current ratio

The current ratio is the most commonly used liquidity ratio. It answers the question, "Does the company have enough financial cushion to meet its current bills?" It's calculated as follows:

Current ratio = Total current assets ÷ Total current liabilities

If Schmocky Corp. (SHM) has $60,000 in current assets and $20,000 in current liabilities, the current ratio is 3, meaning the company has $3 of current assets for each dollar of current liabilities. As a general rule, a current ratio of 2 or more is desirable.

A current ratio of less than 1 is a red flag that the company may have a cash crunch that could cause financial problems. Although many companies strive to get the current ratio to equal 1, we like to see a higher ratio (in the range of 1–3) to keep a cash cushion should the economy slow down.

# Quick ratio

The quick ratio is frequently referred to as the "acid test" ratio. It's a little more stringent than the current ratio in that you calculate it without inventory. We'll use the current ratio example discussed in the preceding section. What if half of the assets are inventory ($30,000 in this case)? Now what? First, here's the formula for the quick ratio:

Quick ratio = (Current assets less inventory) ÷ Current liabilities

In the example, the quick ratio for SHM is 1.5 ($30,000 divided by $20,000). In other words, the company has $1.50 of "quick" liquid assets for each dollar of current liabilities. This amount is okay. *Quick liquid assets* include any money in the bank, marketable securities, and accounts receivable. If quick liquid assets at the very least equal or exceed total current liabilities, that amount is considered adequate.

The acid test that this ratio reflects is embodied in the question, "Can the company pay its bills when times are tough?" In other words, if the company can't sell its goods (inventory), can it still meet its short-term liabilities? Of course, you must watch the accounts receivable as well. If the economy is entering rough times, you want to make sure the company's customers are paying invoices on a timely basis.

# Operating Ratios

Operating ratios essentially measure a company's efficiency. "How is the company managing its resources?" is a question commonly answered with operating ratios. If, for example, a company sells products, does it have too much inventory? If it does, that could impair the company's operations. The following sections present common operating ratios.

## Return on equity (ROE)

*Equity* is the amount left from total assets after you account for total liabilities. (This can also be considered a profitability ratio.) The *net equity* (also known as shareholders' equity, stockholders' equity, or net worth) is the bottom line on the company's balance sheet, both geographically and figuratively. It's calculated as

Return on equity (ROE) = Net income ÷ Net equity

The net income (from the company's income statement) is simply the total income less total expenses. Net income that isn't spent or used up increases the company's net equity. Looking at net income is a great way to see whether the company's management is doing a good job growing the business. You can check this out by looking at the net equity from both the most recent balance sheet and the one from a year earlier. Ask yourself whether the current net equity is higher or lower than the year before. If it's higher, by what percentage is it higher?

For example, if SHM's net equity is $40,000 and its net income is $10,000, its ROE is a robust 25 percent (net income of $10,000 divided by net equity of $40,000). The higher the ROE, the better. An ROE that exceeds 10 percent (for simplicity's sake) is good (especially in a slow and struggling economy). Use the ROE in conjunction with the ROA ratio in the following section to get a fuller picture of a company's activity.

## Return on assets (ROA)

The ROA may seem similar to the ROE, but it actually gives a perspective that completes the picture when coupled with the ROE. The formula for figuring out ROA is

Return on assets = Net income ÷ Total assets

The ROA reflects the relationship between a company's profit and the assets used to generate that profit. If SHM makes a profit of $10,000 and has total assets of $100,000, the ROA is 10 percent. This percentage should be as high as possible, but it will generally be less than the ROE.

Say the company has an ROE of 25 percent but an ROA of only 5 percent. Is that good? It sounds okay, but a problem exists. An ROA that's much lower than the ROE indicates that the higher ROE may have been generated by something other than total assets — debt! The use of debt can be a leverage to maximize the ROE, but if the ROA doesn't show a similar percentage of efficiency, then the company may have incurred too much debt. In that case, investors should be aware that this situation could cause problems (see the section "Solvency Ratios" in this appendix). Better ROA than DOA!

## Sales to receivables ratio (SR)

The sales to receivables ratio (SR) gives investors an indication of a company's ability to manage what customers owe it. This ratio uses data from both the income statement (sales) and the balance sheet (accounts receivable, or AR). The formula is expressed as

Sales to receivables ratio = Sales ÷ Receivables

Say you have the following data for SHM:

Sales in 2009 are $75,000. On 12/31/09, receivables stood at $25,000.

Sales in 2010 are $80,000. On 12/31/10, receivables stood at $50,000.

Based on these data, you can figure out that sales went up 6.6 percent, but receivables went up 100 percent! In 2009, the SR was 3 ($75,000 divided by $25,000). However, the SR in 2010 sank to 1.6 ($80,000 divided by $50,000), or was nearly cut in half. Yes, sales did increase, but the company's ability to collect money due from customers fell dramatically. This information is important to notice for one main reason: What good is selling more when you can't get the money? From a cash flow point of view, the company's financial situation deteriorated.

# Solvency Ratios

*Solvency* just means that a company isn't overwhelmed by its liabilities. Insolvency means "Oops! Too late." You get the point. Solvency ratios have never been more important than they are now because the North American economy is currently carrying so much debt. Solvency ratios look at the relationship between what a company owns and what it owes. Here are two of the primary solvency ratios.

## Debt to net equity ratio

The debt to net equity ratio answers the question, "How dependent is the company on debt?" In other words, it tells you how much the company owes and how much it owns. You calculate it as follows:

Debt to net equity ratio = Total liabilities ÷ Net equity

If SHM has $100,000 in debt and $50,000 in net worth, the debt to net equity ratio is 2. The company has $2 of debt to every dollar of net worth. In this case, what the company owes is twice the amount of what it owns.

Whenever a company's debt to net equity ratio exceeds 1 (as in the example), that isn't good. In fact, the higher the number, the more negative the situation. If the number is too high and the company isn't generating enough income to cover the debt, the business runs the risk of bankruptcy.

## Working capital

Technically, working capital isn't a ratio, but it does belong to the list of things that serious investors look at. *Working capital* measures a company's current assets in relation to its current liabilities. It's a simple equation:

Working capital = Total current assets – Total current liabilities

The point is obvious: Does the company have enough to cover the current bills? Actually, you can formulate a useful ratio. If current assets are $25,000 and current liabilities are $25,000, that's a 1-to-1 ratio, which is cutting it close. Current assets should be at least 50 percent higher than current liabilities (say, $1.50 to $1.00) to have enough cushion to pay bills and have some money for other purposes. Preferably, the ratio should be 2 to 1 or higher.

# Common Size Ratios

Common size ratios offer simple comparisons. You have common size ratios for both the balance sheet (where you compare total assets) and the income statement (where you compare total sales):

- ✔ **To get a common size ratio from a balance sheet,** the total assets figure is assigned the percentage of 100 percent. Every other item on the balance sheet is represented as a percentage of total assets. For example, if SHM has total assets of $10,000 and debt of $3,000, then debut equals 30 percent (debt divided by total assets, or $3,000 ÷ $10,000, which equals 30 percent).

- ✔ **To get a common size ratio from an income statement (or profit and loss statement),** you compare total sales. For example, if SHM has $50,000 in total sales and a net profit of $8,000, then you know that the profit equals 16 percent of total sales.

Keep in mind the following points with common size ratios:

- ✔ **Net profit:** What percentage of sales is it? What was it last year? How about the year before? What percentage of increases (or decreases) is the company experiencing?

- ✔ **Expenses:** Are total expenses in line with the previous year? Are any expenses going out of line?

✔ **Net equity:** Is this item higher or lower than the year before?

✔ **Debt:** Is this item higher or lower than the year before?

Common size ratios are used to compare the company's financial data not only with prior balance sheets and income statements but also with other companies in the same industry. You want to make sure that the company is doing better not only historically but also as a competitor in the industry.

# Valuation Ratios

Understanding the value of a stock is very important for stock investors. The quickest and most efficient way to judge the value of a company is to look at valuation ratios. The type of value that you deal with throughout this book is the *market value* (essentially the price of the company's stock). You hope to buy it at one price and sell it later at a higher price — that's the name of the game. But what's the best way to determine whether what you're paying for now is a bargain or is fair market value? How do you know whether your stock investment is undervalued or overvalued? The valuation ratios in the following sections can help you answer these questions. In fact, they're the same ratios that value investors have used with great success for many years.

## Price-to-earnings ratio (P/E)

The price-to-earnings ratio can also double as a profitability ratio because it's a common barometer of value that many investors and analysts look at. The formula is

P/E ratio = Price (per share) ÷ Earnings (per share)

For example, if SHM's stock price per share is $10 and the earnings per share is $1, the P/E ratio is 10 (10 divided by 1).

The P/E ratio answers the question, "Am I paying too much for the company's earnings?" Value investors find this number to be very important. Here are some points to remember:

✔ Generally, the lower the P/E ratio, the better (from a financial-strength point of view). Frequently, a low P/E ratio indicates that the stock is undervalued, especially if the company's sales are growing and the industry is also growing. But you may occasionally encounter a situation where the stock price is falling faster than the company's earnings, which would also generate a low P/E. And if the company has too much debt and the industry is struggling, then a low P/E may indicate that the company is in trouble. Use the P/E as part of your analysis along with other factors (such as debt, for instance) to get a more complete picture.

✔ A company with a P/E ratio significantly higher than its industry average is a red flag that its stock price is too high (or that it's growing faster than its competitors).

✔ Don't invest in a company with no P/E ratio (it has a stock price, but the company experienced losses). Such a stock may be good for a speculator's portfolio but not for your retirement account.

✔ Any stock with a P/E ratio higher than 40 should be considered a speculation and not an investment. Frequently, a high P/E ratio indicates that the stock is overvalued.

When you buy a company, you're really buying its power to make money. In essence, you're buying its earnings. Paying for a stock that's priced at 10 to 20 times earnings is a conservative strategy that has served investors well for nearly a century. Make sure the company is priced fairly, and use the P/E ratio in conjunction with other measures of value (such as the ratios in this appendix).

## Price to sales ratio (PSR)

The price to sales ratio (PSR) helps to answer the question, "Am I paying too much for the company's stock based on the company's sales?" This is a useful valuation ratio that we recommend using as a companion tool with the company's P/E ratio. You calculate it as follows:

PSR = Stock price (per share) ÷ Total sales (per share)

This ratio can be quoted on a per-share basis or on an aggregate basis. For example, if a company's market value (or market capitalization) is $1 billion and annual sales are also $1 billion, the PSR is 1. If the market value in this example is $2 billion, then the PSR is 2. Or, if the share price is $76 and the total sales per share are $38, the PSR is 2 — you arrive at the same ratio whether you calculate on a per-share or aggregate basis. For investors trying to make sure they're not paying too much for the stock, the general rule is that the lower the PSR, the better. Stocks with a PSR of 2 or lower are considered undervalued.

Be very hesitant about buying a stock with a PSR greater than 5. If you buy a stock with a PSR of 5, you're paying $5 for each dollar of sales — not exactly a bargain.

# Price to book ratio (PBR)

The price to book ratio (PBR) compares a company's market value to its accounting (or book) value. The book value refers to the company's net equity (assets minus liabilities). The company's market value is usually dictated by external factors such as supply and demand in the stock market. The book value is indicative of the company's internal operations. Value investors see the PBR as another way of valuing the company to determine whether they're paying too much for the stock. The formula is

Price to book ratio (PBR) = Market value ÷ Book value

An alternate method is to calculate the ratio on a per-share basis, which yields the same ratio. If the company's stock price is $20 and the book value (per share) is $15, then the PBR is 1.33. In other words, the company's market value is 33 percent higher than its book value. Investors seeking an undervalued stock like to see the market value as close as possible to (or even better, below) the book value.

Keep in mind that the PBR may vary depending on the industry and other factors. Also, judging a company solely on book value may be misleading because many companies have assets that aren't adequately reflected in the book value. Software companies are a good example. Intellectual properties, such as copyrights and trademarks, are very valuable yet aren't fully covered in book value. Just bear in mind that, generally, the lower the market value is in relation to the book value, the better for you (especially if the company has strong earnings and the outlook for the industry is positive).

# Appendix B

# Resources for Stock Investors

• • • • • • • • • • • • • • • • • • • • • • • • • • • • • • • • • • • • • • •

*G*etting and staying informed is an ongoing priority for you as a careful stock investor. The lists in this appendix represent some of the best information resources available.

## Basics of Investing

These resources will help you learn about the basics of stock investing and your rights as an investor.

### Canadian Securities Institute
www.csi.ca
The CSI provides many of the courses and exams you need to work in Canada's securities industry.

### InvestorWords
www.investorwords.com
We know that it sometimes feels like investing has its own language. Consider Investor Words your rosetta stone. This site is a financial glossary, defining terms you need to know.

### Financial Industry Regulatory Authority (FINRA)
www.finra.org
The FINRA is a US-based independent regulator that oversees nearly 4,800 brokerage firms. Its site offers many tips on how you can protect yourself as an investor.

### The Investment FAQ
www.invest-faq.com
The most commonly asked questions about investing are housed on this site, which is has a long history, having started in the early days of the Web.

### The Motley Fool
www.fool.com
Founded by David and Tom Gardner, this site provides investing news, recommendations, and commentary.

# Financial Planning Sources

To find a financial planner to help you with your general financial needs, consider the following organizations and resources.

### Advocis
www.advocis.ca
(Advocis is the brand name of the Financial Advisors Association of Canada. As the voice of over 10,000 of Canada's financial gurus, it's the largest voluntary professional membership association of financial advisers in the country. Advocis serves financial advisers and their clients with information and other services.)

### Canadian MoneySaver
www.canadianmoneysaver.ca
A subscription-based Web site, Canadian MoneySaver offers members financial advice, Non-subscribers, however, will find many useful articles and lists here.

### Financial Advisor Pages
www.fapages.com
If you're looking for a financial advisor, this site will come in handy. It offers a directory of advisors, along with resources for investors.

# General Investing Supersites

These are one-stop investing information supermarkets, and they have everything but the kitchen sink. Most investing supersites have comprehensive stock investor services including stock quotes, charts, portfolio tracking, stock screening, investment articles, discussion forums, company profiles, company press releases, stock market statistics, economic data, and more.

### Adviceforinvestors.com
www.adviceforinvestors.com
The Web site of MPL Communications, the publisher of *The Investment Reporter* and *Investor's Digest of Canada.*

### Bloomberg
www.bloomberg.com
This massive site offers news, information, stock quotes, market information, and even live television.

### CNN Money.com
money.cnn.com
You'll find all of CNN's financial news here, along with stock quotes and portfolio tracking.

**Invest$Link**
www.wwfn.com/links.html
This bare-bones site offers a collection of helpful links.

**InvestorLinks.com**
www.investorlinks.com
This site offers even more links to over 12,000 Web sites.

**MarketWatch**
www.marketwatch.com
Affiliated with the Wall Street Journal, this impressive site offers the usual: news, commentary, stock quotes, and portfolio tracker.

**MSN Money**
money.ca.msn.com
Prominent Canadian commentators such as Patricia Lovett-Reid and Deirdre McMurray set this site apart from its US competitors.

**Silicon Investor**
www.siliconinvestor.com
The draw here is the message board, where the site's members can discuss investments.

**Stockhouse Canada**
www.stockhouse.com
Stockhouse promises to foster an online investing community that creates content to benefit its paying members.

**Yahoo! Canada Finance**
ca.finance.yahoo.com
With news from Forbes, the Canadian Press, and Canadian Business Online, this portal offers a wealth of information in addition to the standard financial supersite features.

# Investor Research and Analysis Resources

No one likes doing homework, but in stock investing, it's worth it. The resources in this section offer valuable commentary, industry- and stock-specific analysis, insight into the economy's performance, and the latest news that could have an impact on your stock.

## Books and pamphlets

***Common Stocks and Uncommon Profits***
By Philip A. Fisher
Published by John Wiley & Sons, Inc.

***Elliott Wave Principle: Key to Market Behavior***
By Robert Prechter and A. J. Frost
Published by New Classics Library

***Forbes Guide to the Markets***
By Marc M. Groz
Published by John Wiley & Sons, Inc.

***How to Pick Stocks Like Warren Buffett: Profiting from the Bargain
Hunting Strategies of the World's Greatest Value Investor***
By Timothy Vick
Published by McGraw-Hill Professional Publishing

***The Intelligent Investor: The Classic Text on Value Investing***
By Benjamin Graham
Published by HarperCollins

***Invest Wisely: Advice From Your Securities Regulators*** (pamphlet)
`www.sec.gov/investor/pubs/inws.htm`
This publication provides basic information to help investors select a brokerage firm and sales representative, make an initial investment decision, monitor an investment, and address an investment problem.

***Secrets of the Great Investors*** (audiotape series)
Published by Knowledge Products
800-876-4332
`www.knowledgeproducts.net/html/inv_files/invest.cfm`

***Security Analysis: The Classic 1951 Edition***
by Benjamin Graham and David Dodd
Published by the McGraw-Hill Companies
This book is a classic, and most investors in this uncertain age should
acquaint themselves with the basics.

***The Wall Street Journal Guide to Understanding Money & Investing***
By Kenneth Morris and Virginia Morris
Published by Lightbulb Press, Inc.

## Special books of interest to stock investors

**The Coming Collapse of the Dollar and How to Profit from It: Make a Fortune by Investing in Gold and Other Hard Assets**
By James Turk and John Rubino
Published by Doubleday

**Crash Proof 2.0: How to Profit from the Economic Collapse**
By Peter Schiff
Published by John Wiley & Sons, Inc.

**The ETF Book: All You Need to Know About Exchange-Traded Funds**
By Richard Ferri
Published by John Wiley & Sons, Inc.
Considering the marketplace, ETFs are better choices than stocks for some investors, and this book does a good job of explaining them.

**Hot Commodities: How Anyone Can Invest Profitably in the World's Best Market**
By Jim Rogers
Published by Random House

**Precious Metals Investing For Dummies**
By Paul Mladjenovic
Published by John Wiley & Sons, Inc.
My shameless plug for another great book. Seriously, the book covers an area that will become an important part of the financial landscape in the coming months and years (can you say "inflation"?). Yes, common stocks and exchange-traded funds (ETFs) involved in precious metals are covered.

**Profit from the Peak: The End of Oil and the Greatest Investment Event of the Century**
By Brian Hicks and Chris Nelder
Published by John Wiley & Sons, Inc.

**Shell Shocked: How Canadians Can Invest after the Collapse**
by John Stephenson
Published by John Wiley & Sons Canada, Ltd.
This book makes the argument that following the collapse of 2008, one of the best places to invest is right here at home.

**Twilight in the Desert: The Coming Saudi Oil Shock and the World Economy**
By Matthew R. Simmons
Published by John Wiley & Sons, Inc.

# Periodicals and magazines

These are classic investment publications.

### Barron's
online.barrons.com
The online home for *Barron's*, the site offers much of the content from the magazine, plus additional content for paid subscribers.

### *Forbes* Magazine
www.forbes.com
Best known for its list of the world's wealthiest people, *Forbes'* online presence offers news, analysis, and commentary and claims to be the most trusted site for executives.

### Investor's Digest of Canada
www.investorsdigestofcanada.com
This Web site is essentially an advertisement for a subscription to this Canadian publication, boasting what you'll gain as a reader.

### *Kiplinger's Personal Finance* Magazine
www.kiplinger.com
This US publication offers investment and money management advice; the site offers some of the magazine's content along with news, podcasts, and other online exclusives.

### SmartMoney Magazine
www.smartmoney.com
Part of the Wall Street Journal network (along with *Barron's*), *SmartMoney* is aimed at the business professional and offers some lifestyle coverage in addition to the usual investment content you'll find elsewhere.

### The Wall Street Journal
online.wsj.com
The most popular paid financial news site online, this site boasts more than 980,000 paid subscribers, who seek the venerable newspaper's content online.

# Company research and analyst evaluations

These sites feature and focus on stock investment analysis, advice, and research.

### Moody's
www.moodys.com

**Morningstar**
www.morningstar.com

**Morningstar Canada**
www.morningstar.ca

**Richard Russell's *Dow Theory Letters***
ww1.dowtheoryletters.com

***The Value Line Investment Survey***
www.valueline.com

# Industry analysis

These sites have great content about the big picture, including economic, political, and geopolitical analysis.

**Hoover's, Research Companies & Industries**
www.hoovers.com/free/tools/bcl

# External factors that affect market value

These statistics about the economy and industry come right from the horse's mouth.

**American Institute for Economic Research (AIER)**
www.aier.org

**Department of Finance Canada**
www.fin.gc.ca

**FreeLunch.com**
www.freelunch.com

**Moody's Economy.com**
www.economy.com

**U.S. Federal Reserve Board**
www.federalreserve.gov

**U.S. Securities and Exchange Commission (SEC)**
www.sec.gov

## Investment news sources

These are online investment news sources and Webcasts that talk stock shop.

**China Online**
www.chinaonline.com

**MarketWatch, TV and Radio**
www.marketwatch.com/tvradio

**The Online Investor**
www.theonlineinvestor.com

**UK Trade and Investment**
www.ukinvest.gov.uk

## Press releases

Access breaking financial news — right from the source — at these media networks.

**Business Wire**
www.businesswire.com

**CNW Group (Canada NewsWire)**
www.newswire.ca

**PR Newswire**
www.prnewswire.com

# Tax Resources

Calculate and minimize your taxes with these resources.

**Canada Revenue Agency (CRA)**
www.cra-arc.gc.ca

**CANTAX (CCH Canadian Ltd.)**
www.cantax.com

**Quicken, QuickTax, QuickBooks (Intuit Canada)**
www.intuit.ca

**Tax and Accounting Sites Directory**
www.taxsites.com

# Stock Investing Web Sites

How can any serious investor ignore the Internet? You can't and you shouldn't. The following are among the best information sources available.

**Allstocks.com**
www.allstocks.com

**MarketHistory.com**
www.markethistory.com

**Reuters Investing**
today.reuters.com/investing

**Standard & Poor's**
www2.standardandpoors.com

## Stock exchanges

These are the homes of Canadian and U.S. stocks, where they're traded.

**Instinet**
www.instinet.com

**Nasdaq**
www.nasdaq.com

**New York Stock Exchange (NYSE)**
www.nyse.com

**OTC Bulletin Board**
www.otcbb.com

**TMX**
www.tmx.com

# Investors' associations and organizations

The goal of these organizations, first and foremost, is enhancing investor confidence through education.

**Canadian Society of Technical Analysts (CSTA)**
www.csta.org

**Investment Funds Institute of Canada (IFIC)**
www.ific.ca

**National Association of Investors Corp. (NAIC)**
www.better-investing.org

# Stock screens

Stock screens are online tools that help you to find stocks that meet your specific criteria.

**Canoe Money**
money.canoe.ca/FinancialTools

**Hoover's**
www.hoovers.com

***SmartMoney Magazine,* Tools**
www.smartmoney.com/tools

**ZacksAdvisor**
www.zacksadvisor.com

# Quotes

Plain and simple quotes can be readily found on these Web sites. Okay — even not so simple ones, too!

**FreeRealTime.com**
quotes.freerealtime.com

**Quote.com**
www.quote.com

**Yahoo! Finance**
finance.yahoo.com

# Charts

See where your stock has been and guess where it may be going with these resources.

**BigCharts**
bigcharts.marketwatch.com

**ChartSmart**
www.chartsmart.com

**ClearStation**
clearstation.etrade.com

**MetaStock (Reuters)**
www.equis.com

**Tradingcharts.com**
www.tradingcharts.com

# Earnings and earnings estimates

These professional sites track analysts' earnings estimates for major companies. Some of these record more than 15,000 such changes made by more than 3,500 analysts at 210 brokerage firms covering 5,000 companies across North America.

**Briefing.com**
www.briefing.com

**Zacks**
my.zacks.com

# Technical analysis

Tools of the technical analysis trade as well as commentary about trading strategy can be found here.

**Elliott Wave International**
www.elliottwave.com

**StockCharts.com**
stockcharts.com

# Insider trading

See what company insiders are doing with their own company stock at these tracking sites.

**Canadian Securities Administrators' System for Electronic Disclosure by Insiders (SEDI)**
www.sedi.ca

**StreetInsider.com**
www.streetinsider.com

**U.S. Securities and Exchange Commission (SEC)**
www.sec.gov

# Fraud

These investor advocacy sites offer fraud-related advice and referrals.

**Canadian Investor Protection Fund**
www.cipf.ca

**Financial Industry Regulatory Authority (FINRA)**
www.finra.org

**National Fraud Information Center**
www.fraud.org

**U.S. Securities and Exchange Commission (SEC)**
www.sec.gov

# Public filings

Check out the latest statutory filings at these Web sites.

**Morningstar Document Research**
www.10kwizard.com
Formerly 10K Wizard (expect that URL to change soon), this site offers a subscription-based search for SEC filings.

**EDGAROnline**
www.edgar-online.com

A pay site for searching SEC filings, which offers customizable data feeds and analytical tools.

**FreeEDGAR**
freeedgar.com
You can find free access to SEC filings here.

**SEDAR**
www.sedar.com
You can access public securities documents filed by public companies with the Canadian Securities Administrators (CSA) here. Best of all, it's free.

# *IPOs*

Not yet extinct, IPOs may one day rise like the phoenix!

**Canadian IPOs**
ipo.investcom.com
A source for Canadian IPO information.

**IPO Monitor**
www.ipomonitor.com
A site that keeps tabs on IPOs, with additional features for paying members.

# Index

## Numerics

*8-K Reports* in EDGAR, 95
*10-K Reports* in EDGAR, 95
*10-Q Reports* in EDGAR, 95
*14-A Forms* in EDGAR, 95
52-week high, 86
52-week low, 86–87
360 Networks, 46–47

## • A •

AAPL (Apple), 51
accelerated depreciation, 177
accelerating sales, 188
accepting some risk, 222
account executive, 98–100
accounting
  aggressive, 185
  big-bath, 198–199
  LIFO (last-in, first-out method), 197
  principles of, 77–78
  red flags, 323–324
accounts
  allowance for doubtful, 196
  brokerage, 108–110
  TFSA (Tax-Free Savings Accounts), 32,
    302–303
accounts receivable, 174, 196–197
accruing cash, 313
accumulate rating, 111
acquisitions, 298
adjusted cost base
  defined, 292
  reducing, 296
advanced orders, 281–282
Adviceforinvestors.com, 344
advisers, investment, 98–100, 261
advisory services, 261

Advocis, 343–344
aggressive accounting, 185
aggressive investing, 44
AIER (American Institute for Economic
    Research), 143, 160, 347
AIG Corp., 64
allocating
  assets, 59–60, 268–270
  income, 295
allowance for doubtful accounts, 196
Allstocks.com, 348
alternative energy, 241
American Institute for Economic
    Research (AIER), 143, 160, 347
American Stock Exchange
  exchange-traded funds (ETFs), 72, 241
  Web site, 77
AMEX banks, 65
amortization, 168
analysis
  balance sheet, 27–28
  cash flow, 32
  dynamic, 147–148
  fundamental, 112, 120
  growth stocks, 119–126
  income stocks, 135–141
  industry, 227–236, 309, 346
  ratio, 184
  resources, 345–348
  of small-cap stocks, 129
  static, 147–148
  technical, 112, 260–261, 351
analysts
  attention of, 122
  evaluations, 346
  overview, 321
annual growth rate, 23
Apple (AAPL), 51
appreciation, 41, 292–293

asset allocation
  relationship with diversification, 268–270
  weighing risk against return, 59–60
assets
  current, 23
  depreciating, 27
  fixed, 176–177
  intangible, 178
  listing, 21–24
  long-term, 23
associations (investing), 349
assurance, 221
atypical events, 170
auditor-switching, 187, 204
Austrian school of thought, 150–151
automotive industry, 235
avoiding
  consumer discretionary sectors, 244
  risk, 222

• *B* •

balance sheet
  accounts receivable, 174, 196–197
  acquisitions, 198
  analyzing, 27–28
  big-bath accounting, 198–199
  buzzwords, 204–205
  cash/cash equivalents, 173–175
  defined, 20
  fixed assets, 176–177
  intangible assets, 178
  inventories, 175–176, 197–198
  investments, 177
  long-term liabilities, 179–180
  materiality, 203–204
  off-balance-sheet obligations, 199–201
  overview, 21–28, 172–173, 195
  owner's equity, 180–181
  payables, 179
  pension plans, 202–203
  smoke and mirrors, 203

Bank of Canada, 162
bankruptcy prevalence, 25
banks/banking
  AMEX, 65
  certificates of deposit (CDs), 135
  industry, 236
*Barron's,* 112, 345
bear market
  considerations for, 250–252
  defined, 11
Bear Stearns (BSC), 47
beta
  defined, 279
  measurement, 279–280
  of stock, 263
big-bath accounting, 198–199
BigCharts, 350
blogging, 226
Bloomberg, 70, 82, 137, 344
BMO InvestorLine, 107
board of directors (BOD)
  overview, 223
  risk management by, 220–221
  role of, 220
BOD. *See* board of directors
Bombay Stock Exchange, 250
bond rating
  overview, 140–141
  red flags, 322
bonds
  investment grade, 140
  junk, 140
book
  conventions, 3
  icons, 7
  organization, 4–7
book value, 180–181
Boston Options Exchange (BOX), 65
BOX (Boston Option Exchange), 65
Briefing.com, 351
broad-based indexes, 62, 65
broker triggers, 315

brokerage accounts
  cash accounts, 109–110
  margin accounts, 110
  option accounts, 110
brokerage orders
  advanced orders, 281–282
  condition-related orders, 276–281
  overview, 261, 274
  time-related orders, 274–276
brokerage reports, 113–115
brokers
  brokerage accounts, 109–110
  brokerage reports, 113–115
  choosing, 102–104
  discount, 98, 100–101
  evaluating recommendations by,
      111–113
  interviewing, 104
  investment advisers, 98–100
  online investing services, 104–109
  role of, 97–98
  types of accounts, 109–110
BSC (Bear Stearns), 47
BSE SENSEX index, 70
bull markets
  considerations for, 250–252
  opportunities, 239–243
Bureau of Labor Statistics, 161
Business Wire, 347
buy rating, 111
buybacks
  disadvantages of, 215
  stock, 213–217
buying
  corporate, 311
  insider
    evaluating company management,
        127–128, 352
    learning from, 210–211
    recognizing, 311
  institutional, 122
  on margin, 282
  preparing for, 12–13
buy-stop order, 287
buzzwords, 204–205

• *C* •

CAC-40 index, 70
Caisse d'Epargne credit union, 137–138
calculating
  annual growth rate, 23
  common size ratios, 338
  company equity, 124
  current ratio, 334
  debt to net equity ratio, 337
  income, 29–30
  market cap, 14
  net income, 78
  net worth, 26, 77–78
  outflow, 30–31
  payout ratio, 139
  price to book ratio (PBR), 341
  price-to-earnings ratio (P/E), 339
  price to sales ratio (PSR), 340
  quick ratio, 335
  return on assets (ROA), 336
  return on equity (ROE), 335–336
  sales to receivables ratio (SR), 337
  working capital, 338
  yield, 42
call option, 259
Canada Deposit Insurance Corporation
    (CDIC), 21
Canada NewsWire, 310
Canada Pension Plan, 327
Canada Revenue Agency (CRA)
  contact information, 348
  income stocks and, 134
  Web sites, 291, 294
Canadian Economics Association, 143
Canadian Economy Online, 143
Canadian insider trading information,
    209–210
Canadian Investor Protection Fund
    (CIPF), 104, 352
Canadian MoneySaver, 344
Canadian National Railway Company, 121
Canadian Securities Administrators
    (CSA), 102, 351

Canadian Securities Administrators' System for Electronic Disclosure by Insiders (SEDI), 351
Canadian Securities Institute, 343
Canadian Society of Technical Analysts (CSTA), 349
Canadian Taxpayers Federation, 162
Canoe Money, 112, 349
CANTAX (CCH Canadian Ltd.), 348
capital appreciation, 117
capital gain/loss, 41, 292–293
capital gains deduction, 293
capitalization-weighted index, 62
capitalizing costs, 189–190
cash
  accruing, 313
  committing, 262
  equivalents, 173–175
  overview, 173–175
  paying with, 188
cash accounts, 109–110
cash flow
  analyzing, 32
  defined, 28
  from financing activities, 183
  inconsistent, 187
  from investing activities, 182
  from operations, 182
  reduced, 187
cash-flow statement, 31
cause and effect, 79, 148
CDIC (Canada Deposit Insurance Corporation), 21
CDs (certificates of deposit), 135
certificates of deposit (CDs), 135
changing auditors, 204
charts, 350
ChartSmart, 350
Chase, 65
Chicago Board Options Exchange, 252, 316
China Online, 347
China's stock market, 248–249
choosing brokers, 102–104
CIBC Investor's Edge, 107

CIPF (Canadian Investor Protection Fund), 104, 352
ClearStation, 350
closing date, 91
CNN, 311
CNNMoney.com, 344
CNW Group (Canada NewsWire), 347
Coca-Cola, 121
COGS (cost of goods sold), 166–167
commitments, 201
committing cash, 262
commodities
  challenges and opportunities of, 329
  overview, 239–240
common size ratios, 338–339
common stock, 12
company
  financial condition analysis, 120
  insiders, 207
  management evaluation, 123–126
  niche, 121–122
  research on, 83, 346
comparative financial analysis, 78
comparing
  growth stocks, 119–120
  yield, 138–139
composite index, 62
condition-related orders
  limit orders, 280–281
  market orders, 276–277
  stop orders, 277–280
Conference Board, 144, 145, 162
conflict of interest, 224
conservative investing, 43, 132
consultant, financial, 98–100
consumer discretionary sectors, 244
consumer groups, 308
Consumer Price Index (CPI), 162
consumer publications, 122
Consumer Reports, 308
contingent liabilities, 179, 201
contribution limits, 297
controlling risky situations, 222
conventions used in this book, 3
corporate buying, 311

corporate governance risk, 220–223
corporate stock buybacks, 213–217
COS (cost of sales), 166–167
cost of doing business, 174
cost of goods sold (COGS), 166–167
cost of sales (COS), 166–167
costs
  capitalizing, 189–190
  of online trading, 105–106
coupon promotions, 189
covered call option, 316
CPI (Consumer Price Index), 162
CRA (Canada Revenue Agency)
  contact information, 348
  income stocks and, 134
  Web site, 291, 294
creating
  cash-flow statement, 31
  revenue, 188–189
credit, 246–247
credit cards, 188
creditworthiness, 109
CSA (Canadian Securities
    Administrators), 102, 351
CSTA (Canadian Society of Technical
    Analysts), 349
current assets, 23
current ratio, 334
customer-receivable balances, 196
cyclical industries, 228–229
cyclical stocks, 247

• D •

date of declaration, 91
date of execution, 91
date of record, 91
DAX index, 62, 70
day last, in stock table, 90
day orders
  overview, 274–275
  using, 315

debt
  analyzing company, 120
  challenges and opportunities of,
    325–326
  excessive, 187
  high-interest versus low-interest, 27
  limited-recourse, 302
  margin, 50
  prevalence of, 26, 246–247
  red flags, 321
  relationship with common size ratios,
    339
debt to net equity ratio, 337–338
defence companies, 243
defence industries, 229
defence stocks, 133
deferred-income tax shelters/plans
  obligations, 302
  Registered Education Savings Plans
    (RESPs), 300–302
  Registered Retirement Income Funds
    (RRIFs), 300
  Registered Retirement Savings Plans
    (RRSPs), 296–299
defined-benefit pension plans, 202
demand
  defined, 79, 122
  overview, 146
demographics, 308
Department of Finance Canada, 347
Department of Justice Canada, 162
depletion, 168
depreciating assets, 27
depreciation, 168, 176, 177
depression, challenges and
    opportunities of, 328
deregulation, 233
derivatives, challenges and
    opportunities of, 326
direct funding, 233
discontinued operations, 172
discount brokers, 98, 100–101
Dismal Scientist, 144
Disnat, 107

distributions
 defined, 296
 receiving, 295
diversifying
 defined, 58, 268
 importance of, 313
 investments, 58
 relationship with asset allocation,
  268–270
 risk exposure, 222
 stocks, 140
dividend income, 291
dividends
 compared with interest, 41
 defined, 37, 132, 136
 income stocks and, 132
 quarterly, 92
 rates, 132
 researching, 90–93
 stock, 292
 in stock table, 87
DJIA (Dow Jones Industrial Average), 61,
  63–65, 68
DJTA (Dow Jones Transportation
  Average), 65
DJUA (Dow Jones Utilities Average), 65
doing a short sale, 285
dollar limits (RRSPs), 298
Dominion Bond Rating Service, 140
Dow Jones Industrial Average (DJIA), 61,
  63–65, 68
Dow Jones Transportation Average
  (DJTA), 65
Dow Jones Utilities Average (DJUA), 65
Duarte, Joe
 *Futures & Options For Dummies*, 316
dynamic analysis, 147–148

## • E •

E*TRADE Canada, 107
earned income limits (RRSPs), 297
earnings
 analyzing company, 120
 defined, 166

estimates, 350–351
 growth in, 125
 net, 124, 172
 red flags, 319–320
 retained, 181
 rise in, 308–309
earnings before interest, taxes,
  depreciation, and amortization
  (EBITDA), 170
earnings per share (EPS), 214
earnings-trend problems, 187
EBITDA (earnings before interest, taxes,
  depreciation, and amortization), 170
economics
 Austrian school of thought, 150–151
 concepts of, 145–148
 effect on stocks, 78–81
 government intervention, 152
 Keynes school of thought, 149–150
 macroeconomics, 144–145
 Marx school of thought, 148–149
 microeconomics, 144
 relationship with inflation, 151–152
 research of, 83–84
 resources, 143–144
economy
 macro effect on, 153
 micro effect on, 153
EDGAR S-1, 95
EDGAROnline, 94–95, 129, 208, 352
effect, cause and, 79, 148
*8-K Reports* in EDGAR, 95
Elliott Wave International, 261, 351
emergency fund, 21, 27
emerging-sectors
 bearish opportunities
  consumer discretionary sectors, 244
  credit, 246–247
  cyclical stocks, 247
  overview, 244
  real estate, 245–246
  stalled economic regions, 248–250
 bullish opportunities
  alternative energy, 241
  commodities, 239–240

defence industry, 243
 gold and precious metals, 241–242
 healthcare, 242–243
 oil and gas, 240–241
 overview, 239
 considerations, 250–252
 overview, 237–239
emotional risk, 55–56
energy
 alternative, 241
 challenges and opportunities of, 329
energy trusts, 142
Enron, 324
EPS (earnings per share), 214
equity
 growth of, 125
 home, 28
 net, 124, 339
 owner's, 180–181
 shareholders', 124
ETFs (exchange-traded funds),
  58, 72, 229
ethical risk
 conflict of interest, 224
 fraud, 223–224
evaluating
 brokers' recommendations, 111–113
 company management, 123–126
 investment tips, 93
exchange-traded funds (ETFs),
  58, 72, 229
ex-dividend date, 91
executive, account, 98–100
expenses
 hiding, 189–190
 operating, 167
 relationship with common size
  ratios, 338
extraordinary items, 170–171

● **F** ●

face rate, 48
Fannie Mae, 246
Federal Reserve, 162
52-week high, 86

52-week low, 86–87
Financial Advisor Pages, 344
financial analysis, comparative, 78
financial consultant, 98–100
financial goals, 33–34, 36–37, 59–60
Financial Industry Regulatory Authority
  (FINRA), 343, 352
financial news, 82–85
financial planning, 343–344
*Financial Post,* 230, 241
financial ratios
 common size ratios, 338–339
 liquidity ratios
  current ratio, 334
  overview, 334
  quick ratio, 335
 operating ratios
  overview, 335
  return on assets (ROA), 336
  return on equity (ROE), 335–336
  sales to receivables ratio (SR),
   336–337
 overview, 333–334
 solvency ratios
  debt to net equity ratio, 337–338
  overview, 337
  working capital, 338
 valuation ratios
  overview, 339
  price to book ratio (PBR), 341
  price-to-earnings ratio (P/E), 339–340
  price to sales ratio (PSR), 340
financial risk, 46–48
Financial Sense, 144, 325
financial services industry, 236
financial situation, assessing current
 establishing starting point, 20–28
 financial goals, 33–34
 funding stock program, 28–32
 overview, 19–20
financial statements
 balance sheet
  accounts receivable, 174, 196–197
  acquisitions, 198
  analyzing, 27–28
  big-bath accounting, 198–199

financial statements *(continued)*
  buzzwords, 204–205
  cash/cash equivalents, 173–175
  defined, 20
  fixed assets, 176–177
  intangible assets, 178
  inventories, 175–176, 197–198
  investments, 177
  long-term liabilities, 179–180
  materiality, 203–204
  off-balance-sheet obligations, 199–201
  overview, 21–28, 172–173, 195
  owner's equity, 180–181
  payables, 179
  pension plans, 202–203
  smoke and mirrors, 203
cash-flow statement, 31
income statement
  aggressive accounting, 185–187
  capitalizing costs, 189–190
  cost of sales, 166–167
  depreciation and amortization, 168
  EBITDA, 170
  extraordinary items, 170–171
  gross margin, 167
  impairments, investments, and other
    write-downs, 171–172
  income from continuing operations,
    169
  interest and taxes, 169
  overview, 165–166
  pro forma reports, 193–194
  research and development (R&D), 168
  reserves, 168, 192
  revenues, 166, 188–189
  selling, general, and administrative
    (SG&A), 167–168
  stock options, 191–192
  tax losses, 193
statement of cash flows
  cash flow from financing activities, 183
  cash flow from investing activities, 182
  cash flow from operations, 182
  "free" cash flow, 183
  overview, 181–182

financing activities, 183
finding
  leaders, 120–121
  megatrends, 120–121
  tax savings, 32
FINRA (Financial Industry Regulatory
    Authority), 343, 352
fixed assets, 176–177
flow-through shares, 294
FNM (U.S. Federal National Mortgage
    Association), 246
footnotes, 204–205
*Forbes* Magazine, 345
foreign-capital shares, 249
Foundation for Economic Education, 144
*14-A Forms* in EDGAR, 95
fraud, 223–224, 351–352
FRE (U.S. Federal Mortgage Assurance
    Corporation), 246
Freddie Mac, 246
"free" cash flow, 183
Free Lunch, 162
FreeEDGAR, 352
FreeLunch.com, 347
Free-Market News Network, 325
FreeRealTime.com, 350
FTSE-100 index, 70
fundamental analysis, 112, 120
fundamentals, 120, 257
funding stock programs, 28–32
funds
  emergency, 21, 27
  mutual, 142, 294–295
Future Source, 240
*Futures & Options For Dummies*
    (Duarte), 316

• *G* •

gains, capital, 292–293
gas stock investments, 294
GDP (gross domestic product), 84,
    160–161
GE (General Electric), 64
General Electric (GE), 64

geographic regions, 248–250
GICs (guaranteed investment
     certificates), 135
*The Globe and Mail,* 82, 85, 160
Globe Investor, 58, 72
goals, 33–34, 36–37, 59–60
going concern, 204
going long, 285
going short, 285
Gold Anti-Trust Action Committee, 241
gold/precious metals, 241–242
good-till-cancelled (GTC) orders
   overview, 275–276
   using, 315
goodwill, 178
governance, senior management's role
     in, 221
government
   bailouts, 156
   economic effects from actions of, 80
   growth of, 328
   intervention, 152
   research, 84
   spending/debt, 155
governmental risks, 53–54
gross domestic product (GDP), 84,
     160–161
gross margin, 167
gross profit, 167
gross revenue, 189
gross unrealized losses, 177
gross-up adjustment, 134
growth
   annual rate, 23
   in earnings, 125
   of equity, 125
   industry, 229–230
   investing, 40–41
growth stocks
   analyzing, 119–126
   comparing, 119–120
   defined, 118
   overview, 117–119
GTC (good-till-cancelled) orders, 275–276
guaranteed investment certificates
     (GICs), 135

• **H** •

"H" shares, 249
Halter USX China Index, 70
Hang Seng Index, 70
healthcare, 242–243
hedging techniques, 262
hiding
   expenses, 189–190
   liabilities, 199–201
high-interest debt, 27
high-yield investments, 27
hold rating, 111
Home Depot, 65
home equity, 28
Hoover's, 230, 346, 349
hostile takeover, 214
*Hot Commodities* (Rogers), 240
HSBC InvestDirect, 99, 107
Human Resources and Skills
     Development Canada, 161

• **I** •

icons used in this book, 7
IFIC (Investment Funds Institute of
     Canada), 349
IIROC (Investment Industry Regulatory
     Organization of Canada), 102
illiquid investments, 21
image, 224
impairments, investments, and write-
     downs, 171–172
income
   allocation of, 295
   attributable to common shareholders,
     172
   calculating, 29–30
   from continuing operations, 169
   dividend, 291
   earned, 297
   interest, 290–291
   investing, 41–43, 131
   net, 78, 172
income investor, 90

income mutual funds, 135
income statement
    aggressive accounting, 185–187
    capitalizing costs, 189–190
    cost of sales, 166–167
    depreciation and amortization, 168
    EBITDA, 170
    extraordinary items, 170–171
    gross margin, 167
    impairments, investments, and other
        write-downs, 171–172
    income from continuing operations, 169
    interest and taxes, 169
    overview, 165–166
    pro forma reports, 193–194
    research and development (R&D), 168
    reserves, 168, 192
    revenues, 166, 188–189
    selling, general, and administrative
        (SG&A), 167–168
    stock options, 191–192
    tax losses, 193
income stocks
    advantages of, 133
    analyzing, 135–141
    basics of, 131–134
    defined, 131
    disadvantages, 133–134
    dividends and, 132
    non-stock alternatives to, 135
    typical, 141–142
    yield, 42–43
Income Tax Act, 295
increasing
    earnings per share (EPS), 214
    profits, 197–198
    sales, 188
index mutual funds, 72
indexes
    broad-based, 62, 65
    BSE SENSEX, 70
    CAC-40, 70
    capitalization-weighted, 62
    composite, 62

DAX, 62, 70
Dow Jones Industrial Average, 63–65, 68
FTSE-100, 70
Halter USX China Index, 70
Hang Seng Index, 70
industry, 65
international, 70–71
investing in, 71–72
market-value-weighted, 62
Nasdaq indexes, 62, 69
Nikkei, 70
performance-based, 62
price-weighted, 62
Russell 3000 Index, 69–70
sector, 65
SSE Composite Index, 70
Standard & Poor's 500, 67
Toronto Stock Exchange/TMX, 65–67
tracking, 71
types, 61–62
using, 71–72
Web sites, 63
Wilshire Total Market Index, 68–69
India's stock market, 248, 250
individual shares, 249
industry
    automotive, 235
    banking, 236
    categories of, 228–229
    defence, 229
    defined, 228
    dependence, 232
    financial services, 236
    growth, 229–230
    indexes, 65
    problems, 323
    publicity, 310
    research, 83
industry analysis
    key industries, 233–236
    overview, 227, 309, 346
    researching, 228–233
Industry Canada, 310

inflation
  challenges and opportunities of, 327
  defined, 52
  income stocks and, 134
  relationship with economics, 151–152
  risk, 52–53
information, gathering
  companies, 77–82
  dividends, 90–93
  EDGAROnline, 94–95
  evaluating investment tips, 93
  financial news, 82–85
  SEDAR, 94–95
  stock exchanges, 76–77
  stock tables, 85–90
information and technology risks
  piracy, 225–226
  privacy, 226
initial public offering (IPO) stock,
  127–128, 352
in-process R&D, 198
insider buying
  evaluating company management, 126
  learning from, 210–211
  recognizing, 311
insider selling
  red flags, 322
  tips from, 212–213
insider trading
  insider buying, 210–211
  insider selling, 212–213
  resources, 351
  tracking, 208–210
insiders, company, 207
instincts, using, 307
Instinet, 349
institutional buying, 122
Institutional Investor News, 312
institutional investors, 311–312
intangible assets, 178
interest
  compared with dividends, 41
  defined, 37, 136
  on income statement, 169
  rates, 134, 155

interest-rate risk, 48–51
intermediate-term goals, 33
intermediate-term investing, 38–39,
  256–257
Internet resources
  Adviceforinvestors.com, 344
  Advocis, 343–344
  AIER (American Institute for Economic
    Research), 142, 160, 347
  Allstocks.com, 348
  American Institute for Economic
    Research (AIER), 142, 160, 347
  American Stock Exchange, 72, 77, 240
  Austrian school of thought, 151
  Bank of Canada, 162
  *Barron's,* 345
  BigCharts, 350
  Bloomberg, 70, 82, 137, 344
  BMI InvestorLine, 107
  Briefing.com, 351
  Bureau of Labor Statistics, 161
  Business Wire, 347
  Canada NewsWire, 310, 347
  Canada Revenue Agency (CRA),
    291, 294, 348
  Canadian Economics Association, 143
  Canadian Economy Online, 143
  Canadian Investor Protection Fund
    (CIPF), 104, 352
  Canadian MoneySaver, 344
  Canadian Securities Administrators
    (CSA), 102
  Canadian Securities Institute, 343
  Canadian Society of Technical Analysts
    (CSTA), 349
  Canadian Taxpayers Federation, 162
  Canoe Money, 112, 349
  CANTAX (CCH Canadian Ltd.), 348
  ChartSmart, 350
  Chicago Board Options Exchange,
    252, 316
  China Online, 347
  CIBC Investor's Edge, 107
  CIPF (Canadian Investor Protection
    Fund), 104, 352

Internet resources *(continued)*
ClearStation, 350
CNN, 311
CNNMoney.com, 344
CNW Group (Canada NewsWire), 310, 347
Conference Board, 145, 162
Conference Board of Canada, 144, 162
Consumer Reports, 308
CRA (Canada Revenue Agency), 291, 294, 348
CSA (Canadian Securities Administrators), 102
CSTA (Canadian Society of Technical Analysts), 349
Department of Finance Canada, 347
Department of Justice Canada, 162
Dismal Scientist, 144
Disnat, 107
Dominion Bond Rating Service, 140
EDGAROnline, 94, 208, 352
Elliott Wave International, 261, 351
The Federal Reserve, 162
Financial Advisor Pages, 344
*Financial Post,* 230, 241
Financial Sense, 144, 325
FINRA (Financial Industry Regulatory Authority), 343, 352
*Forbes* Magazine, 345
Foundation for Economic Education, 144
Free Lunch, 162
Free-Market News Network, 325
FreeEDGAR, 352
FreeLunch.com, 347
FreeRealTime.com, 350
Future Source, 240
*The Globe and Mail,* 82, 85
Globe Investor, 58, 72
Gold Anti-Trust Action Committee, 241
gold market, 241
Hoover's, 230, 346, 349
HSBC InvestDirect, 107
Human Resources and Skills Development Canada, 161

IFIC (Investment Funds Institute of Canada), 349
IIROC (Investment Industry Regulatory Organization of Canada), 102
indexes, 63
Industry Canada, 310
Instinet, 349
Institutional Investor News, 312
Invest$Link, 344
The Investment FAQ, 343
Investment Funds Institute of Canada (IFIC), 349
Investment Industry Regulatory Organization of Canada (IIROC), 102
Investopedia.com, 57
InvestorLinks.com, 344
*Investor's Digest of Canada,* 112, 345
InvestorWords, 343
IPO Monitor, 352
*The Kiplinger Letter,* 311
*Kiplinger's Personal Finance Magazine,* 345
Marketocracy, 57
MarketWatch, 347
MarkeyHistory.com, 348
MetaStock (Reuters), 350
The Mises Institute, 144, 325
Money Canoe, 137
Moody's, 160, 346, 347
Morningstar, 72, 346
Morningstar Canada, 346
The Motley Fool, 343
MSN Money, 344
NAIC (National Association of Investors Corp.), 349
Nasdaq, 69, 77, 280, 349
National Association of Investors Corp. (NAIC), 349
National Bank Discount Brokerage, 107
National Fraud Information Center, 352
*National Post,* 82, 85, 240
New York Stock Exchange (NYSE), 77, 349

NYSE (New York Stock Exchange), 77, 349

The Online Investor, 347

Options Industry Council, 252, 316

OTC Bulletin Board, 349

PR Newswire, 348

Qtrade Canada, 107

Quicken, QuickTax, QuickBooks (Intuit Canada), 348

Quote.com, 350

RBC Action Direct, 107

RBC Economics Research, 160

real estate, 246

Realtor.com, 327

*Report on Business,* 230

Reuters Investing, 348

Richard Russell's *Dow Theory Letters,* 346

RRSP.org, 344

Russell indexes, 70

Scotia iTRADE, 107

ScotiaMcLeod Direct, 107

SEC (Securities and Exchange Commission), 347, 351, 352

Securities and Exchange Commission (SEC), 347, 351, 352

SEDAR (System for Electronic Document Analysis and Retrieval), 94, 352

SEDI (System for Electronic Disclosure by Insiders), 351

Silicon Investor, 345

Simplystocks.com, 348

*SmartMoney Magazine,* 345, 350

Standard & Poor's, 67, 140, 230, 348

Statistics Canada, 160, 161, 308

*Stock, Futures and Options* (magazine), 261

Stock House, 212

Stock Trading Canada, 261

StockCharts.com, 351

Stockhouse Canada, 345

Stocks.com, 348

StreetInsider.com, 351

System for Electronic Disclosure by Insiders (SEDI), 351

System for Electronic Document Analysis and Retrieval (SEDAR), 94, 352

Tax and Accounting Sites Directory, 348

Tax-Free Savings Account, 303

TD Waterhouse, 107

*This Magazine,* 311

THOMAS, 162

TMX, 349

Tradingcharts.com, 350

TSX, 77

UK-Invest.com, 347

U.S. & World Early Warning Report, 243

U.S. Department of Commerce, 160, 162

U.S. Federal Reserve Board, 347

U.S. House of Representatives, 162

U.S. Securities and Exchange Commission (SEC), 347, 351, 352

U.S. Senate, 162

*The Value Line Investment Survey,* 346

Value Lines, 129

*Wall Street Journal,* 230, 346

Yahoo! Finance, 212, 230, 280, 345, 350

Zacks, 351

ZacksAdvisor, 350

interviewing brokers, 104

inventories

increasing profits through, 197–198

overstated, 187

overview, 175–176

Invest$Link, 344

investing. *See also* investment(s)

activities, 183

aggressive, 44

association, 349

compared with trading, 255–260

conservative, 43

considerations for selling, 271

defined, 34

for growth

growth stocks, 118–126

overview, 40–41, 117–118

investing *(continued)*
  small-cap stocks, 126–129
  speculative stocks, 126–129
history of, 123
for income, 131
in indexes, 71–72
intermediate-term, 38–39
with less than $10,000, 268–270
long-term, 39–40
with more than $50,000, 269–270
organizations, 349
for personal style, 43–44
for a purpose, 40–43
reasons for selling, 271
red flags, 319–324
resources for basic, 343
short-term, 37–38
stock, 41–43
supermarkets, 344–345
with $10,000 to $50,000, 269
by time frame, 37–40
The Investment FAQ, 343
Investment Funds Institute of Canada
    (IFIC), 349
investment grade bonds, 140
Investment Industry Regulatory
    Organization of Canada (IIROC), 102
investment(s). *See also* investing
  advisers, 98–100, 261
  on balance sheet, 177
  diversifying, 58
  illiquid, 21
  low-yield versus high-yield, 27
  news sources, 347
  skills, 15–16
  style, 129
  tips, 93
  trusts, 142
Investopedia, 57
investor, institutional, 311–312
investor profile, 59–60
investor research, 345–348
InvestorLinks.com, 344
*Investor's Business Daily* (O'Neill),
    82, 85, 278

*Investor's Digest of Canada,* 112, 345
InvestorWords, 343
IPO (initial public offering) stock,
    127–128, 352
IPO Monitor, 352

## • J •

J.P. Morgan, 65
junk bonds, 140

## • K •

Keynes school of thought, 149–150
*The Kiplinger Letter,* 311
*Kiplinger's Personal Finance* Magazine, 345

## • L •

Labour Force Survey, 161
large cap, 14
last-in, first-out method (LIFO) of
    accounting, 197
Latin America's stock market, 249–250
laws, effect on investing of, 155
leadership, 120–121, 221
leading economic indicators (LEI), 84,
    145
leasing transactions, 200
Lefevre, Edwin
    *Reminiscences of a Stock Operator,* 263
legal-person shares, 249
LEI (leading economic indicators), 84,
    145
leverage, 282
liabilities
  contingent, 179, 201
  defined, 24
  listing, 24–25
  long-term, 179–180
lifestyles
  married with children, 266–267
  ready for retirement, 267
  retired, 267–268
  young and single, 266

LIFO (last-in, first-out method) of accounting, 197
limit orders, 262, 280–281
limited-recourse debt, 302
line items, 165
liquidity, 21
liquidity ratios
  current ratio, 334
  overview, 334
  quick ratio, 335
listing
  assets, 21–24
  liabilities, 24–25
LM (Lucin-Muny), 48
locating
  leaders, 120–121
  megatrends, 120–121
  tax savings, 32
locked-in RRSPs, 299
long on stocks, 285
long-term, 39
long-term assets, 23
long-term goals, 33
long-term investing, 39–40, 256
long-term liabilities, 179–180
long-term stock price appreciation, 166
losses, capital, 292–293
low-interest debt, 27
low-yield investments, 27
Lucin-Muny (LM), 48
Lynch, Peter (investor), 307

### • *M* •

macroeconomics, 144–145, 153
magazines, 345–346
Magna International (MGA), 49–50
management role in controlling risk, 222–223
mania, 235
margin
  defined, 27, 282
  maintaining balance, 284
  outcomes of buying on, 282–283
  trading on, 103

margin accounts, 110
margin debt, 50
market
  bear, 11, 250–252
  bull, 239–243, 250–252
  moving, 262
  risk, 51–52
market capitalization (market cap)
  calculating, 14
  defined, 37
  effect on stock value, 14–15
market orders, 276–277
market perform rating, 111
MarketHistory.com, 348
Marketocracy, 57
market-value-weighted index, 62
MarketWatch, 347
Marx school of thought, 148–149
materiality, 203–204
McCain, 121
measuring
  annual growth rate, 23
  common size ratios, 338
  company equity, 124
  current ratio, 334
  debt to net equity ratio, 337
  income, 29–30
  market cap, 14
  net income, 78
  net worth, 26, 77–78
  outflow, 30–31
  payout ratio, 139
  price to book ratio (PBR), 341
  price to sales ratio (PSR), 340
  price-to-earnings ratio (P/E), 339
  quick ratio, 335
  return on assets (ROA), 336
  return on equity (ROE), 335–336
  sales to receivables ratio (SR), 337
  working capital, 338
  yield, 42
Medicare, 327
mega cap, 14
megatrends, 120–121, 310
metals, 241–242

MetaStock (Reuters), 350
MGA (Magna International), 49–50
micro cap, 14
microeconomics, 144, 153
Microsoft, 65, 121
mid cap, 14
mineral stock investments, 294
minimizing
  risk, 56–59
  transaction costs, 262
misconduct
  corporate governance risk, 220–223
  ethical risks, 223–224
  information and technology risks,
    225–226
  reputational risk, 224–225
The Mises Institute, 144, 325
Mises, Ludwig von, 144, 150–151, 325
mission statement, 221
Mladjenovic, Paul
  *Precious Metals Investing For Dummies*,
    242
Money Canoe, 137
money supply, effect on investing of, 155
Montreal Exchange, 65
Moody's, 160, 346, 347
Morningstar, 72, 346
mortgage resets, 245
The Motley Fool, 343
moving
  averages, 260
  markets, 262
  revenue, 189
MSN Money, 344
Murphy, Bill (Gold Anti-Trust Action
    Committee), 241
mutual funds
  compared with REITs, 142
  income, 135
  index, 72
  overview, 294–295

**• N •**

NAIC (National Association of Investors
    Corp.), 349
name, in stock table, 87
Nasdaq
  indexes, 69
  Web site, 77, 280, 349
Nasdaq 100 Index, 69
Nasdaq Composite Index, 62, 69
National Association of Investors Corp.
    (NAIC), 349
National Bank Discount Brokerage, 107
National Fraud Information Center, 352
*National Post,* 82, 85, 160, 240
Natural Gas Exchange (NGX), 65
needs
  compared with wants, 146–147
  relationship with income stocks,
    136–137
negative coverage, 322
net change, in stock table, 90
net earnings, 124, 172
net equity, 124, 339
net income
  calculating, 78
  defined, 78
  overview, 172
net profit, 338
net revenue, 189
net worth
  calculating, 26, 77–78
  defined, 20
neutral rating, 111
New York Stock Exchange (NYSE),
    62, 77, 349
newsletter recommendations, 122
NGX (Natural Gas Exchange), 65
niche companies, 121–122
Nikkei index, 70
nominal rate, 48

non-recurring events, 170
nonsystemic effects, compared with
    systemic effects, 158–159
notes receivable, 175
NYSE (New York Stock Exchange),
    62, 77, 349

## • *O* •

off-balance-sheet obligations, 199–201
Office of the Superintendent of
    Bankruptcy Canada, 25
oil
    overview, 240–241
    prices, 329
    stock investments, 294
Old Age Security, 327
on account, 174
O'Neill, William
    *Investor's Business Daily*, 278
The Online Investor, 347
online investing services
    costs of, 105
    discount, 105–106, 107
    opening accounts, 108–109
    overview, 104–105
    special features, 106, 108
opening online brokerage accounts,
    108–109
operating expenses, 167
operating ratios
    overview, 335
    return on assets (ROA), 336
    return on equity (ROE), 335–336
    sales to receivables ratio (SR), 336–337
opportunity, 222
opportunity cost, 175
option accounts, 110
Options Industry Council, 252, 316
orders, brokerage
    advanced orders, 281–282
    condition-related orders
        limit orders, 280–281
        market orders, 276–277
        stop orders, 277–280

overview, 274
    time-related orders
        day orders, 274–275
        good-till-cancelled (GTC) orders,
            275–276
ordinary stock splits, 216
organization
    design, 221
    investing, 349
    of this book, 4–7
OTC Bulletin Board, 349
"other interests," 204
outflow
    calculating, 30–31
    defined, 21
oversight, 221
owner's equity, 180–181

## • *P* •

P/E (price-to-earnings ratio)
    defined, 89
    overview, 339–340
    in stock table, 89–90
paid-in capital, 180
payables, 179
payment date, 91
payout ratio, 139
PBR (price to book ratio), 341
pension plans, 202–203
pension tension, 172
pensions, challenges and opportunities
    of, 327–328
performance-based index, 62
periodicals, 345–346
personal investing style, 102–103
personal risks, 54
Petro-Canada, 121
PG (Proctor & Gamble) stock, 19
piracy, 225–226
planning
    importance of, 262
    strategic, 265–268
political research, 84
political risks, 53–54

politics
  climate of, 156–157
  red flags, 323
  relationship with stocks, 154–160
  resources, 160–162
  tracking, 310–311
PP&E (property, plant, and equipment), 176–177
PR Newswire, 348
*Precious Metals Investing For Dummies* (Mladjenovic), 242
preferred stock, 12
preparing to buy stocks, 12–13
press releases, 347–348
price to book ratio (PBR), 341
price controls, 159–160
price-to-earnings ratio (P/E)
  defined, 89
  overview, 339–340
  in stock tables, 89–90
price to sales ratio (PSR), 340
price-weighted index, 62
privacy, 226
pro forma reports, 193–194
Proctor & Gamble (PG) stock, 19
product selection, 106
profit
  defined, 165
  increasing through inventories, 197–198
  net, 338
  overview, 262
  protecting, 313–317
  short-swing, 209
profitability, 333
property, plant, and equipment (PP&E), 176–177
protecting profits, 313–317
protective put, 316
PSR (price to sales ratio), 340
psychology factor of trading, 257
public filings, 352
publications
  *Barron's,* 112, 345
  *Dow Theory Letters,* 346
  *Financial Post,* 230, 241
  *Forbes* Magazine, 345
  *Futures & Options For Dummies* (Duarte), 316
  *The Globe and Mail,* 82, 85, 160
  *Hot Commodities* (Rogers), 240
  *Investor's Business Daily* (O'Neill), 82, 85, 278
  *Investor's Digest of Canada,* 112, 345
  *The Kiplinger Letter,* 311
  *Kiplinger's Personal Finance* Magazine, 345
  *National Post,* 82, 85, 160, 240
  *Precious Metals Investing For Dummies* (Mladjenovic), 242
  *Reminiscences of a Stock Operator* (Lefevre), 263
  *Report on Business,* 230
  *SmartMoney Magazine,* 345, 350
  *Stock, Futures and Options* (magazine), 261
  *Stock Options For Dummies* (Simon), 110, 131, 316
  *Technical Analysis For Dummies* (Rockefeller), 260
  *The Value Line Investment Survey,* 346
  *Wall Street Journal,* 82, 85, 230, 346
publicity industry, 310
purchasing power risk, 52
put option, 259, 316

Qtrade Canada, 107
quarterly dividend, 92
quick ratio, 335
Quicken, QuickTax, QuickBooks (Intuit Canada), 348
Quote.com, 350
quotes, stock, 350

R&D (research and development), 168, 198

rates
  dividend, 132
  interest, 134, 155
ratings
  accumulate, 111
  analyst, 111–113
  bond, 140–141, 322
  buy, 111
ratio analysis, 184
ratios, financial
  common size ratios, 338–339
  liquidity ratios
    current ratio, 334
    overview, 334
    quick ratio, 335
  operating ratios
    overview, 335
    return on assets (ROA), 336
    return on equity (ROE), 335–336
    sales to receivables ratio (SR),
      336–337
  overview, 333–334
  solvency ratios
    debt to net equity ratio, 337–338
    overview, 337
    working capital, 338
  valuation ratios
    overview, 339
    price to book ratio (PBR), 341
    price to sales ratio (PSR), 340
    price-to-earnings ratio (P/E), 339–340
RBC Action Direct, 107
RBC Dominion Securities, 99
RBC Economics Research, 160
real estate
  challenges and opportunities of,
    326–327
  industry, 234–235
  overview, 245–246
  stocks, 142
real estate investment trusts (REITs),
    142, 295–296
realized gains/losses, 171
reallocating, 28

Realtor.com, 327
reasonable reserve, 293
receivables, 174, 187, 196–197
receiving distributions, 295
recession, challenges and opportunities
    of, 328
recessionary, 161
recognizing
  corporate buying, 311
  insider buying, 311
  stock value, 13
red flags, 196–197, 319–324
reducing adjusted cost base, 296
Registered Education Savings Plans
    (RESPs), 300–302
registered rep, 98–100
Registered Retirement Income Funds
    (RRIFs), 300
Registered Retirement Savings Plans
    (RRSPs)
  compared with Tax-Free Savings
    Account (TFSA), 303
  contribution limits, 297
  dollar limits, 298
  earned income limits, 297
  locked-in, 299
  overview, 296
  retirement allowances, 299
  self-directed, 298–299
  Spousal Registered Retirement Savings
    Plans, 298
regulations, effect on investing of, 155
REITs (real estate investment trusts),
    142, 295–296
related party, 190
relative strength indicators (RSI), 260
*Reminiscences of a Stock Operator*
    (Lefevre), 263
*Report on Business,* 230
reports, brokerage, 113–115
reputational risk, 224–225
research and development (R&D),
    168, 198

researching
  dividends, 90–93
  financial news, 82–85
  industries, 228–233
reserves, 168, 192, 293
resource trusts, 142
resources
  economic, 143–144
  financial planning, 343–344
  investing basics, 343
  investing supermarkets, 344–345
  investor research/analysis, 345–348
  politics, 160–162
  stock investing Web sites, 348–352
  tax, 348
response time, of online investing
    services, 106
RESPs (Registered Education Savings
    Plans), 300–302
restricted stock, 208
restructuring charges, 171–172
retained earnings, 181
retirees, income stocks for, 132
retirement allowances (RRSPs), 299
retirement planning, 267–268
return. *See also* risk
return on assets (ROA), 336
return on equity (ROE), 123–124, 335–336
Reuters Investing, 348
revenue
  creating, 188–189
  manipulation of, 188–189
  moving, 189
  overview, 166
reverse stock splits, 216–217
reviewing reserves, 192
Richard Russell's *Dow Theory Letters,* 346
rise in earnings, 308–309
risk
  accepting some, 222
  avoiding, 222
  corporate governance, 220–223
  diversifying exposure, 222
  emotional, 55–56

  ethical, 223–224
  financial, 46–48
  governmental, 53–54
  inflation, 52–53
  information and technology, 225–226
  interest-rate, 48–51
  management role in controlling,
    222–223
  market, 51–52
  minimizing, 56–59
  personal, 54
  political, 53–54
  reputational, 224–225
  sharing, 222
  tax, 53
  transferring, 222
  types, 46–56
  weighing against return, 59–60
risk management, 220–221
risk versus return equation, 45
ROA (return on assets), 336
Rockefeller, Barbara
  *Technical Analysis For Dummies,* 260
ROE (return on equity), 123–124, 335–336
Rogers Communications, 121
Rogers, Jim
  *Hot Commodities,* 240
royalty trusts, 142
RRIFs (Registered Retirement Income
    Funds), 300
RRSP.org, 344
RRSPs (Registered Retirement Savings
    Plans)
  compared with Tax-Free Savings
    Account (TFSA), 303
  contribution limits, 297
  dollar limits, 298
  earned income limits, 297
  locked-in, 299
  overview, 296
  retirement allowances, 299
  self-directed, 298–299
  Spousal Registered Retirement Savings
    Plans, 298

RSI (relative strength indicators), 260
rules of trading, 262–263
Russell 3000 Index, 69–70

## • S •

S&P/TSX 60, 66–67
sales
  accelerating, 188
  analyzing company, 120
  red flags, 320
sales to receivables ratio (SR), 336–337
saving, 34
Scotia iTRADE, 107
ScotiaMcLeod Direct, 107
SEC (U.S. Securities and Exchange
    Commission), 347, 351, 352
sector
  defined, 228, 268
  indexes, 65
securitization transactions, 200
SEDAR (System for Electronic Document
    Analysis and Retrieval), 94–95, 129,
    224, 352
SEDI (System for Electronic Disclosure
    by Insiders), 209–210, 351
selecting brokers, 102–104
self-directed RRSPs, 298–299
sell rating, 111
selling
  considerations for, 271
  insider, 212–213, 322
  knowing when, 270–272
  to protect profits, 317
  reasons for, 271
selling, general, and administrative
    (SG&A), 167–168
selling short, 285
senior management governance role, 221
services, advisory, 261
setting up short sales, 286
settlement date, 91
SG&A (selling, general, and
    administrative), 167–168

share float, 66
shareholders, 41
shareholders' equity, 124
shares, flow-through, 294
sharing risk, 222
sharpening investment skills, 15–16
Shorcan, 66
short sale
  mistakes with, 286–287
  overview, 285
  setting up, 286
  short squeeze, 287
short squeeze, 287
shorting a stock, 285
short-swing profit, 209
short-term
  defined, 37
  goals, 33
  investing, 37–39, 256–257
Silicon Investor, 345
Simon, Alan R.
  *Stock Options For Dummies,*
    110, 131, 316
Simplystocks.com, 348
skills, investment, 15–16
small-cap stocks
  analysis of, 129
  defined, 14, 126
  IPOs, 127–128
  overview, 126–127
  tips, 128
*SmartMoney Magazine,* 345, 350
smoke-and-mirrors, 203
Social Security, 327
solvency, 333
Solvency ratios
  debt to net equity ratio, 337–338
  overview, 337
  working capital, 338
sources and uses of funds, 181
special-purpose entities (SPEs), 201
speculating
  defined, 34
  short-term investing, 39

SPEs (special-purpose entities), 201
splits, stock, 292
Spousal Registered Retirement Savings
 Plans (RRSPs), 298
SR (sales to receivables ratio), 336–337
SSE Composite Index, 70
stagflation, 233
stakeholders, 225
Standard & Poor's, 140, 230, 348
Standard & Poor's 500 (S&P 500), 67
state shares, 249
statement of cash flows
 cash flow from financing activities, 183
 cash flow from investing activities, 182
 cash flow from operations, 182
 "free" cash flow, 183
 overview, 181–182
Statement of Trust Income Allocations
 and Designations (T3), 292
static analysis, compared with dynamic
 analysis, 147–148
Statistics Canada, 160, 161, 308
stock exchanges, 76–77, 349
*Stock, Futures and Options* (magazine), 261
Stock House, 212
stock investing basics, 12
stock markets
 China, 248–249
 India, 248, 250
 instability of, 17
 Latin America, 249–250
stock options, 191–192
*Stock Options For Dummies* (Simon),
 110, 131, 316
stock splits
 defined, 215
 ordinary, 215
 overview, 292
 reverse, 216–217
stock tables, 85–90
Stock Trading Canada, 261
stock value
 effect of market capitalization on, 14–15
 recognizing, 13

StockCharts.com, 351
Stockhouse Canada, 345
stock(s)
 beta of, 263
 buybacks, 213–217
 categories of market capitalization, 14
 common, 12
 cyclical, 247–248
 defence, 133
 defined, 12
 diversifying, 140, 313
 dividends, 292
 effect of economics on, 78–81
 fundamentals, 257
 growth
  analyzing, 119–126
  comparing, 119–120
  defined, 118
  overview, 117–119
 income
  advantages of, 133
  analyzing, 135–141
  basics of, 131–134
  defined, 131
  disadvantages, 133–134
  dividends and, 132
  non-stock alternatives to, 135
  typical, 141–142
  yield, 42–43
 matching strategies with goals, 36–37
 paying with, 188
 preferred, 12
 preparing to buy, 12–13
 program, 28–32
 quotes, 350
 relationship with politics, 154–160
 restricted, 208
 screens, 349–350
 small-cap, 126–129
 trading history, 262
stop orders, 277–280
stop-loss, 262
stop-loss orders, 277–280, 314–315
straight-line depreciation, 177

strategic planning, 221

strategies
asset allocation, 268–270
matching with goals, 36–37
overview, 16–17
planning, 265–268
when to sell, 270–271

StreetInsider.com, 351

strong buy rating, 111

sunrise industry, 231

sunset industry, 231

superficial losses, 293

supply
defined, 79
overview, 146

switching auditors, 204

symbol, in stock table, 87

System for Electronic Disclosure by Insiders (SEDI), 209–210

System for Electronic Document Analysis and Retrieval (SEDAR), 94–95, 224, 352

systemic effects, compared with nonsystemic effects, 158–159

### • T •

T3 (Statement of Trust Income Allocations and Designations), 292

tactics, 16–17

takeover bids, 214

Tax and Accounting Sites Directory, 348

Tax Free Savings Account (TFSA), 32, 302–303

tax shelters, deferred-income
obligations, 302
Registered Education Savings Plans (RESPs), 300–302
Registered Retirement Income Funds (RRIFs), 300
Registered Retirement Savings Plans (RRSPs), 296–299

taxable capital gain, 292

taxes
capital gains/losses, 292–293
decreases, 233
deferred-income tax shelters and plans, 296–302
dividend income, 291
finding savings, 32
implications, 270
on income statement, 169
interest income, 290–291
legislation, 155
losses, 193
mutual funds, 294–295
oil, gas, and mineral stock investments, 294
REIT, 295–296
resources, 348
risk, 53
stock dividends, 292
stock splits, 292
TFSA, 302–303

TD Waterhouse, 107

TD Waterhouse Private Investment Advice, 99

technical analysis, 112, 260–261, 351

*Technical Analysis For Dummies* (Rockefeller), 260

technology industry, 235–236

technology and information risks
piracy, 225–226
privacy, 226

*10-K Reports* in EDGAR, 95

*10-Q Reports* in EDGAR, 95

TFSA (Tax-Free Savings Account), 32, 302–303

*This Magazine,* 311

THOMAS search engine, 162

360 Networks, 46–47

time frame, investing by, 37–40

time-related orders
day orders, 274–275
good-till-cancelled (GTC) orders, 275–276

TMX, 349

tools, trading, 260–261

top line, 166
Toronto Stock Exchange/TMX, 65–67
tracking
    indexes, 71
    insider trading, 208–210
    politics, 310–311
trading
    compared with investing, 255–260
    history, 262
    insider
        insider buying, 210–211
        insider selling, 212–213
        resources, 351
        tracking, 208–210
    psychology factor of, 257
    rules of, 262–263
    tools, 260–261
trading on margin, 103
Tradingcharts.com, 350
trailing stops, 125, 278–279, 315
transaction costs, 262
transferring risk, 222
Treasury securities, 135
trend research, 84–85
triggers, broker, 315
trusts, resource, 142
TSX Venture Exchange, 65
TSX Web site, 77

### • *U* •

UK-Invest.com, 347
ultra cap, 14
unconsolidated entities, 201
unemployment, 161
unfunded liabilities, challenges and
    opportunities of, 327–328
U.S. & World Early Warning Report, 243
U.S. Department of Commerce, 160, 162
U.S. Federal Mortgage Assurance
    Corporation (FRE), 246
U.S. Federal National Mortgage
    Association (FNM), 246
U.S. Federal Reserve Board, 347

U.S. House of Representatives, 162
U.S. insider trading information, 208–209
U.S. Library of Congress, 162
U.S. Securities and Exchange
    Commission (SEC), 347, 351, 352
U.S. Senate, 162
using instincts, 307
utility stocks, 141

### • *V* •

valuation ratios
    overview, 339
    price to book ratio (PBR), 341
    price-to-earnings ratio (P/E), 339–340
    price to sales ratio (PSR), 340
value, stock
    effect of market capitalization on, 14–15
    recognizing, 13
Value Line, 129
*The Value Line Investment Survey,* 346
vision statement, 221
volume
    defined, 88
    in stock table, 88–89

### • *W* •

*Wall Street Journal,* 82, 85, 230, 346
wants, compared with needs, 146–147
watching megatrends, 310
Web sites
    Adviceforinvestors.com, 344
    Advocis, 343–344
    AIER (American Institute for Economic
        Research), 142, 160, 347
    Allstocks.com, 348
    American Institute for Economic
        Research (AIER), 142, 160, 347
    American Stock Exchange, 72, 77, 240
    Austrian school of thought, 151
    Bank of Canada, 162
    *Barron's,* 345
    BigCharts, 350

Bloomberg, 70, 82, 137, 344
BMI InvestorLine, 107
Briefing.com, 351
Bureau of Labor Statistics, 161
Business Wire, 347
Canada NewsWire, 310
Canada Revenue Agency (CRA),
    291, 294, 348
Canadian Economics Association, 143
Canadian Economy Online, 143
Canadian Investor Protection Fund
    (CIPF), 104, 352
Canadian MoneySaver, 344
Canadian Securities Administrators
    (CSA), 102
Canadian Securities Institute, 343
Canadian Society of Technical Analysts
    (CSTA), 349
Canadian Taxpayers Federation, 162
Canoe Money, 112, 349
CANTAX (CCH Canadian Ltd.), 348
ChartSmart, 350
Chicago Board Options Exchange,
    252, 316
China Online, 347
CIBC Investor's Edge, 107
CIPF (Canadian Investor Protection
    Fund), 104, 352
ClearStation, 350
CNN, 311
CNNMoney.com, 344
CNW Group (Canada NewsWire), 347
Conference Board, 145, 162
Conference Board of Canada, 144, 162
Consumer Reports, 308
CRA (Canada Revenue Agency), 291,
    294, 348
CSA (Canadian Securities
    Administrators), 102
CSTA (Canadian Society of Technical
    Analysts), 349
Department of Finance Canada, 347
Department of Justice Canada, 162
Dismal Scientist, 144
Disnat, 107

Dominion Bond Rating Service, 140
EDGAROnline, 94, 208, 352
Elliott Wave International, 261, 351
The Federal Reserve, 162
Financial Advisor Pages, 344
*Financial Post,* 230, 241
Financial Sense, 144, 325
FINRA (Financial Industry Regulatory
    Authority), 343, 352
*Forbes* Magazine, 345
Foundation for Economic Education, 144
Free Lunch, 162
FreeEDGAR, 352
FreeLunch.com, 347
Free-Market News Network, 325
FreeRealTime.com, 350
Future Source, 240
*The Globe and Mail,* 82, 85
Globe Investor, 58, 72
Gold Anti-Trust Action Committee, 241
gold market, 241
Hoover's, 230, 346, 349
HSBC InvestDirect, 107
Human Resources and Skills
    Development Canada, 161
IFIC (Investment Funds Institute of
    Canada), 349
IIROC (Investment Industry Regulatory
    Organization of Canada), 102
indexes, 63
Industry Canada, 310
Instinet, 349
Institutional Investor News, 312
Invest$Link, 344
The Investment FAQ, 343
Investment Funds Institute of Canada
    (IFIC), 349
Investment Industry Regulatory
    Organization of Canada (IIROC), 102
Investopedia, 57
InvestorLinks.com, 344
*Investor's Digest of Canada,* 112, 345
InvestorWords, 343
IPO Monitor, 352
*The Kiplinger Letter,* 311

Web sites *(continued)*
*Kiplinger's Personal Finance Magazine,* 345
MarketHistory.com, 348
Marketocracy, 57
MarketWatch, 347
MetaStock (Reuters), 350
The Mises Institute, 144, 325
Money Canoe, 137
Moody's, 160, 346, 347
Morningstar, 72, 346
Morningstar Canada, 346
The Motley Fool, 343
MSN Money, 344
NAIC (National Association of Investors Corp.), 349
Nasdaq, 69, 77, 280, 349
National Association of Investors Corp. (NAIC), 349
National Bank Discount Brokerage, 107
National Fraud Information Center, 352
*National Post,* 82, 85, 240
New York Stock Exchange (NYSE), 77, 349
NYSE (New York Stock Exchange), 77, 349
The Online Investor, 347
Options Industry Council, 252, 316
OTC Bulletin Board, 349
PR Newswire, 348
Qtrade Canada, 107
Quicken, QuickTax, QuickBooks (Intuit Canada), 348
Quote.com, 350
RBC Action Direct, 107
RBC Economics Research, 160
real estate, 246
Realtor.com, 327
*Report on Business,* 230
Reuters Investing, 348
Richard Russell's *Dow Theory Letters,* 346
RRSP.org, 344
Russell indexes, 70

Scotia iTRADE, 107
ScotiaMcLeod Direct, 107
SEC (Securities and Exchange Commission), 347, 351, 352
Securities and Exchange Commission (SEC), 347, 351, 352
SEDAR (System for Electronic Document Analysis and Retrieval), 94, 352
SEDI (System for Electronic Disclosure by Insiders), 351
Silicon Investor, 345
Simplystocks.com, 348
*SmartMoney Magazine,* 345, 350
Standard & Poor's, 67, 140, 230, 348
Statistics Canada, 160, 161, 308
*Stock, Futures and Options* (magazine), 261
Stock House, 212
Stock Trading Canada, 261
StockCharts.com, 351
Stockhouse Canada, 345
Stocks.com, 348
StreetInsider.com, 351
System for Electronic Disclosure by Insiders (SEDI), 351
System for Electronic Document Analysis and Retrieval (SEDAR), 94, 352
Tax and Accounting Sites Directory, 348
Tax-Free Savings Account, 303
TD Waterhouse, 107
*This Magazine,* 311
THOMAS, 162
TMX, 349
Tradingcharts.com, 350
TSX, 77
UK-Invest.com, 347
U.S. & World Early Warning Report, 243
U.S. Department of Commerce, 160, 162
U.S. Federal Reserve Board, 347
U.S. House of Representatives, 162

U.S. Securities and Exchange
Commission (SEC), 347, 351, 352
U.S. Senate, 162
Value Line, 129
*The Value Line Investment Survey,* 346
*Wall Street Journal,* 230, 346
Yahoo! Finance, 212, 230, 280, 345, 350
Zacks, 351
ZacksAdvisor, 350
weighing risk against return, 59–60
weighting, 62
Wilshire Total Market Index (Wilshire
5000 Equity Index), 68–69
window dressing, 185
working capital, 338
write-downs, 171

## Y

Yahoo! Finance, 212, 230, 280, 345, 350
yield
comparing, 138–139
defined, 42, 89, 137
of income stock, 42–43
income stocks, 137–139
in stock table, 89

## Z

Zacks, 351
ZacksAdvisor, 350

# Notes

## BUSINESS & PERSONAL FINANCE

978-0-470-83878-5

978-0-40-83818-1

**Also available:**

- Bookkeeping For Canadians For Dummies 978-0-470-73762-0
- Buying and Selling a Home For Canadians For Dummies 978-0-470-83740-5
- Investing For Canadians For Dummies 978-0-470-16029-9
- Managing For Dummies 978-0-7645-1771-6
- Money Management All-in-One Desk Reference For Canadians For Dummies 978-0-470-15428-1

- Negotiating For Dummies 978-0-470-04522-0
- Personal Finance For Canadians For Dummies 978-0-470-83768-9
- Small Business Marketing For Dummies 978-0-7645-7839-7
- Starting an eBay Business For Canadians For Dummies 978-0-470-83946-1

## EDUCATION, HISTORY & REFERENCE

978-0-470-83656-9

978-0-7645-2498-1

**Also available:**

- Algebra For Dummies 978-0-7645-5325-7
- Art History For Dummies 978-0-470-09910-0
- Chemistry For Dummies 978-0-7645-5430-8
- French For Dummies 978-0-7645-5193-2

- Math Word Problems For Dummies 978-0-470-14660-6
- Spanish For Dummies 978-0-7645-5194-9
- Statistics For Dummies 978-0-7645-5423-0
- World War II For Dummies 978-0-7645-532-3

## FOOD, HOME, GARDEN, & MUSIC

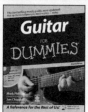 978-0-7645-9904-0

 978-0-470-15491-5

**Also available:**
- 30-Minute Meals For Dummies
  978-0-7645-2589-6
- Bartending For Dummies
  978-0-470-05056-9
- Brain Games For Dummies
  978-0-470-37378-1
- Gluten-Free Cooking For Dummies
  978-0-470-17810-2

- Home Improvement All-in-One
  Desk Reference For Dummies
  978-0-7645-5680-7
- Violin For Dummies
  978-0-470-83838-9
- Wine For Dummies
  978-0-470-04579-4

## GREEN/SUSTAINABLE

 978-0-470-84098-6

 978-0-470-17569-9

**Also available:**
- Alternative Energy For Dummies
  978-0-470-43062-0
- Energy Efficient Homes For
  Dummies 978-0-470-37602-7
- Green Building & Remodeling For
  Dummies 978-0-470-17559-0
- Green Business Practices For
  Dummies 978-0-470-39339-0

- Green Cleaning For Dummies
  978-0-470-39106-8
- Green Your Home All-in-One For
  Dummies 978-0-470-40778-3
- Sustainable Landscaping For
  Dummies 978-0-470-41149-0

## HEALTH & SELF-HELP

 978-0-471-77383-2

 978-0-470-15732-9

**Also available:**
- Breast Cancer For Dummies
  978-0-7645-2482-0
- Depression For Dummies
  978-0-7645-3900-8
- Healthy Aging For Dummies
  978-0-470-14975-1
- Improving Your Memory For
  Dummies 978-0-7645-5435-3

- Neuro-linguistic Programming For
  Dummies 978-0-7645-7028-5
- Pregnancy For Canadians For
  Dummies 978-0-470-83945-4
- Understanding Autism For
  Dummies 978-0-7645-2547-6

## HOBBIES & CRAFTS

 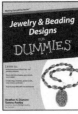

978-0-470-28747-7  978-0-470-29112-2

**Also available:**
- Crochet Patterns For Dummies
  97-0-470-04555-8
- Digital Scrapbooking For Dummies
  978-0-7645-8419-0
- Home Decorating For Dummies
  978-0-7645-4156-8
- Knitting Patterns For Dummies
  978-0-470-04556-5

- Oil Painting For Dummies
  978-0-470-18230-7
- Origami Kit For Dummies
  978-0-470-75857-1
- Quilting For Dummies
  978-0-7645-9799-2
- Sewing For Dummies
  978-0-7645-6847-3

## HOME & BUSINESS COMPUTER BASICS

978-0-470-49743-2  978-0-470-11806-1

**Also available:**
- Blogging For Dummies
  978-0-470-23017-6
- Excel 2007 For Dummies
  978-0-470-03737-9
- Office 2007 All-in-One Desk
  Reference For Dummies
  978-0-471-78279-7

- PCs For Dummies 978-0-470-46542-4
- Web Analytics For Dummies
  9780-470-09824-0

## INTERNET & DIGITAL MEDIA

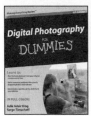 

978-0-470-25074-7  978-0-470-52567-8

**Also available:**
- eBay For Canadians For Dummies
  978-0-470-15348-2
- Facebook For Dummies
  978-0-470-52761-0
- Search Engine Marketing For
  Dummies 978-0-471-97998-2
- The Internet For Dummies
  978-0-470-12174-0

- Twitter For Dummies
  978-0-470-47991-9
- YouTube For Dummies
  978-0-470-14925-6
- WordPress For Dummies
  978-0-470-40296-2

## MACINTOSH

978-0-470-27817-8

978-0-470-43541-0

**Also available:**
- iMac For Dummies
  978-0-470-13386-6
- iMovie '09 & iDVD '09 For Dummies
  978-0-470-50212-9
- iPhone For Dummies
  978-0-470-53698-8
- MacBook For Dummies
  978-0-470-27816-1
- Mac OS X Leopard For Dummies
  978-0-470-05433-8
- Macs For Seniors For Dummies
  978-0-470-437797-7
- Office 2008 For Mac For Dummies
  978-0-470-27032-5
- Switching to a Mac For Dummies
  978-0-470-46661-2

## PETS

9780764584183

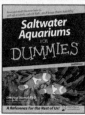

9780470068052

**Also available:**
- Birds For Dummies 9780764551390
- Boxers For Dummies
  9780764552854
- Cockatiels For Dummies
  9780764553110
- Ferrets For Dummies
  9780470127230
- Golden Retrievers For Dummies
  9780764552670
- Horses For Dummies
  9780764597978
- Puppies For Dummies
  9780470037171

## SPORTS & FITNESS

978-0-471-76871-5

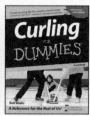

978-0-470-83828-0

**Also available:**
- Exercise Balls For Dummies
  978-0-7645-5623-4
- Coaching Hockey For Dummies
  978-0-470-83685-9
- Fitness For Dummies
  978-0-7645-7851-9
- Rugby For Dummies
  978-0-470-15327-7
- Ten Minute Tone-Ups For
  Dummies 978-0-7645-7207-4
- Yoga with Weights For Dummies
  978-0-471-74937-0